History, Literature, and Identity

History, Literature, and Identity

FOUR CENTURIES OF SIKH TRADITION

J.S. GREWAL

OXFORD
UNIVERSITY PRESS

OXFORD
UNIVERSITY PRESS

YMCA Library Building, Jai Singh Road, New Delhi 110 001

Oxford University Press is a department of the University of Oxford. It furthers the University's objective of excellence in research, scholarship, and education by publishing worldwide in

Oxford New York
Auckland Cape Town Dar es Salaam Hong Kong Karachi Kuala Lumpur Madrid Melbourne Mexico City Nairobi New Delhi Shanghai Taipei Toronto

With offices in
Argentina Austria Brazil Chile Czech Republic France Greece Guatemala Hungary Italy Japan Poland Portugal Singapore South Korea Switzerland Thailand Turkey Ukraine Vietnam

Published in India
by Oxford University Press, New Delhi

First published 2011
Digitally Printed in 2025

ISBN-13: 978-0-19-807074-0
ISBN-10: 0-19-807074-8

Typeset in 10/13.2 Minion Pro
by Excellent Laser Typesetters, Pitampura, Delhi 110 034
Printed in India by Artxel, New Delhi 110 020
Published by Oxford University Press
YMCA Library Building, Jai Singh Road, New Delhi 110 001

To
Indu Banga
for her constructive and critical input
into all the books that I have written
in the past four decades.

Contents

PART FOUR
In the Context of Sikh Rule (1765–1849)

PART FIVE
In the Context of Colonial Rule (1849–1947)

Illustrations

Figures

Note: All the figures are from *Gurshabad Ratanakar Mahān Kosh*, 1930.

Plates (*between pages 162–3*)

Preface

When I look back I find that I developed interest in Sikh literature quite early in my academic career. My article on the *Prem Sumārag* appeared in 1965 (rewritten all afresh for the Oxford University Press in 2009). Working on the British historians of medieval India, I had discovered that the worldviews, the assumptions, and the attitudes of the historians were embedded in their historical situations. I realized that a literary work was similarly embedded in the historical situation of the author. The works of literature even more than the works of history tell us much about the social situation in which they are produced.

My interest in Sikh literature then got linked up with the work I undertook to do on Sikh history. In connection with a biographical study of Guru Gobind Singh, published in 1967, I analysed the *Bachittar Nātak*, the *Zafarnāma*, and the *Srī Gur Sobhā*. For a study of Guru Nanak, published in 1969, I analysed the compositions of Guru Nanak in detail and studied the compositions of his four successors, the Vārs of Bhai Gurdas and the Janamsakhis known as the *Purātan* and the *Miharbān*. Subsequently, I studied the compositions of Guru Tegh Bahadur for a book published in 1776 on the treatment of Guru Tegh Bahadur by the Persian chroniclers. Working on *The Sikhs of the Punjab* for the New Cambridge History of India in the 1980s I thought of studying in detail the eighteenth century *Bansāvalīnāma* of Kesar Singh Chhibber and the early nineteenth century *Panth Prakāsh* of Ratan Singh Bhangu. For the colonial period I analysed the *Ham Hindu Nahīn* of Bhai Kahn Singh Nabha. As Visiting Professor at the Punjabi University, Patiala, in 2006–8, I got the opportunity to lecture on all the major works of Sikh literature from Guru Nanak to Bhai Kahn Singh. This literature produced in its various forms in different historical situations reflects the views, attitudes, and concerns of the authors in those situations.

Fourteen works taken up in the present volume represent the whole range of Sikh literature from the early sixteenth to the early twentieth centuries. These essays are placed in five parts, each indicating the historical context of the works analysed. The titles of the essays indicate the major thrust in each case. It is possible to see a close connection between the context and the character of the work. Significantly, all these works reflect identity consciousness in different phases of the precolonial period. To stay close to the idiom of the writer and flavour of the times, many of the Punjabi words have been used in the course of the discussion, with a glossary given at the end.

Over the decades I have become indebted to such a large number of institutions and scholars that I cannot thank them adequately. I must, however, name Indu Banga as the scholar who has remained associated with all stages of the present study. In recent years I have gained much from discussions with Balkar Singh and Gurinder Singh Mann. I am thankful to them for their interest. The invitation from Patiala to be Visiting Professor at the Punjabi University provided a great opportunity to think and rethink, and to write and rewrite. I am grateful to the then Vice Chancellor of the University, S. Swarn Singh Boparai.

I am thankful to Sheena Pall and Karamjit Kaur Malhotra for their help in preparing this volume for publication. I am also thankful to Parneet Minhas for preparing the manuscript with diligence and care.

J.S. GREWAL

Introduction

History and literature are so intertwined that historical analysis of a literary work becomes a study in history. The vast range of literature produced by the Sikhs from the sixteenth to the nineteenth centuries has been studied by a few Sikh historians, but only partly. A historical analysis of this literature can bring out new dimensions of the Sikh tradition, leading to a better understanding of Sikh history.

Guru Nanak witnessed the transition from the Afghan to the Mughal rule. Therefore, comments on the politics of his times may be expected. But he comments on polity too, and much more on his social and religious environment. In this wider context he advocates a path to liberation that is different from that of his contemporaries. The reign of Akbar, which was marked by the growth of an empire, development of agriculture, trade in agricultural produce and manufactured goods, a great spurt in urbanization, and a policy of cross-cultural toleration, provided a milieu in which the movement initiated by Guru Nanak could flourish in the Punjab. The compositions of Guru Amar Das, Guru Ram Das, and Guru Arjan dwell as much on the Sikh faith as on the Sikhs to place them in the contemporary context. They constructed a self-image that had a direct bearing on their consciousness of identity.

The first part of the book relates to the compositions of the first five Gurus as the articulation of a new dispensation. Guru Nanak refers to his path as the 'Gurmukh *panth*' to distinguish it from the Brahmanical, the ascetical, and the Islamic tradition of his days. His first successor, Guru Angad, reinforced his ideas and institutions and gave expression to his own understanding of the basic significance of the compositions (*bāṇī*) of Guru Nanak. His second successor, Guru Amar Das, elaborated his ideas, expanded their institutional scope, and underscored the exclusive validity of the path of Guru Nanak for the Kaliyuga. Guru Ram Das refers to Guru Nanak and his successors as the 'House of Nanak', and presents their dispensation as an expression of God's grace for the redemption of the world. Finally, Guru Arjan uses the phrase *'halemī rāj'* (mild rule) for the ideology, institutions, and the organized followers of Guru Nanak and his successors as a new order parallel to the political order, a dispensation that was not bound by the political boundaries of the state. The Granth compiled by Guru Arjan in 1605 was seen by him as the means of universal redemption.

The period of peaceful development of the Sikh movement ended with the martyrdom of Guru Arjan early in Jahangir's reign in 1606. His son and successor, Guru Hargobind, adopted martial measures, and fought several battles against the Mughal *faujdār*s before leaving the province of Lahore to establish his headquarters at Kiratpur in a hill principality. Prithi Chand, the elder brother of Guru Arjan, did not recognize Guru Hargobind's authority and started his own line of Guruship. Dissension within the Sikh community was reinforced by a further split under the leadership of Dhir Mal, a grandson of Guru Hargobind who did not recognize the seventh Guru, Har Rai. Ram Rai, the elder son of Guru Har Rai, did not recognize Har Krishan as the eighth Guru. By 1675, when Guru Tegh Bahadur was martyred, there were four lines of succession to Guruship among the Sikhs.

The second part of the book relates to this phase of confrontation with the state. Bhai Gurdas upholds the defiant stance of Guru Hargobind towards the state against the pliant attitude of Prithi Chand and his son Miharban who are denounced as 'rebels'. The compositions of Guru Tegh Bahadur reveal a profound concern with fearless activity in the right cause, which explains his deliberate martyrdom for the freedom of conscience.

Guru Gobind Singh transformed his followers into a political community to meet the challenge of external interference and internal disunity. He came into armed conflict with the neighbouring hill chiefs and the Mughal state. The issue was still unresolved when he died in 1708. This was followed by the revolt of the Sikhs against the Mughal empire under the leadership of Banda Bahadur and the establishment of sovereign Sikh rule in a large part of the Punjab for a few years. Coins were struck as the formal declaration of sovereignty.

The third part of the book relates to the mission of Guru Gobind Singh declared in the *Bachittar Nātak* as an irrevocable commitment to *dharmyudh* (righteous war) in order to safeguard the tradition of his predecessors. The *Vār Bhagautī* of 'Gurdas' Singh expresses the triumphant spirit of this phase. The distinctive role of the Khalsa and their distinctive identity is found sharpened in Sainapat's *Srī Gur Sobhā*. The *Rahitnāmas* of this phase postulate a Sikh social order with a sharp political edge.

For half a century from 1716, the year in which Banda Bahadur was executed at Delhi, and 1765, the year in which the Khalsa struck the coin again as a formal declaration of their sovereign rule, the Sikhs continued their political struggle against the Mughal authorities first and then against the Afghans. The literature produced in this phase is not as voluminous as the literature produced in the earlier phase. Under Sikh rule from 1765 to 1849, however, literary activity was revived on an extensive scale and Sikh writers of the period adopted different attitudes towards the Sikh past, giving expression to some new concerns.

The fourth part of the book relates to Sikh literature of this period of Khalsa Raj. Kesar Singh Chhibber's *Bansāvalīnāma* was written after the establishment of Sikh rule and Ratan Singh Bhangu's *Guru Panth Prakāsh* was written after the formation of a large Sikh state. Chhibber was concerned with the ten Gurus, the Khalsa, the Guru Granth, and the contemporary Sikhs. Bhangu was concerned primarily with Sikh sovereignty as an essential feature of the Sikh movement, and the doctrines of Guru-Panth and Guru Granth. Though Chhibber was socially conservative and Bhangu was rather radical, their works have a direct bearing on the socio-religious identity of the Sikhs.

The annexation of the sovereign Sikh territories to the British Indian empire finally in 1849 changed the situation radically for the Sikhs. There was a sudden recession in their fortunes in the early decades of British rule. Gradually, however, a religious resurgence began to take shape in the wake of economic and social changes to become the basis of political articulation. Religious identity came to the fore among all the communities of the Punjab, and identities began to be defined, redefined, and sharpened. In this process arose the issue of Hindu–Sikh identity. Bhai Kahn Singh Nabha's *Ham Hindu Nahīn* presented a comprehensive view of Sikh identity as distinct from Hindu and Muslim.

In the fifth part of the book an analysis of Bhai Kahn Singh Nabha's work shows that he is not concerned with Sikh identity per se but with the recognition of Sikhs as a political community on the basis of their distinct identity which had developed under the Gurus. What was new in the colonial situation was this conscious political perspective on Sikh identity.

In the Epilogue there is essentially a summing up of the ideas in each chapter and the issue of identity in Sikh literature is highlighted. The self-image of the Sikhs and their objective differences from their contemporaries made them increasingly conscious of their identity in the sixteenth century. In the early seventeenth century then, Bhai Gurdas gives eloquent expression to a distinctive identity of Gursikhs. The literature produced at the court of Guru Gobind Singh embodies a pronounced consciousness of distinction. The Khalsa Panth is emphatically called the Third Community (*tisar panth*). The Sikh writers of the eighteenth and the early nineteenth centuries continued to use *tisar panth* in their works to distinguish the Khalsa from Hindus and Muslims. Bhai Kahn Singh Nabha, at the end of the nineteenth century, argues that the distinctive identity of the Sikhs entitled them to be regarded as a nationality and a constituent of the Indian Nation, like the Hindus and Muslims.

PART ONE

Articulation of a New Dispensation (*c*.1500–1605)

1
The Gurmukh Panth
Guru Nanak

Three Religious Systems in Contemporary India

The compositions of Guru Nanak are marked by two basic features: a comprehensive comment on the political, social, and religious environment of his times, and proclamation of a set of interrelated ideas which constitute an ideology independent of the existing systems of religious belief and practice. These two features are in fact two sides of the same coin: his comment is the reverse of his ideology. These two features, often projected together, are a key to the compositions of Guru Nanak.

Even in the *Japu,* which relates primarily to theology, three religious traditions provide the frame of reference for contention and transcendence, as in the statement that the time of creation was not known to the *pandits*, the *qāzīs*, and the *jogīs*.[1] The pandit represented the Brahmanical tradition in all its forms; the qāzī represented the Islamic tradition; the jogī represented the ascetical traditions of India. Elsewhere in his compositions Guru Nanak looks upon all the three traditions as fruitless. 'The qāzī speaks falsehood and eats dirt; the Brahman bathes and kills living beings; the jogī is blind to the real skill; all the three follow the path of ruin.' Only he is a real jogī who realizes that he needs the Guru's grace to recognize the One; only he is a real qāzī who turns his back (on *māyā*) and through the Guru's grace becomes dead while alive; only he is a real Brahman who meditates on God, liberates himself, and leads others to liberation.[2] Evidently, Guru Nanak has no appreciation for any of the three traditions.

The Brahmanical Traditions

In the *Āsā dī Vār*, Guru Nanak appears to equate Hindus with those people who followed the Brahmanical systems of religious belief and practice—the Hindus praise God as laid down in the shastras; they bathe at sacred places and worship idols, burning incense. They cherish the sacred thread and the sacred mark on their forehead. However, for Guru Nanak, neither the sacred thread nor the sacred mark has any merit in comparison with the true Name.[3]

The kingpin of the Brahmanical system is the pandit, and Guru Nanak has much to say about his role. The Brahmans were associated with learning. For Guru Nanak, however, learning in itself was not enough. It led to pride and self-centredness and, thus, became a hindrance. The more learning one acquires the more anxiety one has to overcome. Reading and writing lead to pride. To read even a cartload and to acquire boatfuls of books was a waste of effort. It is of no use even if one reads books all the year round, all the months of a year, and with each breath. What matters essentially is dedication to God and faith in him. The foolish pandit flaunts his wisdom and skill in arguments but his real purpose is to garner wealth.[4]

There is a whole *shalok* on the Brahman—he reads books, performs worship, and engages in contention; he worships stones and adopts the posture of meditation, like the heron; he tells lies in a palatable manner; he recites the Gayatri three times a day; he wears a necklace of beads around his neck and puts a paste mark on his forehead; he keeps two *dhotīs* and a cloth to cover his head. If his idea is to please God, his acts are surely futile. The only way to please God is to meditate on him with complete sincerity. This path cannot be found without the true Guru.[5]

Guru Nanak tells the Brahman that the sacred thread he wears, and he puts on others has no spiritual or moral efficacy. The only sacred thread that does not get soiled and does not snap is the one prepared with mercy as the cotton, contentment as the thread, self-control as the knot, and ethical living as the twist. 'If you have such a *janaeu* O *pānde* then put it on me.' The sacred thread that the Brahman put on others in the *chaukā* is bought for four cowries; he whispers in their ears that henceforth he is their gurū. When the Brahman dies the thread falls away and he departs without it. The thread is spun from cotton and the Brahman gives it the twist; a goat is slaughtered and cooked; everyone who eats it says that the thread ceremony has been well performed; when it is worn out it is thrown away and replaced by another. Had it possessed any power of its own, it would not have snapped. Honour comes by appropriating the Name; the adoration of God is the true thread. The honour received in God's court is the sacred thread that never snaps.[6]

Useless for the life hereafter, to Guru Nanak, the sacred thread of the Brahman does not serve any moral purpose in life on this earth. It does not restrain him from scandalous indulgence. 'His feet and his hands, his tongue and his eyes are not restrained. He wanders around without a restraining thread. He performs marriages for money, and gives direction to others as an astrologer. Look at the strange spectacle O people: the one who is blind in mind is called wise'.[7] Guru Nanak did not have any appreciation for astrology because it stood opposed to his faith in God's will and grace.

There was yet another dimension to the Brahman's life. He taxes cows and Brahmans and yet plasters his chaukā with cowdung. He wore dhotī, the sacred mark and the rosary, and he received sustenance from those whom he called 'unclean' (*mlechh*). He performed Hindu services in his home but read books of Muslims in public and adopted their ways. He was far away from the path of liberation.[8]

The wearing of sacred thread by the Khatris, according to Guru Nanak, did not stop them from pandering to the rulers whom they regarded as 'unclean'. They wore the thread, and wielded the butcher's knife. Brahmans blew conches in their homes and ate their food. False is the commerce and false the sustenance derived. The mark on their forehead and the dhotī with its stuck-up end does not stop them from butchering the world. To become acceptable to the rulers they wore blue dress; they would perform worship according to the Puranas but eat the mlechh's food. Indeed, they ate the meat of goats slaughtered in the Muslim fashion. And yet they ate in their chaukā and told others not to come near so that their food was not polluted. Guru Nanak says that they practised sinful hypocrisy and rinsed their mouth with falsehood in their hearts.[9]

Equally sinful was the Brahman's performance at *shradhs*. If a burglar stole from a house and used the stolen goods to offer charity in the name of his ancestors, the goods are identified, the dead ancestors become a party to the theft, and the hands of the guilty are chopped off. If the earnings of a *jajman* are unlawful and he feeds Brahmans for the benefit of his dead ancestors, the whole exercise, too, is futile; the ancestors cannot derive any benefit. Guru Nanak adds that the Brahman who serves as the 'broker' is equally guilty. Reward is received only by those who give charity from lawfully earned profits or wages.[10]

The notion of impurity (*sūtak*) to which the Brahman attaches vital importance is rejected by Guru Nanak. Impurity is everywhere: inside cowdung, in wood, in every grain, and even in water which is the source of life. Impurity enters the kitchen itself. The only way out is to discard the very notion through proper awareness. Guru Nanak elaborates: the impurity of the mind is avarice; the impurity of the tongue is falsehood; the impurity of the eye is to look at women with lust; the impurity of the ear is to listen to slander. The human beings caught in these impurities are bound for hell. The whole idea of sūtak is an illusion. Birth and death occur through God's will. Things created by God to eat and drink are pure. They who realize this are free from the superstition of sūtak. Food, water, fire, salt, and *ghee* are regarded as holy; the Brahman eats them and they turn into offal. Therefore, what deserves to be denounced is the mouth that does not utter the Name and partakes of food without devotion to the Name.[11]

Guru Nanak brings in the question of gender in connection with the idea of impurity. Women are regarded as impure because of menstruation and for giving birth to a child. However, there can be no reproduction without women, and there can be no humanity without reproduction. Human beings are conceived by women; they are born to women; men are betrothed to women and marry them; new generations are born; if one woman dies, man seeks another. Why should they be denounced who give birth even to the *rājān*?[12] They are equal partners in life.

The scholars who look at the Bhaktī movement as a monolithic whole, miss the point that Guru Nanak was very critical of the Vaishnava worship of Rama and Krishna. In the first place there is no room for incarnation in Guru Nanak's conception of God who is not subject to birth and death. To him, Rama is the dust of God's feet. Krishna seduced Chandraval and stole the wish-fulfilling tree (*pārjāt*) for a *gopī*, and engaged in alliance in Brindaban. There were numerous other legends of Krishna. Guru Nanak says that many danced to music and whirled about, performed the role of kings and queens in public places, wearing earrings and necklaces worth lakhs, but idle chatter and clever devices do not lead to enlightenment. It comes only through God's grace.[13]

Guru Nanak tells the Vaishnavs that the whole universe dances in praise of God. The *gharīs* are Krishna's milkmaids, and the *pahars* are Krishna and his cowherds; the sun and the moon are as Vishnu's incarnation, with air, water, and fire as the decking ornaments.[14] With reference to this cosmic dance, Guru Nanak refers to the dance-dramatic representations of Krishna and Rama, which are pointless.

The disciples play on musical instruments and the *gurūs* dance; they move their feet and their heads; dust flies and falls into their hair; the people feel amused and go home (after the performance). The performers keep to the measure for bread, striking their feet on the ground; they sing as *gopīs* and *kāhn;* they sing as Sita and Raja Ram.[15]

For Guru Nanak this is no worship. The whole universe is the creation of the Fearless and the Formless One who alone is True. His worship alone leads to liberation.

Loving devotion (*bhāo*) to God, says Guru Nanak, arises from the awe (*bhau*) of his power and greatness. He describes dancing and jumping as sources of passing pleasure. All bound in the bonds of deeds are whirling around, enacting a kind of dance. Endless is their enumeration: the oil-press, the spinning wheel, the grind stone, the potter's wheel, the whirlwind, the top and the churning wheel, the bullocks yoked to the device for separating grain from the chaff, the winged creatures ceaselessly whirling, and the living beings whirling on the pike. In the same way 'the learned dance, play on instruments and deck themselves for histrionic postures, shouting aloud and singing tales of the past heroes, their fight and their contention'.[16]

In the rest of his bāṇī too, Guru Nanak has much to say about the Brahman and his beliefs and practices. In his view, the Brahmans confused the creator with his created beings: the Master who created air, water, and fire also created Brahma, Vishnu, and Mahesh. He alone is the giver of gifts; all others are beggars. There are thirty-three-crore gods who beg from the Master whose stores suffer no decrease. Nothing can be received in an inverted vessel; nectar falls into the vessel held upright. In other words, nothing comes out of worshipping God's creatures, the so-called gods, including Brahma, Vishnu, and Mahesh. Indeed, like the rest of the world, Brahma, Vishnu, and Rudra remain subject to death.[17]

The Vedas inculcate belief in the One whose limits cannot be known. The only creator of the universe, he has established the earth and the sky without any visible support. He is known through the bāṇī and his true ensign is the *shabad*; he is known through the Guru. While the Vedas talk of bhaktī which shows the light, the shastras and smritis talk of the Name that leads to peace through the Guru's instruction, their recitation, however, leads to pride and contention, a chain (that keeps one bound to death and rebirth). Millions of lessons in the shastras and millions of recitations of the Puranas are of no use if one does not find honour (in God's court). Such honour, says Nanak, comes from the Name through God's grace. Guru Nanak exhorts the pandit to show him the way to God. The question carries the implication that the pandit does not know. Indeed, fools are called pandits, he says. They merely talk and never reflect. A learned pandit is he who acquires *giān*; who can see the One in all human beings and who is free from *haumai*. While some recite the Veda or the Puranas, and some count beads, 'I recognize only the Name.'[18]

Guru Nanak does not appreciate the practices followed or recommended by the Brahmans. *Hom*, *jagg*, and *pāṭh* of the Puranas have value only if they are acceptable (to God). Liberation comes through the Name by turning to the Guru and not through jagg, hom, *pun*, *tap*, or *pūjā*. If the whole body is cut into pieces and offered to the fire like ghee, if the mind and the body are offered like firewood, and even if the act is repeated a million times, it will not have the merit of appropriating the Name.[19] 'The gods and goddesses of stone that you worship, what can they give? You wash them in water; if you were to leave them there, they would sink.'[20]

Guru Nanak says that if the idol itself has no relevance for genuine worship of God, an *āratī* offered to the idol can have no meaning. In the true āratī for the bestower of liberation, the sky is the platter, the sun and the moon are the lamps, the stars are the pearls, the fragrant air is the incense, the entire vegetation, with flowers and fruits, are the *chaur*, and the unstruck music is the drum played for him. Similarly, bathing at sacred places is of no use when the mind is filled with the dirt of pride. The object of pilgrimage is within oneself. The merit attributed to pilgrimage at all the sixty-eight places is at the Guru's feet. The real pilgrimage is the Guru's sight and the company of *sants*. If you wish to go on pilgrimage, the Name is the *tīrath*, the *shabad* is the tīrath, the giān is the tīrath. The giān given by the Guru is the real place of pilgrimage with the merit attributed to bathing on all the ten auspicious occasions. There is no tīrath like the Guru's feet.[21]

Fig. 1.1 Gurdwara Janam Asthan (the place of birth) of Guru Nanak at Nankana Sahib, Pakistan

Fig. 1.2 Darshani Darwaza (entrance gate) of Gurdwara Janam Asthan

The popular practice of floating lamps in water induces Guru Nanak to talk of the lamp of giān which cannot be put out by the wind or water, and which leads to liberation. Lamps were lighted for the dead as obituary rites. Guru Nanak says that his lamp is the Name, with suffering as the oil. Its light ends all sorrow. The people are asked not to laugh at the idea: a single spark can burn a whole heap of wood. He adds, God alone is his rice ball (*pind*) and the platter (*pattal*); the true Name of God is his refuge in this world and the next. The rice balls are offered to the gods and to the ancestors of the deceased; the Brahmans eat them. They cannot exhaust the ball of God's kindness.[22] In other words, God's grace does not depend on the Brahman's performance.

Guru Nanak takes up the issue of eating meat against the Vaishnava insistence on vegetarian diet. The debate about the spiritual merit of diet was rather misplaced, he believed. Meat was offered to gods in sacrifice. The Puranas talk of meat and the semitic books talk of meat; in all the cosmic ages (*yugas*) meat was eaten. They who close their nose to avoid the smell of meat enjoy human flesh at night. The pandit claims to be clever but he forgets that human beings are conceived in flesh, they are born through flesh, and they are made of flesh. He regards the animal flesh as bad but loves the flesh of his wife. It was strange that the jajmān who ate meat was supposed to go to hell and the pandit who received charity from him was supposed to go to heaven. He uses the analogy of water and says, if water is regarded as pure it cannot become impure when it changes form.[23]

Guru Nanak tells the Vaishnavas to dance to the tune of the musical instrument (*wājā*) of understanding and the drum (*pakhāwaj*) of the loving devotion; the mind absorbed in this dance is the source of happiness; this bhaktī covers austerities; this is the way to dance. The praise of God is the real dance; all else is sensual pleasure. To go to the *sangat* of the Sikhs and to hear the true Name is the real dance. The Vaishnava dance is associated with the supposed incarnations of Vishnu as Rama or Krishna. The creator of the universe does not become great by killing Ravana. He who is all pervasive, who created all living beings, and who runs the universe does not become great by subduing the serpent Kali, or by killing Kansa.[24]

Guru Nanak tells the pandit that he reads books but does not understand; he teaches others as a gainful occupation; his talk is false and his actions show no awareness of the shabad. There are many pandits who practise astrology and talk of the Veda; they sing of contention and remain subject to death and rebirth. Without the Guru's grace, they can never attain liberation. He who knows Brahm is a real Brahman; he remains immersed in loving devotion and realizes that God is near, in every human being; greatness comes from the Name and from recognizing the Guru's shabad. He who knows Brahm is a real Brahman; he exercises restraint and regards contentment as his *dharam*; he breaks the chain of death and rebirth to attain liberation; such a Brahman is worth worship.[25]

In the *Slok Sanskritī*, Guru Nanak describes the multifarious activities of the Brahman to tell him that he cannot find the right path without the true Guru. There is only one God, and no gods or goddesses are to be worshipped. Liberation comes through the Guru's grace. There is only one shabad for all, and not different *dharma*s for Brahmans, Kshatriyas, Vaishyas, and Shudras.[26]

The Ascetical Traditions

In the *Japu*, Guru Nanak tells the jogī to have the earrings of contentment, the begging bowl of productive work, the ashes of meditation on God, the cloak of the fear of death, the staff of trust, and the skill of keeping his body free from evil. To regard all human beings as equal is to belong to the highest order of the jogīs; to conquer the self is to conquer the world. The jogī should hail the Eternal Lord who has been there from the very beginning, who is without blemish, who is indestructible, and who remains the same throughout the cosmic ages. The jogī should make giān his food and mercy the female-in-charge of the store; instead of blowing the horn he should hear the unstruck music (*nād*) within himself; he should dedicate himself to the master of all human beings instead of seeking supranatural powers; God alone determines union or separation and one receives what he ordains. The jogī should hail the Eternal Lord who has been there from the very beginning, who is without blemish, who is indestructible, and who remains the same throughout the cosmic ages.[27]

In the *Āsā dī Vār*, the jogīs meditate on the void and refer to God as invisible (*alakh*); he has a subtle form; he is not affected by māyā; the whole universe is his visible body. Then there are other ascetics in various garbs who inflict physical pain on themselves. Some go without eating, others without any clothes. There are some who observe silence, and others who go barefoot. There are some who eat dirty food and put ashes in their hair. They are blind and they lose all honour. Without the Name, none can find a place of honour. Some live in the wilderness or in cremation grounds. They all regret in the end.[28] Common to them all are ascetical practices, renunciation, and mendicancy. Guru Nanak was opposed to all these.

In the rest of his bāṇī, Guru Nanak uses metaphors from the ideas and practices of the jogīs, which show his thorough familiarity with their system and also his anxiety to underscore its inadequacies. By smearing ashes on one's naked body, pride does not vanish; this is not the way to *jog*; why forget the name of God, which alone is helpful in the end? Why not remember him who is the giver of the body and the life. Jog is not to be found in *maṛhīs* and *masāṇs*. God bestows gifts in accordance with his greatness; when he is kind he bestows the great gift of the Name. Compared with this gift no power is of any value: the power to create fire out of ice, to eat iron for food, to drink all suffering like water, to goad the earth as a mount, to weigh the skies in a balance, to become so large as to be contained nowhere, to have power over everyone, to do whatever one likes or make others do what one likes. Guru Nanak has no appreciation for the concern of the jogīs with supranatural powers for they have no ethical merit.[29]

Guru Nanak tells the jogīs what jog is not and what it should be. Jog does not consist in donning the cloak, holding the staff, or smearing the body with ashes. It does not consist in wearing the earrings, shaving the head, or blowing the horn (*singī*). The secret of jog lies in remaining detached-in-attachment. Jog does not consist in mere talk; only he can be called a real jogī who regards all human beings as equal. Jog does not consist in living outside (habitations) in maṛhīs and masāṇs; it does not consist in deep meditation. Jog does not consist in wandering in different countries in all the ten directions; it does not consist in bathing at sacred places. Jog is attained by remaining detached-in-attachment. All illusions vanish on meeting the true Guru and the mind is restrained. The ambrosia begins to drop down, the unstruck music is heard, and God is recognized within oneself. Jog is attained thus by remaining detached-in-attachment. Jog should be pursued in such a way that one becomes dead-in-life. The state of fearlessness is attained when the singī produces music unblown. Jog is attained by remaining detached-in-attachment.[30]

Guru Nanak tells Machhandar Nath to control the five senses as the right way to jog; he should try to liberate others as well as himself. The one who does this remains absorbed in God all the time. He should beg for loving devotion to God and his awe. His thirst would be quenched and contentment would well up. He should meditate on God to become one with him. He should meditate deeply on the true Name. The real *avadhūt* remains hopeless-in-hope, and recognizes God. The union of human being with the divine is the secret that Guru Nanak reveals.[31]

Guru Nanak talks of *bhagtī-jog* which, for him, is real jog. The earrings are internal to the body which itself is the cloak; the mind itself is the staff to control the five senses; this is the way to jog. There is one Word and no other; dedication to it is the food of roots and fruits. If by shaving the head one finds God, there are many who would do so on the banks of the Ganges. The blind do not turn to the only Master of the three worlds. The fear (of death) is not removed by sham talk. Take refuge in the One, forsaking greed. Remember the Pure One O' jogī, why indulge in false talk. They who adopt forgiveness, their fast is contentment; they get rid of the disease and do not suffer death. They attain liberation to be assimilated to the formless one. The real jogī has no fear. In plants and trees, inside and outside, is God. The fearless jogī invokes the Pure One; keeps awake to meditate on truth; that is the kind of jogī who is appreciated. He burns death in the fire of giān; he gets rid of pride on the path of death; he attains liberation for himself and his forebears. He who serves the true Guru is the real jogī. Immersed in awe he becomes fearless; he is assimilated to the one he serves.[32]

In a number of verses Guru Nanak uses the terminology of the Gorakhnāthī Jogīs to convey his own message and to express his own values. The shabad is the real jogī's horn and through it he hears the unstruck divine music. The Guru's shabad is the *mundrā* in his heart; forgiveness is his cloak; he accepts what God does as the best for him; he finds the treasure of *sahaj-jog*. He who is linked with God is the real jogī; the name of the Pure One is his nectar and he tastes the juice of giān. Meditating on God, he discards all contention; the shabad is his singī to hear sweet music day and night. Reflection is his begging bowl and giān his staff; awareness of God's presence is his *bibhūt*. Guru

Nanak tells Barthari Jogī that the object of his devotion is the Only One. In an *Ashtpadī*, Guru Nanak recommends to the jogīs praises of God, meditation on him, the shabad of the true Guru, his bāṇī, service, acceptance of God's will, and his Name. The real *jogī* regards all human beings with equal consideration, receives alms of the shabad, and attains the state of sahaj.[33]

Asceticism, renunciation, and mendicancy were some of the characteristics of the jogīs, but not peculiar to them. There were other categories of renunciates who practised austerities, generally known as *bairāgīs* and *sanyāsīs*. Guru Nanak makes a similar comment on them. The fire is not quenched by wandering in all the ten directions; the inner dirt is not removed by roaming in various garbs. The instruction of the true Guru leads to *bhagtī*; the thirst of haumai is quenched by what the Guru says. Austerities in the cave of a mountain of gold or in deep waters, hanging upside down between the earth and the sky, covering the entire body with dresses of all kinds, or remaining deliberately dirty (like the Jain monks) are due to *durmat*. The real bairāgī is one with whom God is pleased. With the awe of God and love of the shabad in his heart he serves the Guru. There can be no bairag in *dubidhā*. He who invokes the one is a real *siddh*, *sādhak*, jogī, and *jangam*. He recites the Master's name and has nothing to do with *jap*, tap, *sanjam*, or *karm*. Through the Guru and the shabad he attains liberation. He who begs for food and clothes remains hungry here and suffers sorrow hereafter. Without *gurmat*, he loses honour. The way of bhagtī is recognized through the Guru's instruction.[34]

The Jain monks are severely criticized. In a verse Guru Nanak calls them pluckheads who drink dirty water and eat leftovers; spread out their offal and smell its bad odour; and are shy of water. They pluck their hair with their fingers smeared with ashes. They abandon their occupation and their family wails for them. They sit together as if in mourning. With cups tied to their waists and threads on their wrists, they move in a single file. They are neither jogīs nor jangams, neither qāzīs nor *mullās*; they are cursed by God, the whole lot of them. They do not realize that God alone gives life and takes it away. They are strangers to *dān* and *isnān*. Water is the source of all food and life. The Guru is the ocean and his Sikhs the streams (for anyone to bathe in their association). If the pluckheads do not bathe, let there be seven handfuls of dust over their heads.[35] To the asceticism, renunciation, and mendicancy of the Jain monks is added their deliberate uncleanliness and atheism. The gulf between the Jain monks and Guru Nanak was surely the widest.

All those people who are alien to the Guru's shabad remain chained to the cycle of coming and going. Among them are siddhs, jogīs, *bhogīs* and *kapaṛīs*, pandits, *pādhās* and *jyotishīs*, the ascetics who live in forests or at sacred places, and those who control the semen to be called *jatī* (caste). They are alien to the Name, the Guru's instruction, the Guru's shabad, and to God within. They never become genuinely detached-in-attachment (*udāsī*).[36]

The Islamic Tradition and the Afghan Rule

In the *Āsā dī Vār,* there is a reference to semitic scriptures (*kateb*). The Musalmans praise the *sharī'at* above all else; they study it and reflect on it. They believe that the servant of God accepts the bonds of the sharī'at to have a sight (*dīdār*) of God in Paradise. In their belief, the non-believers are destined to suffer the torments of hell. However, it was commonly observed that the clay of the graveyard was kneaded by the potter to make pots and bricks; when fired, the Musalman's clay flies in flames and cinders fall from it. Guru Nanak says that only God knows what would happen to human beings after death.[37] The Muslims' claim to an exclusive possession of true faith is misplaced.

In the rest of his compositions, Guru Nanak comments more elaborately on contemporary Islam. He defines *maulā* (an epithet for Allah) as the master who created the world with all that flourishes in it. The mullā and the qāzī should recognize God; their learning would not save them from death. The real qāzī discards 'self' and makes the Name his sole refuge. The true creator is there now and shall be there when all else has perished. The learned Musalman performs five daily prayers and reads the *Qur'ān* and other books; when the call from the grave comes all is left behind.[38] The practices of the *'ulamā* do not earn any merit for the life hereafter.

Guru Nanak refers to the various categories of religious persons among Muslims. Apart from the prophets, there were *pīrs* and *shaikhs*, qāzīs, and mullās, *sāliks*, *sādiqs*, and *shahīds*, and there were *darveshes* at God's door. For abundance of blessings, they recited special prayers. However, God does not consult anyone when he creates or destroys, when he gives or takes away. His power is known only to him and he does what he likes. He watches everyone and bestows his grace on anyone he likes. His *hukam* cannot be measured, and none can describe it. Even a hundred poets together cannot describe even a small part (of his power); they can only cry in despair. Allah is unfathomable and limitless, the true patron whose name is pure and whose abode is pure.[39] The implication is clear: the Musalmans may claim to know Allah and his true worship, but Allah, even of their scripture, is inscrutable and none can anticipate what he would do.

Guru Nanak advises Musalmans to recite the name of Khuda with inner faith and not for the sake of appearance. This advice is preceded by the statement that a cloth soiled by blood is regarded as impure (*palīt*); how can the heart of a person who drinks human blood be pure (*nirmal*)? If one regards mercy as the mosque, sincerity of faith as the prayer mat, honest earning as the *Qur'ān*, modesty as the circumcision, and good will as the fast, only then one becomes a real Musalman. Good conduct should be his pilgrimage, truth his pīr, and compassion his *kalma* and *namāz*. 'What pleases God' should be his rosary. Such a Musalman receives honour from God.[40]

The importance of honest living and action is emphasized in similar terms. What belongs to others should be regarded by a Musalman as pork; even the pīr would intercede on behalf of the one who does not eat honestly earned food. Not by mere profession, but by true actions he can go into heaven. Unlawful food does not become lawful if spice is added to it. Falsehood begets only falsehood. The first of the five daily prayers should be 'truth', the second 'what is lawful', and the third 'good will for all'. 'Right intention' should be the fourth prayer, and the fifth should be 'the praises of God'. Only if 'good conduct' is one's kalma can one be called a Musalman.[41]

The Islamic values mentioned in these verses are those of the '*ulamā* or the orthodoxy. In one verse there is a suggestion that Guru Nanak appreciates the ways of the Sūfis more than those of the 'ulamā. 'It is not easy to be a Musalman; one should be called so if one is a real Musalman'. First of all he should adopt the path of the *auliyā* and remove all impurities to clear the mirror of his heart. He should submit to the guide so as to obliterate the difference between life and death. He should accept the will of God as the doer above him, and he should lose all sense of self. He should be compassionate towards all human beings. Only then can he be called a Musalman.[42] Here, some of the basic values of the Sūfīs are brought into focus.

However, Guru Nanak's appreciation for the Sūfīs was not unqualified. There were certain practices of the Sūfīs which he did not appreciate. There is a strong denunciation of the practice of the Sufi shaikhs to bestow caps upon their disciples by way of authorization to guide others. This, in Guru Nanak's eyes, is presumptuous. Only God knows whether or not one is acceptable in his court. The shaikh presumes that he is and he thinks that he has enabled others to find the goal who can guide still others to the goal. The shaikh is compared to a rat that is too fat to enter the hole and yet attaches a winnowing basket to its tail. All those who give and receive such blessings are spirituality dead, Furthermore, Guru Nanak says that his summer harvest is the only Name and his winter harvest is the true Name; he has received this grant from the door of the Lord. There are numerous doors in the world and there are innumerable beggars who beg there at. The shaikhs do not beg at God's door. They receive grants of revenue-free land from the earthly rulers.[43]

Three *pauṛīs* of the *Āsā dī Vār* contain what may be called political comment. One of these refers to the human frame and beauty being left behind after death and reward or punishment being received according to one's good or bad deeds; it refers to orders having been given at pleasure; the former potentate has now to tread the narrow path; he stands exposed now and looks frightening as he goes to hell; one has to regret one's evil deeds in the end. The language used in this pauṛī suggests that the potentate is a ruler and a Muslim. In another pauṛī, the reference to the Muslim ruler is explicit when he is called the *sultān*. Disgraced by God he becomes lighter than the blade of grass and receives no charity when he begs from door to door. They who had caparisoned horses running fast like the wind, who had colourful harems, who were proud of their splendid palaces and tall mansions, and who did whatever they liked, have wasted their lives without knowing God; issuing commands to others they had forgotten death. Old age has overtaken them'. After death, they would face judgement not only for what they did as individuals but also for what they did as rulers.[44]

Contemporary rule is commented upon in the shaloks as well. In fact, there is an explicit reference to the rule of Muslim Pathans (*turk-pathāṇī 'aml*). It is seen as a characteristic of the Kaliyuga; the name of God now is Allah and the favourite dress is of blue colour. An assessment is built into this close association of Afghan rule with the worst of the cosmic ages. In the Kaliyuga the famine of truth has occurred and falsehood has spread all around; human beings have turned into goblins. The seed is crushed, and it cannot sprout. Greed, evil, and lust are dominant like the *rājā*, *mehtā*, and *sikdār* (*shiqdār*). The chariot in the Kaliyuga is the fire of passion and the charioteer is falsehood. The assessment is not always implicit. It comes to the surface with the statement that 'they who perform *namāz* can yet eat human beings'.[45] This can be seen as a reference to oppression under the rule of the Afghans who profess to be Muslim.

The political comment is far more prominent in the rest of the bāṇī of Guru Nanak than what we find in the *Āsā dī Vār*. It covers the rulers as sultāns, *bādshāhs*, and rājās; it covers the ruling class as *nāibs*, *khāns*, *maliks*, shiqdārs, and the *umarā*. The intermediaries between them and the subject people (*rai'yat*) are referred to as *chaudharīs* and *muqaddams*. The rulers and the other representatives of the state die in the end, like the common people, leaving all their possessions behind; they remain entangled in death and rebirth. The armies and palaces provide no support without the true Name. The horses and elephants, and spears and trumpets are false without the remembrance of the Lord, and there is no liberation without the Guru's shabad even for rājās, khāns, and malik. Millions may stand up to salute the masters of vast armies, and millions may obey them, but all this is futile without honour in God's court. Like the ordinary people, the rulers suffer from the disease of haumai. Unlike the ordinary people, however, the rulers can collect wealth (due to their power), and their thirst for power is never quenched.[46] If anything, the rulers and the state functionaries are more disadvantaged than the ordinary people for the pursuit of ethical and spiritual life.

'Indeed, the rulers are butchers; they suck human blood. The rājās act like lions and the muqaddams act like dogs; they fall upon the people any time; the agents of the rulers inflict wounds and the blood is licked by the dogs.' Justice is administered not in the name of God (as a primary duty of the rulers) but only when their palm is greased. There is discrimination on the basis of faith. 'Now that the turn of the *shaikhs* has come, Ād Purkh is called Allah; it has become customary to tax gods and their temples'.[47] There is no recognition of the principle of the freedom of conscience.

The verses known as Bābar-bāṇī contain among other things a political comment. The army of Babur is called the marriage party of sin; brides are demanded by force; the rites of marriage are performed by Satan and not by Brahmans and qāzīs. The reference clearly is to rape. No distinction was made between women of low and high caste, or between Muslim and Hindu women. Khurasan (Kabul) was occupied in a friendly manner but Hindustan was threatened with violence; the Mughals descended as the agency of Death; the people cried in suffering. God is the creator of all human beings. If the mighty strike the mighty, the fight is equal. But if a lion falls upon a herd of cattle, the master is accountable. The reference is to the unarmed, civilian, people who were killed. The rulers of the land could not protect them against the invaders. Thus, the Afghan ruler and Babur are blamed. The Afghans suffered for their political failure. Gone are the sports and stables of the rulers, their sword-belts and red tunics, their palaces and tall mansions, and their harems in which the beautiful women banished their sleep. Wealth cannot be amassed without sins and it leads to misery. God takes away the goodness from those whom he wishes to mislead. Their tall mansions have been razed to the ground and even the princes have been cut into pieces. The women of the ruling classes, oblivious of God, lived a life of luxury and indulgence, their beauty and wealth became their enemy. They suffered with their men. They were dishonoured. Had they thought beforehand they would not have suffered.[48] Thus, there is a moral dimension, too, to the political situation in which men and women suffer because of the sins of omission and commission.

Theology in the *Japu* and the *Āsā dī Vār*

Regarded among 'the foremost of the world's religious compositions', the *Japu* is meant to guide men on the spiritual path leading to 'total absorption in God-consciousness'. It embodies deep reflection on one of the most important aspects of human life: how to bridge the gulf between human beings and God? Or, as Guru Nanak puts it, how to demolish the wall of falsehood to become true? The *Japu* provides an elaborate and clear answer to this basic question.

At the outset the *Japu* underscores the essential character of the Supreme Being as existing before the beginning of time, through all the cosmic ages, in the present, and to remain in existence when there is nothing else. Identification with this True Being and living in accordance with the divine ordinance (hukam, *razā*) is the objective of human life. This is how the wall of falsehood is demolished. Acceptance of the divine ordinance is of fundamental importance in the religious thought of Guru Nanak.

Human beings sing of the greatness of the Supreme Being but only inadequately. By reflecting on his eternal Name and his greatness early in the morning through his gift of love one may find the door to liberation through his grace, and realize that only the True One is everything. He is self-existent. Only by serving him through singing his praises in awe one may attain peace (*sukh*) through the Guru. The Supreme Being can never be described. The imporant thing is to remember him as the only bestower of all gifts. Nothing can be achieved without his grace. The highest spiritual exaltation is made possible by listening to the praises of the Supreme Being and reflection on the Name to destroy all suffering and sin. The person who has appropriated the Name sees the Supreme Being in the entire creation. He grasps the essence of dharam, attains liberation, and gets recognition in this world as well as in the divine court.

The physical and moral universe in all its multitudinous forms has been created by the divine ordinance. The power of the Supreme Being cannot be described. The mortal beings are nothing in comparison with the everlasting Formless One. He is worshipped in innumerable ways but only that which pleases him is good. There are millions of false, ignorant, and depraved sinners in his creation. There is no word or numeral appropriate for the whole creation. All his creation is his *nām*; there is no place without the Name and there is no place beyond it. Sins are washed away through the Name. One who appropriates and follows the Name with love bathes in the inner tīrath, the divine presence within human beings. This happens through God's grace.

The known scriptures of the world (*Ved* and *Kateb*) have described the greatness of the Supreme Being but only inadequately. There is no limit of any kind in relation to him. To know him one has to be as high, which is impossible. Only he knows how great he is. All gifts are the result of his grace and there is no limit to his grace. It is his pleasure to liberate or to keep one chained (to the wheel of death and rebirth); none else has any say in this matter. He who receives the gift of his praises is the king of kings. He can become as great as he pleases. Any pretention to know his greatness is the height of ignorance.

The earth is a *dharamsāl*, a place to cultivate dharam. True justice is done in the court of the True One. Recognition is given to the true devotees. The true and the false stand distinguished. This is the realm of dharam (dharam *khand*). The other four realms, those of giān, *saram*, *karam*, and *sachch* are described in the last four pauṛīs of the *Japu*. Generally interpreted in terms of ascent towards a higher spiritual state, the five khands are related to the conception of the goal and the means of liberation-in-life.[49]

The first three pauṛīs of the *Āsā dī Vār* refer to the creation of the physical and the moral world. God created himself and his power; he looks at his creation with pleasure. He is the giver and the doer; he gives life and takes it away; pervasive everywhere, he enjoys his sport. He created human beings and made them responsible for their actions: an account is taken and justice is done according to their deeds. When a man dies he has to render account; only good deeds and God's praises count in the hereafter.[50]

In three other pauṛīs Guru Nanak dwells on God's greatness, his will, and his grace. His grace enables human beings to do what God likes; they act in accordance with his hukam; by doing this they become acceptable in God's court. He who does what pleases God finds all his wishes fulfilled; he goes to God's court with honour. God gives life and takes it away; some have the chains of slavery on their necks and others ride horses; he himself is the doer of everything, to whom can one complain? Only the doer can take care. His greatness cannot be described; he is the doer, all powerful, and merciful (*kartā, kādar, karīm*) who sustains life in the world; all the created beings do what he ordains for them; apart from him there is no refuge.[51]

A crucial role is given to the true Guru in three other pauṛīs. One may meet the true Guru (*satgurū*) through God's grace (*nadar*). Having wandered through many lives one may listen to the word (shabad) of the true Guru. None is a greater giver (*dātā*) than the true Guru: on meeting him one finds the truth and the self is eliminated; the whole truth is revealed by the true Guru. Without the true Guru; no one can find God; the true Guru himself removes the chain of attachment (*moh*) and leads to liberation. The *manmukh* who does not turn to the true Guru wastes his life because only by meeting the true Guru can one find the truth by lodging it in his heart. The only true master has promulgated the truth; only they find it to whom he gives, and who then live by the truth.

Through God's grace (karm) and the grace (*kirpā*) of the Guru one may find God and be absorbed in the truth. Through the instruction (*updes*) of the true Guru one receives the collirium of giān to see God; the true Guru is the boat which enables one to cross (the ocean of transmigration) through his grace. Through God's grace one may meet the true Guru who removes evil from human beings by placing his hand on their forehead; they find all the nine treasures (*naunidh*).[52]

Human life is a rare opportunity for liberation. Old age comes inevitably; one should serve one's interest by doing good deeds before it is too late. The body and the soul belong to God, the 'formless' (*nirankār*); one is saved from hell by remembering him. They who meditate on the only eternal truth serve God; they earn merit by doing good deeds; praising God for his grace, they find him. God likes the devotees who sing his praises. The devotees of God cherish the dust of the feet of those who have found God; they discard greed and meditate on the invisible God; one reaps the fruit of one's deeds. What matters is not learning or lack of learning but what one does to earn merit. None should be called bad; everyone has to account for what he does; there is no reason for pride on the basis of self-assessment. Everyone has to depart, and none should forget the Master who gave life and breath. We have to account for everything; we should make such a move that obviates defeat: we should only do good. The servant who does what the Master likes receives honour and enhanced salary; he who tries to rival the Master loses the salary he has earned and suffers humiliation; one does not dictate to the master: the only proper way is supplication (*ardās*).[53] The references to the Guru and the devotee in these pauṛīs could include Guru Nanak himself and his disciples.

Turning to the shaloks of Guru Nanak in *Āsā dī Vār* we find that he underscores God's greatness and his attributes. Everything related to him is true: the worlds, the continents and the forms he has created; his decree and his court, his ordinance and his command, and his grace. His praise is holy. They who meditate on him become holy. Great is God's exaltation; his Name is mighty; his justice is true; his station is immutable; he knows everyone's innermost thoughts and desires; he confers favours of his free will; he is the sole reality; all that happens is due to his will (razā).[54]

Marvellous is God's creation: the varied forms of speech and scripture; the multiplicity of creation and its distinctions; the created forms and their variety; air, water, fire, the earth, and the sources of life; pleasures in which the human beings are involved; union and separation; hunger and indulgence; some straying away and others following the straight path; some close to God and others far away. Fortunate are they who understand this mystery.[55]

God's power is manifest everywhere: in the nether regions and the skies, in the Vedas, Puranas, and semitic scriptures; in eating, drinking, and wearing of apparel; in love, in fear, and joy; in groups, species, and forms; in living beings all the world over, in good and evil, in honour and dishonour, in air, water, fire, and the dust-laden earth. God (kartā, kādar) watches all creation operating in accordance with his ordinance (hukam). He alone is everywhere. Having brought forth creatures he looks after them all. The creator who made them is mindful of them. He feels concerned for them.[56]

God alone is the true formless one, without fear of annihilation. Everything else is subject to fear: the wind that blows, the rivers that flow, fire, the earth, the sun and the moon, the skies, mighty heroes, and swarms of beings coming and going, Indra, Dharm Raj, Siddhas, Buddhas and Nathas. The writ of fear has been recorded over the head of all. Everything is false and short-lived: the ruler and the ruled, gorgeous theatres and bowers of ease and those who live in them, gold and silver and those who wear them, the human frame, beauty and the raiment, the relationship of husband and wife, the false attached to the false and oblivious of the creator, the whole world. However, the false objects of the world are sweet like sugar and honey, and boatfuls are ruined in attachment to them.[57]

Human beings remain preoccupied with themselves, suffering from the malady of self-centredness (haumai) which keeps them away from God. In egoism they come into the world and depart; they are born and they die; give away and receive; make gain and incur loss; seek to be truthful and remain false; enter hell and heaven; experience joy and sorrow; become covered with sins and wash them off; stick to folly and acquire wisdom. They know nothing of the essence of liberation. Only truth leads to liberation and in order to be true one should bear truth in one's heart; one should be washed clean of impurity and falsehood; one should be devoted to truth in love; the door of liberation becomes accessible to one who listens to the Divine Name: he comes to understand the way of union of the self with the Absolute.[58]

Several shaloks in *Āsā dī Vār* relate to the Guru who in no time 'turns men into gods'. They who have not turned to the Guru are like the seedless sesame plants left standing in the field; they flower and blossom but only to be filled with ash. Contemplation comes through the Guru's teaching; they who receive it through his grace are liberated. They who meet the true Guru obtain peace; in their minds is lodged the Name of God; they receive this boon to whom God is gracious; no longer concerned with hope or fear, they get rid of self-centredness (haumai) through the shabad. Through the true Guru's guidance one may receive true instruction and become true, abiding in the inner tīrath of the self with compassion for living beings and charity towards all. There can be no giān without the Guru. The path to God lies in sincere dedication, but this path cannot be found without the true Guru.[59]

In the shaloks of Guru Nanak, God's devotees perform his laudation and the eternal Name is their prop. In the hereafter is valued neither caste nor power; there is a new species of beings; only they are considered pure whose devotion to God is recognized. Where pleasure is, devotion is not. Only they swim across who practise devotion. In sweetness and humility lies the essence of merit and virtue. Outwardly clad in rough quilts, they who have the softness of silk within them are the good ones on this earth. They are attached to God in love. They care for none else. God has fashioned the vessels; some are filled with milk and others remain on the hearth-fire; some sleep under quilts and other stand guard over them; only they are exalted who receive God's grace.[60]

Equality, Caste, and Gender

Guru Nanak shows no appreciation for the distinctions of caste. 'If you wish well of yourself, do good deeds and call yourself low'. Guru Nanak refers to himself as a ministrel (*dhādī*) and the only boon he seeks is that he may meditate on God. The dhādīs were regarded as low (*nīch* jāt) and there were others who regarded themselves of high caste (*uttam* jāt). But they did not meditate on God and, therefore, Guru Nanak did not want to be like them. In other words, it is better to be of low caste and remember God than to be of high caste and forget him. There is no consideration for caste in God's court. The good are they who receive honour from God. The light of God is in the whole universe and in every created being. Only he who is devoted to God in love and calls himself low attains liberation. Sweetness lies in lowliness, which is the essence of goodness.[61]

'There is only one giver for all living beings, should I never forget him'. This is the refrain of a stanza in the *Japu*. The same light is in everyone and all belong to God. He has no form and no caste. In his court, birth and caste are of no count. In the social order, however, innumerable people stake their claims on the basis of caste and there are many others who have no caste. There is contention between those who claim caste status and those who do not have any. At one place Guru Nanak appears to regret that distinctions of caste have been obliterated. But this is the view of those who uphold the *varna* ideal. For Guru Nanak, there is no high or low. He appreciates those who rise above the distinctions of caste. He who forgets God is of low caste; he who is without the Name is an outcaste. Regard everyone as higher than yourself, and no one lower. Guru Nanak identifies himself with the lowest of the low.[62] Thus, he subscribes to the idea of equality and we may be sure that his path was open to all.

The path of Guru Nanak was open to women as well. 'How can I live without God, O' mother; praise be to God that I cannot live without praising him'. The woman is thirsty for God and waits for him throughout the night. He has captivated her heart and he knows her pain. The pain is due to his absence. 'May he be merciful to me and may I remain absorbed in him'. The woman with beautiful eyes who looks beautiful and lovely in her full *sigār* (*shringār*) would be perpetually humiliated if she does not remember God. 'I am the *cherī* (*chelī*) of my Thakur; I have caught the feet of the Master who gives life to the world, and I got rid of *haumai*'. 'We are all his slaves (*dāsīs*) and he is our master (*khasm*)'. We know that Guru Nanak is using the female voice, but it carries the implication that women as well as men could turn to God. More often, the metaphors come from conjugal relationship. 'The woman who is genuinely devoted to the Beloved is dear to the Master'. 'If a woman finds God-Husband in the home she attains peace'.[63]

Because of the patriarchal framework of the family, the metaphors pull the woman into subordination. The woman who is separated from her husband is unfortunate; she falls gradually but all the time like the wall of saline earth. The woman who is alone at night cannot sleep; she is afraid whether or not the husband would come; she cannot enjoy adornment or food; she is afraid that she may never conceive; without the husband she cannot go to sleep. When she comes to the conjugal bed, he may or may not like her. She does not know what would happen. She has not tasted love and her thirst is not quenched; her youth is gone and she is full of regret. The woman can find a husband by losing herself; if he looks with favour, she finds all the nine treasures; only that woman is *suhāgan* who is loved by her husband. How can a woman without merit have union with the husband? She is not beautiful, her eyes are not beautiful; she does not have good manners and she does not have a sweet tongue. She can adorn herself but she cannot become a suhāgan if she is not liked by her husband. The ill-mannered woman is equated with one who fails to have union with her husband, and the cultivated woman is equated with the one who finds union with her husband; the former is duhāgan and the latter suhāgan.[64] Love for God gets equated with conjugal love in which the initiative for union and separation remains with the husband. The grace of God gets transformed into the grace of the husband. Though the unequal institution of patriarchal family is reinforced in the process, the path of liberation is thrown open to women.

A New Path

We have seen that the *Japu* and the *Āsā dī Vār,* which are generally regarded as the two most important works of Guru Nanak, embody his theology and reflect his social awareness. The *Japu,* regarded as the most important expression of his theology brackets the Brahmanical, the ascetical, and the Islamic traditions as equally devoid of authority for him. The terminology of the jogīs is used to convey his own message. The *Āsā dī Vār* dwells on God, the Guru, and the way of liberation, and it contains extensive comment on contemporary religious beliefs and practices, social order, and polity.

The comment on the Brahmans includes scriptures, sacred places, worship of idols, cooperation with the rulers who are otherwise regarded as mlechh, the sacred thread, the shradhs, and the notion of pollution and purity. The comment on Vaishnava bhaktī underscores the rejection of incarnation and the futility of dance and drama as a form of religious worship. The comments on the jogīs relate to austerities, renunciation, and mendicancy as the common denomination of the ascetical traditions. The Muslim beliefs and practices include the scripture, the law, and the burial. The rulers are denounced for oppression, injustice, and discrimination on the basis of the differences of faith. Discrimination in the social order on the basis of caste and gender is also debunked.

In the other compositions of Guru Nanak the Brahmanical tradition is ridiculed as spiritually bankrupt and ethically neutral. Guru Nanak's comprehensive comment on the tradition includes recitation of scriptures, belief in gods and goddesses, worship of idols, ritual charity, and pilgrimage to sacred places, hom, āratī, funerary rites, vegetarian diet, dance and drama related to the human incarnations of Vishnu, the idea of purity and pollution, the varna ideal, the differential system of ethics for the castes, and an in-built discrimination against the outcastes and women.

The ascetical traditions, with their common denominator of renunciation, mendicancy, and austerities, are denounced in more or less strong terms. The jogī aspiration to acquire supranatural powers is debunked as devoid of any ethical content or merit. The denial of God's grace implicit in the attitude of the jogīs is only a reflection of their misconception of the attributes of God. The lack of concern for the common people on their part is yet another aspect of their attitudes. The Jain monks come in for severer criticism because of the added features of deliberate uncleanliness, extreme notion of *ahimsa* (non-violence), and virtual atheism. Against the ascetical ideal of celibacy, Guru Nanak shows a clear preference for the life of the householder. His own ideal is to remain detached-in-attachment and hopeless-in-hope.

The practices of the *'ulamā* (the qāzī and the mullā) in religious and social terms are seen as devoid of merit. The shaikhs are presented in a better light in comparison with the 'ulamā, but this relative appreciation is qualified by criticism of their dependence on state patronage and their presumption that they have reached the goal and they can authorize their disciples to lead others to the goal. There is adverse comment on the rulers, and the ruling class, and the intermediaries. What is denounced in strong terms is oppression, injustice, and discrimination on the basis of differences in religious affiliation of the subject people. The verses called *Bābar-bāṇī* contain political and moral criticism of the rulers, both Mughal and Afghan. The ruling class is bracketed with the rulers, whether Hindu or Muslim.

We can see that Guru Nanak's critique of his milieu is not confined to religious systems; it is extended to polity and social order. This was not incidental but a logical outcome of his ideology which advocated belief in one God, his adoration through the singing of Guru Nanak's hymns in congregation and to reflect on them individually, to earn one's living through honest means, to honour social commitments and act in a detached manner, to lead an ethical life, and to help others irrespective of their caste, creed, or gender. This ideology created the possibility of social regeneration on the basis of equality. Indeed, a socio-religious fraternity came into existence in the lifetime of Guru Nanak. Significantly, when the Siddhs ask Guru Nanak about his path (panth) he refers to his path as '*Gurmukh Panth*' or the path of those who have turned to the Guru, that is, to the worship of God introduced by Guru Nanak. He talks of the praises of God as 'our capital' and his all pervading light as 'our support'. They who drink the nectar of the Guru's instruction become acceptable in the divine court and attain liberation. The Guru and the Sikhs, together, constitute a new kind of association called *Gur-sangat, Gursant-sabhā, sant-sabhā, sādh-sabhā*, or *Sikh-sabhā*.

The statements related to this association (sangat) leave no doubt that Guru Nanak is talking of the Sikh congregation. In the sant-sabhā one finds the Guru and receives the gift of liberation. The One Name is recited in the sat-sangat and the True Guru gives the understanding that the Name alone is ordained by God. The praises of God in the sant-sabhā become the best of acts in accordance with Gurmat. The manmukh remains alien to nām, dān, and isnān, without the sweet taste of sahaj in the sādh-sabhā. By turning to the Guru in the sangat of sants one acquires the merit of pilgrimage to sixty-eight places. The *sevaks* of the Guru reflect on his shabad in sat-sangat, realize the divine presence within, attain liberation, and become the means of liberation for others. The fruit of truth is found in the sat-sangat where God's praises are sung. Misery and suffering end with joining the gursant-sabhā; one is united with God. The Guru is like a sacred river that removes the dirt of sins; all sins are washed away by joining the sant-sabhā and acting in accordance with the Guru's guidance. In the gur-sangat one recognizes God by recognizing his presence within.

The way in which Guru Nanak refers to the Sikhs, the Guru, and the sangat enables us to appreciate some of the other verses which have a close bearing on the new dispensation. The one who is bestowed with the gift of God's praises (*sifat-sālāh*) is the king of kings. All the sixty-eight places of pilgrimage are at the feet of the Guru. They who praise the One Lord are good; they are imbued with the love of the shabad; their sangat is the source of bliss; they are honoured with the order of truth and the banner of the True Name; they recognize hukam and live in accordance with it. The *girhī* sevak who is attached to gurmat is a Sikh who practises bhagtī through nām, dān, and isnān as a householder; has found the true door and the true home from the Guru; he worships none but God and does not go to any maṛhī or maṣāṇ.

The Sikh of the Guru rises above the considerations of caste (*jāt-baran*) and family (*kul*) by reflecting on the shabad in accordance with the Guru's instruction. The rare persons who have discarded the distinctions of caste are actually the Sikhs of the Guru. In the Guru's presence, as in the court of God, there is no consideration for caste or birth. The ones who are alien to the Name have no honour. They who forget God are of low caste. In the bāṇī of Guru Nanak there are clear intimations of the kind of life pursued by his followers. They have lodged the True One in their hearts and they are never forgetful of the Name. They sing God's praises in congregation in the Guru's presence. The Sikhs, sevaks, and *bhagat*s have found the Guru's door; they are dedicated to bhagtī through nām, dān, and isnān. They are householders, truly detached-in-attachment.

Guru Nanak's comment on certain customs and ceremonies suggests their rejection in favour of new beliefs and practices. The traditional songs for marriage should be replaced by the hymns on union with

Fig. 1.3 Dehra Guru Nanak at Kartarpur (founded by Guru Nanak) where he was cremated in 1539

God. The singing of Guru Nanak's *Alāhaṇiān* was meant to replace the traditional modes of lamentation. People are anxious about the disposal of the dead body; no one knows or wants to know where the soul has gone. What a person does in his lifetime is far more important than the way in which his body is treated after death. Equally futile is the performance of *kiryā* (rituals) by the Brahmans for the dead man's sojourn to the next world which involves the feeding of Brahmans and the floating of lamps. There is no room for these traditional rites and rituals in the ideology of Guru Nanak. His comment carries the implication that singing of Guru Nanak's hymns relating to these rites and rituals are the alternative for his followers.

There is divine sanction behind Guru Nanak's dispensation. He is called by God to his court and given the robe of true adoration with the nectar of the true name. They who taste it through the Guru's instruction attain peace. The ministrel spreads the message of the shabad. He utters the divine bāṇī as he receives it from the Lord. 'I have spoken what you have made me speak'. They who follow the Guru's path reap the profit of liberation through the bāṇī and the shabad of the Guru. 'Regard the *bāṇī* of the true Guru as nothing but true; he is one with God'.

Guru Nanak looked upon the new dispensation as distinct from the known religious traditions. The Vedas are compared with the giān of Guru Nanak's conception. The Vedas talk of virtue (pun) and vice (*pāp*) and of heaven and hell: good and bad deeds are the basis for this treatment after death. The giān of Guru Nanak involves adoration of the greatness of the True One and the True Name. Truth is reaped by sowing truth and the devotee finds a place in the divine court. The Vedas stand for trade, but giān is the capital received through God's grace. Without this capital no trader can carry any merchandise with him. People talk of the four cosmic ages, each with its own way laid down in the Veda for the age. For the Kaliyuga, the Veda prescribed was the *Atharvaṇa* which recommended ritual worship. For Guru Nanak, however, the way to liberation in the Kaliyuga is the one advocated by him: appropriation of the Name, recognition of hukam, and living in accordance with the divine will.

Notes

1. Sahib Singh, *Japujī Sāhib Steek*, Amritsar: Singh Brothers, 1995 (26th impression), pp. 96–9.

2. *Shabdarth Sri Guru Granth Sahib Ji*, 4 Vols, Amritsar: Shiromani Gurdwara Prabandhak Committee, 1999 (standard pagination of Ādi Srī Gurū Granth Sāhib), p. 662.
3. Sahib Singh, *Āsā dī Vār Steek*, Amritsar: Singh Brothers, 1995 (19th impression), pp. 44, 56.
4. Ibid., pp. 59–60, 70.
5. Ibid., pp. 85–6.
6. Ibid., pp. 87–90.
7. Ibid., p. 91.
8. Ibid., pp. 92–3.
9. Ibid., pp. 93–4.
10. Ibid., p. 97.
11. Ibid., pp. 99–103.
12. Ibid., p. 104.
13. Ibid., pp. 37–8.
14. Ibid., p. 40.
15. Ibid., p. 41.
16. Ibid., pp. 42, 70.
17. *Shabdarth*, pp. 504, 1153.
18. Ibid., pp. 358, 413, 416, 432, 831, 876, 1171, 1188, 1288.
19. Ibid., pp. 62, 1127, 1257.
20. Ibid., p. 637.
21. Ibid., pp. 13, 61, 147, 152, 597, 663, 687, 1328–9.
22. Ibid., pp. 358, 878.
23. Ibid., pp. 1289–90.
24. Ibid., pp. 350–1.
25. Ibid., pp. 56, 68, 1411.
26. Ibid., p. 1353.
27. Sahib Singh, *Japujī Sāhib Steek*, pp. 121–5.
28. Sahib Singh, *Āsā dī Vār Steek*, pp. 44, 60–1.
29. *Shabdarth*, pp. 147, 1189, 1190.
30. Ibid., p. 730.
31. Ibid., p. 877.
32. Ibid., pp. 155–6, 223–4, 1170.
33. Ibid., pp. 351, 359–60, 411–12, 879.
34. Ibid., pp. 22, 139, 634, 878–9.
35. Ibid., pp. 149–50.
36. Ibid., pp. 418–19.
37. Sahib Singh, *Āsā dī Vār Steek*, pp. 44–8.
38. *Shabdarth*, p. 24.
39. Ibid., p. 53.
40. Ibid., pp. 140–1.
41. Ibid., p. 141.
42. Ibid.
43. Ibid., p. 1286.

44. Sahib Singh, *Āsā dī Vār Steek*, pp. 87, 96, 98.
45. Ibid., pp. 70, 78–80, 93–5.
46. *Shabdarth*, pp. 16, 63–4, 141–2, 148, 225–7, 358, 1342.
47. Ibid., pp. 142, 145, 350, 1191, 1288.
48. Ibid., pp. 360, 417–18, 722.
49. For all the foregoing paragraphs in this section see Sahib Singh, *Āsā dī Vār Steek*.
50. Ibid., pp. 24, 29, 34.
51. Ibid., pp. 39, 49, 58, 92, 116–17.
52. Ibid., pp. 73, 83–4, 101–2.
53. Ibid., pp. 54–5, 58, 63, 67, 73, 87, 88–9, 92, 105, 108, 110, 114.
54. Ibid., pp. 25–9.
55. Ibid., pp. 30–3.
56. Ibid., pp. 33–4, 55–7.
57. Ibid., pp. 35–7, 63–5.
58. Ibid., pp. 50–4, 65–7.
59. Ibid., pp. 22–3, 41, 43, 61–2, 66–7, 76, 86.
60. Ibid., pp. 45–7, 72, 84–5, 107, 116–17.
61. Ibid., pp. 44, 63, 72, 74, 80, 84.
62. *Shabdarth*, pp. 2, 7, 15, 18, 53, 62, 349, 414, 663, 1188, 1198, 1328, 1330–1, 1345.
63. Ibid., pp. 225, 729, 1108–9, 1197.
64. Ibid., pp. 17, 18, 242, 356–7, 722, 750, 762–3.

2

In the Master's Footsteps

The *Shaloks* of Guru Angad

Sahib Singh was the first Sikh scholar to publish the shaloks of Guru Angad in a single volume. He thought of extending this method to the *bāṇī* of the other Gurus.[1] More recently, the Department of Guru Granth Sahib Studies, Punjabi University, Patiala, has published a series of line-and-word index of the bāṇī of each Guru. For the volume on Guru Angad, the text is also published.[2] The assumption seems to be that scholarly study of the bāṇī of each Guru can enhance our understanding of the historical development of the Sikh tradition.

In the Gurū Granth Sāhib, there are only sixty-three *shaloks* of Guru Angad, integrated with nine *Vārs*: thirty-two with the Vārs of Guru Nanak, nineteen with those of Guru Amar Das, and twelve with those of Guru Ram Das. The shalok at the end of the *Japu* is also included by Sahib Singh in the shaloks of Guru Angad. The total number of lines in these shaloks does not exceed 240. But their importance is out of all proportion to their volume. Guru Angad was the first successor of Guru Nanak; his understanding of Guru Nanak is of great historical significance.

Despite the thin volume of the shaloks of Guru Angad, their scope is quite wide. He talks of God, his *hukam*, and his *nadar*. He talks of the Guru and his grace, and he talks of the *nām* and the *shabad*. The *manmukh* and the *Gurmukh* figure prominently in his shaloks and he talks of the path and the goal of liberation. He refers to the Sikhs in a very significant way, and he reflects on the position of Guru Nanak in the Kaliyuga. Thus, Guru Angad projects his theology, dwells on liberation in life, and pays homage to Guru Nanak.

Guru Angad's Theology

God is one (*eko*). 'Ek Krishanan' is the God of gods, the soul of the god of gods. Guru Angad is a servant (*dās*) of those who know this, and they are like God (Niranjan) himself.[3] God alone is the creator, and he alone is the preserver. He creates all living beings and he destroys them. He is all in all.[4] Even in water, where there are no shops and no cultivation, no transactions and no sale or purchase, God provides sustenance to the living beings which feed on living beings. He takes care of them. The import is very clear: 'Do not worry about sustenance, God himself takes care of it'.[5] There is no need to speak; he knows all. God is the only object of praise. The creator of a wondrous world should be praised.[6] Think of the one who brings the spring (Basant); praise him who is the support of all.[7] Do not praise the creation but the creator. He is the only giver of gifts and no other. Praise the creator, and the bestower of all gifts. He alone is eternal and his store-house (*bhandār*) remains full. Praise only him who knows no limits.[8]

Guru Angad emphasizes the power of God. He is the one master whose order cannot be disobeyed. The *mīrs*, *maliks*, and *sālārs* are subject to his order. Human beings have no power of their own; they do what is ordained for them. God sends them into the world, and he calls them back. Only what pleases him is good.[9] Think of the one who created the universe and who has the power to control.[10] Human beings are pushed by their deeds; the rope in the noose is in the hands of God. They eat what he ordains.[11] The right attitude towards him is that of supplication (*ardās*) for he can never be compelled. The ignorant behave according to their own understanding and do not turn to God. False deeds multiply falsehood; only the praises of God result in flowering of the spirit.[12] He knows and he does what is right: 'stand before him in supplication (*ardās*)'.[13] To recognize his hukam and to die unto oneself (*jīvat marnā*) are the means to meet God. In this state of total dedication one sees without eyes, hears without ears, walks without feet, works without hands, and speaks without the tongue. In other words, he follows the will of God.[14]

God's power is matched by his grace. This world is the cabin of the True One; he abides in it. Some are saved through his hukam and others destroyed by his hukam. He is pleased to take some out and keep others engrossed in *māyā*. No one knows who would be saved or destroyed.

By turning to the Guru one realizes that only they are saved whom he himself shows the light.[15] The *sāhūkār* gives capital to the *vanjārās* to trade for profit. Some gain profit and others lose even the capital. They all work for gain. But only they who make the right investment receive God's grace (nadar).[16] The right investment is indicated in another shalok. They who keep the flag of nām flying receive God's grace. They are the treasurer (*potedār*) of the gift of the praises of God; they are given the key to the store-house (bhandār). The store-keeper of merit becomes acceptable to God.[17]

Guru Angad talks of the grace (karm) of the perfect Guru whose speech is perfect; they who are made perfect by him remain in perfect balance. They alone are the perfect sāhūkārs who find the Perfect One. They remain in the same state all the time. They are among those few who have God's *darshan*.[18] Through the Guru's grace (*prasād*), one who turns to the Name finds recognition; all other means are superfluous.[19] Through the Guru's grace one swims across the ocean of transmigration; the life is fruitless if one does not realize God.[20]

Guru Angad refers to the Name in a few of his shaloks which highlight its importance. Mediation on the Name is the source of merit.[21] The nectar (*amrit*) of nām is received through the Guru's grace. They who praise the greatness of the Name of God are dyed in his love. There is only one nectar, no other. It is found within. They drink it in love for whom it is ordained.[22] The Name is forgotten in worldly pursuits.[23]

The importance of the shabad is highlighted in a similar way. One cannot be on the right side of God through one's own effort, howsoever hard one may try; his side is won through right intention and reflection on the shabad.[24] The duties traditionally assigned to various categories of people are restricted to them: pursuit of knowledge (giān) for the *jogīs*, mastery of the Vedas for the Brahmans, courage and valour for the Khatris, and service of others for the Shudars. But the shabad (of the Guru) is for all. Guru Angad is the servant (dās) of those who know this; they are like God.[25] The shabad of the Guru is appropriated through divine grace.[26]

Liberation-in-life

Human beings remain engrossed in māyā, oblivious of the higher purpose of life. They garner wealth for a life which is comparable to a single night; they leave in the morning. Nothing goes with them and they regret in the end.[27] Forgetful of the departure they pursue worldly affairs, but they who are aware of the end do not widen their engrossment.[28] Set fire to all worldly aspirations.[29] Sensual pleasures do not quench the thirst. The eyes are never satiated by attractive sights, the ears are never satiated with sweet melodies, the tongue is never tired of utterance. The seekers of sensual pleasures are all the same. Hunger is never appeased by mere words. The hungry is satiated only by appropriating the praises of God's attributes.[30]

Māyā is all around, but there is an inner adversary too. It is *haumai*. It is comparable to a chronic disease. Its essence is to attribute actions to the self as a separate entity from God. This keeps the human being bound to chain of death and rebirth. Where does it come from and how does it disappear? Haumai is linked with the law of *karma* and the cycle of transmigration, but it has its remedy within itself. One may appropriate the Guru's shabad through God's grace. This is the remedy for the chronic disease of haumai.[31]

Generally, human beings remain engrossed in māyā, and captivated by haumai they remain blind to nām and shabad. The blind have no idea of the jewels; they expose their ignorance when they try to assess the jewels.[32] The blind follow the wrong path, but they who have sight do not follow the path that leads to wilderness. The blind are not they who do not have eyes but they who turn away from God; they are really blind.[33] The master who has taken away their sight may restore it (through his grace). Otherwise, they do not listen to anyone and go on their wrong path. One does not purchase the article that one cannot see.[34] Do not call them blind who have not been given eyesight by God; the really blind are they who do not recognize his hukam.[35] There is no point in befriending them as there is no point to be in love with the worldly great. Any advice given to them is like a line drawn on water that leaves no effect.[36]

The blind cannot appreciate the pearl because they cannot see its beauty. The dealer in jewels has opened his bag of jewels; it is prized equally by the seller and the buyer. Only they who possess merit, buy jewels.[37] The reference here is to the shabad and bāṇī of the Guru. The real assessor assesses himself just as the wise physician (*vaid*) diagnoses the disease and prescribes the right medicine. He regards himself as a guest (in a *sarāi*) and does not entangle himself with the other wayfarers; he speaks to like-minded people and associates with them. Not greed but truth makes him acceptable. (He is on the side of God for he knows that) an arrow shot at the sky comes back to the earth; the archer should know that God is inaccessible.[38] Through an extended metaphor Guru Angad makes it clear that a real physician is he who can get rid of his own disease.[39] Not mere verbal profession but actual conduct is important. Having sown poison one cannot reap nectar (amrit).[40]

Only dedicated and voluntary service can be rewarded. The servant who shows obedience and questions the orders of the master is lost from the very beginning; his obedience is false and his disobedience brings demerit; he can hold no place in the end.[41] The servant who performs service in pride and talks too much is not liked by the master. Only the one who renders selfless service receives honour. He becomes acceptable to his master.[42] What kind of a service is it that does not remove the fear of the master? A distinguished servant is he who is absorbed in his master and becomes one with him.[43] The servant who performs service unwillingly as if he is forced into service earns no merit and is of no use to others. Only that service is appreciated which is gladly rendered.[44]

Indeed, what is required of a devotee is total dedication in love. One dies to the self in love for the beloved; to live without him is a curse.[45] True love is exclusive. What kind of love is it that has another object of love? The true lover remains absorbed (in God) all the time. He accepts good and bad alike as coming from God.[46] His longing for God is commendable. The head that does not bow to the master is better cut off; the body that has no longing for God is better burnt in fire.[47] People are inevitably known by what they do. To be regarded as beautiful, a body has to be whole. A true human being is the one who desires God and reaps the fruit.[48] They who are in awe of God have no fear; they who do not entertain the awe of God live and die in fear. In the divine presence one realizes that there is nothing to fear.[49] He who receives honour in the divine court is not affected by worldly considerations, just as fire is not affected by the cold, the sun is not affected by the night, the moon is not affected by darkness, and air and water are not affected by the caste (of those who use them).[50]

The last shalok of the *Japu*, which is regarded as embodying the essence of Sikh theology, refers to air as the Guru, water as the father, earth as the mother, day and night as the nurses, and the whole world playing. The good and bad deeds of human beings are closely watched in the divine court, and they are close to or distant from God in accordance with their deeds. They who meditate on the Name, their labour bears fruit. Their countenances are bright and they become the means of liberation for others.[51] What remains unsaid in this shalok is that being close to God is being one with him, and this is the state of liberation. The other terms used for this experience are knowledge, enlightenment, sight, and meeting or union.[52] Guru Angad talks of meeting (*milnā*) in a manner that suggests union. It is a meeting of the spirits, not a physical union, and therefore it is a true meeting.[53]

Guru Angad talks of the Sikhs without using the term 'Sikh'. A shalok starts with the statement that earth is conventionally divided into nine *khands*. But the human body may be seen as the ninth khand which has all the nine treasures of the earth in the form of nām. Praise be to those fortunate ones who find God by turning to 'Nanak as *gur, pīr*'. In the fourth quarter (*pahar*) of the night (early in the morning), love wells up in their hearts for they have friendship with those who have the true Name in their hearts and on their lips. Amrit is disbursed (where they meet) through God's grace. Their bodies shine like pure gold and, through the grace of God (*sarrāf*), they do not need the heat of the furnace again. This appears to be a reference to the Sikhs meeting for congregational worship in the morning. For the remaining seven pahars of the day and night, they conduct themselves well; sitting with the learned (in Gurbāṇī) they learn how to make a distinction between vice and virtue; the false are discarded there and the true ones are praised. They realize that *dukh* and *sukh* are in the hands of the Master.[54] This long shalok indicates the importance which Guru Angad gave to congregational worship and the Sikhs who participated in it. Possibly, prayer (ardās) was performed in congregation.

When the metaphor used for God is 'husband' (*kant*) the meeting becomes a metaphor for union. We can see, hear, and know God in and from his creation but this is not experiencing God. We cannot embrace him because we do not have the feet, the hands, and the eyes to reach him. If we make God's awe our feet, his love our hands, and meditation on him our eyes we can meet 'the husband'.[55] Guru Angad uses the female voice in a few other shaloks too. God is 'my only support'; that is why 'I wail and cry' if he is not remembered.[56] If you wish to meet the husband (*sauh*, kant), enjoy him in sukh and remember him in dukh.[57] The Sawan has come and I long to meet the husband (kant); the duhāgans who are attached to others have nothing but suffering.[58] They who have the husband in the home celebrate the spring season; they whose husbands are away suffer all day and night.[59] The Sawan has come and it is raining; the suhāgans who love their husbands (sauh) sleep in peace.[60] These shaloks carry the implication that the path of liberation is open to women.

Guru Angad's attitude towards those who have not turned to the Guru is important to note. The blanket term manmukh is used for them. If the *mantrī* (*madārī*) who knows how to handle scorpions takes it into his head to handle cobras, he ignites his own funeral. If a manmukh opposes the Gurmukh he is bound to go down for his fall accords with the Master's hukam. However, God is the master of both and watches them. In other words, whatever happens is due to his will (*razā*).[61] The manmukh appreciates the gift more than the bestower. He thinks he is clever. What he does secretly becomes known everywhere. They who practise virtue are known as righteous (*dharmī*), and they who practise vice are known as sinners (*pāpī*). God himself is the creator of this sport (*khel*), there is no other. Human beings speak so long as the light placed in their frames is there; without that light, they can do nothing. By turning to the Guru one realizes that there is only one God who is all-wise.[62] God creates all but in different forms. They all have one Master; therefore there can be no inferior. They pursue different vocations but they all have only one Master. Some have more and other have less, but none is totally empty. They come naked into the world and they leave it naked. But they remain engrossed (in māyā). Without recognizing hukam one cannot hope for a happy end.[63] On the whole, Guru Angad has everything good to say about those who turn to the Guru (Gurmukh), and he has nothing good to say about the manmukh who follows his own inclinations, but there is no condemnation of the manmukh who too is a part of God's creation. To condemn others is to go against the divine will.

Homage to Guru Nanak

By turning to the Guru one comes to know the reality of Kaliyuga: now the beggar is called *pātshāh*; the fool is called pandit; the blind is called 'the assessor' (*pārkhū*); the perpetrator of mischief is called chaudharī; and the false woman sits in front.[64] For this yuga, the amrit-bāṇī (of Guru Nanak) has come as the means of regeneration. The Vedas introduced instruction in terms of pāp and pun, transmigration, and heaven

Fig. 2.1 Khadur Sahib, associated with Guru Angad (1539–52)

and hell; they introduced the differences of high and low among castes and kinds, resulting in delusion. Springing from meditation and knowledge, the amrit-bāṇī reveals the essence of things. Uttered by the Guru it is understood by those who turn to the Guru, and by God's grace they meditate on it. They realize that God created the world by his hukam, keeps it under his hukam, and looks after it through his hukam. This realization removes haumai and makes human beings acceptable to God.[65]

'If a hundred moons were to rise, and a thousand suns, despite their light there would be darkness without the Guru'.[66] This is how Guru Angad looks upon Guru Nanak in the context of Kaliyuga. They need no instruction who have been instructed by Guru Nanak; they have been taught to appropriate truth through adoration of God.[67] The office of Guru Nanak has now devolved upon Guru Angad. 'What kind of a gift is it that one gives to oneself? The miracle is to receive it from the master through his grace'.[68] This shalok enunciates the principle that no one can claim Guruship as a matter of right without being installed or designated by a predecessor. The use of 'Nanak' in the shaloks of Guru Angad makes him one with Guru Nanak, underlining not only the unity of Guruship but also its continuity. Guru Angad was installed as the Guru in the lifetime of Guru Nanak.

We can see that Guru Angad's conception of God is the same as that of Guru Nanak. God is the only deity who is all powerful and compassionate, the only creator, sustainer, and destroyer of what he creates. His creation is real in itself but false in comparison with the eternal truth of God. Like Guru Nanak, Guru Angad uses the concepts of Hukam, Nadar, Nam, Shabad, and Guru, and his conception of liberation is the same as that of Guru Nanak. Like Guru Nanak, he gives great importance to ardās. The path is open to all, irrespective of caste, creed, or gender.

On the whole, Guru Angad pays a profound homage to Guru Nanak by walking in his footsteps. His shaloks reinforce the ideology of Guru Nanak and strengthen the institution of dharamsāl for congregational worship. We know from a near contemporary source that the *langar* for community meal became more remarkable in the time of Guru Angad. What is even more significant, Guru Angad's wife, Mata Khivi, used to look after the langar with its rich fare of *khīr* enriched with ghee.[69] Guru Angad's understanding and interpretation of Guru Nanak's position gave right direction to the Sikh movement.

Guru Angad pays even a more profound homage to Guru Nanak by equating the 'shabad' with his bāṇī and by equating the 'Guru' with Guru Nanak. He projects Guru Nanak as the founder of a new dispensation based on divine revelation.

Notes

1. Sahib Singh, *Slok Gurū Angad Sāhib Steek*, Amritsar: Singh Brothers, 1992 (4th edition; first published in 1948), pp. 5–7.
2. Balkar Singh, ed., *Bāṇī Gurū Angad Dev Jī dā Tuk-Tatkarā*, Patiala: Punjabi University, 1997.
3. Sahib Singh, *Slok Gurū Angad Sāhib Steek*, pp. 79–80. The pages in all cases cover not only to the text but also the annotation, which may be helpful to the reader for appreciating our interpretation.
4. Ibid., pp. 88–9.
5. Ibid., pp. 108–11.
6. Ibid., pp. 95–6.
7. Ibid., pp. 97–8.
8. Ibid., pp. 118–19.
9. Ibid., pp. 119–21.
10. Ibid., pp. 69–70.
11. Ibid., p. 90.
12. Ibid., pp. 84–6.
13. Ibid., p. 112.

14. Ibid., pp. 55–6.
15. Ibid., pp. 73–5.
16. Ibid., pp. 115–16.
17. Ibid., pp. 121–2.
18. Ibid., pp. 58–9.
19. Ibid., pp. 102–3.
20. Ibid., p. 69.
21. Ibid., p. 113.
22. Ibid., p. 117.
23. Ibid., p. 131.
24. Ibid., pp. 93–4.
25. Ibid., pp. 78–9.
26. Ibid., p. 75.
27. Ibid., pp. 91–2.
28. Ibid., p. 91.
29. Ibid., pp. 63–4.
30. Ibid., pp. 64–5.
31. Ibid., pp. 72–5.
32. Ibid., pp. 103–4.
33. Ibid., pp. 105–7.
34. Ibid., pp. 107–8.
35. Ibid., p. 108.
36. Ibid., pp. 86–7.
37. Ibid., pp. 104–5.
38. Ibid., pp. 67–8.
39. Ibid., pp. 126–7.
40. Ibid., pp. 83–4.
41. Ibid., pp. 81–2.
42. Ibid., pp. 82–3.
43. Ibid., pp. 87–8.
44. Ibid., pp. 92–3.
45. Ibid., p. 51.
46. Ibid., pp. 50–1.
47. Ibid., pp. 51–2.
48. Ibid., pp. 124–5.
49. Ibid., p. 91.
50. Ibid., pp. 70–1.
51. Ibid., pp. 62–4.
52. Ibid., pp. 55–6, 58–9, 69–70, 73–5.
53. Ibid., pp. 98–9.
54. Ibid., pp. 59–62.
55. Ibid., pp. 57–8.
56. Ibid., pp. 99–100.
57. Ibid., pp. 100–1.
58. Ibid., p. 127.

59. Ibid., pp. 96–7.
60. Ibid., pp. 127–30.
61. Ibid., pp. 65–7.
62. Ibid., pp. 53–5.
63. Ibid., pp. 114–15.
64. Ibid., pp. 130–1.
65. Ibid., pp. 122–3.
66. Ibid., p. 73.
67. Ibid., pp. 71–2.
68. Ibid., p. 87.
69. In the *Ramkalī Vār,* Balvand refers to Mata Khivi as the shade of a tree with thick leaves. *Ādi Srī Gurū Granth Sāhib,* p. 967.

3

An Exclusive Path for the Kaliyuga

Guru Amar Das

God and Liberation-in-life

In the compositions of the Guru Amar Das, God is uncompromisingly one. He created himself and, therefore, there is no other. The One alone is eternally true and there is no one else. Before the creation of the three worlds there was only the formless one (*nirankār*). He created the universe and became the creator. He is the only doer (*kartār*). He does not consult anyone; whatever he wills comes to pass. He is *sarguṇ* and *nirguṇ* at the same time. The elements like air, water, and fire, and all forms spring from him. All living beings are his and he is of everyone. He is out there in the universe and he is within every human frame. There is no other entity even remotely comparable with him.[1]

In the writings of Guru Amar Das two attributes of God are referred to very frequently: his omnipotence expressed in his *hukam* and *bhāṇā*, and his omnipresence which finds specific expression in his grace. The Fearless One (*nirbhau*) is always kind. The body and the soul are his gifts; he is the only giver of gifts for all and he shows the right path to those who go astray. He does everything and his hukam prevails everywhere. He whom God shows his grace (*nadar*) attains liberation. They who recognize God's hukam receive peace and comforts of all kinds. The only giver is the only friend. Everything appears and disappears through his hukam. He is the God of all, there is no other. All have only one Master, that is, God. Through his grace he shows the right path.[2]

Comparing God to a king, Guru Amar Das says that God is the True King. His rule is eternal. In the all the four *yuga*s there is only one kingship (*pātshāhī*) and only one command (*amr*). God is the King of kings. There is no one above him. He is the only one who heads the government of the universe and he alone issues orders. All the rulers of the world pale into insignificance. 'Do not call them Rājās who fight and die on the field of battle; they assume birth again and again' (like ordinary men). God has spread the true umbrella over the heads of the *bhagats* who enjoy real pātshāhī. He who turns to the Guru gets rulership of the world. The real pātshāhs are they who are dyed in the Name of God; all other pātshāhīs are false.[3] Incidentally, the 'service of the other' (*vidāṇī chākarī*) acquires a certain degree of political significance in this context. Primarily, the phrase refers to the spiritual realm in which God alone is to be worshipped (and not any god or goddess); 'the other' is equally applicable to *māyā* or God's creation as distinct from God. At the same time, the service of a temporal king does not command the sole affiliation of God's devotee, his servant. 'For me, there is no one else like you; there is no one else so great'. The Name of God is my father, my mother, every kin and my brother. 'For me, there is only one giver and no other'. 'I have seen the whole world; there is only one giver'. 'My prayer is to the Lord; you are the true Master'. 'Keep me as you wish, my Master'.

Guru Amar Das's personal statements indicate his disposition towards God as much as his conception of God. Brahma, Vishnu, and Mahesh are God's creation. Guru Amar Das' devotion cannot be addressed to any of them, or their incarnations. Indeed, *rāg* and *nād* as symbols respectively of Vaishnava *bhaktī* and Gorakhnāthī *yoga* are discarded in favour of the service of God and his shabad.[4]

This does not mean, however, that Guru Amar Das discards the idea of *bhagtī*. It is commendable that one should perform bhagtī in love and awe, and feel the presence of God all the time. Adornment with love and awe is commendable for following the right path. Two shaloks of Guru Amar Das underscore the importance of awe (*bhai*). Bhagtī is found by turning to the Guru and dying in life. Bhagtī does not spring without awe and the mind does not become pure. Adorned with awe and bhagtī one may attain the state of a suhāgan by turning to the Guru. Bhagtī becomes possible by turning to the Guru and one dies to live through bhagtī. True bhagtī transforms men into gods. Bhagtī cannot be performed without awe; love and awe inculcated by the shabad lead to bhagtī.

Through God's grace one may perform bhagtī and obtain eternal peace.[5] On the whole, thus, bhagtī in the *bāṇī* of Guru Amar Das is associated with awe in acknowledgement of the omnipotence of the one and only Lord. What is more important, the way of bhagtī is found from the Guru and through the Guru's shabad. In other words, Sikh bhagtī is not the same thing as Vaishnava or Shaiva bhagtī.

The *bhagat* of Guru Amar Das is a Sikh of the Guru. The Name of God is the only source of honour and status (*jāt-pat*) for the bhagats; they are adorned with the Name. 'My true Lord is the destroyer of demons; the bhagats are saved through the shabad of the Guru'. Singing praises of God in accordance with Gurmat, the bhagats look beautiful. The bhagats are happy, being dyed in the true shabad. They meditate on the Name. One may be called bhagat by everyone but bhagtī is not found without serving the True Guru and then one may have the perfect fortune of meeting the Lord.[6] Evidently, according to Guru Amar Das, all Sikhs of the Guru are bhagats.

Guru Amar Das refers to the path and the goal for the Sikh of the Guru. The mind is conquered through the shabad of the Guru. Haumai is eradicated by recognizing the shabad. One prays for being enabled to sing the praises of him who is the bestower of the body and the mind. The great warrior is he who destroys the enemy known as *ahankār* (pride). The detached devotee meditates on the Name of God. The object is to remain pure amidst the impurities of the world so that one's light mingles with the divine light. One becomes liberated by serving the liberated one. Lodging God in the heart by the instruction of the Guru, one becomes indifferent to joy and sorrow. The awe of the True Guru removes all illusion and fear, and one recognizes the shabad through God's grace. The goal is liberation-in-life. The servants of God concentrate on the feet of the Guru. The Guru's *darshan* leads to the state of liberation. The devotee takes refuge in the True Guru and dedicates his body and mind to him; he gives up his caste. He bathes in the pool of nectar that is within him. By recognizing the divine hukam, one does not entertain any hope for oneself. One should be ready to give one's head. The service of the Guru is labour of love; one serves in awe of the Lord. The service of another is a curse. The *jan* of God attains liberation and enables others to attain liberation. Liberation-in-life is attained through the divine Name and the Guru's shabad. The cup of the love of the Master is drunk through God's grace. They who conquer their mind conquer the world. They who have lodged God in their hearts by turning to the Guru, for them there is always the season of regeneration.[7]

What is emphasized by Guru Amar Das more than anything else is dying-unto-self and attaining liberation-in-life. The terms often used by Guru Amar Das are *jīvat mare, shabad mare, Gur ke shabad jīvat mare, āp chhoṛ jīvat mare, jīvan marnā, mar mar jīve, jīvat mare mare phun jīve, shabad maro phir jīvo sad hī tā phir marn nā hoi, mūe tin nā ākhiyae je Gur ke shabad samayae, mar jīvīyā* and *jīvatiān mar rahiyae.*[8] Eradication of haumai by recognizing God's hukam and accepting his will is the basic idea of dying unto self. The devotee who dies unto himself has no desires and aspirations of his own. He is detached completely from the world; he lives in the world not for himself so much as for others. The terms frequently used for this state by Guru Amar Das are *ghar hī māhi udās, greh kutumb māhi sadā udās, bikhiā māhi udās* and *viche greh udās.*[9] The basic idea is that the Sikh of the Guru experiences liberation-in-life as a state of bliss but he does not become inactive; he performs his social duties in a spirit of detachment for the welfare of others. He approximates to the divinity; he worships and conducts his life in accordance with God's will.[10]

The opportunity for liberation-in-life was open to all. Guru Amar Das rejects the differences of caste in this connection. Like the human frame, caste (jāt) does not go with one after death. He who recognizes the essence is the real pandit. He who serves the True Guru is dear to God, he is high *(uttam)*, and his caste is the highest. Neither beauty nor caste goes with one to the next world; there, everyone is treated in accordance with his deeds. Since all belong to God and to no other, none can be called bad or inferior (*mandā*). The caste (jāt) and status (pat) of the bhagats is the Name of God. The worldly fame and caste will not go with you. By taking refuge in God the lowest become the highest. The same God is in all. None should be proud of one's caste. He who recognizes Brahm is a Brahman. Only fools take pride in caste and this pride is the source of all evil. Everyone talks of four varnas but all human beings have been created by God. The whole world is made of the same clay. Guru Amar Das talks of God as the Potter who makes pots of various kinds and none has the power to change their equal status. Guru Amar Das talks explicitly of both men and women in connection with the path of liberation.[11]

The Guru, *Nām, Shabad,* and *Bāṇī*

The terms *Guru* and *Satguru* are frequently used interchangeably in the compositions of Guru Amar Das. One should serve the True Guru with single-minded devotion. The True Guru is the master who is true and pure. The service of the True Guru is hard: one has to give one's head and annihilate the self. By serving the True Guru all attachment is burnt and one becomes a renunciate in the home. They who turn away from the True Guru, their foreheads are blackened. By serving the True Guru we receive eternal peace, and light is mingled with the divine light; they who take refuge with the True Guru deserve all praise. By meeting the True Guru one may receive the Name and one's thirst and attachment may end. Without the Guru there can be no peace and the cycle of death and rebirth never ends. The Guru lights the fire of knowledge and the darkness of ignorance vanishes. He who walks in accordance with the Guru's will suffers no sorrow; there is nectar in the Guru's will and one attains the state of bliss. Without the Guru the self is never eradicated. The gift is in the hands of the giver and it is received through the Guru. There can be no bhagtī without the Guru and no gift of bhagtī without the Guru, howsoever one may wish for it. On meeting the True Guru one obtains this wealth by lodging the divine Name of God in the heart. Without the Guru, one cannot find the Name and the right place; one should look for the True Guru from whom one can receive the truth.[12] We can see that Guru and Satguru are interchangeable terms and both refer more frequently to the personal Guru, that is, Guru Nanak and his successors. In the compositions of Guru Amar Das, primacy is given to the human Guru who has an aura of divinity.

Similarly, nām, shabad, and bāṇī appear to be used interchangeably. Human beings are exhorted to meditate on the Name, ask for the Name, and attain the state of bliss through the Name. He who serves the True Guru receives the treasure of the Name. He who has the light of the Name within lasts for ever. The divine Name is the ocean of bliss. If we meditate on the Name, we attain truth. The term shabad appears to be used more frequently than the Name. In any case, the mind is conquered through the shabad of the Guru. One attains God through the shabad, and service of God receives true reward. They who reflect on the Guru's shabad, their countenances are bright. By lodging the shabad of the Guru within oneself, God is lodged in the heart. Both the mind and the body become pure when the shabad of the Guru is lodged in the heart; by praising God through the Guru's shabad one is dyed in bliss.[13] The phrases *Gur kā shabad* and *Gurshabadī* occur frequently in the bāṇī of Guru Amar Das.

Though less frequent, there are a number of references to bāṇī in the writings of Guru Amar Das. True is God and true the bāṇī; he is realized through the shabad. True is the bāṇī and true the shabad when one loves the truth. The bāṇī is revealed for all the four ages; it reveals the truth. Very often, the term bāṇī is found in association with the Guru. Gurbāṇī is the light of the world. In pursuit of devotion to God one sings the bāṇī of the Guru day and night. The bāṇī of the Guru is the sweet nectar. One receives bāṇī from the perfect Guru. The term bāṇī occurs in association with nām, shabad, and Guru. They who love the Name are the true singers of God's praise; they appropriate the true bāṇī and reflect on the shabad.[14]

There are verses or even single lines in which two or more of the terms are used. These lines and verses clarify the usage further. True is the bāṇī and true the shabad; this realization comes through the Guru's grace. There is one bāṇī, one Guru, and one shabad for reflection; true is the shop and true the merchandise; the store-house is full of jewels. True is the praise, true the bāṇī, and peace comes through the shabad. The gift of the Guru is bāṇī-shabad. The bāṇī of the Guru is meant for all the four directions; by listening to it one is absorbed in the true Name. The bāṇī of the Guru is understood through the Guru by getting dyed in the shabad.[15] Thus, shabad and bāṇī become synonymous and tend to become synonymous with nām. Reflection on shabad-bāṇī is a way of meditation on the Name. The equation of the Name with God and of shabad with God's revelation is not discarded, but there is much greater emphasis on the equation between shabad and bāṇī, that is, between the shabad of the Guru and Gurbāṇī.

The *Sangat* and the *Sikhs*

In the bāṇī of Guru Amar Das, the existence of congregational worship becomes emphatic. He refers to it as *sādh-sangat, sat-sangat, sachchī sangat, sachch sangat, sant-sangat,* or *Gur-sabhā*. The Gur-sabhā associates congregational worship clearly with the Guru. The terms sādh and sant are used commonly for the Sikh. The most frequently used term is sat-sangat which emphasizes the character of the congregation as seen by the Guru. As the 'true association' it stands distinguished from others. There can be no sangat without the True Guru, just as there can be no liberation without the shabad.[16]

For Guru Amar Das, the importance of the sangat is linked up with its nature and character. They who are perfectly fortunate attain *bairāg* through sādh-sangat. They who reflect on the shabad of the Guru, begin to entertain the awe of God; they come to the sat-sangat and sing the praises of God. By lodging God in their hearts they get rid of duality (*dubidhā*). By sitting in the true sangat one appropriates the true Name of God and the mind gains poise. The place where the praises of God are sung in sat-sangat is beautiful and is dear to God. They who are immersed in truth turn to true devotion; to their great good fortune they appropriate the Name; they realize God through the true shabad sung in the sat-sangat for the adoration of God. All awareness comes by joining the sat-sangat where devotion to God is expressed through the shabad of the Guru; one learns to accept the will of God and remains in peace, absorbed in the truth.[17]

The centrality of congregational worship in the Sikh way of life becomes evident from what Guru Amar Das says about the true association. He who is God-dyed by God in his colour meets the sat-sangat. True association springs from the True Guru and it leads to inclination towards the truth. All those who remain alien to this sangat live at the level of brutes. In the House of the Guru there is the treasure of the Name and its store-house is filled with bhagtī. Day and night there is *kīrtan* through the medium of the Guru's shabad which has been spoken for all the cosmic ages. He who turns to the Guru reflects on the shabad of the Guru and gets rid of disease. God himself enables one to meet the sat-sangat and bestows greatness on him who lodges the divine Name in his heart. He who accepts the Guru's instruction never leaves the sat-sangat, and meditates on the Name day and night. He who turns to the Guru receives the shabad in the sat-sangat. Guru Amar Das prays to God. 'I will sit where you ask me to sit and I shall go where you tell me to go. But, pray, keep me where I can sing of truth and attain bliss'. This obviously refers to the sat-sangat.[18]

Guru Amar Das uses several terms for those who follow the Guru's instruction. We have already noted sadh and sant in connection with the sangat. The other terms used are bhagat and bairāgī. In a general way they are referred to as God's servants (*Har ke chākar*) or the people of God (Har-jan). The servants of God are always in comfort; they concentrate their minds on the feet of the Guru. The people of God reflect on the Guru's shabad and aspire to attain the truth. They who serve God are *Har ke log*. Yet another term used for the Guru's disciple is *sevak*. He serves the only God through the shabad. Adorned by the shabad of the Guru, day and night through the Guru's grace, he becomes pure and casts away the self; he sings the praises of the True One. He alone can be called sevak who is prepared to give his head. The term sikh is also used: 'they who live in accordance with the Guru's will are *sikh*, *sakhā* and *bandhap*'. A little more clearly it is stated that the Guru enables the Sikh to mingle with the divine light. Finally, Guru Amar Das talks of the riddle (*mundāvaṇī*) of three things in the platter which, if eaten, lead to liberation: this rare food is found only in reflection on the Guru. This riddle was presented by the True Guru and it was solved by the Sikhs of the Guru.[19] They attained liberation.

However, the term used most frequently for the Sikh by Guru Amar Das is Gurmukh. More than 350 lines of his bāṇī open with Gurmukh. The term is used not only in the sense of 'by turning to the Guru' but also for the person who has turned to the Guru. We may cite a few examples. The Gurmukh remains absorbed in the shabad day and night. He casts away the self. He who turns to the Guru meditates on the Name. The Gurmukh gets rid of his haumai. Adorning himself with awe (bhai) and loving devotion (bhagtī), the Gurmukh is comparable to a woman who never loses her husband. The Gurmukhs live by the shabad of the Guru and look beautiful at the divine door. Absorbed in the truth, the Gurmukh dies while still alive. Dedicated to the divine Name, the Gurmukh recognizes his real self. The Gurmukh accepts God's will. The Gurmukh gains the real wealth by reflecting on the shabad of the Guru. At a few places in his bāṇī, Guru Amar Das dwells on the Gurmukh in several lines. For example, in *Rāg Mārū* he talks of the Gurmukh in fifty consecutive lines.[20]

The Others

The Gurmukh of Guru Amar Das stands opposed to the manmukh. About 200 lines in the compositions of Guru Amar Das start with manmukh. As we go through his bāṇī we find that certain traits of the manmukh are repeatedly mentioned. He remains attached to the world and does not cultivate detachment (bairāg, *udās*). He remains alien to the True Guru. His adornment is like that of a duhāgan (who never meets her husband). He is punished in the divine court for his misdeeds. Engrossed in falsehood, he never finds a place (in the divine court). The manmukh is alien to the shabad and the divine Name. He is comparable to a plant that withers without giving any fruit or shade. He incurs only suffering by acting in self-conceit (ahankār). He is ignorant and follows the wrong path (*kumārg*). Blind to the right path he comes and goes (bound to the chain of death and rebirth); out of ignorance and pride he follows *durmat*. The more he reads the more he suffers because there is no liberation without the True Guru. Oblivious of the end, the manmukh regrets in the end. Devoid of *giān*, he is attached to other than God. He suffers in the world due to his hostility towards the sants. Unaware of the thing within himself, the manmukh dies barking in darkness. He is selfish to the core and does nothing for others. He lacks understanding and goes out to search (for truth). He is hard-hearted and evil-minded. The manmukh offers devotion without the True Guru; but without the True Guru there can be no bhagtī. His life is a waste. He is a field in which suffering is sown and reaped. He loses all honour by indulging in slander. The manmukh does not realize that the Name has been revealed through the instruction of the Guru; he remains subject to haumai and māyā. He is foolish enough to talk ill of those who have been set right by the true shabad. He thinks that he is clever.[21] Thus, in every conceivable way the manmukh represents the opposite of the Gurmukh. Without a single trait of the Gurmukh, he is all that the Gurmukh is not.

Significantly, the learned *pandit* is explicitly mentioned as manmukh. The manmukh is associated with *sūtak*, which again takes us back to the Brahman. There is hardly any doubt that the manmukh pandit follows the wrong path (kumārg). In fact, the manmukh, being the opposite of the Gurmukh, represents 'the other'. This is evident from a juxtaposition of the two.[22] It is important in this context to know what Guru Amar Das thought of the representatives of the other religious beliefs and practices in India during the sixteenth century.

The pandit is mentioned in various contexts in Guru Amar Das's writings. He reads and debates much, but spreads illusion without the Guru; without the shabad he cannot attain liberation; he remains chained to the cycle of eighty-four lakh births. The pandit reads the Vedas and gives elaborate expositions but he remains entangled in māyā. He remains oblivious of the divine Name and receives punishment. He recites loudly and does not search for the Brahm within; he teaches others but he himself does not understand. He wastes his life and is reborn again and again. He expounds the Vedas, Shastras, and Smritis but he remains in illusion and does not grasp the essence. Without serving the True Guru he gains no peace and multiplies suffering. Because of what he says and does, the pandit cannot attain the 'fourth stage' (which is beyond the three qualities of māyā). The Vedas talk loudly of the three qualities. He who remains attached to māyā cannot have understanding. The essence of gods and goddesses is māyā which inspires Shastras and Smritis. The lust and anger prevalent in the world perpetuate the suffering of transmigration. The learned pandit remains alien to his own 'self'. The four Vedas were given to Brahma and he reflected on them. But poor Brahma could not understand the divine order (hukam) and remained occupied with hell and heaven, and incarnations. The pandit sets himself up as the teacher (*pādhā*) without having the qualifications of a teacher. Himself entangled in māyā he keeps others entangled. The daughter of his jajmān is like his own daughter, but he receives remuneration for performing her marriage ceremony. The reading of the Vedas does not remove the dirt. His pride is the result of his entanglement in māyā. The learning of the pandit does not lead to contentment. The study of the Vedas does not lead to understanding of the Name. The Vedas dwell merely on good and evil deeds. The Shastras and Smritis do not lead to the goal of life. The pandit is advised to appropriate the way meant for the followers of the Gurus.[23]

An obvious implication of the invitation to the pandit to adopt the Sikh way of life is the futility of his practices in the compositions of Guru Amar Das. The *karm-kānd* is mere entanglement in māyā. He who entertains the notion of impurity (sūtak) can never perform a commendable deed or right worship. Pride (ahankār) is not eradicated by bathing at tīraths. Right thinking does not come by going to Kāsī, nor does one get rid of one's wrong thinking. The Kāsī is in the mind. All the sixty-eight tīraths accompany him who has lodged God in his heart. Only that *sandhya* is acceptable which leads to the remembrance of God. Without realizing God, sandhya, *tarpan*, and *gayatrī* lead to nothing but suffering. Drawn by consciousness of the divine is the true *chaukā*; the divine Name is the true food as the basis of human life. 'Were I to become a *pandit-jotkī* and read all the four Vedas, were I to be known in all the nine regions of the earth for my good conduct and intelligence, and were my *chaukā* never made impure, and forget the true word (it would be disastrous); all *chaukās* are false, the only true entity is God.' Guru Amar Das advises the *pāndā* to replace the fasts of Naomi, Dasmi, Ekadasi, and Duadasi by appropriation of the truth to control his senses and to find the way to liberation.[24]

However, the pandit, the pādhā, and the pāndā are not the only ones to be invited to the new path. In the writings of Guru Amar Das, the worshippers of Krishna are told to recognize God (Bhagwant) and their own self through the Guru's grace; they should control their mind and concentrate on the One; they should die in life; they should meditate on the Name so that they may attain liberation. There is no bhagtī in dancing and jumping; only he who dies through the shabad practices true bhagtī. There is a whole composition on dance in *Rāg Gujrī*. One should 'dance' for the Guru and in accordance with the Guru's will to get rid of the fear of Death. He who turns to the Guru becomes absorbed in the shabad and 'dances' through God's grace. They whom God enables to live in accordance with his hukam are the real bhagats and real *giānīs*.[25]

There are others who are bracketed with the pandit by Guru Amar Das. They are in different garbs (*bhekh*), including jogīs and sanyāsīs. Then there are *siddhs*, sādhaks, and *mauṇ-dhārīs*. If the pandit is engrossed in māyā, the jogīs, jangams, and sanyāsīs suffer from pride; their demand for alms is not confined to food and dress; they waste their lives in proud obstinacy (*hath*). Only he meditates truly who meditates on the Name by turning to the Guru. He who receives the Name by turning to the Guru is the real jogī and knows the real technique; one does not become a jogī by adopting the garb of a jogī. One may learn all the postures of the siddhs and control one's senses but the dirt of the mind is not removed so long as one does not get rid of haumai. Brahma, Bishan, and Mahadeo remained engrossed in the three qualities and strengthened the hold of attachment. Like the pandit, the *mauṇī* remained attached to 'the other' due to his pride. On this wrong path remained the jogīs, jangams, and sanyāsīs: without the Guru they remained alien to the truth. The jogī, the pandit, and the bhekh-dhārī stand bracketed as engrossed in māyā. And so are the pandit, the mauṇī, and the bhekh-dhārī.[26]

Like the pandit, the jogī is addressed several times alone in the bāṇī of Guru Amar Das. He who reflects on gian gets rid of haumai and does not thirst for māyā is the real jogī. There is no jog in the saffron garb and no *jog* in dirty clothes. 'If I were to become a *jogī*, wander over all the earth and beg from every home, what would be my answer in the divine court where account is taken? The Name is my alms and contentment my cremation ground (*maṛhī*); the truth is my companion all the time. Nothing is gained through a garb and everyone remains subject to Death. Stick to the Name which alone is true.' In about fifty lines of *ashtpadīs* in *Rāg Rāmkalī*, Guru Amar Das enumerates nearly all the features of yoga and all the features of the Sikh way of life to invite the jogī to adopt the Guru's path.[27] This comprehensive statement is very much similar to what we find in the bāṇī of Guru Nanak. However, there is a significant difference. Guru Nanak's invitation to the jogī to adopt the true path is implicit. In the bāṇī of Guru Amar Das it is made explicit. Rejection of yoga is built into the invitation.

We can see that the two major religious traditions of India, the Brahmanical and the ascetical, are rejected by Guru Amar Das. Less frequently though, the Vaishnava bhaktī is bracketed with them. We are left with the Islamic tradition. Guru Amar Das refers to *darveshī* to say that real *darveshe*s are rare. They who beg from door to door are a blot on their garb and their life is a curse. They who discard hope and fear and turn to the Guru receive the alms of the Name. Is it an invitation to the Muslim mendicant to appropriate the Guru's path? Guru Amar Das addresses the '*saikh*', asking him to discard the pride of power and to entertain the fear of God. He should pierce his hard heart with the (arrow of the) shabad so that peace is lodged in his heart. He who acts with peace in his mind finds a place with the Master. The saikh who wanders in all the four directions is asked to concentrate his mind on the One. He should forget 'here and there' and recognize the shabad of the Guru; prostrate himself before the True Guru who is the knower of everything; burn all hope and fear and live like a guest in this world. He should walk in accordance with the True Guru's will so that he may receive honour in the divine court. They who do not remember the Name, accursed is what they wear and what they eat.[28] There is hardly any doubt that Guru Amar Das invites the representatives of Islam to follow the Guru's path.

Significantly, Guru Amar Das compares well-water and rain, which has been interpreted as referring to the difference between the scriptures in Sanskrit and the bāṇī of the Guru. This comparison has a social dimension too: in one case the scripture is meant for a limited number of people and in the other, it is meant for all, including the lower castes and even the outcaste. Furthermore, the persons who turn to this bāṇī are transformed into gods or superior human beings. The tables are turned: those who do not appropriate the Name are low (in comparison with the Sikhs). 'We have become *uttam* by taking refuge in God; we are no longer *nīch*'.[29]

There is some social comment in the compositions of Guru Amar Das. Drunkenness is injurious for both physical and spiritual health. There is adverse comment on the red colour for dress: it symbolizes sensual pleasures. There is adverse comment on the notion of auspicious and inauspicious days and times, which throws astrology overboard. This notion of heavenly objects affecting human affairs is opposed to the shabad of the Guru. There is condemnation of female infanticide. There is disapproval of the practice of *satī* much against the cherished ideal of the Brahmans and the upper-caste people. Devotion to the living husband is preferable to becoming satī. There is no doubt that this idea gives strength to the family as a patriarchal institution but it does not minimize the importance of the disapproval of the practice. Then there is a reference to the various modes of disposing the dead. It may be merely contextual but the implication that these rituals were regarded as important cannot be ruled out. Altogether, the social comment in the bāṇī of Guru Amar Das is quite considerable. It is indicative of his social concerns particularly of the Sikhs.[30]

The *Rāmkalī Sadd* of Sunder should be seen in this context. Guru Amar Das clearly rejected the Brahmanical funerary rites and favoured their substitution by a ceremony which can certainly be seen as a Sikh ceremony.[31] It is important to add that formal mourning of the traditional kind had been debunked by Guru Nanak. Guru Amar Das may be seen as taking the next logical step.

There is one small point which may be mentioned in connection with the appreciation of Guru Amar Das for the city of Lahore. In *Slok Vārān Ton Vadhīk*, there is a single line: '*Lahaur sahr amritsar siftī dā ghar*'. In the bāṇī of Guru Amar Das, as in the bāṇī of Guru Nanak, *amritsar* is used as a metaphor.[32]

There is one category of people who are appreciated. In the past ages, there were true worshippers of One God. In the Kaliyuga itself there were bhagats before the time of Guru Nanak. The fact that they belonged to the lowest castes showed that caste did not stand in the way of liberation, and that the low caste were as dear to God as the high caste. They figure for the first time in the bāṇī of Guru Amar Das. They are seen as important individuals but not as the precursors of the Sikh movement in any sense.

In the compositions of Guru Amar Das there is an acute awareness of the slanderers of the *sādhūs* (the Sikhs of the Guru). Guru Amar Das reassures his followers them that God is on the side of the bhagats. One of God's concerns is to protect his devotees. He is the protector of the bhagats and has been protecting them in all the yugas. God is the protector of his bhagats and saves their honour. It is in this context that Guru Amar Das gives an extended reference to Prahlad. He whose Master is all powerful cannot be destroyed by anyone. Since there is no one above him, his devotee does not have to be afraid of anyone. There is also the prayer to the True Master that he may punish those who slander his slave (dās).[33]

The *Ānand* and its Significance

We may now turn to the *Ānand* which is not only the most lyrical but also the most representative composition of Guru Amar Das. He sings of happiness and bliss on realizing God. All sorrows are forgotten on remaining with God. With God on his side all his affairs are set right. All gifts come from him and he bestows the supreme gift of singing divine praises with the name lodged in the heart. The true Name removes all hunger, and peace comes to the mind. With the Name as their support, the sants should love the shabad. They should overpower the five adversaries and subdue the fear of Death. The Name is received through God's grace and one attains peace and bliss.

Elaborating on ānand Guru Amar Das says that people talk of ānand but ānand is found through the Guru and his grace. All sins are washed away and the eyes are opened to giān. Attachment to worldly things is removed. This is the ānand that one experiences through the Guru. Only they know it who receive it. through God's grace by appropriating the Name and accepting his will.

Guru Amar Das invites his dear sants to sing the praises of God together. We may realize God by entrusting our body and mind, and all our material resources to him, and by obeying his hukam. To sing the true bāṇī is to obey the Guru's hukam. This is the way to sing praises of the ineffable One. God is not found by clever talk. The attractive māyā, the source of illusion, is created by him to lure human beings. Guru Amar Das admires God for creating this sweet attachment, which is difficult to discard. He cannot be found by clever talk. One has to appropriate the truth. The family does not go with anyone and there is no reason to remain attached to it. The instruction of the Guru alone helps in the end. Therefore one should appropriate the truth.

God is inaccessible and unseeable and he alone knows himself. The living beings are his creation, his sport. He cares for them. The nectar which the *munī*s seek is found from the Guru. Through his grace he lodges the True One in the heart. They who find the True Guru become free from greed, attachment, and pride (*labb,* moh, ahankār). Only through God's grace one receives the nectar from the Guru. The way of the bhagats is different from that of all others. They follow the hard path. They discard greed, attachment, pride, and thirst in a quiet way and follow the path which is sharper than the edge of the double-edged sword and narrower than the width of a hair. They discard their self through the Guru's grace and are consumed by the desire to realize God. The way of the bhagats has been different from that of others throughout the ages. Guru Amar Das prays to God that he may follow his will. They, whom he shows the right path, follow his will. Only they meditate on God whom he attaches to the Name through his grace. We walk on the way which the True Lord determines for us.

This song of joy is the shabad heard from the True Guru. It is lodged in the hearts of those for whom it is decreed from the divine court. There are some who indulge in much talk but no one can realize God through mere talk. The True Guru proclaims the shabad as the song of joy. They who meditate on God by turning to the Guru become pure, and all those who associate with them become pure. They who recite, they who hear, and they who lodge it in the heart become pure. The state of bliss (*sahaj*) does not spring from karm-kānd; without attaining this state the fear of Death does not vanish. The mind made impure by this fear cannot be washed clean by any other means. It is washed by attachment to the shabad and meditation on God. The state of bliss springs from the grace of the Guru and only then the fear vanishes.

Those who are outwardly clean but dirty within, their life is wasted in a gamble. The thirst for māyā is a serious disease; it makes one oblivious of death. One does not listen to the supreme Name and wanders aimlessly. Those who discard the truth and attach themselves to the false world, waste their life in a gamble. The inward and outward purity is obtained by following the way of the Guru. Absorption in the truth keeps all falsehood away. The real vanjārās gain the jewel, the true purpose of life. Those whose minds are pure remain with the Guru all the time. The Sikh of the Guru remains in his presence and concentrates his mind on him. Discarding his self, he devotes himself to the Guru and knows no one else. Guru Amar Das tells the sants that such a Sikh is face to face with the Guru (sanmukh). Those who turn away from the Guru find no refuge. They find no liberation. They wander from birth to birth and find liberation only when they turn to the True Guru and listen to the shabad. If you think deeply you realize that there is no liberation without the True Guru.

Guru Amar Das invites the Sikhs, who are dear to the True Guru, to sing the true bāṇī, the bāṇī of the Guru, which is supreme. It is lodged in the hearts of those to whom God is gracious. Drink this nectar, remain dyed in the love of God, and sing his praises. Always sing the true bāṇī. All bāṇī other than that of the True Guru is unripe. Unripe is bāṇī other than the bāṇī of True Guru; all other bāṇī is unripe. Unripe are those who recite the unripe bāṇī and those who hear it; unripe is its exposition. They utter 'God' from their lips without knowing him. Their minds have been captivated by māyā and what they say does not carry conviction. Guru Amar Das reiterates that other than the bāṇī of the True Guru all bāṇī is unripe. The shabad of the Guru is the precious jewel. He who appropriates this shabad is absorbed in it. When the mind is attached to the shabad, one turns to the True One in loving devotion. God himself is the diamond, he himself is the jewel, and he himself bestows the gift of understanding. The shabad is the jewel and the diamond.

Guru Amar Das emphasizes the role of the Guru in his compositions. God himself created Shiv and Shakti and he himself governs the universe. He himself disposes, and watches his sport. Only a few understand this by turning to the Guru. Those who lodge the shabad in their heart, their attachment to māyā is snapped and they attain liberation. Through God's grace alone one turns to the Guru and dedicates oneself to the One.

The doer (kartā) himself makes his devotees understand his hukam. The reality is not known by reading Smritis and Shastras or by notions of pāp and pun; the reality is not known without the Guru, it is never known. The world is in the illusion of the three qualities, and the whole life passes in illusion. He who is awakened by the Guru's grace dedicates himself to God and sings the nectar-like bāṇī. Only he comes to know the reality who keeps awake throughout his life and remembers God day and night. The giver of all gifts should never be forgotten. He who remembers him comes to no harm. God himself leads to loving devotion through the Guru. The giver of such gifts should never be forgotten. The distraction of māyā leads to thirst; attachment to māyā results in a different affiliation (*dūjā* bhāo). They who are dedicated to God through the Guru's grace realize God in the midst of māyā. God is a priceless treasure. He is found by meeting the True Guru to whom one offers one's head and annihilates one's self. Only the fortunate ones find this priceless treasure.

The mind is the *vanjārā* and God is the capital. This capital is found from the True Guru. All profit comes from the remembrance of God. This wealth comes through God's grace. With God as the capital, the mind becomes a true vanjārā. The thirst of the tongue is not slaked by things other than the taste of God. After the gift of the taste, there is no thirst. This gift is received through God's grace by meeting the True Guru. All other pleasures are forgotten when God is lodged in the heart.

Talking about the importance of human body Guru Amar Das says that it comes into the world after the divine light is placed in it by God. He himself is the mother and the father; he created the soul and showed the world. Through the Guru's grace comes the realization that the world is ephemeral. What is everlasting is the light which is placed in the body at the time of creation. Love springs from the realization of God within. He has made the body a temple. By singing his praises all suffering and sorrow stays away. Realization of God comes by attachment to the Guru's feet. The divine music is heard through the Guru's shabad and by tasting the divine Name. God himself is the doer and only through his grace one finds him. Only he who devotes himself to the Guru becomes acceptable to God.

The light in the eyes has been placed to see nothing but God. The eyes should see God everywhere. The world around is a form of God; through it can he be seen. Through the grace of the Guru it is realized that God is one and there is no other reality. Without this realization the eyes remain blind; by meeting the True Guru the eyes are opened to the reality. The ears are meant to hear the praises of the True Lord. They should hear the true bāṇī. He who hears the true bāṇī, his mind and body are regenerated. The state of the unknowable cannot be described. By listening to the nectar-like Name the ears are purified; they are meant to hear the praises of the True Lord. Placing the soul in the body as a cave, God has breathed air into it. The nine doors were made manifest by striking the musical instrument of the air. The tenth door was kept concealed. It is revealed to some through the Guru. They see God in innumerable forms, and there is no limit to his manifestation. In his compositions, Guru Amar Das highlights the importance of using our senses correctly.

The *Ānand* projects a whole theology of liberation. Guru Ram Das says that this true song of joy (Ānand) should be sung in the true house where truth is meditated upon. Through God's grace the truth is realized through the Guru. This truth is the Master of everyone and the Master bestows it upon those whom he likes. This true song of joy should be sung in this true house. This true house may be the dharamsāl where the Sikhs gather for congregational worship.

Guru Arjan invites the Sikhs to listen to the *Ānand* so that all their wishes are fulfilled. They realize God and all their sorrows vanish. By listening to the true bāṇī, all sorrows, disease, and curses vanish. Through the perfect Guru, the sants are drenched in joy. The True Guru himself is present in this bāṇī; he who listens to it and utters it becomes pure. By attachment to the feet of the Guru the divine music of joy is struck within.[34] With its celebration of liberation, the literary excellence of the *Ānand* soon made it a liturgical composition, like the *Japu* of Guru Nanak.

An Exclusive Path

Guru Amar Das leaves no doubt that the dispensation of Guru Nanak was meant to transcend all the known religious traditions. This becomes clear from his references to the Kaliyuga. *Kīrat* (singing God's praises) is the light in the Kaliyuga. There is no other karma or dharma for the Kaliyuga: there is no liberation without the Name. In the Kaliyuga, only those who turn to the Guru cross to the other bank. In this yuga, the divine Name is the remover of fear; it is found by reflecting (on the shabad of the Guru). Appropriation of the Name of God involves acceptance of the divine will. In the Kaliyuga, the Name is the treasure that is found through bhagtī and leads to bliss. *Jam* (Death) is all powerful in the Kaliyuga but he is not outside the Divine Order. He punishes the manmukh but those who turn to the Guru are safe. In all the four yugas there is one treasure for the devotees of God. It is the divine Name. The dharma in the first three yugas, respectively, was jat, *sanjam*, and tīrath; in the Kaliyuga it is the praises of God through the divine Name. In this yuga, the wealth of the divine is gained through bhagtī; the rest of the world remains an illusion. They who appropriate the Name attain liberation. But no one finds the Name without the Guru. Dharma stood firmly on four feet in the Satyuga. In the Tretayuga it stood on three feet and in the Duapur it was left with two. In the Kaliyuga it has only one foot. Its power is reduced to one-fourth. Māyā reigns supreme. The only source of redemption is the Name which is appropriated by meeting the True Guru. There is only One True Lord in all the four yugas and the Name is supreme. It is the only source of liberation in the Kaliyuga. Not karm-kānd but the divine Name is efficacious in the Kaliyuga. There is no other way (to liberation). There is no liberation without the Name. The greatness of the Name for the Kaliyuga is well recognized. It is received through the perfect Guru.[35]

Significantly, the season of Basant, which is the season of regeneration, reminds Guru Amar Das of the mind regenerated through the divine Name. They who sing God's praises remain in the Basant season all the time. The regenerated world is liked by the True Guru. The world is a garden and God is Basant. By implication, the Kaliyuga is the age of regeneration. In any case, the divine Name in the Kaliyuga, becomes manifest by turning to the Guru; the treasure of the Name is made manifest in the hearts of those who have taken refuge with the Guru.[36]

Guru Amar Das talks of the world on fire (*jagat jalandā*) in one of his verses. He says that he has woken up on hearing the shabad of the True Guru and a new feeling has sprung up within him. May the body without any merit burn because it does not work in the Guru's way. Engrossed in haumai and attached to 'the other', the world is burning. Guru Amar Das prays that God may save the world on fire through his grace. He goes on to add that God may save the world by whatever the means of redemption (*jit duāre ubre tite lehu ubār*). The 'means' here is sometimes interpreted as any other religious dispensation. This interpretation does not harmonize with the emphatically expressed view of Guru Amar Das that the only means of redemption in the Kaliyuga is the Name, that is, the dispensation of Guru Nanak. In fact, the '*jit duāre*' line itself is followed by the statement that the True Guru has shown peace through reflection on the true shabad. Other than Guru Nanak there is no redeemer now.[37] This verse expresses Guru Amar Das' concern with universal redemption through the dispensation of Guru Nanak and his successors.

Notes

1. *Ādi Srī Gurū Granth Sāhib*, pp. 27, 30, 113, 128–9, 425, 427–8, 508–9, 663, 757, 769, 842, 947, 953–4, 1044, 1051. For the bāṇī of Guru Amar Das in a single volume, see Balbir Singh Dil, *Bāṇī Gurū Amar Das Jī dā Teekā*, Patiala: Punjab Languages Department, 2004.
2. *Ādi Srī Gurū Granth Sāhib*, pp. 27, 36, 65, 86, 122, 127, 232, 440, 512, 556–7, 951, 1094, 1421.
3. Ibid., pp. 425, 590, 648, 769, 842, 947, 1046, 1055, 1413.
4. Ibid., pp. 112, 163, 365, 441, 509–10, 517, 849, 949, 1333.
5. Ibid., pp. 34, 112, 149, 245, 426, 428, 589, 850, 911, 1333.
6. Ibid., pp. 69, 429, 770, 956, 1055, 1131.
7. Ibid., pp. 26, 67, 85–6, 90, 111–12, 116, 122, 157, 161, 311, 362–3, 423–4, 549, 586, 664, 770, 947, 1089, 1420.
8. Ibid., pp. 33, 110, 123, 128–9, 159, 245, 554, 600, 604, 643, 910, 956, 1066, 1132, 1170, 1174, 1257.
9. Ibid., pp. 26, 29, 123, 161, 232, 425–6, 851, 949.
10. Ibid., p. 549.
11. Ibid., pp. 111, 128, 362–3, 424–5, 429, 514, 565, 663, 1128.
12. Ibid., pp. 26–7, 29–32.
13. Ibid., pp. 26–32.
14. Ibid., pp. 32–6, 67, 110, 113, 115, 158.
15. Ibid., pp. 33, 67, 115, 158, 638, 645, 753, 770, 1044, 1065, 1286.
16. Ibid., p. 1068.
17. Ibid., pp. 35, 69, 114, 120, 363.
18. Ibid., pp. 427, 593, 956, 1130, 1258, 1276.
19. Ibid., pp. 111, 117–18, 246–7, 599, 601, 602, 645, 755, 768, 1172, 1247.
20. Ibid., pp. 125, 158, 230, 362, 428, 591, 650, 910, 1058–9, 1063, 1262, 1414.
21. Ibid., pp. 29, 31, 33–4, 37, 66, 87, 89, 231, 314, 435, 441, 569, 570, 590, 643, 754–5, 768, 852, 947, 1046, 1249, 1414.
22. Ibid., pp. 85, 128, 229–31, 317, 319, 337, 423, 559, 1277.
23. Ibid., pp. 67, 85, 114, 116–17, 127–9, 231, 423, 434, 647, 1049, 1061, 1261.
24. Ibid., pp. 162, 229–30, 491, 554, 603, 1048, 1090, 1245.
25. Ibid., pp. 88, 116, 136, 158, 1054.
26. Ibid., pp. 67, 123, 513, 555–6, 851, 1128, 1246.

27. Ibid., pp. 908–9, 911, 1088, 1420.
28. Ibid., pp. 550–1, 646.
29. Ibid., pp. 90, 162, 426, 427, 565.
30. Ibid., pp. 426–7, 554, 565, 648–9, 772, 785, 787, 842–3, 1413.
31. Ibid., pp. 293–4.
32. Ibid., p. 1412.
33. Ibid., pp. 516–17, 587–8, 601, 768, 842, 1154, 1155.
34. Ibid., pp. 917–22.
35. Ibid., pp. 145, 160–1, 229, 365, 513, 588, 797, 851, 880, 1129–31, 1175–7, 1334.
36. Ibid., pp. 651, 853.
37. Ibid., p. 852.

4

The 'House of Nanak'—An Expression of Divine Grace

Guru Ram Das

The *bāṇī* of Guru Ram Das is incorporated in the Gurū Granth Sāhib in thirty *Rags*, besides the *Rahirās* and the *Kīrtan Sohilā*. The bāṇī of Guru Nanak and Guru Amar Das is in nineteen *Rāgs*: *Srī Rāg, Mājh, Gauṛī, Āsā, Gujarī, Vadhans, Sorath, Dhanāsarī, Tilang, Sūhī, Bilāval, Rāmkalī, Mārū, Tukhārī, Bhairon, Basant, Sārang, Malār,* and *Parbhāti*. For the bāṇī of Guru Ram Das there are eleven more Rāgs: Devgandhārī, Bihāgarā, Jaitsarī, Todī, Bairārī, Gaund, Nat-Nārāyan, Mālī-Gauṛā, Kedārā, Kānaṛā, and Kalyān. The addition of Rāgs is an important contribution in itself. Apart from *Ashtpadīs, Chhants, Solhe,* Vārs, and *shaloks,* Guru Ram Das uses *pahrei, vanjārā, karhale,* and *ghoṛiān* as poetic forms. Two modes of rendition are specifically mentioned: *kāfi* and *paṛtāl*. The bāṇī of Guru Ram Das reflects his deep interest in both poetry and music.

Many of the metaphors and similes in the composition of Guru Ram Das relate to his physical, economic, social, cultural, and political environment. The reflection of this environment is partial but nonetheless important. The contextual statements are sometimes conventional but mostly empirical. Besides the physical world and the flora and fauna, there are metaphors and similes from a large number of occupations. Trade and agriculture figure most frequently in these metaphors/similes. The other occupations are those of the potter, oil-presser, dyer, *vaid,* fisherman, gardener, boatman, water-diviner, *sūtardhār,* and the prostitute. Some of the metaphors and similes come from the human body itself: eyes, ears, nose, tongue, teeth, head, hair, nakedness, and lifelessness.

In the bāṇī of Guru Ram Das, socio-religious life, the ceremonies of betrothal and marriage, the dowry, and the bridal bed are important metaphors. The devoted wife is preferable by far to the indifferent. The wife adorns herself to please the husband. The family is clearly patriarchal. The social order is inegalitarian. There are rich, propertied persons who enjoy high social status. There are the high caste Brahmans and Khatris, and the low caste Vaishyas and Shudras. Then there are the outcastes like the Chandāls. There are professional scribes, personal servants, wageless labourers, grooms, thieves, beggars, and slaves. Some of the similes come from the wrestling arena, gambling, and the place of learning.

The religious life reflected in the bāṇī of Guru Ram Das relates largely to the Brahmanical dispensation: *tīrath*, *barat*, *jagg*, *pun*, and *pūjā*. Apart from the four Vedas, eighteen Puranas, six *darshans*, Smritis, and Shastras, there are references to *jap*, *tap*, and *sanjam*, thirty-three crores of gods, sixty-eight places of pilgrimage, and the most sacred rivers. Brahma, Vishnu, and Mahadev appear as God's creatures. Apart from the Pandit, there are Siddhs, Munīs, Sadhs, Sanyāsīs, Jogīs, and Jangams. Transmigration is taken for granted. The presence of Vaishnava *bhaktī* is indicated by references to singing and dancing for worship. There is no reference to Islam.

The representatives of Islam figure in connection with the state as emperors. There are other categories of people who wield power, like the *dīwāns*, the *khāns*, the *maliks*, and the *umarā*. Then there are Bhūpats, Rājās, Rāos, and Rānās. There are local administrators (*shiqdārs* and *chaudharīs*) and there are collectors of tax (*jagātī*). Courts are held and orders are issued. Justice is sought and punishment inflicted. There are forts, palaces, gates, and pillars. There are mints for striking coins.[1]

Theology of Guru Ram Das

The theology of Guru Ram Das is essentially the same as the theology of Guru Nanak. It forms the core of his bāṇī. The basic ideas are put forth in the *So-Purkh*. The Supreme Being is the one Supreme Reality, the Primal Purkh who has no equal. He is immaculate, inaccessible, immeasurable, ever constant, immutable, and changeless. He is the sole creator and the sole provider. He is pervasive everywhere, and abides within all. None besides him operates in the universe. What he wills comes to pass. All creation is brought into being by him and disappears into nothingness by his decree. Some he makes donors and others he makes beggars. He annuls all suffering. He is free from fear and they who meditate on him become free from fear. Union and alienation are in his power. Realization of God comes to those who by him are enlightened. He is made manifest by the Guru's grace.[2]

The ideas expressed in the *So-Purkh* are reinforced in many other compositions of Guru Ram Das, with a slightly greater emphasis on God's immanence than his transcendence. The Primal Purkh is beyond all reach; He is the sole Formless Absolute. He is the sole creator, the sole cause, and source of all things. He himself creates and dissolves creation. None but he has power and his ordinance is operative in the universe. He alone confers greatness. He has no form or feature and yet he pervades all creation. He himself shows his form and meditates on it. He himself is the Silent One and discourses on enlightenment. He himself is the voluptuary and the anchorite. He himself is Brindaban's milkmaids and Krishna grazing cows in the forest. He himself is the child who destroys Kansa.[3] The depiction of God's immance in the bāṇī of Guru Ram Das is both detailed and frequent.

Guru Ram Das gives great importance to the Name. Like God, the Name at one level is immaculate and inaccessible; it is also pervasive and operative in all spots. The Name is our Lord; nothing is supreme over it. To be indifferent to the Name is to be indifferent to God. They who are forgetful of the Name are thoughtless and unfortunate egoists; they remain in the grip of māyā. The jewel of the Name is found by God's grace. Meditation on the Name comes through God's grace. By putting faith in the Name one's clan and family are saved; one's suffering and hunger vanish. By fixing faith in the Name foul thinking is cast off, understanding dawns, the ego is shed, and all maladies are cured. Doubt is annulled by devotion to the Name and no suffering comes thereafter. The Name of the Lord is our father, mother, helper, and friend.[4]

Guru Ram Das highlights the importance of the Name in his bāṇī. The Name is enshrined in the shabad. The Name annuls fear and one acquires bliss through the Guru's shabad. By 'listening to the Name' one finds peace; one's life is fulfilled, and all sorrow vanishes. Here the Name is assumed to be the Guru's shabad. All supranatural powers come from 'listening to the Name', and all one's desires are fulfilled. By 'listening to the Name' comes poise, and from poise comes joy. By 'listening to the Name' comes purity and self-restraint; the self is illumined and realized; sins are annulled and truth is attained.[5]

The equation of the Name with the shabad brings in the Guru. Devotion to the Name is acquired through the Guru's grace. Only they who turn to the Guru meditate on the Name. Only those who are linked to the Guru adore the Name. By the Guru's guidance comes meditation on the Name. The Name is obtained from the Perfect Guru who reveals it in the heart. The gracious Guru instructs us in the Name. Rare are those who contemplate the Name by the Guru's guidance. The Name is uttered in the presence of the Guru. They who adore the Name by the Guru's guidance are universally acclaimed. The Name is lodged in the heart by the True Guru and its repetition leads the mind to bliss. Through great good fortune is the Name obtained by the Guru's guidance. They who are deprived of the touch of the Guru remain ignorant reprobates; by the guidance of the True Guru is tasted the nectar of the Name.[6] The Name signifies God at one level; at another, it signifies the shabad which is identified with the shabad of the Guru or Gurbāṇī.

Guru Ram Das uses 'shabad' for the Divine Ordinance. It is the same ordinance (eko shabad) everywhere. All are covered by his ordinance (shabad). The other terms used for the Divine Ordinance are hukam, bhāṇā, and razā. Nothing can be done on one's own; God keeps us as he likes. He who accepts the will (bhāṇā) of the True Guru attains union with God. He alone is the Master and everyone is subject to his ordinance (hukam); he does what he likes (*bhāvai*) and all have to submit to his will (razā).[7] Here hukam, bhāṇā, and razā are used as synonyms.

God's bhāṇā tends to merge with his grace in Guru Ram Das' bāṇī. Whomsoever God likes he unites with himself'. By living in accordance with the will of the True Guru one may receive a berth in the boat. The terms generally used for grace are *nadar*, *kirpā*, *prasād*, and *dayā*. One may receive the gift of loving devotion through the Guru's grace (nadar). The one on whom the beloved looks with grace (nadar) meditates on the feet of God. Through the grace (kirpā) of the True Guru one may meet God; through the grace (dayā) of the Guru one may meet God. It is through God's kirpā that one serves the True Guru. It is through the Guru's kirpā that one realizes the eternal, inscrutable, and infinite beloved. Through the kirpā of the bestower of peace (*sukhdātā*) one may receive the word (*bachan*) of the True Guru. Everyone wishes to see God but only they see him whom he shows himself; only through the grace (nadar) of the beloved one turns to God.[8] The phrase 'Gurprasādī' occurs frequently in the bāṇī of Guru Ram Das. The Guru's grace is as important as the grace of God. The emphasis on grace is slightly more than on the divine ordinance.

Successors as One with the Founder

Guru Ram Das refers to himself as the *dhādī* of God who was allowed access to the divine court and honoured with the robe of the divine Name. As the dhādī of God, he sang his praises and invited others to meditate on the Name by turning to the Guru, the True Guru, and the Perfect Guru. There is hardly any doubt that any of these terms can refer to God. It is even more certain that each one of these three terms can refer to the personal Guru, that is, Guru Nanak and his successors. Indeed, most of the time Guru Ram Das appears to refer to the personal Guru. We may refer to some of the statements actually made in his bāṇī. God himself is the True Guru; he himself is the disciple; he himself gives instruction. As the True Guru, God himself effects the union. Liberation is not possible without the True Guru. Govind is the Guru and the Guru is Govind: there is no difference between them. Guru Ram Das refers to *Gurū kā bhāṇā* just as he refers to *Gurū kā shabad* or *Gurū kā bachan*. The service of the True Guru is real service only when one lives in accordance with the wishes of the True Guru. The True Guru is the real *sādhū* (saint). The Guru is the real sādhū. The disciple of the Guru dedicates his life to the Guru: 'I have placed my body and mind at the disposal of the Guru; I have sold my head at a very high price'. This high price is nothing short of liberation. Only through God's grace may one sell one's head to the Guru. The Perfect Guru reveals God; union is attained by selling the head to the Guru. We are like uninstructed children; the Guru, the True Guru, is the instructor who makes us wise through his instruction. The Guru instructs that māyā does not go with you in the end. The Guru gives the sword of *giān* to kill death itself. On meeting the Perfect Guru, one may see God's presence. The love of the Name comes through the True Guru.[9]

Significantly, Guru Ram Das refers to his predecessors. The use of the term 'Guru Nanak' in the last line of a hymn may refer to Guru Ram Das as well as to Guru Nanak. One finds Nanak as the Guru through the divine writ. The servants of God seek refuge in Nanak as the Guru. Through the divine writ in one's favour, Nanak the Guru becomes gracious and effects union with God. By divine writ one may meet Guru

Nanak. Guru Nanak seems to represent his dispensation through his bāṇī and his successors. Great indeed is Guru Nanak who looks upon all with the same concern and who is above praise and blame. Nanak is the Perfect Guru; one meditates on the Name by meeting the True Guru. Guru Ram Das refers to the House of the Jagat Guru Nanak and its four generations from Guru Nanak to Guru Ram Das himself. The generations from 'Guru Baba' and 'Guru Angad' to the third and the fourth are mentioned elsewhere too.[10] Obviously, Guru Ram Das is quite conscious of his office as a personal Guru.

As it may be expected, Guru Ram Das talks about his immediate predecessor, Guru Amar Das, as frequently as about the founder of the House. The epithet 'true Guru' is used for Guru Amar Das. There is a reference to his langar. There is a reference also to a hostile ascetic who sends his son to participate in the celebration of the completion of the *baolī* at Goindval. The most important statement refers to Guru Amar Das' visit to the traditional places of pilgrimage. He visited Kurukshetra at the time of the solar eclipse (in 1553), accompanied by numerous disciples. 'In order to redeem the world did the True Guru undertake the pilgrimage to this bathing place'. The whole world came out to behold him. Annulled were the sins of those who had the touch of the Perfect

Fig. 4.1 Baoli Sahib at Goindval, the headquarters of Guru Amar Das (1552–74)

Guru. Jogīs, Sanyāsīs, and Jain monks, the followers of the six orders, had dialogue with him. The Guru then chanted the Divine Name on the Jamuna; all who followed him were exempted from toll. On the Ganga, the eminent people of the town sought shelter with the True Guru, seeing in him the image of God. Through the Guru's shabad and his teaching they became devotees of God.[11] It is clear that the purpose of his visit to the sacred places was to spread the message of the Sikh faith.

A verse of Guru Ram Das is addressed to the son. It is interpreted as his admonition to Prithi Chand.[12] Possibly, Prithi Chand did not accept with grace the nomination of his younger brother to Guruship. The installation of Arjan as the Guru was an important event of the life of Guru Ram Das. What he had received from his father-in-law he passed on to his son, initiating the line of Sodhi Gurus. Evidently, Guru Ram Das feels much concerned about the House of Guru Nanak.

Bāṇī is Guru and Guru is Bāṇī

Paradoxically, Gurbāṇī comes into parallel prominence with the personal Guru in the compositions of Guru Ram Das. There is no doubt that shabad is used for divine self-revelation, as for *hukam* at places. Greatly fortunate are they who serve the True Guru and remain absorbed in the One through the true shabad. Here the shabad may be taken to refer to divine self-revelation. Elsewhere, however, the shabad is equated clearly with the shabad of the Guru when the terms used are Gur-vāk, Satgur-bachan, and Gurshabad in the context of sat-sangat. Similarly, the word bāṇī may be treated as a synonym for shabad. The sants are told, for example, to serve God whose bāṇī is supreme. The bāṇī of the one who has turned to the Divine Preceptor is the Name. The bāṇī of the True Guru is a gift coming from God. However, like the shabad, bāṇī is used also for the bāṇī of the Guru in the context of *sat-sang*.[13]

Indeed, shabad and bāṇī for Guru Ram Das are most often simply Gurbāṇī. Jan Nanak utters the bāṇī replete with merit; through Gurbāṇī one is absorbed in the Name. The bāṇī of the True Guru is the nectar-word (*amrit-bachan*); whoever recites it quaffs amrit. The bāṇī of the *bhagat-jan* is supreme. By listening to the amrit-bāṇī of the bhagat-jan one contemplates God. The Har-jan is supreme and so is his bāṇī; he utters it for the benefit of others. The use of the terms bhagat-jan and

Har-jan does not mean that the reference is not to Gurbāṇī. In any case, there is a direct reference to *Gur kī bāṇī*: they who turn to it in love are redeemed in this world and the next through the grace of the Creator. By constant uttering of Gurbāṇī, God is lodged in the heart. Devotion arises from tasting the shabad of the Guru in the sangat; both the body and the mind are regenerated by praising God through Gurbāṇī. Gurbāṇī and Gurū kā shabad stand equated here, and elsewhere too. Through great good fortune we may meet the Guru and be redeemed through the Guru's shabad. We may know God through the Guru's bachan. Gurbāṇī shows the unseeable God. The bāṇī of the True Guru is the embodiment of truth, and through it one becomes true. Gurbāṇī is one's support and one should remain attached to it.[14]

Guru Ram Das refers to the imitators and their raw and false compositions. The Gursikhs are told to regard the bāṇī of the True Guru alone as true: God himself inspires him to speak. Indeed, 'bāṇī is the Guru and the Guru is bāṇī; all amrits are in the bāṇī itself.'[15] Just as in the equation of God with the True Guru the institutional Guru is brought to the fore, so in the equation of the Guru with the shabad the shabad as Gurbāṇī is brought to the fore.

The attitude of Guru Ram Das towards the Rāgs in relation to Gurbāṇī is highly significant. *Sorath*, for example, is fine if it helps one to search for the Name, celebrate the Guru, and meditate on God through Gurmat. Elsewhere Guru Ram Das says: 'I have sung the praises of the Supreme God using the *Bilāval Rāg* as my blowing horn'. The implication is clear: a Rāg has no sanctity in itself; it is sanctified only when it is used for praising the Lord. This attitude is in consonance with the attitude of Guru Nanak and Guru Amar Das. The point is explicitly made: 'Of all musical measures that one is noble wherewith the Lord abides in the heart. Such melody and music has value beyond expression. But the Lord is above the reach of melody and music. Realization of his ordinance does not come through them. Blessed is music for those who realize the ordinance. Such realization comes from the True Guru.'[16] This sets the relationship between Gurbāṇī and the Rāg on a firm footing: primary in Gurmat *sangīt* is Gurbāṇī itself; the Rāg is secondary. The Rāg acquires relevance and significance only to the extent it serves the basic purpose of Gurbāṇī. This may be treated as the fundamental principle of Gurmat sangīt.

Sikh is Guru and Guru is Sikh

The Sikh of the Guru (Gursikh) has a distinct identity in the bāṇī of Guru Ram Das. We are familiar with the hymn which refers to the daily routine of the Sikh: 'The disciple of the True Guru must rise at dawn and meditate on the Name. At dawn he must rise and cleanse himself in the Name of God, bathing in the pool of nectar. As by the Guru instructed he should then repeat the Name. All his sins shall be washed, all his evil and foul doings. With the rise of the day he must chant the Guru's *shabad*. He should meditate on the Name in rest and in movement.'[17]

This is only one of the numerous references to the Gursikh in the bāṇī of Guru Ram Das. The Sikhs of the Guru have love of God in their hearts; they come to the Guru for worship and take away the Name as their profit; they listen to the instruction of the Guru, and their haumai and *dubidhā* are eradicated; their faces are radiant with love. The Sikhs of the Guru have found that wonderful place where the True Guru sits; their labour has become fruitful through the Name; they who worship Guru Nanak are themselves worthy of worship. Through the grace of Guru Nanak they meet God. Praise be to those Sikhs who fall at the feet of the Guru, recite the Name of God, listen to the Name of God, appropriate the Name by serving the Guru, and live in accordance with the Guru's bhāṇā. The Sikh of the Guru propagates his instruction and there is no difference between them any longer: 'The Guru is Sikh and the Sikh is Guru'. Through his instruction, the Guru assimilates the Sikh with himself; some remain in his presence to serve him, while others are sent away to perform tasks for the Guru. This comes very close to saying that Guru Ram Das appointed his representatives to look after Sikh sangats at places away from Ramdaspur. Elsewhere, *Gur kī kār* is equated with *Har kathā*, making it an essential activity of the sangat.[18]

In a stanza of the *Vār* of *Sorath*, the bhagat, sant, sādh, Gurmukh, and Gursikh are mentioned together. Gurbachan Singh Talib makes no distinction between them in his translation. They refer indeed to one and the same entity: the Sikhs of the Guru. It is important to note in the first place that Guru Ram Das refers to the Sikhs at places without using any of these terms. 'We are called the slaves of the True Guru'; 'we bear his mark branded on our foreheads'. As the slaves of the Guru they join the sangat and the bitter becomes sweet for them. The reference here is obviously to the Sikhs. In *Rāg Dhanāsarī*, the sants and bhagats refer to the Sikhs. Guru Ram Das prays that the sins of all those who serve God may be washed and they be kept in the sangat dear to God. The sant-jan meditate on God and their suffering, illusion, and fear disappear through the instruction of the Guru (Gurmat). In *Rāg Rāmkalī*, a number of terms are used for the Sikhs: Har ke log, Har-jan, Har Rām-jan, Rām-jan, sant, sant-jan, *sādh*, *sevak*, and Gurmukh. Association with them turns crows into swans. The men of God (Har-jan) meditate on the Name; Har and Har-jan become one. God himself is the Guru, he himself is the disciple (*chelā*). They who find God sweet are eminent among men; they are the supreme men of God; greatness and peace come through the Name of God, and this juice is tasted through the shabad of the Guru. It is clear that Guru Ram Das refers to the Sikhs when he talks of sants, bhagats, and sādhs. The Guru himself is referred to as sādhū or sant.[19]

The Sikhs represent a distinct tradition. In the Kaliyuga, *dharam* has only one leg to stand upon; peace comes by singing the praises of God through the shabad of the Guru which serves as the medicine (*aukhad*). Without the seed of the Name there can be no harvest in the Kaliyuga. The Perfect Guru lodges the Name in the heart. The message of the Guru, thus, serves as the only leg of *dharam* in the Kaliyuga. Guru Ram Das makes the explicit statement that the service of the Guru, instruction of the Guru, and bhāṇā of the Guru represent a distinct way (*eh chāl nirālī gurmukhī*). Only they find the Perfect Guru in the Kaliyuga on whose forehead it was written from the very beginning. The foremost boon in the Kaliyuga is the Name. The highest state in the Kaliyuga is attained through the kīrtan of God, and we find God through the True Guru. Praise be to the True Guru who has made the Name manifest. The best form of worship in the Kaliyuga is to praise God in accordance with the teaching of the Guru (Gurmat). The best way to adore the Lord in the Kaliyuga is the Name: it is obtained through the teaching of the Guru. The Name of God protects the honour of God's devotees in the Kaliyuga.[20] These references leave no doubt that the path of the Gurus is the most efficacious in the Kaliyuga, if not the only efficacious path, in the eyes of Guru Ram Das.

The goal is liberation-in-life. The *sākat* is indifferent to God and remains entangled in māyā. The manmukh suffers from haumai. The shabad of the Guru is the antidote to the poison of haumai and māyā. By dying to self, one lives to quaff the nectar of love, and through the Guru's grace attains liberation-in-life (*jīvan mukt*). To attain this objective, one should be ready to offer one's head to the True Guru. To live in accordance with the Guru's bhāṇā is to die while living; by dying-in-life one crosses the ocean of life and through the Guru's grace is absorbed in the Name. The prayer of Guru Ram Das, therefore, is: 'keep me as you wish'. The antidote to māyā is renunciation, but renunciation-in-the-home (*vichche girh udās*). Another word for it is *alipt* (detached). An alternative phrase for the ideal is: *vich āsā hoi nīrasī*. Indeed, the life of a householder is better than that of an ascetic who begs from door to door. That the Sikhs are and should be householders is taken for granted. In fact the compositions like the '*ghoṛiān*' can be appreciated in this context. The caparisoned mare, the saddle and the whip, the songs sung for the bridegroom, the marriage party, and the bride serve as metaphors or similes for the human birth, shabad of the Guru, the Name, Gur-giān, loving devotion, and meeting with God. The marriage symbolizes union with God: it brings in the bridegroom, the marriage party, the bride and her friends, the natal home and the home of the in-laws, the ceremony of marriage, and the dowry. The ceremony of betrothal is followed by the *pādhā* opening his *patrī* to look for the auspicious time (*lagan, mahūrat*), the marriage party coming home, and the performance of the wedding rite in which the bride and the bridegroom take rounds. After this comes the composition known as *lāvān* which is now used for the Sikh wedding ceremony called 'Ānand'.[21] This rite of the passage appears to be important to Guru Ram Das precisely because the Sikhs are householders.

Householding for the Sikhs stands sanctified. Normally, the hoarding of wealth brings torment. Mansions and palace do not go with anyone and steeds are of no use. However, they who are devoted to the Name, their wealth, raiment, and food are sanctified. Approved are their homes, mansions, palaces and abodes. Approved are their steeds, saddles, and haversacks. The sacred rivers like Ganga, Jamuna, Godavari, and Sarsuti yearn for the dust of the sādhū's feet to get purified. All the places of pilgrimage yearn for the dust of the sādhū's feet. In fact the whole creation yearns for this dust. It is received through God's grace. They who have the support of God are no longer dependent on other people. 'We wash the dust of their feet and drink the water'. Praise is to those who volunteer to serve the Guru. They serve the sangat and think of the welfare of others.[22]

Guru Ram Das recommends respect for everyone. The same light is in all, as all have been created by the same God; 'place your head underneath the feet of everyone'. All can attain liberation, whether they are Khatri, Brahman, Sood, Vais, or Chandāl. It is in this context that Guru Ram Das gives the example of Namdev, Kabir, Trilochan, Ravidas, Dhanna, and Sain. Ravidas is mentioned as a Chamiar. Namdev is mentioned as a Chhipa. This was a declaration that the path of the Guru was open to all, including the lowest of the low. In the human body is the light of the True One. All are equal in the eyes of the True Guru who is compassionate towards all.[23] The True Guru himself looks upon all with concern and consideration. He is *par-upkāriā*.

Nevertheless, there were detractors (*nindak*) of the Guru. There were some who obliged the Sikhs to render services to them without any authority from the Guru. The Sikhs of the Guru who believe that God is on their side are dear to God. The Guru was prepared to forgive the detractors if they repented: they could still be redeemed. This was the greatness of the True Guru who was devoid of enmity (*nirvair*). Opposition to Guru Ram Das appears to have come from rival claimants to the office of Guruship. But they could approach the administrators too for support. Guru Ram Das refers to the earthly kings as subject to God's power who protects his devotees. The Guru and his Sikhs were under God's protection. God is the sword and armour of the True Guru; they who think ill of him shall themselves be destroyed by God.[24]

God in the Sangat

There are references to the sangat of sants or sādhs but far more frequently the term used is sat-sangat, the true association of the Guru and his Sikhs. One listens to the *kathā* of God in the sangat and meditates on the ineffable God. The bāṇī is recited in the sangat and the praises of God are sung; this medicine (aukhad) removes all kinds of disease and suffering. Daily one listens to the kathā of the Divine Name in the sangat; by singing the praises of God one swims across the ocean of life; one utters Gurbāṇī in the sangat and quaffs the nectar of Har-kathā. It is quite obvious that sangat meets in the *dharamsāl*. The Guru gives instruction in the kathā of God; one meditates on God in the sangat, and meets God.

The Guru utters amrit-bāṇī and his Sikhs love it; the True Guru gives instruction in the interest of others. As Bhai Gurdas actually tells us, we can visualize Guru Ram Das performing kīrtan in the midst of the amritsar in Ramdaspur. The sangat, by implication, is the divine court. One joins the sangat through great good fortune and all one's affairs are set right by the Name. One meets other Sikhs in the sangat to sing the praises of God, and everyone yearns to see the Guru. Desolate is the life of those who have not taken refuge in the Guru's sangat. Through great good fortune one joins the sangat and cultivates the love of God; day and night one remains absorbed in God and regards joy and sorrow alike; the love of God is cultivated in the sangat through great good fortune. The treasure of the Name is in the sangat where one meets God; through the Guru's grace one's innerself is lighted and all darkness disappears; iron is transmuted into gold by the touch of the True Guru. Only in the sangat does one find the wealth of the Name; it never diminishes, is never stolen, and never taxed. The true sangat of the Guru where one tastes the pleasure of God is dear to God.[25]

Guru Ram Das looks upon worship in the sangat as the only form of worship that leads to liberation. In any case, it is more efficacious than the way of the Jogīs and the path of the Vaishnavas. The Jogī strums the gut but his harp sounds hollow. His heart can be drenched in joy only by the Guru's instruction. The songs that the Jogī sings and his manifold utterances are only a play of the mind: the bullocks he yokes to the wheel to irrigate the field eat away the tender shoots. Guru Ram Das prays to God that the heart of each may bend to divine devotion. It takes long to bring bells and cymbals and to tune the rebeck. Far better it is to use this time in contemplation of the Name. It takes long to collect notes and to tune melody of the measure. Far better it is to use this time for adoration of the Lord. It takes long to stretch hands to form poses. Far better it is to use this time to contemplate the Divine Name. In the true association of God's devotees should one sing the praises of God. Thereby illumination would come and darkness would be lifted. The devotees of God should 'dance the dance of contemplation'. The Sikh way is far preferable to that of the Jogīs and the Vaishnava bhagats. The sangat is the school (*chatsāl*) of the True Guru: one learns to appreciate the attributes of God in the sangat.[26] In the sangat is God. Like Gurbāṇī and the Sikh, the sangat comes to the fore in the compositions of Guru Ram Das.

An Expression of Divine Grace

Guru Ram Das occupied the office of Guruship for about seven years from 1574 to 1581. Two major works are attributed to him by the historians: excavation of the *sarovar* known as 'amritsar' or 'Ram Das sarovar', and founding of the township known as Ramdaspur. The reflection of this environment in the bāṇī of Guru Ram Das is partial but nonetheless important. Daily *kīrtan* of Gurbāṇī was performed in the midst of the sarovar in which the Sikhs bathed, participated in the congregational worship, and ate food in the *langar* that was maintained by their voluntary contribution in cash, kind, and service. This place for earning merit (dharamsāl) served as a model for other dharamsāls established by the representatives of the Guru. All human beings were welcome to join the congregational worship and to eat food in the langar.

The central dharamsāl in Ramdaspur was unique due to the presence of the personal Guru but the kīrtan of Gurbāṇī in other dharamsāls made them equally sacred. The equation of the shabad with Gurbāṇī, and of Gurbāṇī with the Guru, becomes extremely significant in this context. The equation of God with the Guru, and of the Guru with Gurbāṇī, made the presence of God felt in the sangat.

The town of Ramdaspur has its own significance. In the first place, the realistic references to trade and artisanal occupations appear to be related

Fig. 4.2 Gurdwara Janam Asthan (the place of birth) of Guru Ram Das (1574–82), Lahore

to the presence of such people in Ramdaspur. Secondly, the earthly possessions of the Sikhs are sanctified. The temporal and spiritual concerns of the Sikhs are thus two sides of the same religious coin.

The immanence and grace of God, which are a little more important than God's transcendence and hukam, have their earthly expression in the dispensation of Guru Nanak and his successors, a dispensation that is the only hope of mankind in the Kaliyuga. In the bāṇī of Guru Ram Das, God enters history through the Guru, his bāṇī, and his Sikhs for the redemption of the world. The whole dispensation of the House of Guru Nanak appears to be an expression of the divine order and divine grace.

Notes

1. Information on environment in the bāṇī of Guru Ram Das comes in bits and pieces. It has been sifted, collected, and classified carefully. But there may be no point in giving a large number of references for information which is of no great significance in bits and pieces. Put together, it does show that Guru Ram Das kept his eyes and ears open to what was around him. All the relevant pages of the Gurū Granth Sāhib are given below: 11, 13, 40–1, 76, 78, 82, 83, 85, 89, 91, 163–70, 173–4, 234–5, 301–10, 312–14, 317, 366–8, 442–3, 447, 449, 452, 493–4, 507, 527–8, 538–40, 550–5, 561, 573–6, 586, 594, 604–7, 642–6, 651, 653, 669–70, 696, 698–9, 711, 719–20, 726, 731–3, 735, 747, 759, 773, 775–6, 799–800, 834–7, 844–5, 849, 851–4, 859, 860–2, 880, 882, 982, 975–6, 980–1, 983–5, 986, 996, 998, 1038, 1071, 1114–16, 1135, 1178–9, 1191, 1200–1, 1245–6, 1248, 1250, 1263, 1265, 1294–6, 1313, 1317–20, 1323–6, 1336–7, 1421, 1423.
2. For the text of *So-Purkh*, Gurū Granth Sāhib, pp. 10–12.
3. Ibid., pp. 83, 129–30, 174, 556, 585, 606.
4. Ibid., pp. 10–12, 86–7, 443, 592, 1241–2.
5. Ibid., pp. 10–12, 129–30, 443, 1239–40.
6. Ibid., pp. 10–12, 42, 129–30, 167–8, 367, 592–3, 1240–2, 1251–2.
7. Ibid., pp. 173, 448, 654, 723, 736, 1245, 1251.
8. Ibid., pp. 39–40, 561–2, 572–3, 604, 1422.
9. Ibid., pp. 41, 167–9, 234–5, 313, 442, 540, 676, 731, 1069, 1115, 1246.
10. Ibid., pp. 452, 539, 594, 732–3, 882, 1264, 1424.
11. Ibid., pp. 303, 306–7, 315–16, 853.
12. Ibid., 1116–17.
13. Ibid., pp. 442, 775, 860, 1070, 1114, 1200, 1239, 1246.
14. Ibid., pp. 82, 366, 493–4, 507, 538, 699, 833, 997, 1238, 1335.
15. Ibid., pp. 304, 608, 759.
16. Ibid., pp. 642, 849, 982, 1423.
17. Ibid., pp. 305–6.
18. Ibid., pp. 172, 444, 450–1, 590–1, 593, 648.
19. Ibid., pp.171, 445, 649, 652, 666–7, 669, 881.

20. Ibid., pp. 314, 446, 697, 977, 986, 995, 1202, 1314.

21. Ibid., pp. 78–9, 300, 447, 528, 575–6, 587, 670, 773–5, 801, 1114, 1249, 1295, 1337.

22. Ibid., pp. 326, 648, 725–6, 1135, 1263.

23. Ibid., pp. 300, 309, 799, 835, 976, 1325.

24. Ibid., pp. 312, 317, 850–1, 854–5, 978.

25. Ibid., pp. 87, 95–6, 175, 311, 492, 651, 690, 734, 1199, 1244, 1296.

26. Ibid., pp. 94, 368, 1316.

5

Halemī Rāj—A Parallel Dispensation

Guru Arjan

The *Sukhmanī*

Composed in thirty *Rāgs*, the *bāṇī* of Guru Arjan forms nearly two-fifths of the Gurū Granth Sāhib. The best known of his compositions, the *Sukhmanī* (Jewel of Bliss), expounds the bliss that comes from the Name Divine and brings peace to the heart of the devotee. Regarded as a comprehensive statement of Sikh philosophy, it dwells on God, the Name, the Guru, the *shabad*, the *hukam*, and the *nadar*. It underscores the conception of God with and without attributes. Contemplation of his attributes is an essential form of devotion. God is the true Guru, but the divinely inspired human Guru is equally important. His teaching is indispensable for liberation. The shabad refers to divine self-revelation, but more emphatically it refers to the utterance of the Guru (Guru's shabad) and to Gurbāṇī. The *Sukhmanī* dwells on hukam and *bhāṇā*, laying equal emphasis on divine power and divine grace. The bhāṇā of the Compassionate Lord tends to merge into his grace (nadar, *kirpā*, *dayā*, *karm*).

Apart from these key constituents of Sikh philosophy, there is a great emphasis in the *Sukhmanī* on *sādh-sangat*, the God-enlightened (*Brahm-giānī*), the liberated-in-life (*jīvan-muktā*), the *sants*, the Sikhs of the Guru, and supplication (*ardās*). The *Sukhmanī* itself is a source of liberation as Gurbāṇī. An ardās of the *Sukhmanī* is now recited as a prelude to the formal Sikh Ardās. Then there are other significant ideas in the *Sukhmanī*: humility is an essential attitude for receiving grace; whoever reckons himself low is really supreme; the true devotee is dust of the feet of all. Worthless is the body that does not engage in doing good to others. For the God-enlightened, all are alike; the true *vaishnav* remains engaged in endeavour without expecting any reward; the true pandit imparts teaching to all the four castes; the Name is open to all the four castes, and the lowest of the low (*chandāl*); there is no rancour in the hearts of those who lodge God in their heart; between the sādh and God there is no distance; God's devotee is in essence identical with God.[1]

The *Sukhmanī* is rightly regarded as the most important composition of Guru Arjan. It does not mean, however, that the ideas and attitudes expressed in the *Sukhmanī* do not occur in the rest of his bāṇī. They do. Indeed they are reinforced and amplified. The key concepts of God, the Name, the Guru, the shabad, the hukam, and the nadar get clarified when we turn to the rest of the bāṇī of Guru Arjan. A large number of references to the sādh-sangat, the Sikhs, ardās, liberation (*muktī*) and the liberated-in-life throw fuller light on these aspects of the ideas and concerns of Guru Arjan. The account we take of these features is not exhaustive, but surely comprehensive. Even so, all these concepts, ideas, attitudes, and concerns do not cover the entire range of his bāṇī. Guru Arjan has much to say about the entire dispensation of Guru Nanak and his successors, which becomes a distinctive mark of his bāṇī.

God, His Power and His Grace

God is one in the compositions of Guru Arjan. There is none except the one. Know him as the one, the only one.[2] He is both *nirguṇ* and *sarguṇ*. He is nirguṇ and sarguṇ at one and the same time. Unmanifest, he is nirguṇ; manifest, he is sarguṇ. The unity of the nirguṇ and sarguṇ God is underscored in a whole shabad. He remained unmanifest in a complete void (*sunn*) and darkness (*dhundūkārā*) and then he made himself manifest all by himself; he alone is the cause of all things. He is the creator of millions of Brahmas, Vishnus, and Maheshes.[3] He alone was before the creation; he alone shall be after his creation is no more. He was at the beginning, he was in the middle, and he shall be at the end. He is the only real entity.[4]

God is unmanifest. He is *agam*, *agochar*, *be-ant*, and *athāh*. He alone knows his power.[5] Manifest in his creation, God can be known through his attributes. The Primal Being (*ād purkh*) is the creator and the doer of everything; he fills everything and he is within everyone. He is ever present (*sadā hadūrā*). He is near, not far; he is the only Master, there is no other. Whatever we see is his form (*rūp*). The light of God is in the high and the low. He is the living element in every human being. He is all pervasive but detached.[6] God assumes multifarious forms but none of them eternally; when they are no more there remains the everlasting one (*ek ankār*). There is unity in diversity. Numerous waves arise from the water; the gold is seen in many shapes; the seeds of many kinds are sown, the fruit ripens and yields the same seed; hundreds of clouds cover the one sky, and we see the same sky when the clouds part. When the illusion is shattered there is ek ankār.[7]

Some of the other epithets used for God in Guru Arjan's bāṇī are *sat* (who exists forever), *kartā* (the doer), *purkh* (all pervasive), *nirbhau* (without fear), *nirvair* (without malice), *akāl* (eternal), *mūrit* (in form), *ajūnī* (who does not take birth) and *saimbhau* (self-existent). He is the knower of innermost secrets (*antarjāmī*), the destroyer of fear (*bhai-bhanjan*), and kind to the lowly (*dīn-dayāl*).[8] God is the treasure of good qualities, the giver of life; he is ever kind and forgiving. He is the Lord of the poor and the helpless. He is always just. What he does is right and just. He is the protector of all. He is the father and mother of all. He is the bestower of liberation.[9] All the attributes of God cannot be known; he is the most high, without an end, without any limit. He stands revealed and yet he is unrevealed; he is within everyone one and yet detached. The individual light mingles with the universal like the ray of the sun and the wave of water.[10]

Two attributes of God are particularly emphasized by Guru Arjan: his power and his compassion. His court is the highest court. Independent of everything, the sovereign Lord is the perfect ruler. Whatever happens is in accordance with his will. Great is his court, and true is his throne. He is the King of kings, with everlasting flywhisk and umbrella. Whatever pleases the Supreme Lord is true justice. Whatever he does is good. He can give an honourable place to one who has no place. His order (*farmān*) is true and none can disobey it. All power (*qudrat*) belongs to him and whatever happens is his doing. He can reduce *sultān*s and *khān*s to mere ants; he can raise the poor to mastery and rulership.[11]

Guru Arjan uses the word hukam (divine order) quite frequently. Two other words for God's pleasure are bhāṇā and *razā*. All the three terms occur alone or in combination. One takes the round of births due to his bhāṇā and everything happens according to his razā. It is through his hukam and razā that one praises God; he who pleases God is the real *giānī*; the real jap is only that which pleases him; through his bhāṇā comes full knowledge. God takes care of his servant and the servant welcomes his hukam. There is only one sign of meeting God: the mind recognizes his hukam. Peace and contentment come through his bhāṇā. His devotee should do what pleases God; wherever he keeps is good. Only he for whom God's hukam is sweet is wise and honourable. 'I live as you keep me, I eat and put on what you give'. Whatever happens is God's bhāṇā; he who recognizes the hukam is absorbed in truth. Handsome is he and wise is he who accepts God's bhāṇā. His bhāṇā comes to pass; none else has the power to do anything. He who is enabled to obey God's hukam is given the gift of the Name.[12]

Whatever pleases God should be acceptable to his devotees. God's bhāṇā is sweet. 'Whatever you do is sweet to me'. 'Whatever you wish is well. All things are set right in accordance with your *bhāṇā*'. 'Keep me as you wish'. Whatever you wish is well; yours is the hukam and razā. Whaterver I do is what you enable me to do, I cannot do anything else. 'Sweet is your *bhāṇā* to me'. 'You yourself are the cause and yourself the doer. Birth and death are due to your *hukam*'. 'We have become fearless with the Name lodged in our hearts'. Due to the bhāṇā of the True Guru, one comes into the world' and leaves it in accordance with his hukam. Union and separation are God's bhāṇā. 'Whatever you do I take it well; there is no pride in my mind'. What pleases God comes to pass. They who accept God's bhāṇā suffer no sorrow or misery. Whether or not one sings and listens to God's praises is God's bhāṇā; by recognizing his hukam one is absorbed in truth.[13]

In a whole *pauṛī* on hukam, Guru Arjan says that one frolics or sits idle according to the hukam; in accordance with the hukam one experiences dukh and sukh. One recites the Name day and night if one receives the gift according to the hukam. In accordance with the hukam one lives or dies; one is small or great according to the hukam. In accordance with the hukam is sorrow, joy, or happiness; one recites the all efficacious *mantar* of the Guru according to the hukam. In accordance with the hukam, one is released from coming and going by being attached to *bhagtī*.[14] Similarly, there is a pauṛī on bhāṇā. The Name is recited if the perfect Guru imparts the teaching. If he pleases one may perform tap or *sanjam* or one may refrain from it. As he pleases, one may wander from birth to birth or one may be liberated. As he pleases, one may be allowed or denied pleasures. As he pleases, one may go to hell or heaven, or one may be cast down on earth. As he pleases, one may be attached to *bhagtī*. Rare are the persons immersed in bhagtī.[15]

The entire universe and all that is therein was created by divine order. 'You are the Master and you have made me your servant. My body and my soul are your gifts. You do and get everything done; nothing is done by us. We come into the world when you send us. We perform the deeds which you desire. Nothing happenes without you. We have no anxiety. There we hear your command; here we sing your praises. You ordain and you undo; there can be no dispute with you. You are the father and all are your children; we play as you make us play. You have created the wrong and the right path to send men on the one or the other. Some are settled in the home and others are sent to places far and near. Some are grass-cutters and others are rulers. Some attain liberation and others are sent to hell. Some are worldly, others are *bhagats*. Some are wise and others are fools; some are wide awake and others are ignorant. Liberation and hell are in accordance with the *hukam*. God has created the mighty ocean. Some are made ignorant *manmukhs* and stand in hell. Some are taken across by the True Guru in the true boat. Creation and destruction are through his hukam. Living beings are created and destroyed. He watches over his sport and enjoys all its states. He has created the universe as a wrestling arena.[16]

Guru Arjan empasizes the relationship between grace and hukam. Nadar (grace) is closely related to hukam. The rain comes through God's hukam; it is also an act of grace. Through God's grace (kirpā), one remembers God. Through his kindness (dayā) one sings his praises. The creator shows kindness and the thirst of all living beings is slaked. Through the Guru's grace (*prasād*) one receives a kind glance (nadar) from God. The Lord shows his kindness and one gets attached to the Guru's feet. Auspicious is the month, the day and the time when the Lord shows his grace (nadar) and through his grace (kirpā) one receives the boon of his sight (*dars*). He to whom God shows his grace utters the Name with his tongue. It is through God's grace that the gift of the Name is received as a treasure. It is through God's grace that one takes the human birth. It is through God's grace that one becomes a bhagat or a giānī. They who take refuge in God have no anxiety; they who receive his grace remain all well. Only he has the Guru's grace who knows the secret of God within human beings. The truth is ever pure and they become pure who receive this truth through the Guru's grace (nadar). Through the Guru's grace the noose of Death is cut and the body and mind enjoy peace. Only he becomes a bhagat, a giānī, or a tapā to whom God is gracious. The gift of the Name comes as God's grace. It is through God's grace that one gets attached to his bhagtī. One turns dead in life and attains to liberation if God shows his grace (karm). It is through God's kindness that one meets the Guru. God shows his kindness to the lowest of the low and they become his devoted servants. The body and the mind become cool through the all satisfying grace (nadar) of God.[17]

In Guru Arjan's bāṇī the Islamic epithets for God include *karīm* and *rahīm*. God is the kind Master (*mihrwān* Maulā). The *mihr* of God and his *bandagi* go together. If God (Maulā) shows his kindness (mihr) one worships the Lord. Man performs deeds ordained by God and through his grace conquers the mind in association with sādhs. Happiness comes through the Guru's sight, and through his grace one escapes the five adversaries (the senses). If one lodges the Guru's feet in one's heart, the Guru shows his grace to lead one to the Lord. Through God's grace one remembers him all the time and acquires his hue.[18]

The idea of grace does not infringe the omnipotence of God: it reinforces the idea that nothing happens in human affairs without his power or compassion. In the bāṇī of Guru Arjan, the greater emphasis is on the acceptance of the bhāṇā of God rather than on his great majesty and power. Expressed in diverse ways, the bhāṇā of God remains close to his kirpā.

Finally, Guru Arjan advises that the one God is the only object of worship. Attach yourself to the one. Dedicate your body, mind, wealth, and your life to Brahm who is everywhere and in everyone. Pray to Kartar and praise him. Remember the Supreme Lord. Remember him in *sukh* and in *dukh*. 'You are my Master; dedicated to you are my body, mind and wealth'. Praise God all the time, when you sit and stand up; by remembering him you receive the gift of poise. Remember God all the eight *pahars* of the day. Not to remember God is to be unfaithful: a person who does not remember God is comparable to a dog. The term sākat is frequently used for him: he forgets the bestower of the body, mind, and life. The mind should be awakened through the praises of God; one should know none other than the Supreme Lord. 'With you as my Lord there can be no fear; I cannot praise anyone except you. When you are there, every thing is there. No other than you I recognize'.[19]

The Name

Closely linked with the conception of God is the concept of the Name (*nām*). It refers to God in his nirguṇ and sarguṇ states at one and the same time. 'Wherever we look there is he, the only one; within everyone he has manifested himself; the concealed is he and the revealed is he; *sarguṇ* and *nirguṇ* are his epithets; the two as one become the Name'.[20]

Guru Arjan highlights the importance of the Name. Without the Name one remains impure, oblivious of God. One may go to all the known sacred places, one may own immense wealth and vast territory, one may wield power without fear of anyone, one may lord over everyone, but one is reduced to dust without the Name. Appropriate the Name so that God may remain with you. Remember and recite the Name of God who is always there to help you. The Name of God is the nectar of immortality (*amrit*). Only they meditate on God who have been dyed in his Name in association with sādhs. The Name of God is like the drop of rain for the thirsty rainbird (*chātrik*). The Name of God is amrit; he who lodges it in the heart becomes liberated (muktā). The Name is the medicine (aukhad) for all ills. From meditating on the name comes great peace (mahā sukh). The place where the Name is recited becomes the site of an eternally shining mansion of gold; the habitation where the Name is not recited becomes a wilderness. He who reflects on the Name in association with sādhs is our beloved friend. He who has lodged the Name in his heart becomes acceptable to God whether he is a renunciate or a householder. The true saviour in all the cosmic ages from the very beginning is the true Name, Kartar. The best gift that one can receive from God is never to forget the Name. By appropriating the Name of God one remains safe from a hot wind.[21]

Like the ship in a fearful sea, like the lamp in darkness, and like the fire in cold weather, the Name brings comfort to the mind. 'Recite the Name by turning to the Guru so that your thirst is quenched, all your wishes are fulfilled and your mind acquires poise'. The medicine of the Name is received as a gift only through God's grace. All sorrow and suffering vanish from the life of the person who has lodged the Name in his heart. The Name of Ram is the nectar of God's bāṇī; this is what one should inscribe on paper with ink. One becomes safe from Death by remembering and reciting the Name of Ram. Māyā cannot allure him.

He redeems himself and leads the world to redemption. Recite the Name of Ram, the only one. Sing the praises of God all the time. Not to recite the Name is to commit suicide. The life is futile without the Name. The Guru's mantar leaves nothing in the heart but the Name. The Name is the life of the bhagat, his support. The Name is his wealth and his trade. It is the source of one's recognition and good name. It is received through God's grace. The Name is the peaceful abode for the bhagat. Dyed in the Name he becomes acceptable. Very rare is the person who remembers the Name with every breath. Perfectly fortunate is he whose mind remains attached to the Name.[22]

'Recite the Name of Ram a million times and drink the nectar that is dear to God'. From the repeated recitation of the Name the highest happiness (*parm-ānand*) comes. The Name leads to the state of liberation (*parm-gat*). The *mahā-ras* of amrit-nām becomes the source of control over kings and emperors. The Name is the destroyer of all fear. Far preferable to Smriti, Shastar and Ved, and to *yoga*, giān and *siddhī* is the recitation of the Name of God. The seeker seeks the Name of the Lord who is within everyone. Redemption comes through his grace. 'Show your grace and bestow the Name' is the prayer of the seeker. The Name of God is the destroyer of sorrow and suffering (dukh). None gets rid of sorrow and suffering without the True Name. He who is drenched in the Name is liberated (*nirbāṇ*). 'The gift of the Name (*nām-dān*) received from the perfect Guru is my only support'. All other than the true Name is dust and ashes. Without the true Name no one ever has saved his honour. The body in which the Name does not spring is a mere dust. The medicine of the Name, a pure water of immortality, is found through the Guru. God alone bestows the gift of the Name, the remover of all suffering.[23]

'Recite the True Name all the time so that your countenance becomes bright in this world and the next by the daily remembrance of the Divine Being who is without attributes'. Pray for the gift of the divine Name, just as the mother prays for the boon of a son. The perfect Guru gives the understanding that search leads to the sādh and there is no other means as efficacious as the Name of God. One is redeemed through it and so is one's family. Sing the Name of Niranjan (Lord) so that you may receive all the treasures through his grace. 'The Name is my caste, the Name is my honour, the Name is my family'. Great is his future who finds the Guru and is taught how to recite the Name of God. Without the Name all talk is false and mean. The Name exalts the low and fills up the empty. The perfect Guru protects the honour of the Name. Worthless are rulership and riches without the Name. A sustained search reveals that everything is false except the Name. The fears of all the three worlds disappear by lodging the Name in the heart.[24]

'May I sing God's praises and recite the Name till the last breath of my life. The perfect Guru has preserved my honour. He has lodged the nectar of the Name in my heart, and removed the dirt of all the previous lives.' The Name of God is the nectar for the Kaliyuga. The sādhūs find this treasure. Only he recites the Name whom God himself enables to recite. Ask for the treasure of the Name so that you may receive honour in the divine court. The Name of God puts an end to the disease of *haumai*. There is direct opposition between the Name and pride. However, haumai is a part of the creation. There is no other means of liberation than the Name. The Name is equally efficacious for the Khatri, the Brahman, the Sūd, and the Vais. By accepting the Guru's guidance one receives the mantar of the Name as the medicine that leads to liberation. 'The egg of illusion is broken and the mind is illumined. The chain on the feet has been cut asunder and the Guru has released me from detention. The coming and going has come to an end. The boiling cauldron has become calm. The Guru has given me the cooling Name'. They who have forgotten the Name have been seen reduced to ashes.[25]

A long statement on the Name in Guru Arjan's bāṇī, equates it with the Sikh way of life. The unstruck melody (*anhad shabad*) is heard in the mind by those who receive the treasure of the Name by meditation on the feet of the sādhū through God's grace. The Name is associated with dān and *isnān*, and *Gur-kathā*. The Name is the only source of redemption in the Kaliyuga. The Name of God is *patit pāwan* or redeemer of the fallen. The essence of the Guru's teaching is praises of God on the lips and the Name in the mind. The Name of Ram is the only basis of true life. The Name is our all-knowing God. The Name is in every hair of the body. It is the gift of the True Guru.[26] The Name is our Ved and Nād. The Name serves all our purposes. The Name is the God of our worship. The Name is the means of the service of the Guru. The Name of God has been promulgated by the Perfect Guru. It is superior to every thing else. The Name is our sacred place of bathing. It is the perfect gift for us. By uttering the Name, all are shorn of sins. They who recite the Name are my brothers and friends. The Name is our *sauṇ* and happy union (*sanjog*). The Name is our satisfying enjoyment (*subhog*). The Name is the whole of our conduct. The Name is our pure trade. All those who have lodged the one in their mind he is their only refuge. They who receive the Name in the sādh-sang sing praises of God.[27]

Guru Arjan says that the shabad of the Guru removes disease and sorrow by placing the medicine of the Name in the mind. Happiness enters the mind on meeting the Guru. The Name of God is the treasure of all treasures. All other than the Name of God is false. The Guru has given his instruction: the treasure of the Name. He who has the Name in his heart finds immense wealth; the life is a sheer waste without the Name. To lodge the Name in the heart is to find millions of soldiers. He who has the Name in his heart attains to the state of *sahaj*; his mind is stilled and he acquires poise. Without the Name, the life is a deadly curse. He who has the Name in his heart is liberated-in-life; he receives the nine treasures; he is without cares; he gains profit all the time; he has a large family; his place is stable; he sits on the throne; he is the true *sāhu*; he is distinguished from all; he is like God; he is the tallest of all; he is rid of darkness; he is acceptable; he sees God in the sādh-sangat; he does not come and go, and he attains peace; his essence mingles with the divine essence. Without the Name one comes and goes, remains ignorant (manmukh), and has no honour or trust; he remains chained to transmigration.[28]

The shopkeeper, the gambler, and the addict remain preoccupied with their concerns; the man of God remains preoccupied with God. The peacock, the lotus, and the mother are happy to see the rain, the moon and the child; the man of God lives in remembrance of God. The lion, the warrior, and the miser are happy with meat, the battle, and wealth; the man of God is happy with the thought of God. All the colours are in one colour, all the comforts are in one comfort, the Name of God. The treasure is received as a gift through the Guru's grace. The only gift which the seeker cherishes is the gracious gift of the Name. The eight powers (*siddhīs*) and the nine treasures (*niddhīs*) are subsumed in the Name received through God's grace. Without the Name, pride is not subdued, and there can be no liberation without the Name. He who takes refuge with the *sant* of God, his sorrow, disease, and fear are destroyed. He recites the Name and enables others to recite the Name; he is redeemed and leads others to redemption. By reciting the Name, with each breath of life, one attains the state of liberation; all troubles come to an end, the fear goes away, and one is attached to the sādh-sang.[29]

Further, in his bāṇī Guru Arjan says that man comes into the world to hear and read the bāṇī, but he forgets the Name and gets attached to other things; he wastes his life. The *simran* of the Name of Ram removes all dirt in a moment; it is more efficacious than millions of conventional charities and bathings (dān, isnān). Attain liberation by reciting the Name of Ram; the rest are meaningless tales. The instruction of the Name is the essence of understanding; the rest is meaningless. Prem, bhagtī, and the Name are prayed for. The treasure of the Name is mentioned in the context of the sādh-sangat. He whom the Guru gives the mantar of the Name becomes the master of all arts. The Name is recited in the company of sants. True is God's form and true his Name. He who sings the praise of the Name of Ram is regarded as pure in the divine court. The nectar of the Name of God is received from the true Guru.[30]

The Name refers to God. It is combined with epithets for God, like the Name of Ram, the Name of Niranjan, or the Name of 'Kartar'. It is also the True Name. Rememberance and recitation of God's Name and reflection on it are strongly emphasized. The Name is mentioned in connection with the shabad and congregational worship. It is thus a comprehensive and a multilayered concept in the composition of Guru Arjan. Indeed, the whole message of Guru Nanak and his successors is nām-dharam.[31]

The Guru

Guru Arjan refers to Akal Purkh as Gurudev.[32] There is a whole stanza at the beginning and the end of the *Bāwan Akharī* which relates to Gurudev. He is the mother, he is the father, he is the Lord Parmesar. He is the friend who destroys ignorance; he is a close relative and the real brother. Gurudev is the giver of the divine Name and the true mantar. He is the embodiment of peace, truth, and wisdom; he is the magic stone that turns others into magic stone by his touch. Gurudev is tīrath with the pool of nectar and bathing as knowledge (giān). Gurudev is the real doer and the remover of all sins; he purifies the sinners. Gurudev was in the beginning, he shall be at the end, he is in all the cosmic ages; his divine mantar redeems all, one prays to Gurudev that he may enable one to meet God in the *sangat* so that through his grace 'a sinner like me is redeemed'. Gurudev is the True Guru, Parbrahm, Parmesar; he is the God of Nanak to whom we bow in salutation.[33] Gurudev here is God; he is the True Guru.

Guru Arjan in his bāṇī says that a kind glance of the True Guru is the source of limitless happiness and rulership: 'my mind and body shall become cool only if he gives the divine Name'. Discard your own wisdom and touch the feet of the Guru so that you may worship the one who is the King of kings, the trust of all. Only he who eradicates his haumai can serve the True Guru. Discard all other means and concentrate on the perfect Guru to be affiliated to the only one. All problems are solved through the instruction of the True Guru: the nectar of the Name of Ram is lodged in your heart by his all satisfying grace. The gift of the Name is received from the perfect Guru through his grace. None is as great as the Guru: only he can lead you to the Truth, and none else. Therefore, turn to the service of the True Guru. Worship Guru-Parmesar with the loving devotion of your mind and body. The True Guru is the giver of life; he is the support of everyone. Guru-Parmesar is one. All curses are lifted by meeting the Guru.[34]

The true Name is found only if the True Guru becomes kind. There is just one way and no other. All other means are futile. Discard every other means and hold on to the feet of the Guru. 'Auspicious was the time when I met the True Guru. All illusions have gone by treading the path of God'. His bāṇī is outside and inside, uttered by him and shown by him. The Guru says that there is one, only one; there shall be no other. He who has recognized the Guru as true does not have to fear anything. A lamp is lighted in the temple of the mind by meeting the True Guru through God's grace.[35]

In the bāṇī of Guru Arjan, Guru Nanak is also the True Guru and, by implication his successors too. It is necessary to keep in view these two levels suggested simultaneously at places. Through God's grace one may obtain all the fruit by serving the fulfiller of wishes and the bestower of the treasure of peace. The True Guru is the Lord, the pool of nectar that remains full all the time. 'So long as I did not recognize the *hukam* I remained miserable. By meeting the Guru I have recognized the hukam and I am at peace. None is an enemy (in my eyes) now, and no opponent, and none is bad. By serving the Guru, Nanak has become a servant of God.' The Guru here is not God. He is the human Guru. Study the Shastar, Ved, and Smriti with care; they have only one message; none attains liberation without the Guru. Reflect on this. Rare in the world are they who remember the Guru in the depth of their being and utter the Name of the Guru with their tongue, who see the True Guru with their eyes and hear the Guru's Name with their ears, who are suffused with the Guru and find a place in the divine court; only he receives this gift to whom God is gracious.[36]

One who studies Smritī and Shāstar comes to know that illusion does not disappear without the True Guru. One may perform countless rituals, there is no release from the chain of transmigration. One may wander in all the four directions, there is no place other than the Guru's place. Through great good fortune one finds the Guru and recites the Name. Truth is ever pure and they to whom God is gracious attain it and become pure. The mind is enlightened by meeting the perfect Guru as a mark of good fortune. There is no liberation without the Guru; the True Guru, Pārbrahm, Parmesar, redeems all. Fear is destroyed by taking refuge in the Guru. One meditates on the True Guru through God's grace. He who is protected by the True Guru comes to no harm. Wonderful is the Guru's greatness; all living beings are redeemed by the Lord through his *darshan*. They who have complete trust in God receive whatever they desire; by meeting the perfect Guru, all anxiety is gone. The service of the Guru and obedience to him saves one from Death. The Guru who shows the path to those who have strayed from the right path in found through good fortune. He who serves the perfect Guru remains stable at God's door. The perfect Guru teaches that peace comes by accepting God's will.[37]

'Perfect is my Guru, my Guru is perfect.' The perfect Guru has destroyed all anxiety. The recitation of God's praises all the time has made him the protector. 'I have seen the True Guru exactly as I had heard of him.' He invites the separated ones as representative of the divine court; he gives the mantar of the divine Name, and cures the disease of haumai. The True Guru has invited those whose union was ordained by God. There is no liberation without the Guru. In a whole pessage on the True Guru, the Guru is equated with God.

My True Guru is not dependent on any one. Whatever is established by my True Guru is true. My True Guru gives the gifts to all. My True Guru is the creator of things. No *dev* is comparable with the Guru. Only the fortunate one serves him. My True Guru looks after all with kindness. My True Guru can give life to the dead. The greatness of my True Guru has become manifest everywhere. My True Guru is the place for those who have no place. My True Guru is like a *dīwān* in the (divine) court. May I be hundred times a sacrifice to the True Guru who has shown the path to liberation. He who serves the Guru entertains no fear. He who serves the Guru faces no sorrow. Study the Smritī and the Ved, says Nanak; there is no difference between the Guru and Pārbrahm.[38]

In another passage the True Being is the True Guru, Parmesar, by meeting whom one crosses to the other bank. The dust of his feet purifies the sinners. The mythical tree and the cow which fulfil all desires are in his court. Contentment comes from his service and one receives from him the gift of the Name. When one meets the perfect Guru, who is the magic stone, one is transformed into a magic stone. There is no desire for Baikunth or even liberation (muktī) when one attains *ek ankār* through the grace of the True Guru. No one knows the nature of the service of the Guru who is the unknowable *Pārbrahm*. He who has good fortune on his forehead is enabled to serve him and become a sevak. The Ved does not know the greatness of the Guru. The True Guru is God.[39]

The Gurbāṇī

The terms used by Guru Arjan for the message of the Guru are shabad, bāṇī, and *bachan*. The shabad of the Guru gives the mantar of the Name. Peace comes through the Guru's shabad. The treasure of the shabad is found by meeting the True Guru. One should discard one's own wisdom and turn to the true shabad. He who lodges the Guru's shabad in his mind finds the treasure of the Name. The unfathomable, unknowable, and the most high is seen through the Guru's shabad; he gives the message of the Name in the Kaliyuga. He who turns to the Guru meditates on the True Lord, and appropriates the shabad of the perfect Guru. God is worshipped through the Guru's shabad; this is the pure mantar.[40]

There is a whole passage on the Guru's bachan in Guru Arjan's compositions. It is indestructible; it cuts the noose of Death; it remains with the individual; it dyes him in the love of God; what is given by the Guru is for the good; regard this as the truth. The Guru's bachan cannot be evaded; it cannot be pierced; it removes all illusions and differences; it is for all times; in accordance with it one sings the praises of God; it is the protector of those who have no protection; due to it one does not suffer hell; the tongue tastes the nectar. The Guru's bachan is manifest in the world; it never suffers defeat. The True Guru is ever compassionate; the one to whom he is kind cherishes his bachan. Taste the nectar of the Guru's shabad; all other effort is futile. Absorb the teaching of the Guru in the mind.[41]

In another passage the Guru's bachan leads to the state of liberation (*param-gat)*. It enables one to recite the Name and meditate on it. By the Guru's grace 'my utterance' is the nectar. The Guru's bachan has obliterated 'my self'; through his grace 'my honour and influence have increased'. The Guru's bachan has removed 'my illusion; I have seen Brahm'. The Guru's bachan has established *rāj-jog;* through association with the Guru the whole world is redeemed. The Guru's bachan has set all things right; 'I have found the nine treasures'. All those who have turned towards my Guru, their noose has been cut. The Guru's bachan has awakened my fortune and the Guru has led me to meet Pārbrahm.[42]

The shabad of the perfect Guru is endless; all ill deeds disappear through living in accodance with it. The Guru's shabad is sweet; it enables one to see God. The True Guru makes one understand the shabad; this is the real *yoga*. The dye of God is fast; it is acquired through the service of the Guru and his shabad. The Guru has given the true mantar of the shabad. May we recite and meditate on the true shabad and sing God's praises so that all anxiety disappears from our mind. By appropriating the Guru's bāṇī, all suffering disappears through the Guru's grace. The Guru speaks as the Lord enables him to speak; he has no power independently of God. 'May I utter the *amrit-bāṇī* in praise of God'. Great is the fortune of one who listens to the amrit-bāṇī. May we always sing amrit-bāṇī. The Lord has uttered the bāṇī-shabad ; sing and read and listen to it every day so that the perfect Guru keeps you under protection. The bāṇī has come from the most High; it has obliterated all anxiety. The merciful and kind God has revealed the Truth. The bāṇī of the perfect Guru is liked by Pārbrahm. In accordance with the Master's will his servant's bāṇī reveals God.[43]

The Guru speaks when God enables him to speak. The Guru's utterance (bāṇī), his word (shabad) and his speech (bachan) are thus divinely inspired and have divine sanction. Therefore, the bachan of the Sādh (Guru) is the nectar of immortality. Whoever recites it is redeemed; he utters the divine Name daily from his tongue. Perfect is the Guru and perfect is his bāṇī; its merits cannot be counted. The shabad of the Guru is inexhaustible; the more it is used the more it remains with you. Its perfection does not decrease. God resides in the Guru's shabad. He who lives by the Guru's shabad is a *pandit*; he gets rid of the three modes of being which govern eartly existence (*gunas*), and the four Vedas take refuge with him. Drink the nectar of shabad so that your soul is purified. The Guru's bachan is the essence of bhagtī. Listen to the Guru's teaching to attain liberation.[44]

Only he reflects on the Guru's shabad whom God wishes to protect; he who is dear to God loves God. Amrit-bāṇī of the perfect True Guru in lodged in his heart to whom God is gracious; he does not come and go any more; he lives eternally in peace. The bāṇī of the perfect Guru is perfect. Its hue becomes increasingly deep and it never decreases in weight. The Guru's bāṇī suffuses everyone; he spoke it himself and heard it too. Whoever meditates on it is liberated and finds an eternal place. He in whose heart is lodged the Guru's shabad, his suffering, sorrow, and illusion vanish; he hears the *anhad* bāṇī in the tune of sahaj, obtains sach, sahaj and ānand, and tastes nām. Amrit-bāṇī of the Guru reveals that there is one God and no other. There is no other means of liberation except through the Guru's bachan. 'The Guru's *shabad* is sweet to my mind; the doors of fortune have opened and I see the light; I see God in everyone'. The True shabad is the eternal Lord's ensign (*nishān*). Sing every morning the bāṇī of the Master; remember God all through the day.[45]

Sangat, Ardās, and Liberation-in-life

Guru Arjan speaks of association with sādhs and sants. The terms used for this association are sādh-sang, sādh-sangat, sant-sang, sant-sabhā, sat-sang, and sat-sangat. The sādhs and sants meet in the dharamsāl to perform *kīrtan*. The Guru may also be present there. There is hardly any doubt that the sādhs and sants are Sikhs of the Guru and they come to the dharamsāl for congregational worship. The dharamsāl is the most important place for the religious life of the Sikhs.

After associating with sādhs one finds peace; in sensual pleasures and rulership lies fear (of Death). The one true Lord is in the sādh-sangat. Associate every day with the sādhs, concentrating your mind on the Guru's feet. Only through God's grace sādh-sang becomes possible. Association with sants enables one to recite the Name of God. Sādh-sang puts an end to birth and death. It is a great fortune to sing the praises of God (kīrtan) in sādh-sang. All kinds of comforts come from the true association (sat-sang). The divine Name is found in the *sant-sabhā* as the support of life. The teaching through which we sing the praises of God is perfect; sādh-sang is found through good fortune. He to whom God is gracious sings the praises of God in sādh-sang. Fear and illusion are removed by sādh-sang. The fire is quenched in the sādh-sang. The sādh-sangat removes the fear of birth and death. Nothing in the universe is eternal, neither Indrapuri nor Shivpuri, nor Brahmpuri. There is only one place which is true and stable, where there is ānand, sahaj, *sifat*, *bhagtī*, and giān. This is where the sādhs meet in association, the 'city without fear' (*anbhau nagar*) that lasts for ever. There is no fear, no illusion, no sorrow, and no anxiety. There is no death. It is the abode of bliss. The devotees of God live there with the praises of God (kīrtan) as their support. He to whom God is gracious attains liberation in this stable place in sādh-sang.[46]

The Name is found in sādh-sang, the association of sants. The place where the praises of God are sung everyday is found from the Guru: the praises of God are sung in sādh-sang. Singing of God's praises in sādh-sangat is preferable to all other places and all other forms of worship. Sādh-sangat is the redeemer of the world. The Name of God is the support of the mind of the sants. The lotus feet of the Guru are dear to the sants who worship God in love. He whom millions of munīs seek, for whom millions perform austerities, rituals, and prayers, and for whom millions wander all over the earth and bathe at sacred places is realized in sādh-sangat through his grace. The true Guru has become kind to Sikhs and given them the love of sant-sang; their honour has been saved by God by nurturing them on the daily kīrtan. 'I pray to God that he may make me the servant of his servants, that I may live by singing his praises even if I get the nine treasures and rulership, that there may be a large measure of the nectar of the Name in the home of your servants, that I may listen to your praises in their company, that I may serve them to purify my frame, that I may wave the fan over them, fetch water for them, grind corn for them and wash their feet; I cannot do all this on my own; be gracious to me, give me a place in the *dharamsāl* of the *sants.*' Evidently, the dharamsāl is the place for sādh-sang. Conversely, the place of sādh-sang is the dharamsāl.[47]

Sādh-sangat or sant-sangat is also the true association (sat-sangat). The path of liberation is hard to tread. It is like walking on the sharp edge of a double-edged sword. One has to discard pride, attachment, and the question of 'mine or your'. They cross the ocean of fear who join the sant-sangat through God's grace. Life eternal is in the sādh-sang where one drinks the nectar of God. *Kathā* and kīrtan through the bāṇī of the perfect Guru in the sādh-sang become the source of peace. To join sādh-sang is a sign of good fortune; they who join it are shorn of durmat; they lodge God in the heart and the dust of their feet is sought by others. Sādh-sang is raised by God on an everlasting foundation so as to redeem all those who join it. Darkness vanishes by joining the sādh-sangat and one attains liberation. By joining the sādh-sangat one dies to self and obtains real life. Peace here and bright countenance in the hereafter is the result of association with sants. Through the Guru's grace is recited the Name, and the being who is the life of the universe is found. Nām, dān, and isnān are associated with sādh-sang. Death does not touch them who sing kīrtan in sādh-sang. There is one God and one way of worship: kīrtan in the sādh-sangat.[48]

Sometimes the term sādh-sangat is not used but the reference is clearly to this institution.

I see the Guru with my eyes and place my forehead on his feet. I go to the Guru on foot and use my hands for waving the fan. Day and night I recite the Name of Akal Purkh. I have discarded all other means and placed my trust in the Guru. He has bestowed the treasure of the Name on me, and all suffering is gone. The treasure of the Name is inexhaustible. Practised here is nām, dān, and isnān, and Guru's kathā is performed here. In the state of peace there is no fear of death.

The word sat-sangat is used for the collectivity of members who come to join it. The dust of their feet rubbed on the forehead earns a merit equal to that of bathing at all the sacred places. The deep hue acquired through the dye of God is so fast that it never fades. Illusion and fear are destroyed by sādh-sang and one attains brahm-giān.[49]

The dharamsāl is also the place where collective prayer is offered. The word ardās occurs frequently in the bāṇī of Guru Arjan. Equally frequent is 'with hands joined'. It is important to note what is so fervently prayed for. At one place Guru Arjan says, 'I want no rāj and no muktī; my mind is concentrated on the lotus feet of the Lord'. Guru Arjan prays for peace by becoming dust of the feet of the sants. The sevak asks for the service of the Guru. One should pray for association with sādh-sangat. One should pray to the true Guru who bestows the gift of the treasure of the Name for union with God. 'Give this *dān* to your servant that he may never forget the Name'. Our ardās before the Lord Master is that he may slake our thirst for māyā. May God hear my ardās and give me the gift of the Name through the grace of the Sant (Guru).[50]

Prayer can be made only to God who is the giver of the body and the soul. 'Listen to the prayer of Nanak: lodge the Name in his heart'. 'With hands joined I pray that I may meditate on my Master'. 'With hands joined I pray to the Merciful one, the Lord of all, that I may instantly attain liberation'. If you wish for a real life, pray to the Guru; discard your own wisdom and dedicate your mind and body to him. 'Save us O'Lord, we cannot do anything on our own, bestow the Name on us through your grace'. 'With hands joined I pray that I may wash the feet of the *sants*; the merciful everpresent Lord may enable me to live by the dust of their feet'. 'Nanak asks for the gift of the Name through God's grace'.[51]

Those who pray to God face no hindrance; sorrow goes away and peace comes in, and all the three fevers (of the body, the mind, and illusion) disappear. With hands joined one prays for the gift of bhagtī and meditation on God all the time. Nanak's only prayer is that he may never forget God. With hands joined, Nanak asks for the gift that he may become a servant of his servants. With hands joined, Nanak asks for the gift that God may keep him close to himself. 'With hands joined, I pray to my Master, the doer of everything, to whom my body and soul are dedicated, that he may purify me by the dust of the feet of *sādhs*, that all evil thoughts may vanish by meditating on God and the dirt of many births may be washed'.[52]

The gift for which one may pray to the powerful Lord is service of the sants. We pray to God earnestly that we may remember him every moment and that through his grace the destroyer of the suffering of the helpless may lead to liberation. Nanak's prayer to God is that he may be given the service of the sants.

> Through your grace O my beloved God give us loving devotion (*bhagtī*) and the Name. What can the helpless pray for'? God is within everyone. Thirst for God is in the mind. Nanak, the servant of God, says 'I am yours... Be gracious O my divine Master so that I may attain liberation by serving the people. With hands joined I pray that I may meditate on God all the time; every morning I may sing his *bāṇī*, and recite his name throughout the day. The Lord is in every place, in everything and outside everything; may he help me wherever I go'.[53]

Many a time the prayer is for liberation. Guru Arjan attaches crucial importance to the ideal of liberation. One term used for the liberated person is brahm giānī. Another is muktā. The state of liberation is *nihchal rāj* or *nihchal āsan*. The state of muktī is not subject to change. Somewhere on the path to liberation one has to die-in-life. It is a state of unison or union with God. It is possible to become liberated in one's life (jīvan-muktā). It is an ever-lasting state (*amrāpad*). It is through the Guru's grace that one becomes a muktā. This state is called *pad-nirbāṇ*. It is a state of fearlessness (nirbhau pad). This is the highest state open to a human being: it is *parm-pad*. By taking refuge in God one may receive the gift of fearlessness (*abhai dān*). One may become liberated-in-life by meditating on God in loving devotion. One becomes a muktā in the world through the instruction of the Guru (*gurupdes*). One may attain liberation while laughing and playing, dressing and eating. In other words, one can become liberated-in-life with all its commitments. In a state of liberation one is devoid of haumai, affection, and attachment. So long as durmat lasts there is no scope of attaining parm-pad. In order to recognize God one has to die-in-life. One can die-in-life and cross the ocean of fear through God's grace. Parm-pad is found at the feet of the sants and in the service of the Guru. By serving the sādhs one may receive abhai-dān. The life of the liberated being alone is real life. The state of liberation is jīvan-pad. The state of liberation is the mingling of light with the divine light. Association with sādhs can be a means of liberation. He who has the Name in his heart becomes liberated-in-life. It is a state in which one remains detached in action (rāj-jog).[54]

Guru Arjan tells the potential novices 'to accept death first, discard all hope of life, and become the dust of the feet of others before coming to us'. The beginning of the journey is the complete negation of self. The end of the journey is liberation, a state of bliss. This state is not an inert state. The liberated-in-life remains active as in *rāj-jog*. They who are acceptable to the Guru remain detached (jog) amidst wordly activities (rāj). This is where the state of fearlessness (nirbhai-pad) becomes relevant. When the sevak and the Master become one the sevak acquires the attributes of God. The Master is nirbhai. Therefore, the liberated-in-life also becomes fearless. God is the giver (dātā) of the state of fearlessness (anbhai).[55]

The activity of the liberated-in-life is not in self-interest alone. He performs services for the Guru and his followers, and for other people. 'My Master is *par-upkārī*', says Guru Arjan. Like God, the Gurus are par-upkārī. Guru Arjan says that the par-upkārī jan give the gift of bhagtī and unite people with God. This can be a reference to the Gurus and their followers. Thus, par-upkār is the concern of the liberated-in-life as much as of the Gurus and God. From God, through the Guru, the liberated-in-life becomes a part of the large dispensation called nām-dharam, the lamp lighted in darkness for the redemption of mankind in the Kaliyuga.[56]

The Followers

Gurmukh and Gursikh are the most familiar terms for the followers of the Gurus. The less familiar are sādh, sant, bhagat, and har-jan. Occasionally, sādh or sant is used for the Guru. To become the dust of feet of the sants is a cherished ideal. The dust of the feet of the sādhū is preferable to millions of pilgrimages, fasts, and penances. God belongs to the sants and they belong to God; they have lodged God in their hearts. God looks after his sants. The sants join the sport with him. They are very dear to God, and he is their life. They show the way towards him. God is the Master and the sants are his servants. God is the helper of his sants.[57]

Guru Arjan poses a number of questions and gives answers which talk of the Gurmukh, the one who has turned to the Guru. He finds the way to liberation and gets liberated. He acquires knowledge and does good to others. He has eradicated haumai. He performs good deeds and remains unattached. He remains in peace, in contrast with the manmukh who remains subject to suffering. The Gurmukh regards sukh and dukh as the same. He meditates on God and sings his praises. The whole world is in fear but not the Brahm-giānī: he is redeemd. There is no difference between Ram and the Sant who is one in millions. Once the disease of haumai is successfully treated, one attains rāj-jog through the Guru's grace.[58]

The Sikh of the Guru is protected by God and is taken out of the ocean of fear through his grace. The dust of the sādh's feet is more efficacious than pilgrimage to all the sixty-eight sacred places. The Sikh sevaks have the treasure of the Name. Devoid of all fear, they are dyed in the hue of the Master. Their association is cherished by the Guru. God's devotees remain steadfast. They are indifferent to joy and sorrow. The Guru himself is their protector. Death does not touch the Sikh of the Guru. The sevak of the Guru performs perfect service. The Sikh of the Guru meditates on God. The devotees of God are saved and their detractors are thrown into hell. The place where the sādhs sit is beautiful. Bhagtī, love, and the state of liberation are found through association with the sādhs.[59]

Guru Arjan addresses the sants at one place. He tells them that the shabad is the support of life. By worshiping the one God their countenance becomes bright and they remain in peace. The True Guru brings all transactions to a good end. All thirst is queched. After great search the treasure of the Name in found, it is priceless. God is their friend, their wealth and youth, and their father and mother. By turning to the Guru, they escape the deadly whirlpool. The sants take refuge with God to be liberated. The haughty suffer destruction. The gift of the Name is found in the sādhū-sangat. There is no high or low: God's light is in all.[60]

The Sikhs have come together like swans on a pool in accordance with God's hukam. They feed on pearls and gems in the pool, and God's will is that they should never part from it. God is under the control of bhagats and he is their strength. The Gursikhs are instructed to meditate on God and to taste the nectar of bāṇī with its nectar of the Name. In contrast with *monīs, tapsīs, brahmachārīs,* sanyānsīs, and others, the sants of God are free from joy and sorrow, greed, and attachment. The dust of their feet is chrished. By meeting the True Guru all their anxiety is gone.[61]

The manmukh, in contrast with the Gurmukh, remains chained to the wheel of death and rebirth and goes through all hells. The Gurmukh is dear to God, and none can injure the one guarded by God. He enjoys eternal bliss as a special robe (*sirpao*). The sevak of the Guru never goes to hell; he meditates on God; he meets the sādh-sang and receives life every day from the Guru. He listens to kīrtan at the Guru's door (*gurdwara*). Guru Arjan takes notice of the detractors of the sant and the bhagat, both of which appear to refer to the Guru and his followers. The bhagats of God are devoid of enmity (nirvair): they who touch their feet are redeemed. The circle (*mandal*) of sants has a stable place. Sins are washed away in the circle of sants. There is pure kathā in the circle of sants; there is no suffering due to haumai in the sant-sang. There is God in the sant mandal. In association with the sādhs one is redeemed and sees none as enemy; the perfect God is in everyone. The people of God sing his praises all the time; they have found a perfect place. All wanderings end in refuge with the sants. The bhagats have no fear of any kind. 'Ever since I have met the sādh-sangat I feel no envy of others: there is no enemy and no stranger, we are on friendly terms with all'.[62]

Guru Arjan takes notice of the bhagats of the myth and legend and of the times closer to him. In the former category are Ajamal, Balmik, Dhruv, Ganika, Gajinder, Sudama, Badhik, Kubja, Bidar, and Dropadi. There are a few female bhagats among them. They were all saved or redeemed. The bhagats closer to the time of Guru Arjan are Dhanna, Trilochan, Beni,

Jaidev, and Sen. Their merit or demerit was not taken into account when they were saved due to their loving devotion to God. Kabir meditated on one God; Namdev lived in association with God. Ravidas meditated on the Beautiful Lord. Guru Nanak Dev was the veritable form of Gobind. Evidently, the former bhagats are equated with the Sikhs as sādhs, sants, and bhagats. Guru Nanak is placed far above them.[63]

The Sikhs have a distinct identity. In the broadest context of his times Guru Arjan makes the position clear in explicit terms: 'The Gusain (of Hindus) and the Allah (of Muslims) is my one God. I have parted from both the Hindu and the Turk. I do not go to the *ka'bah* for *hajj* and I do not go to a *tīrath* for worship. I worship the one and no other. I do not worship (any idol in a temple) and I do not perform *namāz*. I bow to the formless one in my heart. We are neither Hindu nor Musalman; our body and its breath are dedicated to Allah-Ram.' This distinct way of the Sikhs is a gift of their Guru.[64]

The Sarovar, the Harmandar, and Ramdaspur

The institutions which served as the instruments of spreading nām-dharam in the world are given great importance by Guru Arjan in his compositions. He makes the explicit statement that all sins are washed away by bathing in Ramdas Sarovar. He exhorts the Sikhs to sing the praises of God everyday in congregation (sādh-sang): 'all one's wishes are fulfilled by lodging the perfect Guru in the heart.' This pool is the work of the creator. There was no shortage of money and materials. This was the will of the Merciful One who completed the perfect design. God himself stood amidst the sants to complete their work and to ensure that everything went right. Beautiful is the earth and beautiful is the pool with its nectar-like water. All objectives have been fulfilled and all sorrows have vanished. True to his nature God bestows all gifts on his devotees. All the merit of bathing at sixty-eight places, all charities, rituals, and good deeds are here. All sins are washed away by bathing in Ramdas Sarovar. This source of purification is a gift of the Perfect Guru. Through the Guru's shabad everything is in the right place. The dirt is removed in the sādh-sang, with God as the kind friend.[65]

Guru Arjan refers to 'the house having been raised'. This may be a reference to the Harmandar. There is a direct reference to God's temple (*harmandar*) erected for meditation on him. The sants and bhagats sing

Fig. 5.1 Sri Harmandar Sahib, originally built by Guru Arjan (1582–1606) at Ramdaspur, Amritsar

his praises here; by meditating on the Master they get rid of all their sins. By singing God's praises through the divine bāṇī they attain liberation. It was a happy conjunction and an auspicious moment when the eternal foundation of God's temple was laid. This could happen only through God's grace.[66] In another shabad, God's abode (*ghar*) is mentioned along with the pool and the garden as the sign of God's pleasure. By meditating on God and singing his praises, all wishes have been fulfilled. By attachment to the Guru's feet the mind is filled with joy. Through the Master's grace, our life is blessed in this world and the next.[67]

The sanctity attached to Ramdas Sarovar and the Harmandar is extended to the town of Ramdaspur. 'I have seen all places,' says Guru Arjan, 'but there is none like you.' Thickly populated, the sprawling Ramdaspur is extremely beautiful since God himself founded it. Through his grace, God has established his own rule in Ramdaspur. In the compositions of Guru Nanak and his successors Ram is a familiar epithet for God. Ram-rāj refers, therefore, to divine rule and not the rule of the Rama of Ayodhya. Nothing untoward happens if we meditate on God; the enemy runs away when the Name is praised.[68] Ramdaspur was an autonomous town with which the Mughal administration had nothing to do. There were other such towns in the country, especially the towns founded by Guru Arjan.

Guru Arjan talks of Abchal Nagar where peace comes through nām, which has been established by the creator and where all one's wishes are fulfilled, where the praises of God are sung and everything falls in place, where God himself is the protector, the father and the mother, where houses and shops look beautiful check by jowl, where the gifts of God increase everyday, where all living beings are at peace under God's own care, where the sants of God exchange their views, where the noose of transmigration is cut off, and where one discovers God through his grace. This eternal city of God reminds one of Ramdaspur, the ideal city in the world.[69]

More significantly, Guru Arjan depicts the ideal city (*abchal nagarī*) in terms of the dispensation of Guru Nanak. There is no room for the five adversaries (kām, *krodh, lobh,* moh, and hankār); all sins are removed through the Guru's instruction; the city wall is made of sachch and dharam; the seed of nām is sown here; the merchant (*sāhu*) and his agents are equally prosperous; the Guru's service day and night is the goods for sale; the shops hold *shāntī*, sahaj, and sukh as merchandise; there is no fine and no taxes; they who trade in nām take large profits

Fig. 5.2 Darbar Sahib Tarn Taran originally built by Guru Arjan (1582–1606)

home; the True Guru is the sāhu and the Sikhs are his *banjārās*. This is the city eternal of Guru Nanak Dev.[70]

Guru Arjan refers to the *Granth* (*pothī*) as the abode of God. Here the equation of bāṇī with the shabad, of the shabad with the Guru, and of the Guru with God is assumed. The pothī contains the Name as the means of redeeming mankind. With truth, contentment, and contemplation, the ambrosial Name sustains all existence and saves all who appropriate it. This is the indispensable means to be cherished by all. When darkness is lifted, the manifestation of God is seen in all that is visible. Characteristically, Guru Arjan attributes the compilation of the Granth to the grace of God. He is grateful for its completion, which could happen only through God's grace. True life is found only in the Name. Like Ramdaspur, the Harmandar and the Ramdas Sarovar, the Granth is the expression of God's grace and the means of spreading the dispensation of Guru Nanak.[71]

A New Dispensation

Teja Singh and Ganda Singh refer to Guru Arjan taking up residence in Ramdaspur to complete the work started by Guru Ram Das on the tank and the city of Ramdaspur. Within a decade then he laid the foundation of the central structure now called the Golden Temple. More than a decade later he completed the greatest work of his life, the compilation of the Holy Granth. After describing the work of organization he had effected among the Sikhs, Guru Arjan observed: 'Now the order of the Merciful has gone forth that no one shall molest another'. The Sikhs had been sufficiently prepared to understand what that order meant for them: to resist all tyranny and oppression. The verse from which Teja Singh and Ganda Singh quote has in it the phrase '*halemī rāj*' (mild rule).[72]

In the *Shabdarth Srī Gurū Granth Sāhib Jī*, Teja Singh refers to the essential significance of the whole shabad which refers to 'halemī rāj'. Dedicated service of the Lord becomes a source of strength. A religious centre was established by the Guru with the support of dedicated Sikhs. The forces of good were organized to resist tyranny and oppression. It seemed as if the Merciful God had issued a command that no one shall be able to oppress another and all would live in peace and harmony. In this way, the Sikhs were inspired to aspire for freedom and look upon themselves as the wrestlers of the Lord.[73] The interpretation does not explain the use of the phrase '*halemi raj*'.

Guru Arjan refers to the ordinance of the Merciful One that none shall oppress another, that all shall live in peace now that the mild rule (halemī rāj) has been established. It has divine sanction. Guru Arjan is a champion wrestler of God. He uses the plough of Truth to sow the seeds of the Name and hopes to raise a heap of God's grace. God has assigned this task to him and he performs it in accordace with his will. Putting on a robe of honour in his court, God has made him the headman. The village is well settled. Guru Arjan's sole occupation is to serve the Master. Evidently, halemī rāj refers to the entire dispensation headed by Guru Arjan. Significantly, he goes on to refer to the dharamsāl of truth that he has established. He seeks Gursikhs to wash their feet and wave the fan over them, and to bow at their feet. They who hear of the Guru come to him and receive the boon of nām, dān, and isnān. A whole world has attained liberation by boarding the true boat.[74]

It is extremely significant that Guru Arjan refers directly to Guru Nanak a score of times. It is absolutely clear that Guru Nanak for him is the founder of a new dispensation. There is limitless joy and no sorrow in 'the house' of Nanak. God has given him an inexhaustible treasure that is meant for all. The eternal foundation laid by Nanak is becoming stronger day by day. His greatness has been made manifest in the entire world. The storehouse of bhagtī which God has entrusted to him is the source of liberation. Greater than all, he is the saviour of all, like God himself. The lamp of the Name has lighted the world and all darkness is gone. Guru Nanak represents the veritable spirit of God.[75]

There is a reference to this dispensation in *Rāg Bhairo*: all brothers, their friends, and their families have attained liberation by being united with the Eternal Father. Others receive this boon from them. Their mansions are the tallest and their realms are endless. This rule is everlasting. Its fame has spread over the world and it is praised in every home.[76]

The dispensation of Guru Nanak has an exclusive validity for the Kaliyuga. The inaccessible Lord has graciously conferred on the Guru the 'devotion of the Name' in order to redeem the Kaliyuga. The lowest of the low have become devoted to it. The other yugas were reckoned noble earlier but now the Kaliyuga is supreme among all the yugas. Every human being is judged on his own merit and the prayers of the devotees are granted. The bliss of God's sight has become possible for all.[77] This idea is reinforced in *Mārū Sohle* where kīrtan is proclaimed to be the supreme means of liberation in the Kaliyuga. Only they attain liberation who receive the boon of the Name through the Master's guidance. They alone are saved who seek the Master's shelter. A seed sown in the wrong season does not sprout. The singing of God's praises in congregational worship (kīrtan) is the supreme act in the Kaliyuga. Through the Master's guidance, the people utter the Name Divine.[78] In *Rāg Basant,* it is emphasized that the Name is the proper seed to be sown in the Kaliyuga. In the spring of spiritual joy, they who are directed by God blossom forth. 'Sow the seed of the Name now that Kaliyuga has come. This is not the season for any other crop'. The Kaliyuga is the Age of the Name.[79]

Opposition to the halemī rāj was an important dimension of the historical situation. Guru Arjan was very much aware of his enemies. In a context of confrontation he refers to an enemy having been burnt in fire. God does perfect justice and protects his servant. A slanderer died of fever. The one who signed a false affidavit (*mahzar*) against the Guru turned out to be false and the sinner suffered for his misdeed. Through the Guru's grace the slanderer was removed by an unseen arrow of fate. In a moment he became all ash and met the end he deserved. God saved the Guru from Sulhi; his hands could not reach the Guru and he himself died. The Master killed him and he became dust in a moment. He died thinking ill of the Guru; the Creator pushed him into the pit of death. The Merciful God listened to the Guru's prayer, saved his servant and filled the mouth of the slanderer with ash.[80] The poison had no effect and the evil Brahman himself died of ache. God protects his devotees. He protected his servant like father and mother. The face of the slanderer was blackened in this world and the next. God listened to the prayer of his devotee and he who thought ill of him was ashamed and disappointed. God takes his servant in protective embrace and throws the slanderer into fire. God protects his devotees from evil-doers. The evil-doer finds no place and comes to his deserved bad end. He meets his desert. The servant of God remains in his refuge. There are general references to divine protection for the devotees of God, for the Sikhs and the Guru. 'All around us is the *chaukī* of the *shabad* of the Guru for our protection'.[81] 'All around us is the protective line of Ram'.[82]

These situations relate to internal opponents and external enemies, and the possibility of a collusion between them. Guru Arjan's safety in all these situations was a sign of God's grace. The specific instances illustrated

Fig. 5.3 Dehra Sahib at Lahore, commemorating the martyrdom of Guru Arjan in 1606

the general idea that God protected his bhagats in all situations. This conviction arose from the increasing realization of God's will through Guru Nanak and his successors, the institutions they established, and the popularity they gained. It was a part of the halemī rāj. The martyrdom of Guru Arjan, instead of shaking this conviction, became rather a part of the faith in halemī rāj.

Notes

1. *Ādi Srī Gurū Granth Sāhibjī*, pp. 262–96.
2. Ibid., pp. 210, 563.
3. Ibid., pp. 184, 897.
4. Ibid., pp. 184, 897, 1071, 1150, 1236, 1385.
5. Ibid., pp. 541–2, 546, 1150.
6. Ibid., pp.184, 1156.
7. Ibid., pp. 70, 523, 713 , 748, 748, 802.
8. Ibid., p. 803.
9. Ibid., pp. 184, 192–3, 376, 391, 530, 1003.
10. Ibid., pp. 45–7, 535, 578, 614, 884–5.
11. Ibid., pp. 827, 846, 964.
12. Ibid., pp. 195, 203, 212, 1076–7, 1121.
13. Ibid., pp. 380, 387, 394, 396, 431–2, 564, 614, 760, 824.
14. Ibid., pp. 101, 103–4, 106–7, 138, 251, 380, 499, 900, 962–3, 1049, 1270, 1281, 1339.

15. Ibid., p. 190.
16. Ibid., pp. 193.
17. Ibid., p. 207.
18. Ibid., pp. 42, 44, 47, 71, 79–80, 104, 609, 615, 678, 710, 737, 777, 801, 815, 828, 896–7, 961, 1020, 1117, 1210, 1270.
19. Ibid., pp. 179–80, 183, 189, 190, 193.
20. Ibid., p. 761.
21. Ibid., pp. 99, 106, 109, 179, 185, 191, 195, 199, 382, 1136.
22. Ibid., pp. 405, 518, 608, 616.
23. Ibid., pp. 639, 670, 674, 676, 713, 715, 804, 807, 810–11, 813, 816.
24. Ibid., pp. 823, 888, 890, 895, 957–8, 986, 999, 1001–2.
25. Ibid., pp. 1006–7, 1083, 1101, 1138, 1142–4, 1146, 1148, 1151.
26. Ibid., pp. 1152, 1155–6, 1180–1, 1184, 1205–6.
27. Ibid., p. 1218.
28. Ibid., pp. 1219, 1221, 1227–8.
29. Ibid., pp. 1268, 1271, 1298, 1362–3, 1386, 1408, 1425.
30. Ibid., pp. 44, 48–50, 52–3, 71, 99, 101.
31. Ibid., pp. 188–9, 194, 197, 201–2, 209–10, 218–19, 385, 387.
32. Ibid., p. 736.
33. Ibid., p. 616.
34. Ibid., pp. 235, 250, 375, 400, 495, 502, 517.
35. Ibid., pp. 608–9, 614–15.
36. Ibid., pp. 616, 618–19, 671, 803.
37. Ibid., pp. 43, 46, 51, 101, 808, 813, 901, 957, 1019, 1078, 1142.
38. Ibid., pp. 130, 137, 177, 178.
39. Ibid., p. 187.
40. Ibid., pp. 208, 235, 239, 259, 387, 508, 543.
41. Ibid., p. 576.
42. Ibid., p. 743.
43. Ibid., pp. 611, 628–9, 744, 805, 816, 828, 888, 891, 895, 924, 960–1.
44. Ibid., pp. 98, 1047, 1075, 1079, 1137, 1186, 1212, 1323, 1340.
45. Ibid., pp. 100–1, 106, 108, 137, 180, 193, 198, 207–8.
46. Ibid., pp. 204, 207, 237, 298, 385, 392–4, 455, 496, 518, 532–4, 563, 616, 618.
47. Ibid., pp. 622, 675, 683, 700, 743, 750, 885.
48. Ibid., pp. 13, 48, 100, 107, 131, 205, 208, 211, 1079, 1101, 1212, 1322.
49. Ibid., pp. 382, 532, 577.
50. Ibid., pp. 519, 635, 676, 682, 710, 714, 737, 742, 749, 979, 1009, 1121.
51. Ibid., pp. 1152, 1210–11, 1219, 1268, 1304, 1338, 1347.
52. Ibid., pp. 13, 43, 70, 79, 176, 185, 188.
53. Ibid., pp. 196, 213, 238, 318, 383, 385, 395, 410.
54. Ibid., pp. 13, 43, 70, 176, 185, 188, 196, 213, 238, 318, 383–4, 395, 410, 498, 508, 519, 522, 542, 736, 741, 777, 780, 820, 828, 848, 1000, 1004, 1156.
55. Ibid., pp. 1102, 1184, 1209, 1236, 1408.
56. Ibid., pp. 627, 749, 1338, 1387.

57. Ibid., pp. 801, 818, 864, 869.
58. Ibid., pp. 577, 801, 818, 864, 869, 916, 960, 962–3.
59. Ibid., pp. 1003, 1073–4, 1145–7, 1151, 1181.
60. Ibid., p. 1299.
61. Ibid., pp. 13, 534, 1192, 1302.
62. Ibid., pp. 43–4, 49, 178–9, 183, 192, 383–4, 499.
63. Ibid., p. 500.
64. Ibid., p. 401.
65. Ibid., pp. 624–5, 783–4.
66. Ibid., pp. 525–6, 781.
67. Ibid., p. 782.
68. Ibid., pp. 626, 817.
69. Ibid,. p. 783.
70. Ibid., p. 430.
71. Ibid., p. 1299. *Shabdarth Srī Gurū Granth Sāhibjī.*
72. Teja Singh and Ganda Singh, *A Short History of the Sikhs*, Patiala: Punjabi University, 1989 (rpt), pp. 25, 27–8, 36.
73. *Shabdarth Srī Gurū Granth Sāhibjī*, p. 73.
74. Ibid., p. 783.
75. Ibid., p. 1429.
76. Ibid., pp. 186, 230–1, 496, 500–1, 611–12, 621, 747, 750, 802, 862–5, 1152, 1192, 1226, 1341, 1387.
77. Ibid., p. 1140.
78. Ibid., p. 406.
79. Ibid., pp. 1075–6.
80. Ibid., pp. 181, 316–17, 381, 507, 647, 687, 825, 887, 1099, 1137–8, 1145, 1151–2.
81. Ibid., p. 626.
82. Ibid., p. 81.

PART TWO
In the Context of Confrontation (1606–75)

6

A Pure and Distinct Panth

Bhai Gurdas

Bhai Gurdas and His *Vārs*

Born around 1550, Bhai Gurdas lost his parents at an early age and he was brought up and educated at Goindval by his uncle, Guru Amar Das. In the time of Guru Ram Das he stayed in Agra, Benares, and Burhanpur to work as a missionary (*parchārak*) of the Sikh faith. In the time of Guru Arjan he was associated with the administration of Ramdaspur and the preparation of the Granth. After the martyrdom of Guru Arjan, Bhai Gurdas became a staunch supporter of Guru Hargobind. He was associated with the construction of Akal Takht, and led a body of Sikhs to Gwalior when Guru Hargobind was detained there early in the reign of Jahangir. Bhai Gurdas died in 1637. For more than half a century, thus, he remained actively associated with three Gurus, including the phase of overt politicization of the Sikh Panth in the time of Guru Hargobind.[1]

Among the works of Bhai Gurdas there are six *shaloks* in Sanskrit to be found in Bhai Santokh Singh's *Suraj Prakash*, and there are 675 *kabitts* and *savayyās* in Braj Bhasha. There are forty Vārs in Punjabi which proved to be more popular than the other two. It is generally agreed that the kabitts and savayyās were written when Bhai Gurdas stayed outside the Punjab as a parchārak of the Sikh faith. The shaloks are believed to have been written in Kashi. The Vārs of Bhai Gurdas were written mostly after the compilation of the Granth in 1604. Regarded as the key to the Granth Sāhib, the Vārs of Bhai Gurdas relate equally well to the Sikh Panth.[2]

Harjot Oberoi has observed the relevance of the Vārs to Sikh identity. He says that there can 'hardly be a better source for understanding early

Sikh identity'.[3] Bhai Gurdas enunciates in his Vārs some of the most enduring themes in Sikh consciousness: faith in the Gurus and their utterances, regular visit to *dharamsāl*, and importance of the *sangat* as a body of the faithful. Bhai Gurdas is not 'unaware of boundaries'. In his view Muslims miss the correct path and Hindus remain entangled in empty rituals and social inequalities. The Sikh way of life is 'a distinctive third path to human problems'. The Gurmukh, a follower of the Sikh Gurus and their doctrines, is the ideal man. To metaphysical differences are added a new idiom, a separate community of believers and a reworking of the social order. But all this does not go very far because, for Oberoi, there are 'no explicit statements of an independent Sikh identity' in the Vārs of Bhai Gurdas.[4]

For W.H. McLeod, the evidence of Bhai Gurdas suggests distinctive ideals for a conscious Nanak-Panthi identity based on common loyalty, association, and practice. The custom of gathering (*sat-sang*) for regular *kīrtan* sessions, at which the compositions of the Gurus were sung, was an essential feature of the Nanak-Panth identity. Caste had 'no place' amongst those who were loyal to the Gurus. Furthermore, the evidence of Bhai Gurdas foreshadows the doctrine of Guru Granth and Guru-Panth to make the line of doctrinal development logical and clear, easily accommodating the final version within the established tradition of the Nanak-Panth.[5]

The Vārs of Bhai Gurdas provide 'an extensive commentary' on the teachings of the Gurus. He mocks external observances 'gently yet effectively', and describes the way of life to be followed by the devout Sikh. McLeod looks upon the Vārs of Bhai Gurdas primarily as the vehicle of the teachings of the Gurus. After detailing the content of the first Vār he makes the explicit statement that the remaining thirty-eight Vārs 'faithfully' reflect the doctrines taught by the Gurus and enshrined in the sacred scripture. There is repeated stress on a cluster of fundamental doctrines; the grace of the Guru, his crucial role, and the sat-sang. The sublime powers of the Guru are contrasted with the futility of 'conventional religious practices'. Bhai Gurdas is vehement about 'the harm' inflicted by the sectarian allegiances of Hindus and Muslims; they should recognize 'the perversity of their mutual antagonisms' and join 'the ironic way of the Guru'. Bhai Gurdas also repeats the Guru's teaching with regard to caste. All these statements are illustrated with quotations from the Vārs.[6] The evidence of Bhai Gurdas can be very useful to 'the historian of the Panth'. As an illustration McLeod quotes the stanza in which the differing policies and lifestyle of Guru Hargobind are contrasted with those of his predecessors.[7]

McLeod is one of the very few historians who have talked about the whole range of the Vārs of Bhai Gurdas. But even he has not studied the Vārs thoroughly from the viewpoint of Sikh identity. With a high degree of convergence on some basic ideas, Bhai Gurdas provides a great deal of information on points consciously or unconsciously raised by Oberoi and McLeod. The questions relevant for Sikh identity may be explicitly stated: what has Bhai Gurdas to say about Guru Nanak and his five successors? what does he say about the institution of Guruship? what does he say about the institution of *sādh-sangat* in the dharamsāl? what is his conception of Sikhism? who is the ideal Sikh for Bhai Gurdas? where do the Sikhs stand in relation to 'others' around them? Answers to these questions can give us a clear idea of Bhai Gurdas' consciousness and conception of Sikh identity.

Guru Nanak and His Successors

For Bhai Gurdas, Guru Nanak is the World-Preceptor (*jagat-gurū*); he is the Manifest Guide (*jāhar pīr*).[8] He was commissioned by God to redeem the world; darkness was dispelled on his appearance, and the world became bright.[9] Regard him as the perfect Guru and everything he instituted as perfect: *satnām-mantar*, shabad, Gurmukh panth, sādh-sangat, and *takht.*[10] In the opening stanza of the first Vār, loving devotion (*bhāv-bhagtī*), celebration of the Guru (*gurpurb*), nām-dān-isnān, and liberation (*mukt padārath*) are mentioned in addition to satnām-mantar and sat-shabad. The path he laid down as the true king was the highway for wheeled traffic (*gādī-rāh*); it obliterated *durmat* and dual affiliation; it taught the Sikhs to live like the lotus in water, to remain detached in māyā, and to cherish humility.[11]

Guru Nanak lived as a householder (*ghar-bārī*) and he made householders his followers who remained detached (*udās*) in their attachment to worldly affairs (māyā).[12] The perfect Guru taught how to live in accordance with divine order (*hukam*); the gur-shabad of *Vaheguru* that he proclaimed was beyond the Veda and the semitic books; it was meant for members of all the four castes (*chār varan*) who, as Sikhs, constituted the sādh-sangat.[13] He established a dharamsāl at Kartarpur for the sādh-sangat as the True Abode.[14] The true Guru was the true king, the king of kings; whatever he instituted was true: takht, *farmān, nīsān,* hukam, shabad, *taksāl, bhagtī,* kīrtan, gurmukh-panth, proclamation (*dohī*), and his rule (*rāj*).[15]

Guru Nanak made the water run upstream by raising Angad as the Guru over himself. During his lifetime he placed the canopy of Guruship over Lehna's head; mingling light with light, the true Guru changed his form. Guru Angad had the same *tikkā,* the same *chhatar,* the same takht, and the same *muhar.*[16] Guru Angad was the master of the spiritual and temporal realms (*dīn-dunī*). His throne was everlasting. The coin struck in the true mint, the true shabad, was entrusted to him. He held sway over Siddhs, Naths, and Avtars.[17] Guru Nanak, the *pīr* of pīrs and the gurū of gurūs, transformed a disciple into the Guru and the gurū became a disciple (*chelā*). The Sikhs of the gurū were amazed to see a Sikh of the Guru becoming the Guru.[18] The Guru and the disciple became one.[19] In the eyes of Bhai Gurdas, the gur-chelā and chelā-gurū syndrome had a distinctive bearing on the Sikh conception of Guruship. A great stress is laid on the interchangeable position of the gurū and the disciple. There is no difference between the Guru and his successor. They represent the same light.[20] The perfect person shows the miracle of gur-chelā, chelā gur.[21] A diamond is cut by the diamond. The same light is in two bodies.[22] The Gurmukh Sikh becomes the Guru and the Guru becomes a chelā.[23] Only among the Sikhs a disciple becomes the Guru of a Guru.[24]

Guru Amar Das received the gift of the light from Guru Angad; the Guru became the disciple and the disciple became the Guru. As the second successor, Guru Amar Das became the 'grandson' of Guru Nanak. He became the true Guru in place of Guru Angad: with the same tikkā, the same seat, and the same authority. He accepted disciples from all the four castes; their *kula-dharam* was replaced by the ideal of detachment (udās) amidst worldly concerns (māyā).[25]

Guru Ram Das received Guruship from Guru Amar Das and followed the practice of rāj-jog, with the same light and the same throne. The great grandson of Guru Nanak was the pillar of both spiritual and temporal realms (dīn-dunī); he was the untouched lotus of the house of Baba Nanak. As a householder he enjoyed the pleasures of life as the master jogī, who is hopeless in hope (*āsā vich nirās*). He was the only master for all; Guru Amar Das was absorbed in him.[26]

After Guru Ram Das, Guruship came to Guru Arjan, a son of Guru Ram Das. None else could bear the unbearable. Therefore, Guruship remained in the house of Guru Ram Das. Guru Arjan belonged to the line of Guru Nanak as much as to the line of Guru Ram Das. He filled the treasure of Gur-shabad and remained absorbed in kīrtan and *kathā*. The sādh-sangat used to meet as Gur-sabhā. With his true standards, true court, true might, and true honour, the everlasting rule established by Guru Nanak became eminently visible under Guru Arjan. Innumerable Sikhs used to come from all the four directions to partake of the *langar* of Gur-shabad which was unknown to the *Veda* and the semitic books. His Sikhs remained detached amidst māyā. Even under tortures he remained calm.[27]

Guru Hargobind, who followed Guru Arjan, was Guru Arjan himself in a different body. He was a great and brave warrior who shattered the ranks of the enemy and made the welfare of others his own concern. But he was no different from his predecessors. He walked firmly on the Gurmukh-*mārg* which was sharp like the edge of a double-edged sword. His Sikhs followed him.[28] There is no difference between Gobind the Guru and Guru Hargobind: both refer to the same light. The principle of chelā-gurū applied to him as well; he was made the Guru by Guru Arjan; there was no difference between the father and the son or the son and the father. His critics maintained that Guru Hargobind did not stay at one

Fig. 6.1 Akal Bunga, built on the site of the Akal Takht originally constructed by Guru Hargobind (1606–44)

dharamsāl; he was imprisoned in Gwalior by the emperor; he was afraid of none; kept dogs and went out for hunt; he did not compose, sing, or listen to *Gurbāṇī*; and he gave preference to others over his old *sevaks*. The critics of Guru Hargobind were almost certainly the rival claimants to Guruship. Bhai Gurdas defends his position as the true Guru; the true Sikhs remained attached to his feet.[29]

Bhai Gurdas goes on to add that a crop needs a hedge, and an orchard needs the hedge of hardy trees. The Sikhs should not be deceived by the appearance of a new role (sāng).[30] Guru Hargobind alone represents the 'sixth generation' of the Gurus.[31]

The Guru, the Gurbāṇī, and the Sangat

The doctrine of the unity of Guruship, which accommodates apparent change in the policies of the Guru, is hammered by Bhai Gurdas. All the five successors are mentioned in the first Vār as an integral part of the account of Guru Nanak: a continuation and extension of his mission. The Guru and the Sikh become one when the Guru so desires. In this connection Bhai Gurdas mentions all the six Gurus together.[32] All the six Gurus are invoked as one.[33] Guru Nanak was made Guru by God himself. Guru Nanak exalted a Gursikh as the Guru, and all the other successors were Gursikhs to be exalted as Gurus. All the Gurusikhs who became Gurus represented the same light, like a candle lighted by a candle, like water mingling with water.[34] The unity of the six Gurus is depicted in several stanzas.[35] Guru Nanak was like God, and so was the sixth Guru, the only true Guru in his turn.[36] Those who did not acknowledge the Guruship of any of the five true successors of Guru Nanak were 'rebels'.[37]

The true merchandise is available only at the shop of the true Guru who is the perfect merchant (*sāhu*).[38] No shabad other than that of the Guru is true.[39] The shabad of the Guru is in fact the Guru.[40] Regard the shabad of the Guru as the Guru.[41] Regard God as the Guru and the Guru as God.[42] The true Guru is a *tīrath* superior to all the sixty-eight tīraths of the Indian tradition. Do not go to any other tīrath.[43] There is no liberation without the perfect Guru.[44] All one's love should be for the Guru; dual affiliation (*dūjā bhāo*) is futile.[45] Without the Guru there can be no liberation.[46] Without submitting to the only true Guru one remains entangled.[47] Without the true Guru there is degradation in the end.[48]

The Guru obliterates durmat and duality. An outward change in the ways of the Guru is a testing time for the Sikh.[49] Dear to the Guru are those who walk in humility, and work for the welfare of others.[50] There is no true master other than the true Guru; none is so kind as the Guru, not even one's mother or father.[51] Bhai Gurdas makes it absolutely clear that exclusive affiliation to the Guru, who stands equated with God and Gurbāṇī, is the only way to liberation.

Gurbāṇī occupies the central place in the Sikh scheme of things. One of the reasons why human birth, out of the 84,00,000 births of the Indian tradition, is the best is that one can understand Gurbāṇī and make others understand.[52] God is praised through the shabad as the perfect Guru, the foremost concern of the Sikhs.[53] The shabad of the Guru is both God and Guru.[54] The shabad of the Guru is not found in the Veda or the semitic books. God himself is present in the Guru's shabad, and not in the Veda or the semitic books.[55] The Sikh lives by the shabad, and drinks Gurbāṇī as the nectar.[56] Significantly, Guru Amar Das is praised for opening the treasure of the shabad, and Guru Arjan is praised for filling the treasure of Gurbāṇī.[57] The shabad is the veritable form of the Guru.[58]

According to Bhai Gurdas the shabad and Gurbāṇī confer a peculiar distinction upon sat-sang and sādh-sangat. The feet that walk to sat-sang are sanctified.[59] The place where sādh-sangat is held is bright like the divine light; lakhs upon lakhs of Vedas and Purānas are nothing in comparison with the kīrtan.[60] All the four castes meet in sat-sang and become Gurmukh.[61] Without the Guru's shabad and sādh-sangat even good persons find no liberation.[62] Truth is praised in the sādh-sangat alone.[63] The sādh-sangat is the abode of truth in which the True Guru abides; God is present in the sādh-sangat.[64] For the true Guru, the sādh-sangat is the only true association; it cannot be adequately praised.[65] There is no true sangat other than the sādh-sangat.[66] The Guru, the Gurbāṇī, and the Sangat are equated with one another, and with God.[67]

The place where the sādh-sangat meets is dharamsāl. It is the Mansarovar lake where the Sikh-swans enjoy kīrtan of the Guru's shabad.[68] It is the place where the Sikhs find *jog* within the home by performing service of Sikhs and listening to Gurbāṇī.[69] The dharamsāl is the place where the Sikhs earn merit; all the four *varnas* become one varna and acquire the *gotra* of Gurmukh; the grandfather and the grandson meet in the sādh-sangat as equals.[70] The Gur-bhāīs look beautiful in the sādh-sangat.[71] Very frequently, the sādh-sangat and dharamsāl are used by

Bhai Gurdas as synonyms. In his view, the offerings that came to the dharamsāl were meant strictly for the Guru and his Sikhs and not for an individual. Personal greed for offerings was a source of sorrow and faithlessness.[72] There is no room for doubt that the dharamsāl was by far the most important Sikh institution. The dharamsāl in which the Guru was present was literally the door of the Guru (*Gurdwār*). In other dharamsāls, the Guru was deemed to be represented by Gurbāṇī and the sangat.

Bhai Gurdas talks of the faith of the Sikhs of the Guru (Gursikhkhī), the path of those who have turned to the Guru (Gurmukh-*panth*) and follow the path (Gurmukh-*mārg*). The Gurmukh-panth is distinct (*nirol*): it cannot be confused with any other. Giānī Hazara Singh equates the pure (*nirmal*) panth of Guru Nanak with the Sikh Panth at one place.[73] More often, however, panth is treated as the path. Gursikhkhī is the instruction of the Guru. It is thinner than a hair, and sharper than the edge of the double-edged sword.[74] The Gurmukh listens only to the instruction of the Guru and worships only One God; *dubidhā* is eradicated by the path he follows.[75] Significantly, the Gurmukh who regards the Guru's shabad and sādh-sangat as the means of liberation discards all rites and ceremonies of kula-dharam: the traditional rites of passage and the traditional observances known as *āchār* and *vichār*. The Gurmukh-panth is based on Gurmat and it is clearly outside the systems of the Veda and the semitic books.[76]

The highway of the Gurmukh is superior to all the twelve panths of the Jogīs put together.[77] No other path can be compared with the Gurmukh-mārg.[78] Bhai Gurdas is explicit on the uniqueness of Sikh faith: there is nothing like it in the Indian religious traditions.[79] The Gurmukh-panth transcends the twelve panths of the Jogīs; the shabad which the Gurmukh sings is not there in the Veda or the semitic books. The salutation of the Gurmukh 'I fall at your feet', makes the prince and the pauper equal, and makes no distinction between the young and the old; this salutation is different from that of the Muslims, the Jogīs, the Sanyāsīs, and the Brahman.[80] Gursikhkhī is attained through the grace of the Guru (*gurduārā*) in the sādh-sangat.[81] The life of Gursikhkhī is marked by the eradication of haumai so that one becomes dead-in-life; to do the bidding of the Guru is the deed of Gursikhkhī; instruction other than that of the Guru is like the light of a firefly before the sun.[82] The Guru-Sikh relationship makes Gursikhkhī pre-eminent in the midst of

Hindu and Muslim systems.[83] Sikhism for Bhai Gurdas is emphatically a distinct system.

The Gursikhs

Highlighting the qualities of a Gursikh, Bhai Gurdas says the Gursikh is one who has received instruction from the Guru.[84] Another term used for the Sikh of the Guru is Gurmukh who follows the Guru's path in association with other Sikhs (sādh-sangat); he knows no distinction of caste; his sight is better than the knowledge of all the six philosophies; his affiliation to Gursikhkhī is exclusive; he lives according to the shabad and cultivates humility; he is dear to the Guru on account of his loving devotion; he adores One God as the source of liberation in life; he appropriates Gur-*updes* and becomes dust-of-the-feet (*pā-khāk*) of others; he discards durmat, dubidhā, and falsehood; he appropriates gurmat, shabad, and the truth; he serves the Sikhs of the Guru and regards them as mother, father, brother, and friend.[85] The devotional life of the Gurmukh covers recitation of and meditation on Gurbāṇī, visit to the dharamsāl, and service of the Guru and his Sikhs.[86] He performs manual services for the sādh-sangat; he writes Gurbāṇī to compile *pothīs*; learns to play musical instruments for kīrtan; he follows an honest profession and feels happy to give something to others; in all humility he regards other Sikhs as far above himself; he walks a long distance to help them; he lives in accordance with the divine order (hukam) and remains detached in the midst of māyā.[87] The social background of the Gurmukhs is diverse but there are no social distinctions in the sādh-sangat.[88] The Gurmukh regards himself as the lowest of the low; he becomes dust-of-the-feet and serves the sādh-sangat; he talks sweetly and walks in humility; he is happy to give something to others; he remains absorbed in the shabad; and he remains hopeless-in-hope. These traits distinguish the Gurmukh from all other categories of people in the world.[89] Bhai Gurdas describes the situation in which people come to the Guru through the mediacy of Sikhs, become Sikhs, and turn into Gurmukhs. Their traits are described in detail.[90] The Gurmukhs regard the Guru and God as one, and know no other affiliation.[91] They are distinct from the rest of the world.[92] The Sikh of the Guru and Gurmukh are synonymous for Bhai Gurdas: all the traits of the Gurmukh are associated with the Gursikh too.[93] They too are distinct from the other peoples in the world.[94]

Common affiliation to the Guru bound the Sikhs with one another in the local sādh-sangat, and the local communities with the Guru at the centre. One Sikh is an individual but two constitute sādh-sang, and in five Sikhs there is God. Bhai Gurdas feels gratified that there are thousands of Sikhs in every city and lakhs in every country.[95] Pre-eminent among these countries was the Punjab where the greatness of the Guru was well recognized. But there were Sikhs in other provinces of the Mughal empire and in its cities. Bhai Gurdas mentions Kabul and Kashmir, Thanesar, Delhi, Fatehpur, Agra, Lucknow, Paryag, Jaunpur, Patna, Raj Mahal, Dhaka, Gwalior, Ujjain, and Burhanpur. Many of the eminent Sikhs of the Gurus are identified as Khatris belonging to a number of gotras: Sehgal, Ohri, Uppal, Julka, Passi, Bhalla, Sodhi, Beri, Kohli, Nanda, Sabharwal, Khullar, Vohra, Puri, Jhanji, Soni, Vij, Chaddha, Handa, Kapur, Behl, Sethi, Marwaha, Seth, and Ghaī. There were some Brahmans, Aroras, Sūds, and Jatts too among the eminent Sikhs. Then there were blacksmiths (*lohārs*), barbers (*nāīs*), tailors (*chhīmbās*), fishermen (*māchhīs*), potters (*kumhārs*), goldsmiths (*suniārs*), and outcastes (*chandāls*). A Muslim, Mian Jamal, is mentioned among the Sikhs who stayed beside Guru Arjan. Some of the Masands of Guru Arjan are also named.[96] The Gurus addressed themselves to both Hindus and Muslims, and to all the four varnas. After joining the Sikh Panth they all become one: they are casteless; they acquire the same colour, like the ingredients of the betel leaf; they are like the metal made out of eight metals.[97] The idea of equality among the Sikhs is stressed by Bhai Gurdas throughout the Vārs. Equally important for him is the idea that the only true relation in the world is that of a Sikh with another Sikh: the relationship of Gur-bhāīs is the true relationship.[98] The ties of faith are stronger than the ties of kinship in the eyes of Bhai Gurdas. It is obvious that he sings of the Sikh Panth as much as of the Sikh faith.

A Distinct Faith

The Sikh faith and those who cherish this faith are distinct from all other people known to Bhai Gurdas. This is one of his major preoccupations. In the first Vār itself, the Indian religious traditions known to Bhai Gurdas are mentioned, followed by various manifestations of the Islamic system. The Hindus and Muslims are explicitly contrasted to draw the conclusion that they have missed the truth. The metaphor of the blind leading the blind is used for both Hindus and Turks. The travels of Guru Nanak are seen as his universal triumph. The Vāhegurū *mantar* symbolized the transcendence of all faiths of the previous *yugas*.[99] The theme of transcendence is taken up again in the eighth Vār. Everything related to Hindus and Muslims is mentioned– all categories of people among them, their beliefs and practices, their occupations and identities. Apart from Muslims, the Jews and Christians are specifically mentioned. All are invited to become Gurmukhs who are different from them all.[100] The Hindus and Muslims are different and distinct from each other but there is one thing common to both: they have missed 'the place'.[101] They are not equal to the hair of a Sikh. This is true of Jews and Christians as well.[102] Significantly, Bhai Gurdas makes no distinction between orthodox Muslims and Sūfis: they all struggle in vain.[103] According to *Vārān Bhai Gurdas* Vishnu, Brahma, and Mahesh could not have the sight of God. The ten incarnations of Vishnu, as well as Brahma and Mahādev, have misled people.[104] The ten incarnations of Vishnu remained in haumai; Mahādev did not know real jog; Indra and Brahma did not attain sahaj; and Narad, though a Munī, could not discard backbiting. Then there were many others who were nothing in comparison with the casteless Gurmukhs.[105]

It is interesting to note what Bhai Gurdas thought of the 'bhagats' who attained liberation: Namdev who brought a dead cow to life, Kabir who came out of the prison walls, the Jatt Dhanna and the butcher Sadna, the cobbler Ravidas who became famous among all the four varnas, Beni who was a selfless devotee, and the low caste barber Sen. The Sikhs of the Guru become dust-of-the-feet and show great forbearance: they have realized God but they do not reveal this secret.[106] It is remarkable that Bhai Gurdas thinks of the bhagats in connection with the Sikhs (and not the Gurus). In another stanza, several bhagats are mentioned to make the point that caste does not matter for liberation: men of caste (jāt), men without caste (*ajāt*) and men of low caste (*sanāt*) are all alike.[107] The low caste Namdev was praised by the high caste Brahmans and Khatris; all the four varnas bowed to him. Indeed, the bhagats have no jāt or sanāt.[108] The bhagats who had turned their consciousness towards God to eradicate haumai are the only category of persons equated with Gurmukhs.

More than one affiliation stands discarded as dūjā bhāo.[109] Those who do not turn towards the Guru are *bemukh*.[110] The most foolish among them are the manmukh. However, the worst among them are the detractors (*nindak*), especially the slanderers of the Gurus.[111] The followers of Prithi Chand and his successors are denounced as *mīṇās* in this context. They claim to be Gurus but their claims are false; their followers believe themselves to be Sikhs but actually they are not.[112] The mīṇās stand outside the pale of Sikhism in the eyes of Bhai Gurdas in terms of doctrines, beliefs, and practices. He draws clear boundaries between the Sikhs of the Gurus and the rest of mankind, except the bhagats. But even they are nowhere near the Gurus who hold a unique position in the world as the only agency of liberation.

A Distinct Identity

The Vārs of Bhai Gurdas leave a very strong impression that he is acutely conscious of Sikh religious identity. He believes in divine sanction behind the path instituted by Guru Nanak and followed by his successors. Central to the system is the doctrine of the True Name which symbolizes the Sikh conception of God. The equation between God and the Guru confers a peculiar importance on the latter. The Guru in turn is equated with shabad and Gurbāṇī and by implication with the Granth compiled by Guru Arjan. The Guru-Chelā syndrome, unique in itself, gives a peculiar importance to the Sikhs and their congregation so much so that the Guru and the Sangat stand equated. The institutions of Guruship and dharamsāl become the hallmark of the distinctive Gurmukh-panth, both in the sense of a path and a community. The egalitarian character of the Sikh Panth distinguishes the Sikhs from all the other communities of the world. The Sikhs of the Guru are householders with a sense of social commitment. The bhagats are seen as forerunners not of the Gurus but of the Gurmukhs in so far as they attain liberation.

The criteria of Sikh identity for Bhai Gurdas are both subjective and objective: the doctrine of the Name, the Sikh scripture, the institutions of Guruship and dharamsāl, and the character of the Sikh Panth. What is said of the path is true of the Panth: it is pure (nirmal) and distinct (nirol). The consciousness of Sikh identity is heightened by the presence of sectarian mentalities.

Evidence of the *Dabistān*

It is important to note that evidence on Sikh identity comes from an outsider too in the middle decades of the seventeenth century; the author of the *Dabistān-i-Mazāhib*.[113] The traits of the Nanak-Panthis, also known as 'Sikhs of the Guru', noted by him distinguish them from all other people mentioned in his work. The Sikhs did not make any distinction between Guru Nanak and his successors, regarding them all as one. Indeed, if any-one of them did not regard Guru Arjan (the fifth *mahal*) exactly as Guru Nanak (the first mahal) he was deemed to be an unbeliever (*kāfir*). Guru Hargobind used the title Nanak for himself in his letters to the author of the *Dabistān*. That explains why every Sikh was regarded as the Sikh of Guru Nanak, and why the Panth was called the Nanak-Panth.

The Sikhs looked upon their Guru as the 'true king' (*sachchā pātshāh*) in contrast with the temporal king. The Guru's representative (*gumāshtā*) was called Masand (from the Persian *masnad*) to indicate his importance. The Masands used to come to the Guru at the time of Baisakhi, bringing with them offerings collected from the Sikhs, and receiving a turban from the Guru as a parting gift. A large number of persons became Sikhs of the Guru through their mediacy. There was hardly any city in the world in which there were no Sikhs, and the Masands used to collect offerings from all the cities and towns. To demonstrate that the Sikhs did not care for the distinctions of caste, the author of the *Dabistān* underlines that a Brahman could accept a Khatri as his leader, and a Khatri could accept a Jatt as his leader, though the latter belonged to the lowest category of Vaishyas. In fact, many of the important Masands of the Guru were Jatts, and the Brahmans and Khatris became Sikhs of the Guru through their mediacy. If a Sikh visited another Sikh in the name of the Guru, he was to be treated like the Guru himself. The collective prayer of the Sikhs was regarded as more efficacious than the prayer of a single person, even that of the Guru.

Like the principle of inequality, the Sikhs rejected the idea of renunciation (udās or *tark-i duniyā*). That was why they took either to agriculture or trade, or service (*naukarī*). Being productive, they could contribute towards the Guru's treasury. The author of the *Dabistān* observed that Guru Hargobind maintained 700 horses, 300 horsemen, and sixty match-lockmen on a permanent basis at Kiratpur. This was the result of a deliberate policy in which hunt, eating of meat, bearing of arms, and martial activities were encouraged. Being a teacher, Guru Hargobind could think of giving practical lessons to his opponents in the effective use of the sword in the field of battle. The Sikhs did not observe any Brahmanical taboos about food and drink. There was nothing of the worship (*ibādat*) and austerities (*riāzat*) stipulated by the law books of the Hindus (*sharab-i Hinduān*) among the Sikhs. The Sikh belief in transmigration distinguished them from Muslims, and the Sikh insistence on the unity of God distinguished them from Hindus. The followers of Guru Nanak had nothing to do with idols in temples. An incident related in the *Dabistān* underlines that the Sikhs had no respect for the Goddess. A Sikh of Guru Hargobind broke the nose of an idol to show how helpless the Goddess was and how foolish were they who believed in her power. The Sikhs never recited the Hindu scriptures (*mantar-hā-i Hunūd*). Indeed, the bāṇī of Guru Nanak was in the language of the peasants of the Punjab (*zubān-i jattān-i Panjāb*). His followers had no concern with Sanskrit which was regarded as the language of gods by the Hindus. Evidently, the Sikhs were not 'Hindu' in terms of their beliefs and practices, their scripture, their institutions, and the character of their social order.

Notes

1. For the life and works of Bhai Gurdas, Ratan Singh Jaggi, *Guru Granth Vishvkosh*, Patiala: Punjabi University, 2002, Part I, pp. 387–90. Oankar Singh, *Kabitt Savayye Bhai Gurdas*, Patiala: Punjab University, 1993, pp. ix–xvi; also, 'introduction' by Balkar Singh.
2. For a belief analysis of the Vārs, J.S. Grewal, 'The Nanak-Panthis', *Sikh Ideology, Polity and Social Order*, New Delhi: Manohar, 2007, pp. 67–77.
3. Harjot Oberoi, *The Construction of Religious Boundaries: Culture, Identity and Diversity in the Sikh Tradition*, New Delhi: Oxford University Press, 1994, p. 50. Oberoi regrets that as yet there is no major translation of the works of Bhai Gurdas into English. By now, however, the Vārs have been translated into English by Jodh Singh as *Vārān Bhai Gurdas*, 2 Vols, Patiala: Vision and Venture, 1998.
4. Oberoi, *The Construction of Religious Boundaries*, pp. 50–1.
5. W.H. McLeod, *Who is a Sikh? The Problem of Sikh Identity*, Oxford: The Clarendon Press, 1989, pp. 18–22, 53–4.
6. W.H. McLeod, *Textual Sources for the Study of Sikhism*, Manchester: Manchester University Press, 1984, pp. 63–9.
7. W.H. McLeod, *The Sikhs: History, Religion and Society*, New York: Columbia University Press, 1989, pp. 92–4.
8. *Vārān Bhai Gurdas*, ed., Giani Hazara Singh. Amritsar, 1962, *Vār* XXIV, Pauṛīs, 2–4.
9. Ibid., I. 23–4, 27.
10. Ibid., VI, I; XXVI, 16.
11. Ibid., V, 13.

12. Ibid., VI, 2.
13. Ibid., XII, 17–18.
14. Ibid., XVIII, 14.
15. Ibid., XXIV, 1.
16. Ibid., XXVI, 1.
17. Ibid., I, 38, 45–6.
18. Ibid., XXIV, 7, 8.
19. Ibid., XXII, 12.
20. Ibid., XIII, 1.
21. Ibid., III, 2, 11.
22. Ibid., VI, 5.
23. Ibid., IX, 8, 16.
24. Ibid., XVIII, 20.
25. Ibid., XI, 11.
26. Ibid., I, 46; XXIV, 9, 10, 12.
27. Ibid., I, 47; XXIV, 14–17.
28. Ibid., I, 47; XXIV, 19–20, 23.
29. Ibid., I, 48; XXIV, 21, 24.
30. Ibid., XXVI, 24.
31. Ibid., XXVI, 25–6.
32. Ibid., XXXIX, 12.
33. Ibid., III, 11–12.
34. Ibid., XIII, 25.
35. Ibid., XX, 1–2.
36. Ibid., XXIV, 25; XXXIX, 2–3.
37. Ibid., XXXVIII, 20; XXXIX, 4.
38. Ibid., XXVI, 32–4.
39. Ibid., III, 6; XIII, 21.
40. Ibid., XXVI, 2.
41. Ibid., IV, 17.
42. Ibid., III, 4; VII, 20.
43. Ibid., XII, 4.
44. Ibid., XV, 2, 10.
45. Ibid., XV, 6, 10.
46. Ibid., XXVII, 16–17.
47. Ibid., XXXVI, 13–16.
48. Ibid., XXXIV, 18.
49. Ibid., VIII, 15.
50. Ibid., VI, 16; XXV, 20–3.
51. Ibid., IV, 5; XVI, 7.
52. Ibid., XXXIX, 20–1.
53. Ibid., I, 3.
54. Ibid., IX, 13.
55. Ibid., XII, 2, 4.
56. Ibid., VII, 11, 18; IX, 1.

57. Ibid., XII, 17; XIII, 21.
58. Ibid., XX, 4.
59. Ibid., XXIV, 9–13, 18–20.
60. Ibid., XXIV, 9–13, 18–20.
61. Ibid., I, 3.
62. Ibid., III, 10.
63. Ibid., III, 16.
64. Ibid., V, 7, 10.
65. Ibid., V, 14.
66. Ibid., IV, 1; VII, 4, 6–7.
67. Ibid., VI, 9, 15.
68. Ibid., XXVI, 17.
69. Ibid., XXXII, 2.
70. Ibid., IX, 14.
71. Ibid., III, 8, 18.
72. Ibid., XXIX, 5.
73. Ibid., XXIX, 6.
74. Ibid., XXXV, 12, 14–15.
75. Ibid., III, 15–16.
76. Ibid., IV, 17–18; IX, 2: XI, 5; XXVIII, 1.
77. Ibid., V, 9.
78. Ibid., V, 10.
79. Ibid., VI, 19.
80. Ibid., VII, 12.
81. Ibid., XIV, 17.
82. Ibid., XVI, 20.
83. Ibid., XXIII, 19–20.
84. Ibid., XXXVIII, 7.
85. Ibid., XXXVIII, 9, 10, 21.
86. Ibid., XXIII, 4.
87. Ibid., XI, 3, 6; XXVIII, 20.
88. Ibid., V, 1–2.
89. Ibid., VI, 3.
90. Ibid., VI, 12–13.
91. Ibid., VII, 4.
92. Ibid., VIII, 24.
93. Ibid., XI, 3–4.
94. Ibid., XIX, 14.
95. Ibid., XXXVIII, 9–12.
96. Ibid., I, 25; III, 8, 19–20; VI, 4–5; IX, 19–20, 22; XII, 1–4, 6; XX, 6, 10, 12–13, 21; XXV, 11; XXVIII, 2; XXIX, 5; XXXII, 1.
97. Ibid., XII, 8–15.
98. Ibid., XIII, 19.
99. Ibid., XI, 13–31.
100. Ibid., XI, 7.

101. Ibid., XXXIX, 18–19.
102. Ibid., I, 18–21, 26, 34, 36, 49.
103. Ibid., VIII, 6–24.
104. Ibid, XXXIII, 2.
105. Ibid., XXXVIII, 9–10.
106. Ibid., XXXIX, 10.
107. Ibid., XIV, 3–4.
108. Ibid., XII, 8–12.
109. Ibid., XII, 15.
110. Ibid., XXIII, 15.
111. Ibid., XXV, 4–5.
112. Ibid., XXXIII, 7, 12, 13–22.
113. 'Dabistān-i-Mazāhib', in J.S. Grewal and Irfan Habib, eds, *Sikh History from Persian Sources*, New Delhi: Tulika/Indian History Congress, 2001, pp. 59–84.

7

'Frighten No One and Be Afraid of None'

Guru Tegh Bahadur

At the top of the first page of a manuscript in the Library of the Panjab University, Chandigarh, there is Guru Tegh Bahadur's *nishān*, that is, the *mūlmantar* written in his hand: 'I *onkār satnām kartā purkh nirbhau nirvair akāl mūrit ajūnī saibhan gurprasādī*'. Below the nishān there is an entry in a very different hand: *'eh darsan nāven pātsāh jī dī hajūrī vich hājar ho ke prāpat kīte gae, sammat 1731 Bikrami punniān Jethe dī, samet sangat de'*.[1] Evidently, a considerable number of Sikhs were present when Guru Tegh Bahadur inscribed the mūlmantar on the full moon day of Jeth in Sammat 1731 (AD 1674). This recension of the Granth contains the *bāṇī* of Guru Tegh Bahadur. This is an indication of the importance attached by Guru Tegh Bahadur to his own bāṇī as much as to the Granth Sāhib.

The bāṇī of Guru Tegh Bahadur, like the bāṇī of Guru Angad, is rather small in volume—fifty-nine *shabads* and fifty-seven *shaloks* of less than 550 lines.[2] However, like the bāṇī of Guru Angad, the bāṇī of Guru Tegh Bahadur has a significance out of all proportion to its volume. If Guru Angad was the first successor of Guru Nanak, Guru Tegh Bahadur was the first to compose bāṇī in a critical situation after the compilation of the Granth by Guru Arjan in 1604.

Nearly a century ago Puran Singh observed that 'the writings of Guru Tegh Bahadur can be recognized at once: they breathe 'a deep and sweet melancholy of a solemn and serene mind that is tired of the fictions of this seeming world'. Guru Tegh Bahadur saw 'nothing tangible in the world, with which he may make relations of love'. He would depend on nothing. He would lean on nothing. Father, mother, friend, brother, wife, offspring, everything in the world for him was 'too slippery a ground to rest upon'. Puran Singh goes on to add that in the bāṇī of Guru Tegh Bahadur we find the spirit of God-realization alternating with a spirit of deep renunciation of the world as if the two were one and the same thing. Guru Tegh Bahadur is 'pessimistic, in order that he may enjoy the highest optimism without interruption'. He was 'a man of iron will'. Nothing could ever daunt him. He expressed the spirit of Guru Nanak in a language that is all his own. We do not find 'such intensity in the writings of any other Guru'.[3]

Professor Harbans Singh has remarked that the *shalok*s of Guru Tegh Bahadur, which form the concluding portion of the Guru Granth, are ceremonially intoned as part of the epilogue for concluding an open congregational reading of the scripture on a religious or social occasion and, consequently, the shaloks are the most familiar fragment of the Granth Sāhib after the *Japjī*. The shabads and shaloks of Guru Tegh Bahadur essentialize the same spiritual experience and insights as does the bāṇī of the preceding Gurus.[4] We know, however, that the situation in which Guru Tegh Bahadur wrote his shabads and shaloks was different from that of the preceding Gurus. His bāṇī can be appreciated better if seen in relation to his life in the context of the politicization of the Sikh movement in confrontation with the state.

The Life of Guru Tegh Bahadur

Guru Tegh Bahadur was born in Ramdaspur in 1621. By this time, the institution of Guruship had become extremely important. Based on the principles of unity, continuity, and indivisibility, it had acquired a uniqueness of its own. The Guru occupied a crucial position in the Sikh movement and the Sikh Panth. He was expected to inspire the Sikhs and to give direction to them in an ever-changing historical situation. In matters of organization, he needed the services and support of the *masands*. Local *sangats,* with the *dharamsāl* as their core institution, were spread all over the Mughal empire, with affluent Sikhs in its major cities. The compilation of the Granth by Guru Arjan in 1604 had given the Sikhs their scripture. Its presence in a dharamsāl assimilated its position to that of a Gurdwara where the Guru was personally present. Ramdaspur, with the Harmandar in the midst of *amritsar,* was a flourishing town. The martyrdom of Guru Arjan in 1606 added a new dimension to the Sikh movement.

By the time of Guru Tegh Bahadur's birth in 1621, Guru Hargobind had developed martial interests, built a fortress in Ramdaspur and founded the Akal Takht. The phase of overt confrontation with Jahangir was over, but temporal pursuits had become a part of Guru Hargobind's regular activities as the Guru. There is no direct information on the early education of Tegh Bahadur. However, it may not be unsafe to assume that he was nurtured on Gurbāṇī. The evidence of his own compositions leaves little doubt that he had internalized the essential ideology of the Granth. Possibly, he was given training in martial arts too. He is said to have participated in the battle of Kartarpur at the age of fourteen. There are indications that he loved horses and horse-riding. For about ten years then he lived at Kiratpur with his father who maintained a contingent of musketeers and horsemen till his death in 1644. At the age twenty-three, he would be aware of Guru Hargobind's prolonged confrontation with Jahangir and Shah Jahan.

By this time, two other developments had taken place within the Sikh movement as a result largely of this confrontation. Guru Arjan's elder brother, Prithi Chand, had contested his succession to Guruship in his life. After his martyrdom he refused to acknowledge Hargobind as the Guru. Prithi Chand's son, Miharban, succeeded his father as the seventh Guru. Like Prithi Chand, Miharban remained on the right side of the Mughal authorities and, with their support, occupied Ramdaspur after Guru Hargobind's departure from the place due to his armed conflict with the Mughal authorities. Miharban and his successor, Harji, tried to consolidate their position in Ramdaspur.

The second development related to Kartarpur in the Jalandhar Doab. Before the death of Guru Hargobind in 1644, his eldest son, Baba Gurditta, had died, and Gurditta's elder son, Dhir Mal, had left Kiratpur to establish his own centre at Kartarpur, seeking patronage from the Mughal Emperor Shah Jahan. Guru Hargobind installed his younger grandson, Har Rai, in his place. Dhir Mal refused to recognize him as the Guru. Thus, two splinter groups came into existence within the Sikh community before 1644, creating a cleavage in the Sikh Panth.

Tegh Bahadur accepted with grace the Guruship of Har Rai in 1644 and moved to Bakala in the Bari Doab. There are two views of his stay at Bakala for twenty years. One, that he lived a life of seclusion and meditation and according to the other version he also travelled to the Gangetic plain. The second view is based on the evidence of Bhatt *vahis* (books).[5]

In any case, these twenty years were marked by important developments. Guru Har Rai maintained the contingents raised by Guru Hargobind. According to Sujan Rai Bhandari, he went to the aid of Dara Shukoh when the latter had come to the Punjab after his defeat at the hands of Aurangzeb. Called to the court by Aurangzeb, probably on this account, Guru Har Rai sent his elder son Ram Rai who made a good impression on the emperor. However, he overstepped the bounds of propriety in his ingenuity to substitute '*be-īmān*' for '*musalmān*' in a shabad of Guru Nanak. Guru Har Rai chose his younger son, Har Krishan, as his successor before his death in 1661. Guru Har Krishan was also called to Delhi. Probably, Aurangzeb wanted to intervene in the succession to Guruship. Guru Har Krishan died of small pox in 1664, indicating that his successor was the Baba at Bakala, that is, Tegh Bahadur.

The acceptance of Guruship by Tegh Bahadur in 1664 was in a sense a challenge to Aurangzeb who was keen on arbitration. Harji at Ramdaspur and Dhir Mal at Kartarpur were not happy with Guru Tegh Bahadur's assumption of the office in their neighbourhood. In any case, Guru Tegh Bahadur left Bakala and founded a new centre at Makhowal, the present Anandpur Sahib, and went to work among the Sikh sangats of the 'east'. He remained in the 'east' from 1665 to 1670, visiting Assam in 1669 with Raja Ram Singh, the son of Raja Jai Singh of Jaipur. He returned to Makhowal in 1671 and toured the Malwa region in 1673–4. In 1675 he was arrested, taken to Delhi, and executed. On the place of martyrdom of Guru Tegh Bahadur on 11 November 1675 now stands the Gurdwara Sisganj. The phase of Guruship from 1664 to 1675 was also the time when Guru Tegh Bahadur composed his bāṇī. We can see that the bāṇī of Guru Tegh Bahadur was composed in a confrontational situation.

This was also the phase of his life when he issued *hukamnāmas* to the sangats in the Punjab and in the 'east'. These hukamnāmas provide valuable insights into the situation. Four of these hukamnāmas were issued to the Masands or eminent Sikhs in the Majha region, indicating that Guru Tegh Bahadur had begun to mobilize support for himself as the Guru. The epithet Ramdas is used for the Masand. Ramdas Uggar Sain is told that his house is the Guru's house. Six of the hukamnāmas were sent to the sangat of Pakpattan where Bhai Batha was made the leader. He was to be treated as the Guru's son and his orders were to be regarded as orders of the Guru. The sangat is expected to send offerings regularly and to have the Guru's *darshan* at the time of Diwali. The sangat of Pakpattan is also told that they are the Guru's *khālsā*.

For the 'east', one hukamnāma was addressed to the sangat of Mirzapur, asking that the offerings be handed over to Bhai Dayal Das who appears to have held a prominent position. The Masands of Benares, the environs of Benares and the province (*sūba*) of Benares are asked to send their offerings through Bhai Dayal Das who is the leader of the sangat of Patna which is the Guru's home. The orders of Bhai Dayal Das are to be regarded as orders of the Guru. A large number of Sikhs are mentioned in the hukamnāmas addressed to the sangats of Benares and Patna. Among the eminent Sikhs of Benares there is a lady. Apart from the regular offerings, called *kār* or *kārbār,* the Sikhs are expected to send their presents or gifts (*bhet*) to the Guru, and also to send what they vow (*mannat*). The articles asked for and received by the Guru include items of ordinary use, particularly for travel, and also costly items. Notable among them are turbans which were generally given to Masands and eminent Sikhs in acknowledgement and appreciation of their services. Apart from references to the Raja (Ram Singh), there is a reference to Nawab Saif Khan, to whom high quality vessels are being sent. Guru Tegh Bahadur stayed at Monghyr for quite some time, asking the sangats to have his darshan there and appreciating all that the sangat of Patna was doing for his son, Gobind Das, and the family of Guru Tegh Bahadur. The hukamnāmas by their very nature relate to practical, mundane matters. But the injunction *'gurū, gurū japṇā'* is not forgotten. It is underlined as the source of liberation.

The hukamnāmas of Guru Tegh Bahadur clearly show him in the light of an organizer, a leader who is very much concerned with the detail of practical matters, and a person who means business. His relations with Raja Ram Singh and Nawab Saif Khan are indicative of his political awareness. He appears to have strengthened the sangats of the east through a certain degree of reorganization. These hukamnāmas reveal the kind of support which these sangats could provide to the Guru. Though these sangats were old, the work of Guru Tegh Bahadur in the east was of a regenerative character.[6] His decision to return to the Punjab in 1670 appears to have been linked with the aggressive policies of Aurangzeb.[7] His tours in the Malwa region were probably meant to give reassurance to the people.[8] In turn, the people could come to him for reassurance and help.[9]

The *Shabads*

Guru Tegh Bahadur uses a number of epithets for God is his shabads: Bhagwan, Bhagwant, Chintaman, Gusai, Gobind, Har, Harji, Kanhai, Murar, Murari, Narayan, Niranjan, Prabh, Prabhu, Ram, and Soami. He is the only real being (*ek purkh*) and he remains the same (*ek rang*). He is the creator of the universe. The whole creation is his māyā and he look on it (with pleasure). He has no form or sign but he is near. He, the many-coloured, appears in innumerable forms but he is without limits, he cannot be seen, and he is without any impurity. He is within human beings, like the image in a mirror and fragrance in a flower. He is within and he is outside. He is detached from his creation. He is everywhere and in everything but he is also detached. He is the Master of māyā. He can raise a pauper into a prince in a moment and degrade a prince into a pauper. He fills the empty and he empties the filled. He is the treasure of compassion, and the succourer of the poor and the meek. He protects his devotees. He is the remover of sorrow and suffering (*dukh-bhanjan*). He is the remover of sorrow and suffering (dukh-bhanjan). He is the remover of fear (*bhai-bhanjan*). He cuts off the noose of Death. Thus, God for Guru Tegh Bahadur is One, both transcendent and immanent at the same time, who is all powerful and compassionate.[10]

In his compositions Guru Tegh Bahadur underscores that God is the only refuge of human beings. Therefore the Guru calls aloud to take refuge in God.[11] In his refuge is real peace.[12] Think of refuge in the Lord.[13] None else comes to your rescue in the end.[14] He is the only true object of worship. Discard all other illusions and concentrate on the feet of God.[15] The foremost duty of human beings is to sing God's praises. The phrases used are *jas, kīrat, guṇ,* and *gīt* of *Gobind, Har*, or *Prabh*.[16] It may be safely assumed that the praises of the Lord are sung in congregation. The term sādh-sangat or sādh-sang is explicitly used for singing God's praises.[17]

The term used mostly frequently in the shabads of Guru Tegh Bahadur is *nām*. The terms associated with nām, or the name of God, are *japṇā, bhajnā*, and *simarnā*, that is, uttering, singing, and reflecting. One in millions receives the gift of Ram-*bhajan*.[18] The man who praises the Lord through Rām-nām remains at peace.[19] The nām of Har is the redeemer of the world.[20] All one's affairs are set right through the bhajan of Rām-nām which is the means of redemption. In the Kaliyuga, the nām of God is the only means of redemption.[21] The whole universe is an illusion without

Rām-nām.[22] One remains in sorrow and suffering without the nām of Har.[23] The man who does no bhajan of Ram wastes his life.[24] The nām of Ram remembered for a moment in a whole day becomes the source of redemption; the fear of Death is destroyed and the objective of life is fulfilled.[25] The nām of Har is the source of peace. 'I have found the wealth of *nām*, O' mother; my mind does not wander any more, it is at peace'.[26] In the Kaliyuga, the nām of the Treasure of Grace is the only means of redemption.[27]

Appropriation of nām and singing of God's praises constitute bhagtī in the shabads of Guru Tegh Bahadur. The bhagtī of Ram is equated with the bhajan of Har.[28] The means of appropriating bhagtī is the nām of God.[29] Without the nām of Har there is sorrow and suffering, without bhagtī the fear of Death is not removed.[30] He who is devoid of the bhajan of Ram is devoid of bhagtī.[31] *Har ko nām* and *Rām-bhagtī* appear to be synonymous.[32] Just as the singing of God's praises in the congregation is equated with nām, so the appropriation of nām is equated with bhagtī.

The way to both nām and bhagtī is shown by the Guru according to Guru Tegh Bahadur. The Guru's updes is to appropriate truth, Rām-bhajan, and nām.[33] The right path is seen through the Guru's grace.[34] The Guru imparts awareness of God within and outside.[35] The one who does not receive the Guru's instruction and remains alien to divine knowledge is no better than a beast.[36] 'Listen O' brother to the Guru's *updes* and take refuge in God'.[37] The Guru reveals the secret that the fear of Death does not vanish without bhagtī.[38] The Guru reveals the secret that liberation in Kaliyuga comes through nām alone.[39] One awakens to the need of Rām-bhajan and Prabh-jas by turning to the Guru's feet.[40] The one who imbibes the Guru's instruction becomes Gurmukh. The path to liberation is extremely difficult (*kaṭhan*); only a few find it by turning to the Guru.[41] By turning to the Guru one follows the path of liberation.[42] God is recognized by one in a million.[43] The wealth of the praises of God is found by a few Gurmukhs.[44] The term Gur-jan is also used, which may refer to both the Guru and his follower. 'I have not taken to *Har-bhajan*, nor have I served the Gur-jan; I have experienced no *giān*'.[45] The Gurmukh of Guru Tegh Bahadur is evidently the Guru's Sikh. The sādh and the sant in his shabads stand both for the Guru and the Sikh.[46] The word '*sikhkh*' is used for the Guru's instruction.[47]

The purpose of human life is liberation. Guru Tegh Bahadur uses various terms for the state of liberation. It is called *pad-nirbāṇā*, muktī, nirbhai pad, *milan*, *gatī*, *achal-amar-nirbhai-pad*, jīvan muktī, and *sachch māhi samāya*.[48] God fills the whole being of the person who experiences muktī.[49] He mingles with God like water in water.[50] The person who attains liberation is muktā or giānī.[51] The path is called muktī-panth.[52] The state of liberation is an everlasting state of peace and fearlessness.[53] Guru Tegh Bahadur prays for the gift of fearlessness. He underscores that it is a state of detachment. Indeed, realization of God is self-realization. The illusion does not depart without knowing the self. 'Why do you wander in wilderness in search of God. The ever-detached omnipresent is within you'.[54] The sādhs (Sikhs) should regard the body as an illusion; they should recognize the Ram within who alone is true.[55]

It is interesting to note that the bhagats who attained to the state of liberation in the past are all legendary and mythical: Ajamal, Ganika, Gaj, Narad, Dhruv, and Panchali. They were given protection or the gift of fearlessness.[56]

Guru Tegh Bahadur dwells on the need of liberation. The path of liberation is found by turning to the Guru.[57] The human birth is a rare opportunity and human beings should find the means to liberation.[58] The soul wanders in many yugas before it is clothed in the human body: this is the only chance for meeting God.[59] It is never too late to turn to the singing of God's praises and his bhajan to attain the state of fearlessness.[60] The way to liberation-in-life lies is the praises of God, nām, and bhagtī, discarding pride and attachment.[61] In a sense, the entire bāṇī of Guru Tegh Bahadur inculcates the need of liberation. Life without liberation is a waste and the path of liberation is shown by the Guru.

Guru Tegh Bahadur underscores that the state of liberation means an attitude of detachment and not renunciation. The Gurmukh seeks pad-nirbāṇā to become indifferent to both sukh and dukh, *mān* and *apmān*, *harkh* and *sog*; he remains totally detached in the world.[62] He who is not affected by harkh and sog is a veritable god; to him heaven and hell, nectar and poison, and gold and copper are the same; alike to him are praise and slander; the *giānī* knows no dukh or sukh.[63] God is completely detached from sukh and dukh (and the liberated-in-life acquires this attribute).[64] The person who experiences God does not experience sorrow and suffering; he is indifferent to peace, affection or fear; he ignores praise and slander alike as he is indifferent to *lobh*, *moh*, and *abhīmān*; he remains detached from harkh and sog and indifferent to mān and apmān; he discards all desires and aspirations (for himself) and remains *niras* in the world; he is not touched by kām and krodh; God dwells within him. This way is recognized through the Guru's grace.[65] Only he who remains detached-in-attachment is a real jogī.[66]

In the shabads of Guru Tegh Bahadur there is no appreciation for renunciation and mendicancy. He is not much concerned with the religious systems of his time but he makes it clear that Jogīs and other ascetics who practised renunciation, celibacy, and medicancy had missed the goal of life. The Jogīs have tried hard but failed to find God. They are not alone: jangams and sanyāsīs are bracketed with them; they are all subject to transmigration. Bracketed with them are *jatīs* and *tapīs*. Then there are those who shave their heads or put on saffron robes. There is hardly any doubt that the ascetical tradition as a whole stands rejected in the shabads of Guru Tegh Bahadur.[67]

In the same way, all Brahmanical practices stand rejected. The merit of nām simarnā subsumes the merit believed to flow from the reading of the Vedas and the Purāṇas. The *jagg* of the Brahmanical tradition is fruitless as it leads to oblivion of the Lord. What is the use of going on pilgrimage (tīrath) or keeping fast (*barat*) when the mind is not under control. Regard this dharma as fruitless (*nihphal*).[68] In fact Guru Tegh Bahadur's insistence on the exclusive efficacy of nām in the Kaliyuga carries the implication that all other dispensations stand transcended.

As we noticed earlier, the path of liberation is tough (*kaṭhan*). Not many people can follow it, though it is open to all. Guru Tegh Bahadur addresses the human beings in general as much as he addresses the Sikhs. The message is the same. The obstacles to the path of liberation are māyā, *mamtā*, and haumai. Guru Tegh Bahadur exhorts the Sikhs to discard mān, apmān, and haumai, and to discard kām and krodh.[69] Human beings remain engrossed in māyā and mamtā, and strengthen the chains which bind them. It is like following a mirage.[70] Thirst occupies the mind and it does not remain stable.[71] One can turn to God only by discarding abhīmān, moh, and māyā. Māyā, lobha, moh, and mamtā are like poison.[72] Men remain occupied with other women and slandering others.[73] The mind remains chained in attachment (moh) and ignorance (*agiān*). It remains inclined towards poison, day and night.[74] Running after others' wealth and women, men waste their lives; maddened by the lure of māyā they remain strangers to giān and oblivious to nām.[75] The world is sold to māyā, attached to kith and kin, and intoxicated with youth, wealth, and power.[76] Engrossed in the pleasure of gold and women, men do not remember God.[77] Lost in the poison of māyā, men do not remember God.[78] Absorbed in māyā they do not take refuge in God.[79]

The importance given to māyā, mamtā, and haumai by Guru Tegh Bahadur is reflected in his exhortation to all and sundry. All customary relationship end with one's life, whether that of mother, father, brother, son, or wife. When one's breath is separated from the body, the corpse is taken out of the home in less than half an hour.[80] The worldly affection is false. Even your wife and friend are attached to you in self-interest. They cannot go with you in the end.[81] Everything in the world is like a dream; it does not take long to vanish. The wall of sand does not last for more than a few days. Similar are the comforts of māyā; 'why are you entangled with it O' fool? Even now there is time to appropriate *nām*'.[82] There is no friend in this world. Everyone is with you when you are in comfort but none is with you when you are in trouble. The wife, the friends, the son, and the relations—all are with you when you are rich; the moment you are rich no more, they leave you.[83] People are attached to you in their own interest; no one is permanently attached to another. In comfort you are surrounded by many, but when you are in trouble no one comes near you. Even the wife cries '*pret, pret*' (ghost, ghost) when the husband is dead. This is how things are but you remain engrossed in them. In the end, only God can help you.[84] This world is a mountain of smoke but you regard it as true. Your wealth, wife, property, and home do not go with you. If anything goes with you it is the bhagtī of Narayan.[85] Except God, none can help you, neither your mother, father, son and wife, nor your brother. Even your body, wealth, and property are not yours for ever. Your wealth and property do not go with you when you are dead. The world is an illusion, like a dream.[86] Why are you holding the poison in your arms? None stays in this world; if one comes, another leaves. Whatever we see disappears sooner or later, like the shadow of a cloud.[87] Take refuge with the sants so that you may attain liberation. Man wastes his life, engrossed in the pleasure of māyā and does not take refuge with God. This world is a dream. No one can stay here. You have put yourself in chains by regarding your body as true.[88] The rulership of the world is like a wall of sand.[89]

On the whole, in the shabads of Guru Tegh Bahadur we find the same conception of a transcendent and immanent God, who is omnipotent, omnipresent, and compassionate, as in the compositions of his predecessors in the Gurū Granth Sāhib. God's attribute as the remover of fear is not new but there is a difference of emphasis. This attribute gets directly linked up with the state of liberation as a state of fearlessness. Again, the idea is not new but there is a difference of emphasis. The path advocated by Guru Tegh Bahadur is emphatically the one advocated by his predecessors, with equal importance given to kīrat, nām, and bhagtī. The obstacles on the path are the same: māyā, mamtā, and haumai. The first two are emphasized a little more than the third, The exclusive validity of the path is clearly stated. Not the way of renunciation or ritual but the path of detached activity and commitment is upheld. In the given situation, the message of Guru Tegh Bahadur is one of firm, even grim, determination and reassurance.

In the foregoing analysis of the shabads of Guru Tegh Bahadur we have paid close attention to the words and phrases used in the shabads in order to construct a coherent picture of his ideas and attitudes. In the process we have missed the richness and flavour of a whole shabad. For this reason, a score of his shabads are given in the Appendix, with English translation in prose.

The *Shaloks*

The shaloks of Guru Tegh Bahadur trenchantly reinforce the ideas and attitudes expressed in the shabads. As it may be expected, some of the shaloks relate to māyā, mamtā, and haumai, along with a comment or a suggestion. Blinded by māyā, a person does not think of God; he is caught by the noose of Death.[90] I have tried hard but failed to get rid of pride; I am caught in durmat, may God save me.[91] My mind is so absorbed in māyā that it does not leave it, as a portrait painted on the wall does not leave it.[92] God is lodged in the heart of one who discards māyā and mamtā to become detached from everyone and everything.[93] The person who discards haumai, recognizing God as the real doer, is verily a liberated person.[94] He who discards mamtā, lobh, moh, and ahankār, gets liberated and liberates others.[95] Fortunate are they who discard the poison (māyā) and put on the garb of detachment.[96]

There are shaloks by Guru Tegh Bahadur on the transience and evanescence of all earthly things, with exhortation to turn to God: 'Wealth, wife, and property, which you regard as your own, will not go with you; this is verily true'.[97] 'Regard the world as a dream; there is nothing everlasting, except God.'[98] 'The world is like a bubble of water that appears and disappears in a trice.'[99] 'All are with you in sukh and none is with you in dukh; recite the name of God who alone is helpful in the end.'[100] 'What for is the false pride when the whole world is like a dream; nothing goes with you.'[101] 'Be not proud of the body which disappears in a moment; the person who sings the praises of God conquers the world.'[102] 'I have seen the world very closely, no one can help another; the bhagtī of God alone is a lasting thing.'[103] 'The whole created world is false; like a wall of sand, it does not last long.'[104] 'Ram left the world and so did Ravan with his large progeny; nothing is stable in this world, which is like a dream.'[105]

A few shaloks of Guru Tegh Bahadur underline the crucial importance of human life as a rare opportunity for liberation: 'In youth you did nothing and old age has overtaken you now; turn to the remembrance of God, your life is reaching its end.'[106] 'The old age has come and you cannot think of anything; why not turn to the remembrance of God?'[107] 'Why don't you repeat the name of Ram who gave you the human frame, wealth, possessions, and tall mansions.'[108] 'He who desires peace should take refuge in Ram; the human birth is a rare opportunity.'[109] 'Boyhood, youth, and old age are the three stages of human life; all these are useless without Har-bhajan.'[110] 'The head trembles, the feet are no longer steady, and eyes have lost their sight; even in this state you have not experienced God.'[111]

There are shaloks on kīrat, nām, and bhagtī also. The life goes waste without singing the praises of God; attach yourself to the remembrance of God, like the fish to water.[112] The ignorant and foolish people pursue māyā and spend their life in vain without Har-bhajan.[113] The person who remembers God day and night is like God; between Har and Har-jan surely there is no difference.[114] The mind is engrossed in māyā and the name of Gobind is forgotten; of no use is life without Har-bhajan.[115] Blinded by the intoxication of māyā, people do not remember God; without Har-bhajan, they find the noose of Death on their neck.[116] Whatever is created disappears sooner or later; sing the praises of God and free yourself from the net.[117] In your heart lodge God, who has no equal; all crises are resolved and you see his face.[118] He who has the simran of Ram to his credit, regard him as liberated; between him and God verily there is no difference.[119] The tongue should sing the praises of God and the ears should hear his name; this way, one does not go to the place of Death.[120] The name of God is the destroyer of fear and the remover of ill-thinking in the Kaliyuga; he who recites it day and night, all his efforts bear fruit.[121] The person devoid of bhagtī is like a pig and a dog.[122]

God is everywhere in the shaloks of Guru Tegh Bahadur as Gobind, Har, Bhagwan, Ram, Harju, Brahm, Narayan, and Raghunath. The redeemer of sinners and the remover of fear, God is the protecting master of those who have no patron; he is always with you.[123] God is the bestower of all peace, there is no other; one may attain liberation by his simran.[124] God dwells within everyone, as the sants proclaim aloud; remember him alone to get rid of fear.[125] Human beings seek comfort and wish to avoid pain, but all that happens is due to God's bhāṇā.[126] The whole world is a beggar and God alone is the bestower of gifts; remember him, so that all your affairs are set right.[127] When all your associates and friends leave you, God alone is your support.[128] God alone is the bestower of gifts, there is no other; by his simran you attain liberation.[129]

Guru Tegh Bahadur lays great stress on liberation in his shaloks as in his shabads. He who is not affected by sukh or dukh and who has no lobh, moh, or abhīmān is like God.[130] Praise and blame, gold and iron, are to him alike; regard him as the liberated one.[131] Happiness or sorrow does not touch him, and the enemy is like a friend to him; regard him as the liberated one.[132] He does not frighten any one, nor is he afraid of anyone; regard him as a giānī.[133] The transience of the world is due to God's will; there is no point in worrying about it.[134] What survives in the end is God as the Guru, his nām, and the sādhū (Sikh) who has attained liberation.[135]

On the whole, thus, the message of the shaloks is one of affirmation. The world is of no count; what really matters is total dedication to God that leads to liberation as a state of bliss and fearlessness. There is melancholy but no pessimism. The grim determination to accept God's will on the path of righteousness comes through the shaloks.

Martyrdom for the Freedom of Conscience

With the life and bāṇī of Guru Tegh Bahadur in view, we may turn to the brief statement on his martyrdom in the *Bachittar Nātak*. It comes at the end of the chapter which refers to the new dharam promulgated by Guru Nanak to show the right path to sādhs in the Kaliyuga. All his successors were one with him: Guru Angad, Guru Amar Das, Guru Ram Das, Guru

Arjan, Guru Hargobind, Guru Har Rai, Guru Har Krishan, and Guru Tegh Bahadur. The sādhs saw them as one, but not the fools.

Guru Tegh Bahadur performed a great deed in the Kaliyuga. He protected *tilak* and *janjū*, and for the sake of sādhs he gave his head without a sigh of pain. This great deed he performed for the sake of dharam. He gave his head but he did not give up his determination. The true devotees of God are ashamed of performing dramatic ill-deeds (of a supranatural kind). Breaking the pitcher of his body on the head of the ruler of Delhi, Guru Tegh Bahadur went to the abode of God. None else has ever performed such a great deed. The world was sorrowful on his departure, and there were loud cries of lamentation. In the heavens, however, there were shouts of applause.[136]

The situation of confrontation with Aurangzeb is clearly alluded to in these lines, and so is Guru Tegh Bahadur's determination to lay down his life for a principle. Tilak and janjū serve as the symbols of Brahmanical dispensation, and dharam and sādhs refer to the dispensation of Guru Nanak. We have seen that Guru Tegh Bahadur had no appreciation for the Brahmanical tradition. Therefore, the principle involved was the freedom of conscience as opposed to the practice of coercion. Martyrdom in the context of confrontation with the ruler of the times on a matter of principle was both religious and political in character.

The *Srī Gur Sobhā* was composed more than thirty years after the martyrdom of Guru Tegh Bahadur. The importance given to the event and the terms used for it indicate that it was never forgotten by the Sikhs. It may not be far-fetched to suggest that the principle for which Guru Tegh Bahadur laid down his life was built into the institution of the Khalsa: willingness to die for a righteous cause.

Selected *Shabads*

1. No one knows the state of God. The Jogīs, the celibates, and they who practise austerities, like other wise people, have tried and failed. In a moment, God turns a prince into a pauper, and a pauper into a prince; He fills the empty, and empties the fully filled: this is his familiar way. He is the creator of māyā and its beholder. He appears in many colours and assumes innumerable forms, but he remains apart (from his creation). He keeps the whole world under illusion, he is incomputable, beyond all limits, unknowable, and immaculate.

Discard all illusions O' mortal, says Nanak, and concentrate your mind on his feet.[137]

2. All the earthly affairs pertain to this life, even the ties with mother, father, brother, son, kith and kin, and wife. When the soul departs from the body, they call it 'ghost'; they do not keep it even for half an hour and take it out of the house. Reflect well in your mind, the world is like a mirage. Recite everyday the name of Ram, the source of liberation. [138]
3. Earthly love has turned out to be false. Everyone thinks of his or her own interest, even a friend or the wife. With their own interest in mind they call you 'mine'. In the end, no one goes with you. So strange is this customary way. My stupid mind does not grasp this and I am tired of giving it instruction every day. He who sings the praises of God, O' Nanak, crosses the ocean of life (to be liberated).[139]
4. What should I say about my degradation? Absorbed in the pleasure of gold and women, I have never sung the praises of God. I regarded the false world as true and fell in love with it. I have never thought of the real friend of the poor, who alone is helpful in the end. Day and night I remain engrossed in *māyā* and the moss (of illusion) is still on my mind. I am left with no other option, says Nanak, than refuge in God.[140]
5. Such is God's creation O' sādhs that one disappears and another thinks he is here for ever; it is strange beyond words. Subject to lust, anger, and attachment, the human being forgets the divine form, and regards his own frame as ever-lasting though actually it is like a dream in sleep. All that we see disappears like the passing shadow of a cloud. Nanak, know the world to be an illusion and seek refuge in God.[141]
6. To whom should I tell the state of my mind? Engrossed in greed it runs in all the ten directions in the hope of wealth. Keen to serve all and sundry, it seeks peace but suffers pain, It goes from door to door like a dog, and does not think of turning to the adoration of Ram. Insensitive to people's ridicule, it wastes the opportunity provided by the human birth. Nanak, why don't you sing the praises of God so that you are rid of your ill-thoughts?[142]
7. You have imbibed ill-thoughts O' my mind; engrossed in pleasure from other women and slandering others, you have not turned to the bhagtī of Ram. Running after wealth and youth, you have remained

a stranger to the path of liberation. You have entangled yourself in vain because none will accompany you in the end. You have never adored God, never served the Guru, and acquired no knowledge of the divine. The immaculate God is within you but you seek him in the wilderness. Wandering through many births to exhaustion you have still not found the abiding state. Now that you have found the human birth, Nanak tells you to turn to the feet of the Lord (for liberation).[143]

8. Human beings do not turn to the praises of the Lord. How can they sing God's praises if they remain engrossed in māyā? Thus, they bind themselves to māyā and affection for sons and friends. They run after earthly things, like a deer after the mirage. The fools forget the Master who is the bestower of all earthly comforts and liberation. One in millions, O'Nanak, receives the gift of singing God's praises.[144]
9. If you have any sense, O' man, remember God day and night. Moment by moment your life is decreasing, like water in a cracked pitcher. Why don't you sing the praises of God, you ignorant fool. You have forgotten death in greedy pursuit of falsehood. Nothing is lost yet if you turn to God's praises. By singing his praises, says Nanak, you may attain the state of fearlessness.[145]
10. On the name of the Lord meditate; this meditation alone can help you. Renounce *māyā* and take refuge in the Lord. The pleasures of the world and your pride are illusory, the whole setup is false. Wealth disappears like a dream, what are you proud of? The rulership of the whole earth is a wall of sand. It vanishes in the end, says Nanak. Yesterday passed away moment by moment so is today passing away moment by moment.[146]
11. Take refuge in the name of God, O' my mind; by meditating on nām you may find the state of liberation. Fortunate is the man who sings God's praises. Sins of many births are washed away and he goes to *Baikunth* (the abode of God). Ajamal thought of God at the last moment and he attained the state which the great Jogīs desire. The elephant had no merit, no learning, and no dharma; it is in the nature of God to be gracious, and he gave the gift of fearlessness to Ajamal.[147]
12. I have found, O' mother, the wealth of the name of God. My mind wanders no more, it is at peace. Māyā and mamtā have left my body and pure knowledge of the divine has welled up. It is no longer

touched by greed and attachment now that I have appropriated the bhagtī of God. By finding the jewel of nām, the fear of death and rebirth has vanished. Māyā lures my mind no more and I am absorbed in my bliss. Only he sings the praises of God to whom the Treasure of Grace is kind. This kind of wealth, says Nanak, is found by a few who turn to the Guru.[148]

13. The Guru reveals the secret that without the name of God there is nothing but sorrow and suffering; without his bhagtī the fear of Death is not dispelled. If you have not taken refuge in God, then pilgrimage and fasting will not help. If you forget to sing the praises of God, then no austerities or ritual sacrifices can help. Discard pride and attachment, and sing the praises of the Lord. In this way, says Nanak, one may become liberated-in-life.[149]
14. I have never sung God's praises with my heart. Day and night I remained under the sway of māyā and did whatever I liked. My ears did not listen to the Guru's instruction, and I remained entangled with other women. I slandered others everywhere and did not heed advice. I wasted my life due to my own deeds. All demerits are in me, says Nanak, but I have turned to you for refuge; save me, O' Lord.[150]
15. You have not appropriated the Guru's instruction, O' my mind. Nothing comes out of shaving the head or donning the saffron garb. Discarding the truth you are attached to falsehood and, thus, you have wasted your life. Every day you fill your belly through deceit and hypocrisy, and you sleep like a beast. Sold to māyā, you remain alien to the way of God's adoration. You have forgotten the jewel of nām in a mad pursuit of poison (māyā). Remaining indifferent to God and never remembering him, you have lived your life in vain. God is always forgiving, says Nanak, and man is always liable to go astray.[151]
16. Save my honour, O' Lord; the fear of Death fills my inside and I have taken refuge with you, the Ocean of Mercy. I am ignorant and greedy, and I am a great sinner, now at my wit's end. The fear of death does not leave me and this worry keeps my body aflame. I have wandered in all the ten directions in search of the means of liberation, unaware of the secret that the immaculate God is within me. I have no merit and no meditation or austerities to my credit, what should I do? I have sought refuge with you at last; give me, O' Lord, the gift of fearlessness (through liberation).[152]

17. Why do you go to the wilderness in search of God? The omnipresent is within you, detached at the same the time. Like fragrance in the flower and like the image in a mirror, God dwells in you; search for him within. The Guru has imparted this understanding that the same God who is outside everywhere is also within you. Without knowing yourself, says Nanak, the moss of illusion is not removed.[153]
18. God dwells in the man who feels no pain while actually in pain, who is not affected by ease, love, or fear; who regards gold as dust; who remains unaffected by praise or blame; who has no greed, attachment, or pride; who remains detached in joy and sorrow; who is indifferent to honour and dishonour; who renounces all hopes and desires for himself; and who is not touched by lust or anger. This way is recognized by the one to whom Guru is gracious. Nanak, he mingles with God like water with water.[154]
19. What should one do to appropriate the bhagtī of Ram and to get rid of the fear of Death? What deeds, what sort of knowledge, and what kind of dharam? What is the name on which one may meditate to swim across the ocean of life? In the Kaliyuga there is only one name, that of the Treasure of Grace, on which one may meditate to attain liberation. Even the Veda tells you that no other dharma is its equal. He who is called the Master of the world remains ever untouched by peace and suffering and he dwells within you, O' Nanak, like the image in a mirror.[155] Renounce pride, O' sādhs (Sikhs); always run away from lust, anger, and association with the evil-minded. He who is indifferent to comfort and pain, to honour and dishonour, and who is not affected by joy or sorrow in this world, knows the essence. He seeks no praise but shuns slander; he pursues the path of detachment. This game is hard O' Nanak, only a few learn it by turning to the Guru.[156]

Notes

1. Panjabi Manuscripts, MS 1192, Panjab University, Chandigarh, seen through the Librarian's courtesy.

2. Five *dohras* are counted among the shaloks of Guru Tegh Bahadur, and his shabads are in 15 Rāgs: *Gauṛī, Āsā, Devgandhārī, Bihāgaṛā, Sorath, Dhanāsarī, Todī, Tilang, Bilāval, Rāmkāli, Mārū, Basant, Sarang,* and *Jaijāvanti*. The last Rāg was his own contribution.

3. Puran Singh, 'The Life and Teachings of Sri Guru Tegh Bahadur, the Ninth King Spiritual', *The Panjab Past and Present*, vol. IX, pt 1 (April 1975), pp. 1–4.

4. Harbans Singh, *Guru Tegh Bahadur*, New Delhi: Sterling Publishers, 1982, p. 119.

5. For the life of Guru Tegh Bahadur, apart from Harbans Singh's work cited above, see Ganda Singh, 'Guru Tegh Bahadur', *The Panjab Past and Present*, vol. IX, pt 1 (April 1975), pp. i–xi; G.B. Singh, 'Sikh Relics in Eastern Bengal', ibid., pp. 82–102; Surya Kumar Bhuyan, 'Guru Tegh Bahadur in Assam', ibid., pp. 125–36; Fauja Singh, 'The Martyrdom of Guru Tegh Bahadur', ibid., pp. 137–57; Ganda Singh, 'The Martyrdom of Guru Tegh Bahadur', *The Panjab Past and Present*, vol. X, pt 1 (April 1976), pp. 191–210.

6. Sabinderjit Singh Sagar, *Hukamnamas of Guru Tegh Bahadur: A Historical Study*, Amritsar: Guru Nanak Dev University, 2002.

7. J.S. Grewal, 'Guru Gobind Singh: Life and Mission', *Journal of Punjab Studies*, vol. 15, nos 1 and 2 (Spring-Fall 2008), p. 5.

8. Sir Attar Singh, 'The Travels of Guru Tegh Bahadur and Guru Gobind Singh', *The Panjab Past and Present*, vol. IX, pt 1 (April 1975), pp. 17–81. See also, Tara Singh Narotam, 'Gurdwāre Nauvīn Pātshāhī' De', ibid., pp. 220–30. Exactly 100 Gurdwaras are listed in order of their association with the life of Guru Tegh Bahadur. Most of these Gurdwaras were in the Malwa region and Haryana; seventy-four of these were under 'Sikh' management, the remaining twenty-six were managed by Udasis (10), Nirmalas (7), Sodhis (3), and one each by Masands, Brahmans, Diwanas, Banias, Bhallas, and Nihangs, Some of the Gurdwaras were in Bengal and Assam. In the Punjab, most of the Gurdwaras were in the Amritsar area, and in Anandpur-Makhowal.

9. Apart from the later Sikh sources which refer to Kirpā Ram Datt, a Brahman of Mattan in Kashmir, who led a deputation of Brahmans to seek help from Guru Tegh Bahadur, the Persian sources refer to his popularity among the people.

10. This para is based on all the shabads of Guru Tegh Bahadur.

11. *Gauṛī* (7), *Ādi Srī Gurū Granth Sāhib* (SGGS), p. 220.

12. *Bihāgaṛā*, SGGS, p. 537.

13. *Sorath* (12), SGGS, p. 634.

14. *Gauṛī* (3), SGGS, p. 219.

15. *Sorath* (4), SGGS, p. 632.

16. *Gauṛī* (8), SGGS, p. 220; *Devgandhārī*, (3), SGGS, p. 536; *Sorath* (1), SGGS, p. 632; *Todī*, SGGS, p. 718; *Tilang* (1), SGGS, p. 729; *Tilang*, (2), SGGS, pp. 726–7.

17. *Sorath* (1, 6), SGGS, pp. 631–2.

18. *Gauṛī*, (3), SGGS, p. 219.

19. *Gauṛī* (8), SGGS, p. 220.

20. *Gauṛī* (9), SGGS, p. 220.

21. *Sorath* (11, 12), SGGS, pp. 633–4.

22. *Jaitsarī* (3), SGGS, p. 703.

23. *Bilāval* (2), SGGS, pp. 830–1.
24. *Bilāval* (3), SGGS, p. 831.
25. *Rāmkāli* (3), SGGS, p. 902.
26. *Basant Hindol* (3), SGGS, p. 1186.
27. *Sorath* (5), SGGS, p. 632.
28. *Sorath* (3), SGGS, p. 632.
29. *Sorath* (5), SGGS, p. 632.
30. *Bilāval* (2), SGGS, pp. 830–1.
31. *Bilāval* (3), SGGS, p. 831.
32. *Jayāvantī* (4), SGGS, pp. 1352–3.
33. *Sorath* (10), SGGS, p. 633.
34. *Sorath* (11), SGGS, pp. 633–4.
35. *Dhanāsari* (1), SGGS, p. 684.
36. *Dhanāsari* (4), SGGS, p. 685.
37. *Tilang* (3), SGGS, p. 727.
38. *Bilāval* (2), SGGS, pp. 830–1.
39. *Bilāval* (3), SGGS, p. 831.
40. *Mārū* (3), SGGS, p. 1008.
41. *Gauṛī* (2), SGGS, p. 219.
42. *Gauṛī* (5), SGGS, p. 219.
43. *Dhanāsarī* (2), SGGS, pp. 684–5.
44. *Basant Hindol* (3), SGGS, p. 1186.
45. *Sorath* (3), SGGS, p. 632.
46. *Gauṛī* (1, 2, 5), SGGS, p. 219; *Sorath* (7,8), pp. 632–3; *Rāmkālī* (2), p. 902; *Sārang* (2), p. 1231.
47. *Devgandhārī* (3), SGGS, p. 536.
48. *Gauṛī*, (1, 7, 8), SGGS, pp. 219–20; *Sorath* (2), pp. 631–2; *Dhanāsarī* (4), p. 685; *Jaitsarī* (2), p. 703; *Tilang* (1), p. 726; *Bilāval* (1, 2), pp. 830–1; *Rāmkalī* (1), pp. 901–2.
49. *Gauṛī* (6), SGGS, p. 220.
50. *Sorath* (11), SGGS, pp. 633–4.
51. *Gauṛī* (7), SGGS, p. 220; *Sārang* (3), p. 1231.
52. *Sorath* (3), SGGS, p. 632.
53. *Jaitsarī* (2), SGGS, p. 703.
54. *Dhanāsarī* (1), SGGS, p. 684.
55. *Basant Hindol* (1), SGGS, p. 1186.
56. *Gauṛī* (5), SGGS, p. 219; *Sorath* (4), p. 632; *Bilāval* (1), p. 830; *Rāmkalī* (1), pp. 901–2; *Mārū* (1), p. 1008.
57. *Gauṛī* (5), SGGS, p. 219.
58. *Gauṛī* (8), SGGS, p. 220.
59. *Sorath* (2), SGGS, pp. 631–2.
60. *Tilang* (1), SGGS, p. 726.
61. *Bilāval* (2), SGGS, pp. 830–1.
62. *Gauṛī* (1), SGGS, p. 219.
63. *Gauṛī* (6), SGGS, p. 220.

64. *Sorath* (5), SGGS, p. 632.
65. *Sorath* (11), SGGS, pp. 633–4.
66. *Dhanāsarī* (3), SGGS, p. 685.
67. *Gauṛī* (4), SGGS, p. 219; *Bihāgaṛā*, p. 537; *Sorath* (1), p. 631; *Dhanāsarī* (1, 3), pp. 684, 685; *Bilāval* (2), pp. 830–1; *Basat hindol* (2), p. 1186.
68. *Gauṛī* (7), SGGS, p. 220; *Bilāval* (2, 3), pp. 830–1.
69. *Gauṛī* (1), SGGS, p. 219.
70. *Gauṛī* (2, 3), SGGS, p. 219.
71. *Gauṛī* (4, 5), SGGS, p. 219.
72. *Gauṛī* (6, 7, 8), SGGS, p. 220.
73. *Sorath* (3), SGGS, p. 632.
74. *Sorath* (7), SGGS, pp. 632–3; *Sārang* (3), SGGS, p. 1231.
75. *Sorath* (10), SGGS, p. 633.
76. *Dhanāsarī* (2), SGGS, pp. 684–5.
77. *Todī*, SGGS, p. 718.
78. *Mārū* (2, 3), SGGS, p. 1008.
79. *Sārang* (3), SGGS, p. 1231.
80. *Devgandhārī* (2), SGGS, p. 536.
81. *Devgandhārī* (3), SGGS, p. 536; *Sorath* (2), SGGS, pp. 631–2.
82. *Sorath* (8), SGGS, p. 633.
83. *Sorath* (9), SGGS, p. 633.
84. *Sorath* (12), SGGS, p. 634; *Tilang* (2), SGGS, pp. 726–7.
85. *Basant Hindol* (4), SGGS, pp. 1186–7.
86. *Sārang* (1), SGGS, p. 1231.
87. *Sārang* (2), SGGS, p. 1231.
88. *Sārang* (3), SGGS, p. 1231.
89. *Jaijāvantī* (1), SGGS, p. 1352.
90. The Shaloks of Guru Tegh Bahadur are on pp. 1426–9 of SGGS. See Shalok, 26.
91. *Shalok*, 34.
92. *Shalok*, 37.
93. *Shalok*, 18.
94. *Shalok*, 19.
95. *Shalok*, 22.
96. *Shalok*, 17.
97. *Shalok*, 5.
98. *Shalok*, 23.
99. *Shalok*, 25.
100. *Shalok*, 32.
101. *Shalok*, 41.
102. *Shalok*, 42.
103. *Shalok*, 48.
104. *Shalok*, 49.
105. *Shalok*, 50.
106. *Shalok*, 3.

107. *Shalok*, 4.
108. *Shalok*, 8.
109. *Shalok*, 27.
110. *Shalok*, 35.
111. *Shalok*, 47.
112. *Shalok*, 1.
113. *Shalok*, 28.
114. *Shalok*, 29.
115. *Shalok*, 30.
116. *Shalok*, 31.
117. *Shalok*, 52.
118. *Shalok*, 57.
119. *Shalok*, 43.
120. *Shalok*, 21.
121. *Shalok*, 20.
122. *Shalok*, 44.
123. *Shalok*, 6.
124. *Shalok*, 8.
125. *Shalok*, 12.
126. *Shalok*, 35.
127. *Shalok*, 40.
128. *Shalok*, 55.
129. *Shalok*, 9.
130. *Shalok*, 13.
131. *Shalok*, 14.
132. *Shalok*, 16.
133. *Shalok*, 17.
134. *Shalok*, 51.
135. *Shalok*, 56.
136. *Srī Dasam Granth Sāhib*, eds, Rattan Singh Jaggi and Gursharan Kaur Jaggi, New Delhi: Gobind Sadan, 1999, vol. I, pp. 142–5.
137. *Rāg Bihāgaṛā*, SGGS, p. 537.
138. *Devgandhārī*, SGGS, p. 536.
139. Ibid.
140. *Todī*, SGGS, p. 718.
141. *Gauṛī*, SGGS, p. 219.
142. *Rāg Āsā*, SGGS, p. 411.
143. *Sorath*, SGGS, p. 632.
144. *Gauṛī*, SGGS, p. 219.
145. *Tilang*, SGGS, pp. 726–7.
146. *Rāg Jaijāvantī*, SGGS, p. 1352.
147. *Rāg Rāmkalī*, SGGS, pp. 901–2.
148. *Basant*, SGGS, p. 1186.
149. *Bilāval*, SGGS, pp. 830–1.
150. *Sarang*, SGGS, p. 1232.

151. *Sorath*, SGGS, p. 633.
152. *Jaitsarī*, SGGS, p. 703.
153. *Dhanāsarī*, SGGS, p. 684.
154. *Sorath*, SGGS, pp. 633–4.
155. *Sorath*, SGGS, p. 632.
156. *Gauṛī*, GGS, p. 219.

PART THREE

In Response to External Threat (1675–*c*.1708)

8

Declaration of 'Righteous War'

The *Bachittar Nātak*

Initially, *Bachittar Nātak* was the title given to a voluminous work which included *Chandī Charitras*, *Chaubīs Avtār*, *Brahma Avtār*, and *Rudra Avtār* as well as the autobiographical *Apnī Kathā*. These works cover more than 600 pages of the standard edition of the *Dasam Granth*. The *Apnī Kathā*, now entitled *Bachittar Nātak*, covers only forty-four pages in *Srī Dasam-Granth Sāhib* edited by Dr Ratan Singh Jaggi and Dr Gursharan Kaur Jaggi.[1] It is not a very long composition, with less than 1,000 lines. Highly significant in itself, it acquires added importance due to its intimate connection with the incarnation literature of all the three major Brahmanical traditions of India: the Vaishnava, the Shaiva, and the Shakta.

The *Bachittar Nātak* (*Apnī Kathā*) consists of fourteen chapters: the praise of Srī Kāl Jī; narrative of the Sodhi dynasty; the war between the descendants of Lav and Kush; the bestowal of rāj for the recitation of the Vedas; an account of the Pātshāhīs (from Guru Nanak to Guru Tegh Bahadur); command of Kāl to enter the world; the birth, rulership, and the battle of Bhangāṇī; the battle of Nadaun; the expedition of the Khānzāda and his retreat; the death of Husain, Kirpal, Himmat, and Sangatia; the battle with Jhujar Singh; the expedition of the Prince and the Ahadīs; and the protection of Sarb Kāl. If we set aside the formal division of these chapters we can see that the major themes of the *Bachittar Nātak* are (a) Guru Gobind Singh's conception of God, (b) his conception of religious dispensations before the time of Guru Nanak, (c) his view of and identification with the Sikh tradition, and (d) his view of his own role in history. With these concerns in mind we may turn to the contents of the *Bachittar Nātak*.

At the outset the author invokes the double-edged sword (*kharag*) with loving devotion. This sword is the slayer of the wicked and protector of the pious. It is symbolic of the power of the creator of the universe, the eternal light, the God of gods and the King of kings, the formless one who wields the sword. He has no form, no sign, no colour, and no garb. He does not take birth. He is free from fear. He was there in the past, he is there in the present, and he shall be there in the future. He alone is the creator and the destroyer. He is kind, compassionate, and graceful; he is fierce in battle. With the sword in hand, he destroys sin. He is the only refuge.

If all the continents turn into paper, all the seven seas turn into ink, and all the vegetation turns into pens, if Sarasvati herself utters the words, and Ganesh writes for ages, even so they cannot please the Time-Sword. Without prayerful surrender to the Lord there is no way.[2]

Guru Gobind asks his followers to take refuge at the feet of the Lord. He is not in stones. He is not be pleased by meditation in silence, by disowning pride, by adopting a garb, or by shaving the head; he is not pleased by wearing a rosary around the neck or by keeping matted hair on the head; to tell the truth, nothing avails but refuge with the compassionate Lord. He is found through love; the compassionate Lord is not moved by mere circumcision. Here, the Brahmanical, ascetical, and Islamic traditions are seen as futile.[3]

Given the monotheistic conception of God and rejection of the Brahmanical tradition, Guru Gobind could not be expected to subscribe to the idea of incarnation. Indeed, in the *Bachittar Nātak* itself there are intimations of his disapproval. God created millions of worms like Krishan; he created numerous Rams and destroyed them; many Muhammads appeared on the earth to leave it when their time came.[4] What is hammered here is the idea that the so-called *avtārs* and prophets were God's creatures, subject to death like all other human beings. The human incarnations of Vishnu, like Ram and Krishan, could not win against death; they were bound to fail. Bracketed with them are the *auliā* (friends of God), the *anbiā* (prophets), and the *ghauses* (mystics of the highest repurte).[5] Like all other gods and demons, the avtārs like Ram and Krishan died in the end. And so did Narsingh, Bāwan, and Machh.[6] God is the only refuge for all creatures, whether Ram or Krishan, the sun or the moon. The only entity that is not subject to death is God himself.[7] The author tells the devotees of Vishnu, Krishan, Ram, Brahma, Shiva, and Rahim, and millions of other gods, that their worship has been futile: they have no power to save their worshippers.[8] Not their past existence but their divinity is denied.

Guru Gobind elaborates the qualities of God. He is beyond praise and none can know his limits; he is God of gods and King of kings; he is kind to the lowly and gracious towards the poor. Through his grace the dumb can utter all the six Shāstras, the lame can climb the mountain, the blind can see, and the deaf can hear. Only he knows his greatness. The son can have no idea of the birth of his father. His subtle form cannot be described, but his manifestation in the universe can be seen. To manifest himself he created the universe from *Oankār*.[9]

Beginning with the mythical creation of the universe, and of the earth (*medhā*), the author states that *devtā* and *asur* are metaphors for the good and the evil. 'They who perform good deeds are called gods in the world and they who do evil deeds are known as demons'.[10]

Talking of the earliest rulers, the author comes to the Suryavanshi Raghu, Ajj, Dasrath, and Ram. Sita's sons Kush and Lav founded Kasur and Lahore in the Madar Des. Their descendants, Kalket and Kalrai, came into conflict, and the former ousted the latter from Lahore. Kalrai went to the country called Sanaud and married its princess. The son born to her was named Sodhi Rai. His descendants came to be known as Sodhis. They conquered many countries and ruled over them. They came into armed conflict with the descendants of Kush, and many of the latter were killed in fierce battles. Those who survived went to Kashi and mastered the four Vedas. They came to be known as Bedis. They were invited to Madar Des by a chief of the descendants of Lav. They recited all the four Vedas. The chief was immensely pleased and renounced rulership in favour of the Bedis. Pleased with the great gift, the Bedis vowed that they would return the compliment in the Kaliyuga when their descendant Nanak would raise the Sodhis to a prime position in the world.[11] This, obviously, is a reference to Guruship of the Sodhis as Guru Nanak's successors.

Earlier Dispensations and Guru Gobind Singh's Mission

For a proper appreciation of Guru Nanak and his successors it is necessary to keep in view the author's presentation of earlier dispensations. He was performing deep meditation at Hemkunt, which is adorned by seven summits and where the Pandus had performed penance. He was commanded by God to take birth in the Kaliyuga, spelling out the reason. God had created demons first; they became mad with the acquisition of power and ceased to worship the Supreme Being. They were destroyed by God, and gods were created in their place. But the gods too were enamoured of their power and claimed to be the Supreme God. Among them were Brahma, Vishnu, and Mahādev. Then God created the five elements, the sun, the moon, and Dharmraj. They began to introduce their own worship, asserting that there was no other Master. Created as witnesses, they claimed to be the Lord. Then God created great human beings; they began to be worshipped as idols of stone. The Siddhs were now created but they failed to find the Supreme Being. Whosoever gained some understanding started his own path. None followed the path of God.[12]

Several other categories of people are mentioned to hammer the point that none of them established the true worship of the Supreme Being. The Rāj Rishīs made their own smritīs current. They who followed them abandoned the worship of God (Brahm). But they who meditated on God (Har) did not follow the path of Smritīs. Brahma composed the four Vedas to induce people to follow the path of ritual. They who meditated on God abandoned the Vedas. They who discarded the Vedas and the semitic books (*kateb*) became the true devotees of God, and became one with him. All others remained entangled in transmigration. Dattatreya started his own panth; he allowed his nails to grow and wore matted hair; he did nothing for the worship of the Master. Gorakh Nath made mighty rulers his disciples; he pierced his ears and put on two earrings; he remained alien to the love of God. Ramanand adopted the garb of a bairāgī; he put a wooden necklace aroud his neck; he did not think of worship of the Master. Whosoever was created by God for his worship started his own panth. Muhammad was made the ruler of Arabia; he started his own panth; all the rulers practised circumcision; all were obliged to recite his name; none promulgated the True Name. All of them remained occupied with themselves and no one recognized the Supreme Lord.[13]

In the author's view, it was left for the Bedi Nanak to promulgate dharam in the Kaliyuga to show the right path to the pious. Whosoever followed his path was shorn of all sins; whosoever joined his panth, his sorrows and sins were removed by the Master. They were not plagued by hunger or sorrow, and they did not remain entangled in the net of transmigration. He gives peace to all the Sikhs and comes to their aid in all situations.

As the author elaborates, the legacy of Guru Nanak had come to Guru Gobind Singh through a line of successors in a manner that made them all one. Guru Nanak adopted the form of Angad and propagated dharam in the world. Then he became Amar Das, just as a lamp is lighted by another. The time had come to return the gift to the Sodhis: Ram Das became the Guru. The pious could see, but not the ignorant ones, that Guru Nanak, Guru Angad, Guru Amar Das, and Guru Ram Das were one and the same. Many regarded them as different but the discerning ones recognized them as one. They who recognized this attained liberation. Without this recognition none can attain liberation. Guru Ram Das gave Guruship to Arjun who appointed Hargobind as the Guru before his departure to the other world. Similarly, Guru Hargobind installed Har Rai in his place. Guru Har Rai was succeeded by Guru Har Krishan who was succeeded by Guru Tegh Bahadur. The idea of the unity of Guruship linked Guru Gobind Singh with Guru Nanak and made them one.[14]

Guru Gobind Singh was ordained by God to protect and propagate the panth (promulgated by Guru Nanak). The purpose of his birth was to spread (his) *dharam* with support from God himself. 'Whoever calls me God shall fall into the pit of hell. Regard me as his slave and entertain no doubt whatever about this. I am a slave of the Supreme Being come into the world to see his sport.'[15] In other words, he should not be regarded as an incarnation of God.

Guru Gobind Singh goes on to add that he would say without any reservation what God has told him. He would not be affected by any garb; he would not worship stones; he would meditate on the Name and realize God. He would not wear matted hair on his head, nor rings in his ears. He would do only what he has been commanded by God to do. He would meditate on the Name which is efficacious in all situations. He would recite nothing else; he would not establish any other path. He would meditate on the Name and find the light. He would not think of anything else; he would not utter any other name. Totally absorbed in God's name, he would not think of any other honour. Meditating on the supreme he would avoid all sins. Absorbed in his form, he would seek no other gift; uttering his Name, he would escape suffering.[16]

To leave the reader or the listener in no doubt, Guru Gobind Singh declares that he who meditates on the Name of the Supreme Being remains immune to sin or suffering, but he who meditates on any other entity would die in contention.

I have come into the world, sent by the Supreme Guru for the sake of *dharam*: 'to spread *dharam* everywhere and destroy the wicked and the enemy. For this purpose I have taken birth. Be assured in your mind O' *sādhūs* of the purpose for which I have taken birth: to propagate *dharam*, to raise the *sants*, and to root out the wicked.

Explaining further Guru Gobind observes that the so-called avtārs who had appeared in the world got their own name recited; they did not destroy the enemies of God; they did not put anyone on the path of dharam. They who became prophets and *ghauses* departed from the world talking about themselves. No one recognized the Great One; no one knew anything of right conduct and dharam. They who recite the *Qur'ān* or read the Purānas are pursuing a futile dharam; they would not be able to save themselves. They should recite the Name of the Supreme who alone can save in the end. All other dharams are futile: they serve no purpose. All the purposes are served by reciting the Name of the Supreme Being. Let everyone be assured that hypocrisy does not lead to God. 'What the Master told me I have told the world.' There is no difference between God and God's devotee; the ripple arises from water and is absorbed in water.[17]

The Martial Measures of Guru Gobind Singh

The chapter on the birth and the early life of Guru Gobind Singh is the shortest. It consists of just one *Chaupaī* of twelve short lines.

My father went towards the east. He visited *tīraths* of all kinds. When he reached Triveni he spent several days there, disbursing charities. I was conceived there; I was born in Patna. I was brought to Madar Des, and nurtured by various kinds of nurses. My body was protected in all possible ways. I was given all kinds of education. When I came to the age of understanding *dharam* and *karam* my father departed from this world.[18]

This brief statement indicates that Gobind was well cared for, and he was well educated and trained.

There is hardly any doubt that the martyrdom of Guru Tegh Bahadur was the most important event in the early life of Guru Gobind Singh. It is recorded in the *Bachittar Nātak*:

Fig. 8.1 Gurdwara at the place of the birth of Guru Gobind Singh at Patna in 1666

The Master saved their *tilak* and *janjū*. He did something great in the Kaliyuga. He did this for the sake of *sādhs*. He gave his head but betrayed no pain. He wrought this event for the sake of *dharam*. He gave up his head but not his conviction. The men of God are ashamed of theatrical demonstration (*nātak, chetak, kukāj*).

He shattered the pitcher of his body on the head of the master of Delhi and went to the abode of the Master of the universe. What Tegh Bahadur did was never done by anyone else. The whole world mourned Tegh Bahadur's departure. 'Hai, *hai*, *hai*' was the cry heard in this world, but 'jai, jai, jai' was the shout heard in the other.[19]

This is a very moving account of the martyrdom of Guru Tegh Bahadur. It is very significant too. There is a probable reference to Brahmans whose sacred mark and sacred thread were saved. The sacrifice was something extraordinary and unique. Knowing Guru Gobind Singh's view of the Brahmanical, ascetical, and Islamic traditions, it is impossible to maintain that he would appreciate sacrifice made for the protection of Hinduism or Hindus. The *sādhs* of Guru Gobind Singh would include the Sikhs and dharam would include the Sikh tradition. The principle for which Guru Tegh Bahadur sacrificed his life included the Sikhs as well as Brahmans and, by implication, it included other religious dispensations.

Whereas Aurangzeb stood for uniformity and coercion, Guru Tegh Bahadur stood for diversity and freedom. He sacrificed his life for the principle of the freedom of conscience. This was the criterion of Guru Nanak's denunciation of discrimination practised by the rulers of his time on the basis of religious differences. There is also the suggestion that wrangling on the basis of religious differences was appreciated neither by Guru Tegh Bahadur nor by Guru Gobind Singh. The responsibility for Guru Tegh Bahadur's martyrdom is squarely placed on Aurangzeb's head. What Guru Tegh Bahadur did was honourable in his own eyes and in the eyes of God. Guru Gobind Singh appreciates the stand taken by Guru Tegh Bahadur. The legacy of the Name was defended at the cost of life.

Guru Gobind Singh succeeded Guru Tegh Bahadur to promote the legacy of Guru Nanak and his successors. 'When *rāj* came to me I propogated *dharam* to the best of my capability'. At the same time he went out hunting in the forest, killing bears, *nīlgāos*, and antelopes. Then he had to leave his des (Makhowal and its environs); he went to Paonta on the bank of the Jamuna where he witnessed many a sport. He killed lions in large numbers, besides bears and *nīlgāos*. Without any apparent cause, Raja Fateh Shah attacked him at Paonta. The battle of Bhangāṇī is described with great gusto. The acts of the brave warriors on both sides are appreciated. Guru Gobind Singh's cousin Sango Shah, who died fighting in the battle, was given the title of 'the king of the battle' (Shah Sangram). Guru Gobind Singh personally participated in the battle at a critical juncture to change its course decisively in his favour. The victorious Guru returned to Kahlur and founded Anandpur (adjoining Makhowal). What happened at Anandpur was even more significant. The men who had not fought in the battle of Bhangāṇī were turned out of the town; those who had fought well were well rewarded. Many days passed in 'raising the *sants* and destroying the wicked'. The fools died the death of dogs.[20] There was no mercy for the traitors to the cause of Guru Gobind Singh.

A long time passed before Mian Khan came to Jammu (as its Mughal *faujdār*) and sent Alif Khan to (the Mughal post at) Nadaun (as his deputy). Alif Khan developed great animosity towards Raja Bhim Chand of Kahlur who approached Guru Gobind Singh for support, himself marching to fight against Alif Khan. Alif Khan fortified the hill top he was occupying. Bhim Chand was supported by Raja Raj Singh, Ram Singh,

Raja Sukhdev of Jasrota, and Prithi Chand Dadhwalia. Kirpal Chand (of Kangra) supported Alif Khan. Bhim Chand and his supporters failed in their assault. They held a consultation to which Guru Gobind Singh was also invited. A pitched battle was fought. Guru Gobind Singh shot one Raja with his musket but he was not killed. Then the Guru used his bow to shoot four arrows with his right hand and three with the left. By this time, the battle was coming to its end. Alif Khan fled the field, leaving all his goods behind. The allies were victorious. Guru Gobind Singh stayed on the bank of the river for eight days and saw all the palaces of Nadaun.[21]

Despite his success in the battle, Bhim Chand came to terms with the Mughal authorities. He did not need Guru Gobind Singh's support any more. Subduing Alsun on the way, the Guru returned to the comforts of Anandpur. Several years passed in punishing the thieves of the area. Dilawar Khan sent his son at the head of an expedition against Guru Gobind Singh. He decided to attack Anandpur at night but the defenders were alerted in time to be ready for meeting the attack. The Khānzāda retreated without a fight. It was due to God's grace that the fools failed to touch the Guru and took to heels.[22]

The Khānzāda ran to his father, but could not give a satisfactory explanation of his shameful retreat. Husaini was now keen to lead the expedition. He plundered villages of the hill chiefs and overpowered the Dadhwalia chief. He enslaved many Rajputs. He plundered the entire valley and no chief dared face him. In order to supply food to his own men he foolishly deprived the people of their food. Raja Gopal, the chief of Guler, and Ram Singh went to see him, but the slave was buffed with pride. They were willing to pay tribute but Husaini demanded more and more. They returned with their wealth towards their homes. The slave demanded ten thousand rupees, which obliged Raja Gopal to revolt. Kirpal Chand Katoch marched against him on behalf of the Mughals. Bhim Chand was also on their side. However, some of the hill chiefs and Guru Gobind Singh supported Raja Gopal. In the battle that followed, Kirpal Chand and Husain Khan were killed; the hill chiefs were victorious against the Mughals. Guru Gobind Singh did not take part in this battle but he had sent Sangatia with seven horsemen to fight in support of Raja Gopal. They all died fighting. When another sevak of Guru Gobind Singh heard of this, he too died fighting. Guru Gobind Singh had no doubt that Husain Khan had been sent against him. But God ensured his protection and 'the cloud of iron burst elsewhere'.[23]

The death of Turk Sardars in the battle infuriated Dilawar Khan. He dispatched a contingent of cavalry against the rebels. The hill chiefs were divided in their support, the Chandels supporting one side and the Jaswals supporting the other. Jujhar Singh, the leader on the Mughal side, killed many warriors but eventually died fighting. Aurangzeb decided to send his son to Madar Des. Out of fear many of the hill chiefs sought safety in the high mountains. Not knowing the mysterious ways of God, many people warned Guru Gobind Singh too of the danger. Many people abandoned him to seek safety in the mountains. A special messenger (*ahadī*) named Mirza Beg, sent by Aurangzeb, destroyed the homes of those who had turned away from the Guru. The Sikhs who stayed with the Guru remained safe. Aurangzeb sent four more ahadīs; they too destroyed the homes of the remaining renegades. Ironically, they had never fought in any battle and they had never earned the merit of charity; even their villages were obscure, but they were discovered by death. The scene of their humiliation was witnessed by the sants (Sikhs). Protected by the Lord himself, the sants suffered no harm.[24]

The renegades are strongly denounced in the *Bachittar Nātak*. Guru Gobind says that 'They who turn away from their Guru their homes are destroyed literally in this world and metaphorically in the next. They are laughed at here and find no place in the next world. All their wishes remain unfulfilled. They who abandon the service of the sants (Sikhs) suffer from hunger and sorrow; their needs are not met in the world and they fall into the pit of hell. They who turn away from the path of the Guru, their faces are blackened in this world and the next. Their sons and grandsons do not flourish; they die as a source of suffering for their parents. They who oppose the Guru die the death of a dog. They regret eternally in the pit of hell. The successors of Baba Nanak and the successors of Babur were established by God, the former as the kings of dharam (*dīn*) and the latter as temporal lords. They who do not pay allegiance to the house of Baba Nanak remain subject to the house of Babur; they are punished and their houses are plundered. Shorn of their means of subsistence, they who turn away from the Guru turn to the Sikhs to beg; the Sikhs who help the renegades are plundered by the *mlechh*. When they are left with no means they turn to the Guru again. When they come for the Guru's darshan he does not see them. They return without grace and nothing turns out to be right for them. Without a place at the Guru's door they find no place in God's court; they lose both the places. They who remain attached to the Guru's feet, they face no hardness. They remain untouched by sin and suffering; they have *riddhī* and *siddhī* (wealth and power). The mlechh fail to touch them and they succeed in all their ventures.[25]

Divine protection for the Guru and his Sikhs is emphatically underscored in the *Bachittar Nātak*. The enemy cannot harm those who are protected by the Friend; the enemy cannot touch even their shadow, and all their hostile efforts are futile. He who takes refuge with the *sādhūs* (Sikhs) does not come to any harm; his enemies are destroyed and he remains safe like the tongue against the teeth. God raises all the sādhs and destroys their enemies. He revealed his wonderous state to the *bhagats* and saved them in all critical situations. He protected the sants in all crises and removed the enemies like the thorns in their path. 'God has helped me as his slave and saved me with his hands'. God showed his grace and 'gave me iron-like protection for all the ages'. 'With God's grace over my head. I have become fearless and I walk in majesty like a king'.[26]

Dharam Juddh: Incarnations Re-interpreted

Guru Gobind Singh's conception of God is uncompromisingly monotheistic, with no room for the idea of incarnation. The foremost duty of God's creatures is his worship, without any intermediary. The mythical and historical figures in the past failed to establish worship of the Supreme Being. This was as true of the Islamic tradition as of the Indian, whether Vaishnava, Shaiva, or Shakta. The true path was laid down by Guru Nanak, and his legacy was carried forward by his successors. Guru Gobind Singh identifies himself with them completely. He appreciates the sacrifice made for the tradition promulgated for the redemption of the Kaliyuga. He has the divine sanction for its protection and promotion. To destroy its enemies is a corollary of its defence. The use of physical force is made legitimate. Guru Gobind Singh fights battles and demonstrates his martial prowess. His safety is ensured by the divine sanction for his mission. They who join him in the righteous cause also remain safe. If they suffer they find honour in the court of God as his true devotees. The Guru and the Sikhs are thus pursuing a path ordained by God.

The *Bachittar Nātak* does not record any appreciation for avtārs. Guru Gobind Singh is keen to hammer the point that he is a servant or slave (das) of the Supreme Being. Therefore, it should be interesting to study the essential character of 'incarnation' literature included in the *Dasam Granth*, that is, the *Chaubīs Avtār*, *Brahma Avtār*, *Rudra Avtār*, and the three versions related to the Goddess. This literature appears to present a comparison and a contrast with the mission of Guru Gobind Singh in the *Bachittar Nātak*.

The twenty-four avtārs of Vishnu taken up in the *Chaubīs Avtār* are Machh, Kachh, Nar, Narayan, Mahāmohni, Baraha, Narsingh, Bavan, Parasram, Brahma, Rudra, Jallandhar, Vishnu, the slayer of Madhu and Kaitabh, Arhant, Manu, Dhanvantri, Suraj, Chandar, Ram, Krishan, Nar, Baudh, and Nihkalanki. The account of Krishan is the longest, followed at a distance by that of Ram, and Nihkalanki.

Before taking up the brief account of Machh, the author talks of the Supreme Being. Whenever the people of the earth are oppressed by evil-doers, God creates avtārs to destroy them. The avtārs themselves are subject to death. God becomes unhappy to see the sants suffering; he shows his grace to them through protection. God is not pleased with *jantar*, *mantar*, or *tantar*, or with any garb (*bhekh*). Some visit *maṛhīs* and some visit graves; by neither of these practices is found God. Both (Hindus and Muslims) are entangled in wrangling but the Master is not affected. He who casts off illusion, for him there is no difference between Hindu and Turk. They who are dyed in the love of the One, dance to him with abandon. They who recognize the One Primal Lord do not think of another. The sādh who is devoted to the Name does not remain concealed. He is distinct from those who deceive and plunder the world through their external garb, like the Jogīs and sanyāsīs, and the Musalmans. They who are devoted to the One practise no hypocrisy. 'They give up their head but not their conviction'. The same light is in all but the forms are different and distinct. People remain entangled in the outward form and fail to find the one who is in every form and yet separate. He creates all forms and destroys them. The blame comes to them and he remains free from all blame.[27]

The *Krishan Avtār* was completed at Paonta in 1688, the year of the battle of Bhangāṇī. It was based on the *Bhagavata Purāṇa*. However, the philosophic expositions are virtually omitted, like the minor episodes. The major difference in the original and the adaptation lies in the fact that Krishan is depicted as a great warrior in the *Krishan Avtār*. At the end of the *Krishan Avtār*, the author says that he has rendered the tenth book of the *Bhagavata* into the vernacular (*bhākhā*) 'with no other desire than that of inspiring *dharam juddh*'. Worthy of great praise in this world are they who utter the Name of Har from their lips and cherish the intent of *juddh* in their hearts.[28] Before 1688, thus, Guru Gobind Singh was preoccupied with the idea of a struggle in the way of righteousness (*dharam-yuddh*). Krishan's role in the world was seen in this light.

At the end of *Rām Avtār*, the author says: 'Ever since I have caught hold of your feet, I have not looked upon another. Many talk of the Purāṇ and the *Qur'ān*, and of Rām and Rahīm, but I do not believe in them. The Smritīs, Shāstras and Vedas talk of many different things but not for me'. The work ends with the couplet: 'Forsaking all other doors I have come to your door. It is for you to protect the honour of one who has sought refuge with you; Gobind is your slave'.[29] Completed in 1698, the *Rām Avtār* was based largely on Balmiki's *Ramāyaṇa*. However, the battle of Lav and Kush against the forces of Ram, which is not there in the *Ramāyaṇa*, is movingly described in some detail. The objective of the work is to present Ram as a great warrior who destroys all his enemies. Again, the inspiration for dharam juddh is the primary purpose.

The *Nihkalankī Avtār* is not based on the *Kālkī Purāṇa*. If there is anything common in the two it is the purpose of Kalki to conquer the whole world, to destroy all sin, and to establish dharam all afresh. However, he becomes oppressive in the end and is killed by Mir Mehdi. The whole tradition of incarnation, or avtarhood, is virtually undermined. Mir Mehdi, in turn, becomes haughty and overbearing and he too is killed. Their only redeeming feature is their martial prowess. The narrative being placed in the future, its imaginary character gets underscored.[30]

The avtārs of Brahma are seven in all: Balmiki, Kasp, Sukr, Baches, Bias, Shastrodharak, and Kalidas. At the back of these incarnations was Brahma's pride. He had composed or created the Vedas on the advice of the Supreme Being but he became haughtily proud. He was sent to the earth. He served the Supreme Being for millions of years to please him. The purpose of his seven incarnations was his own redemption. Brahma was redeemed only through his seven incarnations.[31] The Supreme Being also told Brahma that he was not different from Vishnu and, therefore, should celebrate the exploits of Vishnu's incarnation. Thus, at the centre of everything is the Supreme Being. Brahma and Vishnu remain totally subordinate to him as his creation. There is no other God and the Name of the Supreme Being alone is efficacious in the Kaliyuga.[32]

Like Brahma, Rudra's incarnations were also due to his great pride. He was so proud of the power obtained through austerities that he forgot the Supreme Being and regarded none as his equal.[33] He was sent to the earth as Datt who adopted twenty-four Gurus to be redeemed. Without recognizing the One Supreme Being and reciting the One Name, no wish can be fulfilled.[34] The second incarnation of Rudra was Paras Nath. He acquires great power and learning by pleasing Bhavani. No one is his equal in the world. However, all this does not satisfy him. Towards the end he is told that all jantars and mantars are futile. Nothing is of any avail except the One Lord and the Name.[35] Paras Nath cremates his body on a huge pyre that keeps burning for years.[36]

The first *Chandī Charitra* opens with an invocation to God who is the Primal Being, who is not bound by any limits, who is beyond description, who is infinite, who is not subject to death, who has no form, who cannot be seen, and who cannot be destroyed; he has created Shiv-Shakti, the four Vedas, the three qualities of being (*rajo*, *tamo*, and *sato*), and he is pervasive in the three worlds; he has created day and night, the lamps like the sun and the moon, and the whole universe from five elements; he has created and increased enmity between gods and demons and he looks on their battles as a sport.[37] This *Chandī Charitra* is based on the 'Durga Saptshati' which occurs in the *Markendya Purāṇa*. However, there is abbreviation, elaboration, or variation in the treatment of themes. The emphasis is on the depiction of the scenes of battle in familiar terms and the martial prowess of Durga who destroys the mightiest of the demons. At the end of this work is the well-known prayer for the boon of victory through a fearless fight or death in the field of battle.[38] This is not a part of the original account in the *Markendya Purāṇa*.

The second *Chandī Charitra* is shorter than the first, with a longer description of the battles than what is there in the *Markendya Purāṇa*. What is highlighted in this version is the image of the Goddess as the destroyer of demons and the protector of the sādhs. These aspects are highlighted even more in *Vār Durgā Kī* which is also known as *Chandī dī Vār* and *Vār Srī Bhagautī Jī Kī*. Written in the Punjabi language, this Vār portrays the destructive and protective aspects of the Goddess much more effectively and economically than the other two versions. It is also clear that she is not the Supreme Deity.

> You who created the *khandā* first and then the universe, who created Brahma, Bishan and Mahesh for displaying your power, who created rivers, mountains

and the earth to set the sky over it without any pillars, who created demons and gods with enmity between them—you yourself created Durga to destroy the demons. Receiving the power from you did Ram pierce Ravan with arrows; receiving power from you did Krishan catch Kans by the hair to dash him to the ground.[39]

Bhagautī symbolizes the power of God. Therefore, the author highlights that Guru Gobind Singh meditates on Bhagautī first and then on Guru Nanak, Guru Angad, Guru Amar Das, and Guru Ram Das who come to his aid. He meditates on Guru Arjan, Guru Hargobind, Guru Har Rai, and on Guru Har Krishan whose sight removes all suffering. He meditates on Guru Tegh Bahadur who is the source of all the nine treasures and who helps in all situations.[40] Significantly, the chaupaī that heads *Vār Durgā Kī* also heads the formal Sikh prayer (Ardās). In any case, Durga is God's creation and not the Supreme Deity of the Shakta tradition. Her status is no different from that of Vishnu, Brahma, or Rudra.

One common focus of much of this incarnation literature is fierce fight, with all kinds of weapons, generally between the forces of good and evil; martial prowess displayed in destroying the evil and protecting the good is highly appreciated, justifying in fact the use of physical force against the oppressors. What is deprecated in the protagonists is pride, arising out of their power or their success, so much so that they became oblivious of God and his supreme power. The avtārs of Brahma and Rudra in particular come into the world as a place of penance for the sake of redemption. Guru Gobind Singh's position in the *Bachittar Nātak* is similar to those of the avtārs: he too is commanded by God to come into the world. The purpose of his birth is to protect and promote the dharam promulgated by Guru Nanak as the most efficacious if not the only valid path to liberation. Those who are hostile to this dispensation represent the enemy and they have to be destroyed or subdued with physical force. Guru Gobind Singh asserts that he is God's servant. His cause is both religious and political: it is *dharam* juddh. The *Bachittar Nātak* can be appreciated as an open declaration of war in the right cause. It is a declaration of dharam-yudh.

Notes

1. *Srī Dasam-Granth Sāhib*, eds, Rattan Singh Jaggi and Gursharan Kaur Jaggi, New Delhi: Gobind Sadan, 1999, vol. I, pp. 104–81. The text and its paraphrase are given on pages facing each other.

2. Ibid., p. 124.
3. Ibid., pp. 122, 124.
4. Ibid., p. 108.
5. Ibid., pp. 108, 110.
6. Ibid., p. 116.
7. Ibid., p. 118.
8. Ibid., p. 122.
9. Ibid., pp. 124, 126.
10. Ibid., p. 126.
11. Ibid., pp. 126–40.
12. Ibid., pp. 144, 146.
13. Ibid., pp. 146, 148.
14. Ibid., pp. 142, 144.
15. Ibid., pp. 148, 150.
16. Ibid., p. 150.
17. Ibid., pp. 152, 154.
18. Ibid., p. 156.
19. Ibid., p. 144.
20. Ibid., pp. 156, 158, 160, 162.
21. Ibid., pp. 164, 166.
22. Ibid., pp. 168, 170.
23. Ibid., pp. 170–82.
24. Ibid., pp. 184, 186, 188.
25. Ibid., p. 186.
26. Ibid., pp. 188, 190.
27. Ibid., pp. 412, 414, 416, 418.
28. Ibid., vol. II, p. 792.
29. Ibid., vol. I, p. 682.
30. Ibid., vol. I, p. 52; vol. III, pp. 110, 112.
31. Ibid., vol. III, p. 172.
32. Ibid., vol. I, p. 53; vol III, p. 114.
33. Ibid., vol. III, p. 184.
34. Ibid., vol. III, p. 370.
35. Ibid., vol. III, p. 376.
36. Ibid., vol. III, p. 380.
37. Ibid., vol. I, p. 192.
38. Ibid., vol. I, p. 258.
39. Ibid., vol. I, p. 314.
40. Ibid., vol. I, p. 314.

9

Triumph of the Khalsa

The *Vār Bhagautī* of 'Gurdas'

The *Vār Bhagautī*

The last composition in the *Vārān Bhai Gurdas* is entitled *Rāmkalī Vār Pātshāhī Dasvīn Kī*. Its author in the text is 'Gurdas' who refers to his work as *Vār Bhagautī*. The editor notes that this work is also known as *Vār Srī Bhagautī Jī Kī Pātshāhī 10*. The association of the Vār with Guru Gobind Singh is interesting. In some manuscripts there is a *dohrā* at the end that mentions 'Gurdas Singh' as the author of this Vār. The editor also notes that a copy of the *Sarab Loh Granth* contained the dohrā which states that 'Gurdas Singh' completed this work in 1700 (Sammat 1757). This would place the Vār in the time of Guru Gobind Singh.[1]

The editor goes on to argue, however, that the Vār was written much later than 1700. In the seventh line of its pauṛī 19 occurs the words '*yeh bārāh sadī nabeṛ ke Gur fateh bulāe*'. These words suggest that this *Vār* was composed after 1787 (AH 1200).[2] Later in the Vār in *pauṛī* 21, there is a reference to Auranga (Aurangzeb) who was responsible for the destruction of his own family due to his enmity towards Guru Har Krishan. The editor thinks that this statement too indicates that the Vār was composed at a time after the family (*vansh*) of Aurangzeb had been destroyed.[3] However, the bulk of the contents of the *Vār* does not appear to fit into the context of the late eighteenth century. In a recent article, Gurinder Singh Mann suggests the possibility of the Vār of Gurdas having been written at the court of Guru Gobind Singh who is referred to in the title of the Vār as the Tenth King (*dasvīn* Pātshāhī).[4]

A composition known as *Ugradantī*, included in a composite manuscript at Patna dated 1698, contains in its title '*Srī Mukhvāk Pātshāhī 10*'.

This work is an expression of praise for the goddess and invokes her for fulfilment of wishes. The epithets used for the goddess are Bhavani, Durga, and Bhagautī, among others. But she is not supreme. She herself worships *Niranjan Purkh* and *Akāl*; she meditates on *Niranjan Purkh* and grants the boon of meditating on the True Guru (Satgurū).[5]

The contents of the composition are important for our present purpose. The 'Hindus' and 'Turks' are seen as purveyors of empty ritual practices and deceptive knowledge. There is a clear disdain for the *Vedas*, the *Purāṇas*, the *Shāstras*, and the *Qur'ān*. Equally futile are the call of prayer (*azān*), the prayer (*salāt*), the circumcision (*sunnat*), and the worship of pirs centred around their tombs (*dargahs*). The destruction of both these panths is prayed for. The Khalsa Panth, as the *tīsar* panth, may then be proclaimed in the world to establish peace and justice. The entire Panth is the Khalsa, the Singhs called to battle are a part of the Panth. The tīsar panth is identified as the victorious political successor to the sovereign rule established by the 'Turks'.[6] Sovereignty of the third panth and liberation for its members, is the concern of the author of the *Ugradantī*.

Sovereignty of the Khalsa Panth and liberation for individuals go together in the *Vār Bhagautī* of Gurdas. It is not a piece of secular literature for him. Its reading could lead to liberation (*amrāpad*), remove all sorrows and bestow bliss (*ānand*). One could see God within oneself and all one's wishes could be fulfilled. He who recites the Vār to others would attain muktī. All his sins would be washed away and Dharmraj (Jamdharm) would not ask him to account for his deeds. At the end, the *Vār* is called '*mahā punīt*'. It washes away all sins by generating trust (*partīt*). He who loves this Vār would have all his wishes fulfilled. All his sorrows are removed and he enjoys peace and happiness. He who recites the Vār day and night would go to the divine court (Har Darbār).[7]

Two refrains divide the Vār formally into two unequal parts. In the first part of twenty pauṛīs the refrain used is '*Vāh vāh Gobind Singh āpe gur-chelā;* in the second part of eight pauṛīs it is '*Ion kar hai Gurdas pukārā, hae satgur muhe lehu ubārā*'. The first six pauṛīs of the first part celebrate the Panth. Praises of God are sung in the eight pauṛīs that follow. The six pauṛīs then celebrate the triumph of the Khalsa. The last eight lines of the twentieth pauṛī relate to the author's view of his Vār already noticed. Similarly, the last pauṛī of the Vār is about the Vār itself.

Of the remaining seven pauṛīs of the second part, three relate to the Gurus and four to God. Thus, the author dwells on three major themes: God, the Gurus, and the Sangat or the Panth.

God and His Attributes

The pauṛīs in *Vār Bhagauti* relating to God depict his essential attributes. God himself is onkār and ākār (transcendent and immanent), who is and shall be. He is the creator who can be known through the shabad of the Guru. He can destroy and create in a trice without the fear of anyone. The whole world is his sport (khel). He is the ocean of virtues. He is the Primal Being (*ād purkh*), the fearless (anbhai), and the boundless preceptor (gurū) whose limits cannot be known. His depth cannot be fathomed. He is everlasting, and gives without asking. His is the true name (sat-nām). He is indestructible (*abnāsī*). He is the one who has appeared in many forms. He is within everyone. He destroys sin (*aghnāsī*). He cannot be deceived. The incomprehensible, immortal, unchangeable God can be known through the shabad of the Guru. He is omnipresent (*sarab-biāpī*) and yet detached (*alep*). Māyā does not affect him.[8] This conception of God is characteristically Sikh.

Indeed, God is formless (nirankār). He is devoid of enmity (nirvair). He is the destroyer of sorrow (dukh-*dalan*, dukh-*bhanjan*). He is the kind master who bestows all kinds of gifts. He is perfect (*puran*), the supreme God (*parmeshar*), the remover of sins (*patit-pāwan*), and the knower of innermost thoughts (*antar-jātā*). He is all-wise (*dānā*) and all-seeing (*bīnā*). He is the forgiver (*bakhsind*), himself the father and the mother. He himself is the male and the female. He is the destroyer of fear (bhai-*bhanjan*, bhai-*nāsan*). He is beautiful in form. He is the bestower of liberation (*mukand*). He himself is the one who leads to union (jogī, *sanjogī*). He is the only protector (*rakhwālā*). He is merciful (*rahīm*). Whatever he wills comes to pass. He is the true merchant (who takes account from his agents). He is the king (pātshāh) who looks after all (his subjects). He is ever-present (*sadā hajūrā*).[9] All these attributes of God in the *Vār* come from the Gurbāṇī, including the compositions of Guru Gobind Singh.

God is the only object of worship. By serving him in the present age (*kalīkāl*), all sorrows are removed. By serving the True Master (*sachchā sāhib*), all one's wishes are fulfilled. Meditation on the Name is the most efficacious path to liberation. Birth as a human being is the precious opportunity to attain liberation. One should worship God, the destroyer of fear (bhai *taras nās*). Liberation depends on God's grace. Gurdas offers a fervent prayer to God in the second part of the Vār. The refrain itself is indicative of the mood: 'lead me to liberation O True Guru'. Even Brahma, Vishnu and Shiva cannot know God (without his grace). 'We are full of lust, anger and falsehood. You are the forgiver and the redeemer'. There is no one else who can lead us to liberation. God's hukam covers the earth and the waters. 'One can swim across the ocean of life only by worshipping him'. The only way to liberation (muktī) is the worship of the one True Lord. 'The humble Gurdas is your devotee. His life has become easy by reciting your Name. Forgive all his sins and omissions and accept him as your slave'.[10]

God is the only truth (*sachch*). His throne is true (sachchā). He is the true master (sachchā sāhib). He is the true merchant (sachchā *vāpārī*). The worldly occupations are all false by contrast. God is the true Guru (satgur, satgur sachchā). He is the object of praise (Vāhegurū). Devotion is to be addressed to the Guru. Gur-bhagtī here is a synonym for Har-bhagtī. The True Name (satnām) is bestowed by God. The Name is priceless. The Name is the name of God (Har-*nām*). As we noticed earlier, God is known through the shabad of the Guru. This statement can refer to divine self-revelation as shabad and also to the shabad of the Gurus, or Gurbāṇī. There is a direct reference to the shabad contained in the Granth. The word nadar is not used, but the idea of God's grace is emphasized by the attribute of rahīm. The word *kirpā* (kindness, mercy) is used in connection with the attainment of liberation.[11]

The idea of grace is closely allied with God's hukam. Since God is all powerful and nothing happens without his will, the way to liberation lies in his grace alone. In other words, grace is an expression of God's will. Gurdas emphasizes the importance of hukam as comprehending grace. In the twenty-seventh pauṛī of his Vār he dwells on both kirpā and hukam. It was God's hukam that through his grace Gurdas should write his Vār. Not even a leaf can move without God's hukam. Only that happens which he commands. All creation is subject to his hukam. Only he who recognizes his hukam can attain liberation. Not only the sun and the moon, but also Brahma, Vishnu, and Mahesh are subject to God's hukam. All cherish the dust of his feet. The earth and the sky are subject to God's hukam, and so is each breath and every morsel. No one is born or dies without his hukam. He who recognizes his hukam acquires stability. 'That is why Gurdas prays aloud: save me O True Guru'.[12] The theology of the Vār, thus, is the same as that of the Gurus from Guru Nanak to Guru Gobind Singh.

The Ten Gurus

Gurdas refers to Guru Nanak at several places in the Vār. At one place, he is simply Nanak. At another, he is Guru Nanak. He does not stand alone. He is at the head of a line of ten Gurus. He is not God but he is closely allied with divinity. His position as the true Guru on the earth assimilates him to the True Guru, that is, God. A new dispensation was initiated by 'Har Satgur Nanak'. He meditated on the Name and worshipped the Creator. By promulgating the path of 'devotion to God' (Har-bhagtī) he saved the earth, and the whole of mankind, in accordance with the command of the ineffable (alakh) and the infinite (*apārā*). All things come to a happy end by serving Guru Nanak. He enabled Guru Angad to recognize God. The second mahal, Guru Angad, sang the praises of God. The third mahal, Guru Amar Das, realized God within himself by serving the true Guru (Angad). The fourth manifestation (*pargāsā*), Guru Ram Das, dedicated himself to God. The fifth, Guru Arjan, compiled a *Granth* of authenticated shabad. The recitation of this Granth was made current so that the whole world was redeemed by reciting the Name day and night.[13]

The sixth *avtār*, Guru Hargobind, held the sword and vanquished many a foe. He gave anxious moments to the Mughals who had started oppressing the devotees of God. The seventh mahal, Guru Har Rai, practised deep and long meditation so as to gather all power unto himself, but without revealing the fact to others. He strengthened the godly side. Guru Har Krishan reached Delhi to give up his life. He adopted the form of a boy to highlight the injustice of the Mughals: his death brought great discredit to them. He was received with honour in the divine court. Aurangzeb, who had shown hostility towards the Guru, ensured the end of his own family; incurring sins, they all went to hell. Guru Tegh Bahadur gave his head to stabilize the world. He did not reveal his power and the Mughals were deceived. He reached the divine court in accordance with God's will. The Mughals incurred blame, which became the cause of their downfall. Thus, the nine mahals adopted the way of devotion to defy and defeat the Mughals. The shouts of victory were heard by the whole world.[14]

Guru Gobind Singh, the tenth avtār, instituted the Khalsa to annihilate the Turks and to make the whole earth a garden of flowers (*gulzār*). None could withstand the Singh warriors. Their victory removed all sorrows and made the worship of Immortal God secure. The followers of the path of devotion started by Guru Nanak were free to pursue it without hindrance.[15] We can see that Gurdas makes no difference between Guru Nanak and his successors. The unity of the Gurus is reinforced by using mahal, pargāsa, and avtār as synonyms. Each carried forward the work of Guru Nanak. The tenth avtār enabled the followers of his predecessors to safeguard their cherished tradition against oppression and external interference. Gurdas does not see any difference between the followers of Guru Nanak and Guru Gobind Singh, between the Sikh and the Singh. In a very real sense they form one and the same entity.

The Khalsa as the Third Panth

The first six pauṛīs of the Vār can be appreciated in this perspective. The true congregation (sat-sangat *melā*) was established by God through Guru Nanak. The members of this congregation were invited by Guru Gobind Singh to taste baptism of the double-edged sword. In this way 'Gur-sangat' was made Khalsa. 'Praise be to Gobind Singh who himself is the Guru and the disciple'. The central point of the institution of the Khalsa for Gurdas is the fact that Guru Gobind Singh accepted *pahul* from the Khalsa, assuming the position of a disciple. By implication, the Khalsa were at par with the Guru. His true injunction must be heard by all who are dear to the Guru; join the true congregation (sat-sangat). They who forget the master find no place in this sangat. They who turn to the Guru, their foreheads shine when they reach the true court. Remember 'Har-Gur-Gobind' in the ambrosial hours. The five adversaries (*kām, krodh, lobh, moh, hankār*) are subdued in the sangat. Only the self-centred (*manmukh*) remain in misery and sorrow.[16]

Gurdas contrasts the manmukh with the Gurmukh, as it is done in Gurbāṇī. It is important to remember, however, that the Gurmukh of the Vār is the Khalsa. The whole creation suffers from haumai but they who are enabled to recognize God's hukam become Gurmukh. Others are misled to remain affiliated to other than God. The gift of the Name is bestowed by God through his grace. The recipients of his grace are Gurmukhs. Their life comes to fruition while the manmukh suffers the sorrow of rebirth. Only the fortunate ones turn to Gurbāṇī. They are Gurmukh. They are comparable with the woman who has a good husband, while the manmukh is like the woman abandoned by her husband. The Gurmukh is a bright swan and the manmukh, a crow. The Gurmukh meets God and the manmukh wanders in transmigration. True is the Master, true his command, and true is Gurbāṇī. They who serve the True Guru receive peace and bliss. The manmukh suffers in the divine court, like sesame seeds in the oil-press. The Gurmukh is found in the true congregation (sat-sangat) where the praises of God are sung and truth is disbursed. He stands distinguished from the manmukh in the true court where true justice is dispensed.[17] The refrain of these pauṛīs reinforces the impression that whatever was true of the Sikh-Sangat is true of the Khalsa-Sangat.

Guru Gobind Singh became manifest (*pragtio*) as the tenth avtār. He worshipped God and started the Khalsa Panth. With the *kesh* on their heads and the sword in their hands the Khalsa vanquished the enemy. They wore the drawers (*kachh*) of restraint and took up arms. They proclaimed the victory (*fateh*) of the Guru and won the field. They annihilated the demon-like enemies. The worship of God was made manifest in the world. Thus rose the Singh warriors in their blue clothes. They proclaimed the Name (Har-nām) by destroying the wicked Turks. No one could withstand them; mighty leaders (*sardārs*) took to their heels; the rulers (*rāje, shāh*) and their nobles (*amīrs*) were reduced to dust. The mountains trembled and the earth shook. People abandoned their homes and the world suffered misery in the clash. 'There is no one except the True Guru who puts an end to fear' (bhai *kāṭanhārā*). No one could stand against the might of the Khalsa. 'Praise be to Gobind Singh who is at once the Guru and the disciple'.[18]

The Khalsa was instituted neither in response to any exigency nor with the idea of capturing political power as an end itself. In accordance with the hukam of Gurbar-Akāl came intuitive understanding and the Khalsa was created in a perfect manly form. When the Singhs rose with a roar, the world was frightened. They killed the sultāns, and the pīrs concealed themselves. The Turks, the Muslims, and all things Islamic lost their former dominance: the *Qur'ān* and the *sharī'at*; the mosque, the prayer, and the call to prayer; the kalmā and the sunnat (circumcision); the qāzī

Fig. 9.1 Takht Kesgarh Sahib at Anandpur, the place where Guru Gobind Singh instituted the Khalsa through baptism of the double-edged sword in 1699

and the mullā; the *fatihā*, the *durūd* (prayers) and the *zikr*; the pīrs and their *mazārs* (mausoleum). The religion and the *'ummat* of Mahāmmad were overshadowed by 'the third religion' (tīsar *mazhab*) and 'the third *panth*' of the Khalsa. The third mazhab was different and distinct from the Indic (*hindak*) tradition represented by the Vedas, the Purāṇas, the Shāstras, the temples and the idols of stone, the jagg and the hom, the Brahman, the Pandit, and the Jotkī. The hukam of Akal was made manifest in the world. The sword taken up by the Khalsa in accordance with the command of Guru Gobind Singh was meant to establish the worship of Akal on a secure footing by eliminating its enemy; the 'victory of the Guru' was meant to make the truth prevail.[19] Misery and sorrow would yield place to peace and bliss. The Khalsa wields power without fear but with true justice. The things associated with Satyuga were made current in the Kaliyuga. The annihilation of the Turks, the mlechh, was to serve as a prelude to the spread of truth. True dharam was made manifest so that the praises of God could be sung freely. Falsehood and deceit vanished before truth when the victory of the Guru ushered light in the world. There was no persecution on the basis of religion. The freedom which the Khalsa won for themselves was extended to others: it became possible now to perform *jagg* and *hom*. The world began to live in happiness. It was made resplendent by the dharam promulgated by the Gurus who remove darkness. Here Gurdas gives a longish comment to the effect that the Sikh faith, that is, the faith of the Khalsa, leads to liberation. He invites others to seek refuge in Guru Gobind Singh.[20]

Guru Gobind Singh commands praise as a disciple of the Primal Being (*mard kā chelā*) who brought about a revolution through the Khalsa. They raise their standards over the earth and become its rulers. They take care of the world and promote happiness. They triumph over the self-centred. They establish true rule, and make true dharam manifest in the world in accordance with the hukam of Akal. Their victory establishes true seats of power. The world is reassured to worship God without fear. The devotees of God can now join the congregation of the Guru's followers (gur-sangat melā). The Sikhs of the Guru (Gursikh) can now promote the way of devotion shown by the Guru (*Gur-bhagtī*). He who appropriates the Name is acceptable to God. He is freed from kām, krodh, lobh, moh, and *ahankār*, and is enabled to practise the inner discipline. Here Gurdas uses metaphors from Yoga to refer to the path of liberation, control of the breath, the six *chakras*, *sunn-smādh* (the void) and ānand.[21] He leaves no doubt, however, that he is talking of the path of Guru Nanak.

Celebration of Sovereignty and Liberation

Gurdas does not provide a description of the institution of the Khalsa. He is emphatic nonetheless about the importance of the baptism of the double-edged sword. He takes it for granted that Guru Gobind Singh accepted *khandedhār pahul* from the Khalsa. Those who taste the pahul keep their kesh uncut, bear the sword, and adopt the name Singh. They also wear kachh as the symbol of sexual restraint. They are manly (*mardānā*) not simply because they are brave warriors but also because they keep flowing beards. They adopt 'Vāhegurūjī kī fateh' as the form of salutation. They wear blue dress. The Khalsa do not represent a new order; they are a continuation of the Sikh Panth instituted by Guru Nanak and nurtured by his successors. Not to belong to the Khalsa Panth is to be a non-Sikh. The identification of the Sikh with the Singh is complete.

Gurdas celebrates the triumph of the Khalsa and provides justification for Sikh rule but not as an end in itself. Attained through martyrdom, Sikh rule is sanctified by the freedom of belief and dispensation of justice.

The faith and ideology of the Khalsa is the same as that of the pre-Khalsa Panth. Both the Sikh faith and the Khalsa Panth had an identity that was different and distinct from that of Muslims and Hindus. The religious faith of the Khalsa is as important as their politics. Gurdas does not pray for power; he prays for the boon of the Name, association with the sangat, eradication of haumai, acceptance of the hukam, and attainment of liberation. Freedom of the conscience is ensured by political freedom. Gurdas sings of the double dispensation of political and spiritual freedom: sovereignty and liberation.

Notes

1. *Vārān Bhai Gurdas*, ed., Giani Hazara Singh, Amritsar: Khalsa Samachar, 1962 (4th edn), pp. 662–76. The Vār does not become unorthodox because of the use of '*bhagautī*'. The word is used by Sainapat in the *Srī Gur Sobhā* for the sword. The epithet 'Kalka' is used for the deity in pauṛī 1 of the Vār, and God is both male and female in pauṛī 13. The conception of God in this Vār is strictly Sikh.
2. Ibid., p. 670.
3. Ibid., pp. 662–3.
4. Gurinder Singh Mann, 'Sources for the Study of Guru Gobind Singh's Life and Times', *Journal of Punjab Studies*, vol. 15, nos 1 and 2 (Spring-Fall 2008), pp. 254, 280n129.
5. Ami P. Shah, '*Ugradanti* and the Rise of Tisar Panth', ibid., pp. 181–3.
6. Ibid., pp. 183–4. For English translation of the text, pp. 189–97.
7. *Vār Bhagautī*, pauṛīs 20, 28. Probably, the Vār was expected to be sung by the *dhādīs*.
8. Ibid., pauṛīs 7–8.
9. Ibid., pauṛīs 9–13.
10. Ibid., pauṛīs 8, 11–13, 25–6.
11. Ibid., pauṛīs 1, 3, 5–7, 9, 12, 14–15, 18, 20–1, 23, 26, 28.
12. Ibid., pauṛī 27.
13. Ibid., pauṛīs 1, 21, 23–4.
14. Ibid., pauṛīs 21–3.
15. Ibid., pauṛīs 2, 4.
16. Ibid., pauṛī 1.
17. Ibid., pauṛīs 2–6.
18. Ibid., pauṛī 15.
19. Ibid., pauṛīs 16–17.
20. Ibid., pauṛīs 17–18.
21. Ibid., pauṛīs 19–20.

10

The Guru-Khalsa

Sainapat's *Srī Gur Sobhā*

The Guru and the Khalsa

The central theme of Sainapat's *Srī Gur Sobhā* is the Khalsa of Guru Gobind Singh as a historical manifestation of his mission in life. The historical character of this work is underscored by the editors of the text.[1] Its importance as the earliest interpretation of the Khalsa has also been underlined.[2] It is a contemporary work,[3] and the author was closely associated with the court of Guru Gobind Singh.[4] The *Srī Gur Sobhā* has a peculiar significance as the first expression of a perspective in which Guru Gobind Singh and the Khalsa occupy the centre of the stage.

Sainapat states that he thought of writing of the creation of the master (*prabh*) (presumably soon after the event). The epithet prabh, used here, may refer to both God and the Guru but at several other places in the text this epithet is used for Guru Gobind Singh. Sainapat invokes the aid of the true Guru for the completion of the 'Gur Sobhā Granth' as a source of liberation for those who may read it or hear it. The other terms used for the work are *upmā*, *sākhī*, and *kathā* of the Guru.[5]

The true Guru of Sainapat has ten names: Guru Nanak, Guru Angad, Guru Amar Das, followed by Guru Ram Das, Guru Arjan, Guru Hargobind, Guru Har Rai, Guru Har Krishan, Guru Tegh Bahadur, and Guru Gobind Singh. In the case of Guru Tegh Bahadur alone something more is stated. He protected the whole creation. He saved the honour of karam and dharam, and established an everlasting tradition. His praises are sung in the universe for saving all dharams. The way in which he preserved honour is praised in all the three worlds. He saved tilak, *janjū*, and *dharamsāl* and of his own accord did something unprecedented. For the sake of dharam he went to the divine abode. The reference obviously is to the martyrdom of Guru Tegh Bahadur.[6]

Guru Gobind Singh was chosen by God to propagate the true worship of God. The instruments of this divine purpose in the past had themselves become the objects of worship. Among them are mentioned Brahma, Vishnu, Mahadev, and Chandi. Guru Gobind Singh was commissioned to establish the panth of dharam. He came into the world for this purpose. The Keshdhari Singhs constituted the panth created in accordance with the divine will. An eternal foundation was laid to create the panth in the image of the Guru: it could not be concealed; it was to increase day by day. Only they would gain peace who took refuge in this panth, called *Khālas* (pure).[7] We can see that the mission of Guru Gobind Singh is the same as in the *Bachittar Nātak*, but with a difference. The panth is explicity stated by Sainapat to be the Khalsa Panth. The chapter itself has the heading 'Panth Pragās'.

The unity of the Gurus is reinforced in the second chapter that postulates their equation with God: 'You are Guru Nanak, you are Guru Angad, you are Guru Amar Das, and Guru Das are you. You are Guru Arjan, you are Guru Hargobind, you are Guru Har Rai, and Guru Har Krishan are you. The ninth *Pātshāhī*, who had the power in the Kaliyuga to protect the world, are you. As the tenth Pātshāhī you are Guru Gobind Singh.' Empowered to establish the true panth, Guru Gobind Singh was the hero (*nāyak*) of the three worlds.[8]

Early Battles

Sainapat does not refer to the early life of Guru Gobind Singh. After several years at Makhowal, he moved to Paonta on the bank of the river Jamuna. His wonderful deeds made Fateh Shah (the Chief of Garhwal) unhappy and he marched against Guru Gobind Singh with a large army. The Guru went out of Paonta to face him, and chose the field of battle. Supported by many chiefs, Fateh Shah in his pride hoped to defeat his adversary in a few hours. He had no idea that the followers of Guru Gobind Singh did not care about their life, like the moth that burns itself on the flame. Mahri Chand, Lal Chand, Dayā Ram, Nand Chand, Sahib Chand, Jit Mal, and Sango Shah are specially mentioned as the brave warriors who fought on the side of Guru Gobind Singh. He himself played a decisive role in the battle. Sango Shah was posthumously honoured with the title of 'Shah Sangram' (the king of the battle). Many commandants on the opposite side were killed, like Najabat Khan, Bhikhan Khan, and Harish Chand. Fateh Shah fled into the hills and Guru Gobind Singh returned to Paonta, beating the drums of victory. The chapter carries the heading 'Teg Pragās: Shāh Sangrām Juddh'. The account of the battle is based largely on the *Bachittar Nātak.* The Guru and his followers are glorified.[9]

The battle of Nadaun, fought several years later, is presented as a battle fought in support of the hill chiefs, especially Bhim Chand of Kahlur (Bilaspur). Mian Khan sent Alif Khan to Nadaun (to collect tribute from the hill chiefs). Bhim Chand, supported by other chiefs, approached Guru Gobind Singh for help (against the Mughal faujdārs). He went to their support with his brave warriors. Guru Gobind Singh's personal participation in the battle, in which he used his musket and arrows, turned the tables against the Mughal commander who was obliged to retreat. The Guru stayed at Nadaun for some days and saw the residential places of its Rajas. On his way back to Anandpur, he 'conquered' the place called Alsun after a battle in which several persons were killed.[10] Sainapat does not mention any cause of this event.

Some years later, Dilawar Khan and his son came with an army. At the head of a thousand horsemen, the son marched towards Anandpur with the intention of attacking it during the night. The Guru was informed of his march up to the bank of the stream (close to Anandpur). He sent his own army to attack the enemy. The beat of drums in the darkness created the impression that the army of the Guru was very large. The Khānzāda was demoralized and made a hasty retreat, destroying a village on his way. Disappointed with the expedition of his son, Dilawar Khan sent his slave, Husain, against Guru Gobind Singh. On his way he was embroiled with the local hill chiefs and killed in a battle. Sangati Singh, sent by Guru Gobind Singh to support the hill chiefs, also died fighting along with his seven companions. Sainapat suggests that Husain Khan's death was the Guru's *kautak.*[11]

In these three chapters of thirteen pages in all, Sainapat's account of the battles and expeditions is based on the *Bachittar Nātak.* It is short but significant. The battle near Paonta, known as the battle of Bhangāṇī, was fought by Guru Gobind Singh in defence but it was caused by the reaction of Fateh Shah to the Guru's (martial) activities on the borders of his state. In the battle of Nadaun Guru Gobind Singh supported Bhim Chand who was the leader of a revolt against the Mughal authority.

The later expeditions were sent against Guru Gobind Singh because he appeared to represent the hard core of resistance.

Institution of the Khalsa

Sainapat gives three chapters to the Khalsa. He mentions Baisakhi, but not the year, as the day on which Guru Gobind Singh made the Khalsa manifest. First of all he declared that the Masands were to be discarded: all Sikhs were to be linked with the Guru directly, like the fish in water. The Sikh sangat was to become Khalsa sangat. The removal of the mediacy of the Masands was the first step towards the redemption of the world. The Khalsa were meant to destroy the wicked demons. What was concealed earlier was made manifest now.

The message of the Guru was to be spread in the world by his Sikhs. They were to have no association with five categories of people. They were to discard *hukkā* smoking and *bhaddar*. Even on the death of the mother and the father they should not shave their heads. Guru Gobind Singh was the mother and the father of the Khalsa. Bhaddar was an illusion (*bharam*); it had nothing to do with true faith (dharam). All offerings were to be taken to the Guru personally: mannat, *golak*, *dasvandh* and *bhet-kār*. The sight (darshan) of the true Guru, Gobind, was a source of liberation.[12]

There was to be only one category of Sikhs: the Khalsa. 'The entire *sangat*, from the beginning till the end, is my Khalsa'. Baptism of the double-edged sword (*khande kī pahul*) was administered to make them strong and powerful, and to make the divine will (hukam) prevail. The 'pure form', the unshorn hair, and holding the sword are mentioned directly; the adoption of the epithet 'Singh' and the salutation of 'Vāhegurūjī kā Khālsā, Vāhegurūjī kī fateh' are taken for granted. The injunctions regarding the essential *rahit* are repeated several times: to discard the Masands, to have no association with five categories of people, never to observe bhaddar, never to smoke, to sing God's praises in the *sat-sangat*, to recite *nām*, to follow the Guru, and to love the sants.[13]

All the Sikhs did not respond to Guru Gobind Singh's declaration with the same enthusiasm. Some became the Khalsa on hearing the Guru, but others, lost their poise. Some obeyed the Guru, but others refused in their ignorance to follow him. 'They who forget the Guru's door find no other place'. Some declared themselves to be the Khalsa, but others remained in the dark well. They who have no love, avoid the *sant sabhā*, they suffer in pain the cycle of death and rebirth, and never attain liberation. They are comparable to the snake that never discards poison even if fed on milk, the ass that rolls in dust even if fragrance is applied to its body, the bitter gourd (*tummā*) that never turns sweet even if filled with sugar, and the tail of the dog that never becomes straight. The crafty people remain engrossed in the world, do not heed the Guru's word, and do not join the sangat of the Khalsa. Only they turn to the Khalsa to whom God is gracious; others are kept in the wilderness of illusion. God is the true doer; his limits are unknowable; the only true creator is the only true preserver. He is one, but he is known to the world by many names. His true nām is the source of redemption. The pure ones recite the name of Gobind and become Khalsa. Sainapat makes use of the term 'Gobind' to postulate an equation of the Guru with God: 'Pārbrahm Parmesar is Guru Gobind'.[14]

Resistance and opposition to 'Vāhegurūjī kā Khālsā' was quite general. After the Baisakhi, some of the Khalsa remained with the Guru and others returned to their own places. Everywhere there was conflict between the Khalsa and the conservative Sikhs. Sainapat gives the example of what happened in Delhi. When the Sikhs who had gone to Anandpur returned to Delhi and informed others of the Guru's injunctions, some accepted them most willingly but others were indifferent. The Khatris and Brahmans in particular refused to accept the new baptism which obliged the Khalsa to discard bhaddar, a practice traditionally cherished by Brahmans and Khatris. The issue of contention, therefore, was this rite. The Sikhs of Delhi were divided into two groups on this issue: the Khalsa, who presumably belonged to the lower castes, and the other Sikhs led by Khatri traders supported by Brahmans.[15]

The Khalsa were dominant in the sangat that used to meet in the dharamsāl. Sainapat regards them as the sangat when he says that there is no difference between the sangat and the Guru. All wishes were fulfilled through the sangat's prayer. The true Sikhs were so dedicated to the sangat that they could not live without it. A Sikh who had observed bhaddar, was turned out of the dharamsāl and also the one who associated with him. Sainapat observes, 'the true Guru and the *sangat* are one'; it is for them to punish or to forgive.[16]

The Khatris and other affluent persons held a fair in Darapur and declared that there was no prohibition on cutting the hair or smoking hukkā. So long as there was no written order from the Guru, no one could impose any such prohibition. Many people liked the idea of continuing the practices of their forefathers. They abandoned the rahit and became *'khulāsā'*. Sainapat observes that to live without the Guru's shabad is to invite death, like the fish without water. Only the ignorant fools ignore the master's words. He is Niranjan and his light shines in all the seven continents and all the nine regions (*khands*) of the earth. He is the redeemer of sinners and the remover of fear; he alone is the source of peace.[17]

God does what he wills; good or bad is ordained by him. Nothing is attained without the sangat. A devout Sikh died and no bhaddar was observed. The *panchas* of the city excommunicated the one who had not observed this traditional practice. The Khalsa sangat encouraged the excommunicated person to defy the panchas. In retaliation, the panchas, decided to close the bazaar. Many people were deprived of their livelihood and were in distress. Some of the Sikhs approached the Mughal administrators for orders to open the shops. The panchas too approached the administrators to represent that some Sikhs had assumed the name of Khalsa on their own and were obliging others to discard their ancestral practices. They should be asked to explain how they had become Khalsa: the ruler of Delhi had his *'Khālisa'* but what was this 'Vāhegurū kā Khālsā'? The Sikhs told the administrators that just as the ruler of Delhi had his nāibs so did the Guru have his nāibs called Masands. They were removed by the Guru and all Sikhs had become his Khalsa. The panchas then bribed the administrators. They took action against the Sikhs 'The Khalsa were on one side, and the whole world on the other'. In this desperate situation the Sikhs prayed to the Guru. He responded to the prayer. The administrators on their own ordered the shops to be opened. Furthermore, the opponents of the Khalsa sangat admitted their fault and sought forgiveness. Those who gave it in writing were readmitted into the sangat and they went to have the Guru's darshan. 'What the *kartā* wills gets done'.[18] The triumph of the Khalsa sangat was due to the Guru's grace.

Contest over Anandpur

The Khalsa sangats triumphed everywhere and replaced the authority of the Masands as the representatives of the Guru. Now the Rajas of the hills sent an ultimatum to Guru Gobind Singh that he should leave their land or pay tribute. The Guru was offended by this challenge to his rāj and *tej*. He was not prepared to pay tribute (which was a token of submission to a superior power). Had the Raja come to him and asked for anything he would have given, but now he could have it only on 'the point of the spear'. The chief of Kahlur wrote to the chief of Hindur (Nalagarh) that they should attack Anandpur from two sides. With their men they laid siege to Anandpur. Guru Gobind Singh sent his son Ajit Singh to attack them. 'Due to the grace of the Guru the Khalsa have no match as warriors in the three worlds'. Ajit Singh fought in such a way that the Rajas lost their sense in surprise. Several battles were fought, ending in the victory of the Khalsa. The Rajas now thought of a stratagem. To appeal to Guru Gobind Singh's sense of honour, they took a cow with them and requested the Guru to leave the land as *'gāo-bhāt'* (feed of the cow). Thus, despite the victory of the Khalsa, 'the first battle of Anandpur' ended in its evacuation by Guru Gobind Singh.[19]

Guru Gobind Singh moved to Nirmoh. The Khalsa 'army' began to plunder the villages of Kahlur. In one skirmish Sahib Chand died fighting. The Khalsa went to his aid, fought hard, and brought his body back to Nirmoh where it was cremated. Sainapat observes that Sahib Chand became *'khalsa'* by giving his life; his fortune became perfect. The Khalsa continued to conquer villages. Raja Bhim Chand became anxious to dislodge Guru Gobind Singh from Nirmoh. He sent his pradhān to the 'Turk' to seek aid. He apprised the Sultan that the Guru had forcibly seized all the villages and now his target was Kahlur. The Sultan sent his messenger to the administrator of Sirhind with the orders to collect an army for attack (on Nirmoh). A sardār in the service of Sirhind fearlessly marched with his soldiers (to the aid of the Guru). Seeing this kautak, the sangat arrived at the court from all sides to be enlisted and given arms. 'The Sikh who lives in the Guru's presence is unmatched'. The governor of Sirhind with Pathans, and the Raja of Kahlur with Gujjars and other villagers, surrounded Nirmoh from all sides. The Khalsa were ready to meet the attack. 'There is no equal of the Khalsa Singh in the whole world'. Much blood was spilt when warriors from both the sides were killed, and the earth became red. The battle went on for twenty-one hours (seven pahars). The army of the Turks retreated and the Guru thought of leaving Nirmoh. Before he crossed the river, he was attacked by Pathans. The battle lasted for about four hours and the Turks were repulsed. They all fled. The Chief of Basali welcomed Guru Gobind Singh (on the other side of the river).[20]

The Khalsa encamped in Basali. The army of Kahlur attacked them. Guru Gobind Singh watched the battle as if it were an elephant fight. The warriors fought like elephants. Defeated by the Khalsa, the army of Kahlur fled like an arrow shot from the bow. 'They who entertain pride are kept lost in illusion; they who cherish God in love are appropriated'. For several days Guru Gobind Singh stayed in Basali. Going out under the appearance of hunting, he led the Khalsa against the haughty men of Kalmot who used to waylay the Sikhs on their way (to Anandpur). The Khalsa beseiged Kalmot and, after some fight, the nishān of the Guru was hoisted on the fort and drums of victory were beaten. The people of Kalmot tried to recover the place, but they fled before the Khalsa. The Raja of Kahlur now submitted to the Guru, discarding his pride. Guru Gobind Singh returned to Basali, and then built Anandgarh all afresh.[21]

The Khalsa began to come to Anandpur from all directions for the Guru's darshan. All the neighbouring villages were 'conquered' by the Khalsa. The Khalsa used to ride out to plunder the villages which refused to offer bhet. This went on for over two years. The rāj of the true Guru was spreading in all the four directions. The Raja felt humiliated. He asked the Guru to leave Anandpur. The Guru prepared for meeting the attack. The Rajas laid seige to Anandpur. They were astonished by the cannon fire from Anandgarh. The Singhs fell upon the army of the Rajas and they lifted the siege.[22]

In view of the unmatched prowess of the Singh warriors who had killed many brave men in the battle, the Rajas held consultations and approached the Turks. Many Mughals and Pathans, Gujjars and Ranghars, the troops of Sirhind and Lahore, and the armies of all the Rajas constituted a huge force. Guru Gobind Singh made preparations to meet their attack. The Khalsa fought so fiercely that the allies were obliged to retreat. They held consultations and decided to lay seige to Anandpur. All communication with the outside world was cut off. The price of grain began to rise and reached one rupee a seer. The Sikhs resorted to raids for food and water. Some of the Singhs resorted to night attacks. The allies began to keep watch. They killed some of the Singhs. The matter was reported to the Guru and he remarked that they should not have gone out without orders. Many days later the people of the town complained of dire shortage of food; they were on the verge of death due to starvation. Guru Gobind Singh gave them the assurance that food would be available after some days. All the Sikhs then submitted to the Guru that there was no harm in leaving Anandpur. The Guru asked them to give in writing that they would be responsible for the consequences. Then the people of the town prepared to leave Anandpur, Guru Gobind Singh distributed the treasury among the Sikhs. The Singh warriors put on five weapons. What was left behind was set on fire. They were ready to leave Anandgarh.[23] Thus, the second battle of Anandpur ended in its evacuation by the Guru and the Khalsa, with many other people of the town.

The *Zafarnama*

After leaving Anandpur, Guru Gobind Singh reached the Shahi Tibbi. The Raja and the Turks were in pursuit. Guru Gobind Singh told Udai Singh to face them. He fought against them for three hours and died fighting along with other Singhs. Meanwhile, Guru Gobind Singh came to Chamkaur where a zamīndār offered a place in the village. The army in pursuit surrounded the village. The Singhs who were with the Guru fought valiantly to die on the field of battle. Guru Gobind Singh asked Sahibzada Ajit Singh to attack the enemy. He killed many Pathans,

Fig. 10.1 Gurdwara Katalgarhi at Chamkaur Sahib where the Khalsa accompanying Guru Gobind Singh, including his two elder sons, died fighting against the Mughal *faujdār* of Sirhind in 1705

Fig. 10.2 Gurdwara at Fatehgarh Sahib where the two younger sons of Guru Gobind Singh were executed by the Mughal faujdār of Sirhind in 1705

brave warriors, and sardārs, before he 'drank the cup of love' uttering 'Vāhegurū' with his last breath. Guru Gobind Singh remarked, 'today he has become Khalsa in the court of the true Guru'. Sahibzada Jhujhar Singh then fought valiantly. He killed many Pathans and died fighting. Another Khalsa who died fighting was Sant Singh. Guru Gobind Singh himself shot deadly arrows and lost a third of one finger in the battle. Then he went out, unseen by the enemy. The other two Sahibzadas were taken to Sirhind where they followed the example of their grandfather, Guru Tegh Bahadur, and died for the sake of dharam.[24] Thus, the battle of Chamkaur ended in the death of the four sons of Guru Gobind Singh as martyrs, besides a number of brave Singhs like Udai Singh and Sant Singh, among others.

Guru Gobind Singh was now alone, without a place, or attachment. He demonstrated the 'ek onkar' aspect of the divine being. Renouncing everything, he appeared in the *nirban* form. He manifested himself again as 'kalādhār' to liberate the world. 'The only one master assumes innumerable forms'. The chapter in Sainapat's work is headed 'Kalā Pragās'.[25]

Guru Gobind Singh arrived amidst the Brars. All Singhs had his darshan. The dust of many births is removed by the sight of the eternal master. They who take refuge with the Guru become pure. He encamped near a large pool of water. The enemy came to know of his presence and came with an army. The Singhs defeated the whole army in a bloody battle. The Turks fled, leaving the field to the Singhs.[26] The reference here is the battle of Muktsar.

Guru Gobind Singh thought of apprising the emperor of what had happened. Dayā Singh was sent with a written message to be delivered personally to Aurangzeb. Accompanied by five other Singhs, he went to Delhi where the Sikh sangat supplied the money they needed. Through Agra, Gwalior, Ujjain, Burhanpur, and Aurangabad, they reached Ahmadnagar and stayed in a dharamsāl. The sangat assured them that the message sent by the Guru would reach the emperor. However, Dayā Singh could not have access to Aurangzeb. He wrote to Guru Gobind Singh, seeking his grace. Guru Gobind Singh wrote five hukamnāmas to be sent with Dayā Singh's messenger. Consequently, the message written for the emperor reached him.[27]

Sainapat refers to the contents of the written message sent to the emperor. Guru Gobind Singh wanted to see Aurangzeb personally but his men had betrayed their solemn promise and attacked the Guru. The

Fig. 10.3 Darbar at Muktsar in commemoration of the Khalsa martyrs of the battle of Khidrana against the Mughal faujdār of Sirhind in early 1706

Mughal faujdārs and *qiladārs* of the provinces on the way to the south could not be trusted. Therefore, a Singh was sent to the emperor with the message. The emperor should pay attention to this urgent matter and send a farmān. After receiving it, the Guru could start his journey. The emperor ordered that the Singh should take an imperial farmān to Guru Gobind Singh. A *gurz-bardār* was sent with the farmān. Sainapat goes on to give a discourse on faith in Guru Gobind Singh.[28]

Guru Gobind Singh started for the south just when Dayā Singh left Ahmadnagar for the north. Sainapat describes the Guru's majestic splendour when he rode his caparisoned horse, fully armed with five weapons, and with a golden aigerette (*kalgī*) crowning his headgear. 'Vāhegurūjī kī fateh' resounded in the three worlds. On hearing the exclamation, Shesh, Mahesh, Suresh, and Shivji on the Kailash trembled out of fear. Dayā Singh met the Guru in Rajasthan, while the gurz-bardār went to Delhi. The chiefs of Rajasthan met the Guru with reverence. Sometimes, however, the Khalsa had to resort to plunder for food and fodder. On his way, Guru Gobind Singh heard of Aurangzeb's death, and decided to return to the north, where the war of succession (*sultānī jang*) was going to be fought.[29]

On the way back, Guru Gobind Singh thought of seeing the land associated with Kichak (who was killed by Krishna for his misbehaviour with

Fig. 10.4 Damdama Sahib at Talvandi Sabo, in commemoration of Guru Gobind Singh's stay there in 1706–7

Daropadi). When the Guru came close to the city of Bhagaur, the people were frightened. Thinking that the place (*dhām*) may be plundered, they made preparations for battle. Guru Gobind Singh sent Dharam Singh to clarify his intention to see the place of 'Kich juddh' (the battle with Kichak). Guru Gobind Singh chose the Singhs to accompany him. Some days later a fight took place between a Singh and the men of a local chief over damage done to his orchard by the camels of the Guru's followers. The other Singhs saw the fight from the top of the hill and joined the fray. The fight went on for two days and two nights. On the third day, Guru Gobind Singh sent Dharam Singh to lead the attack. The Singhs burnt the gates and entered the city. There were pitched battles, and many warriors were killed. Guru Gobind Singh advised the Singhs to carry a cannon to the top of the hill and fire. The enemy took to flight. Guru Gobind Singh left the place, but the Sikhs who were in the rear were attacked by the enemy. The Guru and Dharam Singh killed their leaders and the army was repulsed. Beating the drums of victory, Guru Gobind Singh marched towards Shahjahanabad.[30] For Sainapat, significantly, this battle is the main theme of the chapter.

Ultimate Triumph of the Khalsa

Aurangzeb died in Ahmadnagar after his stay there for thirteen months. His son, Ā'zam, crowned himself and sat on the throne. Prince Mu'azzam marched (towards Agra). When he reached Delhi, he wrote to Guru Gobind Singh for help in the war of succession. Guru Gobind Singh told him to have no doubt about his success: 'regard the *rāj* as yours.' Mu'azzam felt satisfied and prepared for war. Sainapat praises Ā'zam Shah Sultan who died fighting in the battle, along with his sons. Mu'azzam thanked God for taking Ā'zam's life and giving the throne to Bahadur Shah (the new title of Mu'azzam). His success was a result of the Guru's blessings. He went to Agra to stay there during the rainy season. By this time, Guru Gobind Singh had reached Delhi.[31]

The sangat of Delhi welcomed Guru Gobind Singh with great enthusiasm. He encamped on the bank of the Jamuna and redeemed the world through his darshan. After some days he left Delhi and reached Mathura and gave charities to Brahmans. Then he went to see Bindraban and its 'Kunj Galī'. From there he marched towards Agra, and encamped at some distance from the city. The Khān-i Khānān, Mun'im Khan, invited him to his place. Then Bahadur Shah expressed his wish to have the Guru's darshan. With some of his warriors, Guru Gobind Singh went to Bahadur Shah's camp. Taking only one Singh with him he went into the emperor's presence fully armed. Bahadur Shah expressed his gratitude for the Guru's blessings and offered a kalgī, a *dhugdhugī*, and a *khil'at* to him. The Guru called in the Singh and told him to carry the presents. He said farewell to the emperor and returned to his own camp. Among the amusements of the Guru in Agra was an elephant fight. 'Sitting in the *jharokha* our king of kings watches the elephant fight' is the refrain of a savvayyā. Sangat from far and near used to come for the Guru's darshan. In this way, several months passed and Bahadur Shah went towards Rajasthan.[32] The meeting of Guru Gobind Singh with Bahadur Shah had not resulted in anything more tangible than a demonstration of appreciation and good will on the emperor's part.

Guru Gobind Singh marched in close proximity to Bahadur Shah's camp, marching stage by stage towards Ajmer, Jodhpur, and Udaipur. The most important event for Sainapat in the context is the fight of Zorawar Singh at Chitor. He had joined Guru Gobind Singh at Itimadpur, near Agra. The incident narrated by Sainapat highlights his bravery in his fight against an overwhelming number of opponents. He died fighting. A few other Singhs were also killed.[33] As pointed out by Ganda Singh, this Zorawar Singh was different from Sahibzada Zorawar Singh. In a Persian source too he is mentioned as 'the son' of Guru Gobind Singh.[34] Like Ajit Singh later, Zorawar Singh was an adopted son.

Bahadur Shah moved towards the south and Guru Gobind Singh remained close to his camp. Sometimes there were skirmishes between the followers of Guru Gobind Singh and the local people over fodder. He met the emperor once again. Eventually, he decided to stay at a place called Nander. As heard by Sainapat, a Pathan came to see the Guru and talked sweetly to him for a short while. He came again after a few days, and then several times more. One evening, when no Singh was around, he attacked the Guru with a *jamdhaṛ*. Some Singhs responded to the Guru's call and killed that Pathan and his accomplice on the spot. The Singhs discovered that the Guru had been wounded and they were filled with dismay. Guru Gobind Singh said that he had been saved by Sri Akal. The wound was washed and sewn. After some days he began to give darshan. Days passed and the end came near: the Guru assumed the form of shabad, uttering 'Vāhegurū kī fateh' for the last time.[35]

Fig. 10.5 Sri Abchal Nagar, Huzur Sahib, at Nander where Guru Gobind Singh resided in September–October 1708 and where he was cremated

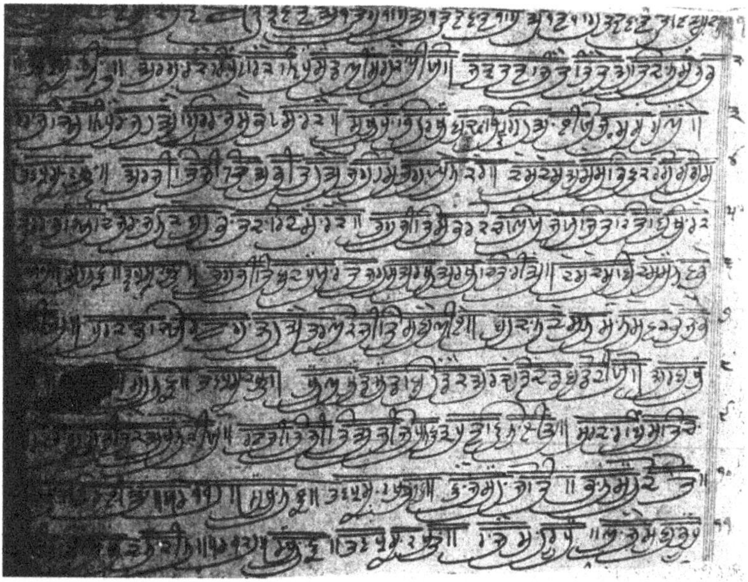

Fig. 10.6 A folio of the Granth Sāhib at Huzur Sahib in the Gurmukhi script popularized by Guru Gobind Singh at Anandpur

This happened on Kattak *sudī* 5 in Sammat 1765 (7 October 1708). A day before the Singhs had asked Guru Gobind Singh what would be his form. He told them that his form was the Khālas, he had bestowed his mantle upon the Khālas. 'The Khālas is my form and I am with the Khālas'. The Khālas have no illusion. Detached from bharam and bhekh, 'the Khālas are our true Guru'. 'Our Guru' is also shabad, the bāṇī that leads to liberation.[36] In other words, Guru Gobind Singh vested Guruship in the Panth and the Granth.

The last chapter dwells on God and his attributes, the need of worshipping the one through bhagtī, nām, and sangat, the indispensability of the Guru, the objective of liberation through the path of love. Peace comes through service of the true Guru; the perfect master is found in sat-sangat. Sainapat has sung his praises inadequately because he has a limited talent.[37] The *Srī Gur Sobhā,* which opens with the manifestation of the Khalsa Panth, ends with a statement of the Sikh faith as the means of liberation. In the author's mind, the two are closely interlinked. The way to liberation lies through the Khalsa who embody the Sikh faith.

In the chapter before the last, Sainapat talks of the future. The last savvayyā of the chapter has the refrain: *'bhal bhāg bhayā tum tahe kaho garh ānand pher basāvenge'*. 'Garh Ānand' is used as a symbol for the triumph of the Khalsa.[38]

The Hallmark of Distinction

The first chapter of the *Srī Gur Sobhā* serves as a kind of prologue, introducing the central theme: transformation of the sangat into the Khalsa as a political community. The last chapter serves as a sort of epilogue, underscoring the relevance of Sikh theology for the life of the Sikhs. Three chapters relate to the battles of Guru Gobind Singh before the institution of the Khalsa. Three chapters on the Khalsa are followed by four chapters on the battles of Guru Gobind Singh which are presented as the battles of the Khalsa too. After the evacuation of Sirhind, two battles fought in the plains are given in two chapters. Four chapters relate essentially to Guru Gobind Singh's attitude towards and relations with the contemporary Mughal emperors. This is also the context in which Guru Gobind Singh's death is related in a separate chapter. The future triumph of the Khalsa is seen as the triumph of Guru Gobind Singh.

There is no doubt that Sainapat is narrating historical events. What he says has a great significance of its own. Combined with evidence from Persian and other Sikh sources, his evidence becomes even more meaningful. He gives only two specific dates but he indicates the passage of time with reference to number of days, months, and years. Consequently, much of what he narrates falls into a chronological order. In terms of events, Sainapat is consciously selective. This selection imparts historical significance to what is narrated. Much of his historical sense comes from his Sikh heritage in the ascending order from the Granth Sāhib, through the *Janamsākhīs*, to the *Bachittar Nātak*. There is little of the supranatural in the *Srī Gur Sobhā* but the kautak of the Guru tends to become a substitute of causal explanation. A strong undercurrent of theology runs throughout the historical narrative.

The *Srī Gur Sobhā* is seen by Anne Murphy as a form of historical representation with a particular rationale within the Sikh religious thought. In consideration of the role of history in relation to social formation, both religious and political, the case of *Srī Gur Sobhā* becomes particularly interesting. The past in the text is chronologically and geographically ordered and located; the Sikh community itself is seen as the creation of a historical process. Three key narrative modes are interwoven in this text: events related to Guru Gobind Singh, his theological and doctrinal pronouncements, and his interaction with his followers who are described. There is more than biography or hagiography at work in the text. The formation of the community stands at its centre, defining its boundaries in relation to others. The sovereignty of the Guru is both territorial and extra-territorial. There is a sense of the connectedness of past, present, and future. Murphy concludes that the *Srī Gur Sobhā* constitutes the Sikh Panth through history, organized around the Guru and defined in relation to the past as well as the presence of the Guru. The narration of the Guru within the world and the construction of the community through this narration are linked with doctrinal and theological concerns.[39]

This perceptive analysis enhances the value of the *Srī Gur Sobhā* as a social document. However, it does not confront the issue of identity. The basis of the excommunication of the five categories of people was both ideological and political. The Khalsa were further distinguished by their baptismal rahit and political aspirations. Sainapat's great interest in battles appears to be a reflection of this concern. The Khalsa stand not merely in opposition to the world but also as distinguished from the rest of the people because of their historical role which is both religious and political. Sainapat is talking of a religious fraternity which has become a political entity. The rāj and tej of the Khalsa, inherited from the Guru, is the hallmark of their distinction.

Notes

1. Ganda Singh ed., *Srī Gur Sobhā*, Patiala: Punjabi University, 1967, pp. 24–7. Shamsher Singh Ashok, *Shrī Gurū Sobhā*, Amritsar: Shiromani Gurudwara Prabandhak Committee, 1967, pp. 3, 5–6.

2. J.S. Grewal, 'Praising the Khalsa: Sainapat's *Gursobha*'. *The Khalsa: Sikh and Non-Sikh Perspectives*, ed., J.S. Grewal, New Delhi: Manohar, 2004, pp. 35–45.

3. Ganda Singh has argued against Akali Kaur Singh's view that the *Srī Gur Sobhā* was written in 1741. He argues in favour of 1711 as the year of its completion (*Srī Gur Sobhā*, pp. 21–3). Shamsher Singh Ashok suggests that Sainapat started writing in 1701 and completed the work in 1711 (*Shrī Gurū Sobhā*, p. 4). Gurinder Singh Mann is in agreement with Ashok about the beginning of the work in 1701 but suggests that it was completed soon after Guru Gobind Singh's death in 1708. Gurinder Singh Mann, 'Sources for the Study of Guru Gobind Singh's Life and Times', *Journal of Punjab Studies*, vol. 15, nos 1–2 (Spring–Fall 2008), p. 252.

4. According to Ashok, the author of the *Shrī Gurū Sobhā* was Kavi Sainapat whose real name was Chandar Sain; he was a resident of Lahore but shifted to Wazirabad due to the persuasion of Pandit Jagat Rai Vaid; he came to be known as Kavi Sainapat Mann of Wazirabad; he lived at the court of Guru Gobind Singh for about fifteen years. Initiated through baptism of the double-edged sword, Sainapat became 'Saina Singh' (*Shrī Gurū Sobhā*, pp. 1–3). Ganda Singh comes to the same conclusion, adding that the internal evidence of Sainapat's work supports the view that he had become a 'Khalsa' (*Srī Gur Sobhā*, pp. 17–20).

5. Ganda Singh, ed., *Srī Gur Sobhā*, pp. 1–2.
6. Ibid., pp. 2–3.
7. Ibid., pp. 4–5.
8. Ibid., pp. 7–8.
9. Ibid., pp. 8–13.
10. Ibid., pp. 14–16.
11. Ibid., pp. 17–19.
12. Ibid., pp. 20–3.
13. Ibid., pp. 24–31.
14. Ibid., pp. 20, 26–30.
15. Ibid., pp. 32–3, 48.
16. Ibid., pp. 34–6.

17. Ibid., pp. 36–40.
18. Ibid., pp. 42–7.
19. Ibid., pp. 48–54.
20. Ibid., pp. 55–61.
21. Ibid., pp. 62–5.
22. Ibid., pp. 66–8.
23. Ibid., pp. 68–73.
24. Ibid., pp. 74–84. Ganda Singh has pointed out Sainapat's mistake about the identity of the Sahibzadas.
25. Ibid., pp. 85–6, 94.
26. Ibid., pp. 86–7.
27. Ibid., pp. 87–90.
28. Ibid., pp. 90–3.
29. Ibid., pp. 93–8.
30. Ibid., pp. 99–105.
31. Ibid., pp. 106–9.
32. Ibid., pp. 110–16.
33. Ibid., pp. 118–22.
34. Ibid., pp. 52–7, 83 n1. In the *Nairang-i Zamāna* of Abdur Rasul the martial exploit and tragic end of a 'son' of Guru Gobind Singh in 1708 in the vicinity of the fort of Chitor in briefly described. There is only a slight variation between his account and that of Sainapat. *Sikh History from Persian Sources*, eds, J.S. Grewal and Irfan Habib, New Delhi: Tulika/Indian History Congress, 2001, pp. 100–3. For my comment, ibid., pp. 15–16.
35. Ganda Singh, ed., *Srī Gur Sobhā*, pp. 120–7.
36. Ibid., pp. 128–31.
37. Ibid., pp. 134–49.
38. Ibid., pp. 132–3.
39. Anne Murphy, 'History in the Sikh Past', *History and Theory*, vol. 40 (October 2007), pp. 345, 349, 351–2, 354, 356–7, 360–2, 364–5. The basic idea put forth by Anne Murphy makes a lot of sense. In matters of detail, however, the arguments are sometimes based on wrong assumptions about the time of Sikh literary works (like the *Rahitnāmas*) and about the relevance of other traditions (like the historiography in Persian) for the Sikh awareness of temporal sequence. Debatable views expressed by some other scholars (like Jeevan Deol) are accepted as valid.

11

The Singh Way of Life

The *Rahitnāmas*

The *Nasīhatnāma*

The work popularly known as the *Tankhānāma* of Bhai Nand Lal is one of the earliest *Rahitnāmas*. A copy of this work dated 1718–19 is in the Library of Guru Nanak Dev University (MS 770) which refers to the work as the *Nasīhatnāma*. The author uses the terms Khalsa and Singh for the Sikh, which indicates that the *Nasīhatnāma* was composed after the formal institution of the Khalsa in 1699. There is no reference to the Khalsa as the Guru; nor is there any reference to *Granth* or Shabad-Bani as the Guru. Therefore, it may be safe to place the original work before the death of Guru Gobind Singh in 1708. Thus, the *Nasīhatnāma* was written between 1699 and 1708, probably close to 1700.[1]

The concern of the author of the *Nasīhatnāma* with religious and ethical life of the Khalsa comes out clearly in the text. More significant, however, is his concern for the political aspirations of the Khalsa. They protect the weak and destroy the wicked. They bear arms, ride horses, fight every day, promote dharam, and die for their faith. The slanderers of the Khalsa shall not be able to oppose them. Guru Gobind Singh himself is presented as enunciating: 'I shall verily establish my own rule. I shall merge the four castes into one'. The Khalsa shall ride horses and keep hawks. The Turks would take to flight on seeing them. 'I shall empower each Sikh to confront a lac and a quarter (of the enemy)'. They who die fighting attain liberation. The spears of the Khalsa shall wave in the air and they shall ride caparisoned elephants. Kettle drums shall be beaten at their doors. They shall acquire arms and establish their rule over the world. 'The Khalsa shall rule and none shall withstand them;

shorn of honour they shall all submit (to the Khalsa) and only they who take refuge (with them) shall be saved.'[2]

Rāj karegā khālsā ākī rahe nā koi
Khuār hoe sabh milenge bache saran jo hoi

These two lines of the *Nasīhatnāma* are familiar to Sikhs all over the world as a part of the 'Sikh anthem' which is recited at the end of every formal occasion after the collective prayer (Ardās). Its occurrence in the *Nasīhatnāma* is the most emphatic expression of the idea of sovereign rule coming down from the days of Guru Gobind Singh. Therefore it has a unique significance of its own.[3]

The *Sākhī Rahit Pātshāhī 10*

Another early Rahitnāma, the *Sākhī Rahit Pātshāhī 10*, emphasizes the unity of God, belief in the Guru and the Shabad-Bani, individual and congregational worship, concern for fellow-Sikhs, the uniqueness of the dispensation of Guru Nanak and his successors. The Brahmanical rites are rejected, taboos against tobacco and beef are underscored, and the sanctity of the *kesh* is highlighted. Much of the content of the *Sākhī Rahit* gets related to the early Sikh tradition. The *bāṇī* is equated with the Guru, and the Granth is assumed to be there in the *dharamsāl*, but there is no reference to Granth as the Guru. The Sikh is equated with the Guru, and a certain degree of sanctity is attached to 'five Sikhs', but there is no reference to the Khalsa as the Guru. There is no feature of the *Sākhī Rahit* that can be seen as later than the lifetime of Guru Gobind Singh. Therefore, the *Sākhī Rahit* may be regarded as originally composed around 1700.[4]

The most remarkable feature of the *Sākhī Rahit* for our present purpose is its conception of the Khalsa as a distinct entity. Amidst an emphatic rejection of the Brahmanical, ascetical and Islamic traditions, the *kesh* are seen as an alternative to the sacred thread as the marker of Singh identity. Indeed, there is the explicit statement that a Khalsa with a turban on his head and a flowing beard could not be concealed amongst a lac of Hindus and Turks. The emphasis is on the visibility of distinct identity rather than on its novelty. For the author of the *Sākhī Rahit*, there is no rupture between the early Sikh tradition and the Khalsa ideals.[5]

The *Prem Sumārag*

The *Nasīhatnāma* and the *Sākhī Rahit* are very short texts. By contrast, the *Prem Sumārag* and the *Rahitnāma* associated with Chaupa Singh are very long. In the introduction to the text of the *Prem Sumārag*, Bhai Randhir Singh argues that it was written by a learned person at the court of Guru Gobind Singh, but after his death. The Sikh is identified with the Singh in the *Prem Sumārag*. However, there is no emphatic statement that the Khalsa is the Guru or the Granth is the Guru. The interest of the author in the ideal Sikh state appears to be a corollary of the idea of 'rāj karegā khālsā' which is explicitly stated in the *Nasīhatnāma*. A later manuscript of the *Prem Sumārag* is claimed to have been copied from a manuscript of 1701–2. Gurinder Singh Mann gets the impression that the *Prem Sumārag* marked the peak of the rahit documents produced at Anandpur and 'it synchronizes well with Sikh religious, social, and political aspirations of the rule of the deg and tegh'.[6]

I have analysed the *Prem Sumārag* all afresh as a Sant Khalsa vision of the Sikh Panth in terms of its roots in the early Sikh tradition, initiation and other rites and ceremonies, occupational and personal life of the Khalsa, the ideal Sikh ruler, the path of liberation, and the character of the envisioned order to bring out its comprehensive scope in terms of the religious, social, cultural, and political life of the Khalsa. It is not necessary to go into all this detail again. However, we may notice the character of the ideal social order and the ideal Sikh state.[7]

The injunctions of the *Prem Sumārag Granth*, like the Khalsa Panth, have divine sanction and they are meant for the Khalsa of Sri Akal Purkh. The Sikh, the Khalsa, and the Singh refer to the same entity, and there is no other category of Sikhs. The injunctions are meant for both men and women, with some modifications. The ideal of equality is modified in some other ways too, but it remains the hallmark of the Khalsa and their distinctive identity. They are emphatically distinct from Hindus and Muslims.

According to the injunctions no compromise is to be made with regard to the religious beliefs and practices of the Khalsa of Sri Akal Purkh. Belief in Akal Purkh to the strict exclusion of all gods and goddesses, and worship of Akal Purkh through Shabad-Bāṇī to the strict exclusion of all other forms of worship define the basic position of the Khalsa. They believe in ten Gurus and after them, in shabad-bāṇī as the Guru; it is embodied essentially in the *Pothī Granth*. To converse with the Guru one could read his shabad. To see the Guru, one could go to a gathering of the Khalsa to see the Guru in the Khalsa. No living person is to be regarded as Guru.

The daily life of the Khalsa is marked by early morning worship after bathing, recitation of the *Japjī*, the *Jāp*, the *Ānand*, the *Sodar Rahrās*, and the *Kīrtan Sohilā*, reading of Gurbāṇī from the Granth, and participation in the kīrtan. The initiation of a person into the order of the Khalsa involves khande dī pahul, wearing a kachh and five weapons, an ardās, and instruction in the essentials of belief and ethics. A married woman and a widow can also take pahul. Apart from some other differences of detail, a baptized male is to bear the epithet 'Singh' and a baptized female the epithet 'Devi'.

The ceremonies of birth, naming, betrothal, marriage, and death do not have any role for the Brahman. To figure largely in these ceremonies are Gurbāṇī, ardās, pahul, and arms. For the marriage ceremony, fire is to be a witness, like the sword and the Khalsa; it is to be fed with ghee at proper moments. On the death of a Khalsa, no traditional mourning is to be observed; there should be no wailing; the ashes are not to be taken to the Ganges.

Ideally, the Khalsa belong to one caste and there are no distinctions of high and low between them. However, the traditional attitudes may be partially and temporarily accommodated. Marriage within the same caste or occupational group is one such compromise. Not eating with the unclean outcastes is another. Remarriage is not allowed to a widow who has children. The ideal of equality is underscored without ambiguity: all are one in the eyes of Akal Purkh; everyone professing to be the Khalsa should be regarded as equal.

All honest occupations are sanctified in the *Prem Sumārag*. However, preference is given to *saudāgarī* and cultivation of land; petty shopkeeping and service are forbidden, except soldiering. A Khalsa must save for the Guru's treasury and spend a portion of his income on the welfare of others. He should share his food with others, whether a Khalsa, a Hindu, or a Musalman. Meat is the most preferred item of food. In certain situations, a Khalsa may eat *halāl* meat. Alcohol is forbidden but, if necessary, opium or *bhang* can be taken privately in a small quantity.

The form of government in the ideal Sikh state is monarchical according to the injunctions of the *Prem Sumārag*. The authority and the orders of the ruler can be disregarded only at the cost of life. The vast territory of the state occupies an imaginary space; its primary, secondary, and tertiary divisions have several common departments. The foremost concerns of the state are the army, revenues, intelligence, and justice. The dominant institutions of the state are *mansabdārī* and *jāgīrdarī*, both of which remind us of the Mughal state. Many terms used for offices and officials come from the Mughal practice. The share of the cultivator in the produce from land is less than a half, which is regarded as lenient. The language of education and administration is to be 'Gurmukhi' (both language and script). The ruler is expected to ensure the worship of Akal Purkh and the propagation of *nām*, *dān*, and *isnān*. Chastity and fidelity in marriage are cherished; illegal sexual intercourse is a criminal offence; prostitution is officially recognized. Monogamy is the ideal, but the ruler can have more than one wife for various reasons, including the need of a male child. In certain situations he may have sexual intercourse with slave girls. The ruler will be judged ultimately on the basis of justice, and not piety. Justice is the *raison d'etre* of the ideal Sikh state.

The path initiated by Guru Nanak and elaborated by Guru Gobind Singh is *sahaj jog* which stands for the total acceptance of God's will. It is the antidote to *haumai*. It leads to liberation or the state of *rāj*-jog. Its essence is the service of others as a sort of selfless social commitment.

The *Prem Sumārag* does not appear to bear any clear imprint of the late eighteenth or the early nineteenth century. There are a few similarities between the ideal Sikh state and the state of Maharaja Ranjit Singh, but the differences between them are more marked. 'Gurmukhi', for example, was not the language of government and administration under Ranjit Singh. The conception of the ideal Sikh state put forward in the *Prem Sumārag* does not appear to represent a reaction to the state in existence. The ideal Sikh social order of the *Prem Sumārag* is for more egalitarian than the Sikh social order of the early nineteenth century. There is no role for Brahmans in the Sikh social order which is exclusively the Khalsa order.

The scope of the *Prem Sumārag* is quite comprehensive. It does present a conception of the ideal Sikh state, but more than that it relates to the ideal Sikh social order. Its author was a learned person, keen perhaps to influence his fellow Sikhs in the interest of Sikh faith and the Sikh community. The adoption of the form of prophecy, which could make his Granth authoritative, also gave him the freedom to bring in the past in a big way. His work does not remain a reflection of his own historical situation because of his concern for the future as well as the past. His vision of the Sikh community and the Sikh state was informed largely by the Khalsa ideology. The *Prem Sumārag* is essentially a Sant Khalsa document.

The *Rahitnāma* Associated with Chaupa Singh

W.H. McLeod has argued that the text of *The Chaupa Singh Rahit-Nama* was originally composed on the basis of oral tradition cherished by the Chhibber family. Since the extant copy was prepared at Jind in 1764–5 the original text was obviously composed earlier. However, it could not have been composed earlier than 1740 because the terms *tankhā* and *tankhāya* which occur in it frequently had come into currency only in the 1730s. The contents on the whole suggested to McLeod that the text was composed around 1750, slightly later than earlier.[8] McLeod argues further that a written text was prepared after 1740 to be used by the compiler of the *Rahitnāma*.

However, the terms tankhā and tankhāya occur in the *Nasīhatnāma* and the *Srī Gur Sobhā*.[9] Therefore, McLeod's inference that the *Rahitnāma* could not have been composed before 1740 is not valid. The colophon of the *Rahitnāma* reads as follows:

> Srī Vāhegurū showed his grace by creating a Panth infused by zeal and good will. The Guru gave the gift of wisdom (*buddh*) to Chaupa Singh (to compose). The signatures of the scribe Bulaka Singh, with authentication by Guru Gobind Singh (were there). The present manuscript (*chiththā*) of the *Rahitnāma* was got written by Gurbakhsh Singh, son of Dharam Chand the Chhibber Brahman who was the treasurer of the Guru.[10]

The colophon, thus, refers essentially to a document prepared by Chaupa Singh, inscribed by Bulaka Singh, and approved by Guru Gobind Singh. Therefore, McLeod's argument that the written source for the *Rahitnāma* was composed after 1740 is not tenable.

The text published by McLeod starts with the statement, '*āgae rahit satgurū kī*' (now begins the rahit of the true Guru). In the translation, the word 'now' is left out. The reader may not realize that the text of the original document was preceded by a statement that has been omitted. This brings in the question of the 'introductory prologue' given by McLeod in his translation as an appendix.[11]

According to McLeod, this prologue evidently draws on the Chhibber tradition because it refers to the role assigned to the *muktā* category of Sikhs (which is peculiar to the Chhibbers). The *Bansāvalīnāma* of Kesar Singh Chhibber could be the source of the distinctive terminology employed in the prologue. McLeod goes on to state that the story of the *Rahitnāma*'s composition given in the prologue deviates from the *Bansāvalīnāma* version, and its language is much later than that recorded in the texts of 1764–5 and 1856–7. The prologue, thus, carries us well into the nineteenth century or even the beginning of the twentieth. According to McLeod, this possibility is suggested by the prologue's support for the Anand marriage ceremony and its opposition to caste discrimination within the Panth. He suggests that the prologue could have been added in the period of the Singh Sabha movement.[12]

However, a composite manuscript of 1887, prepared by a person who had little to do with the Singh Sabha, contains the prologue.[13] McLeod himself notices that the prologue contradicts the standard claim that the first *Rahitnāma* was prepared by Chaupa Singh. According to the prologue, the *Rahitnāma* was composed by a group of muktā Sikhs. The prologue also contradicts the main text by prohibiting recourse to Brahmans for ceremonial purposes. On the point of 'Ānand marriage', which appears to be anachronistic, the text says that the only consideration for a matrimonial tie is that the other party should be Sikh, whether Khatri, Shudar, or Vaish, without any consideration for *jātī* or *varna*. There was no need for *janjū*, *tikkā*, *dhotī*, and *kiryā-karam*. Shabads were to be sung and the *Ānand* was to be recited. It is not the recitation of the *Ānand* which makes the ceremony 'Sikh'. The essence of a 'Sikh' marriage lies in being non-Brahmanical. We have seen that neither the *Sākhī Rahit* nor the *Prem Sumārag* assigns any role to a Brahman in the rites and rituals of the Khalsa.

McLeod has given the content of the rahit in the Chaupa Singh text under thirteen main headings, containing a number of sub-headings. The main themes listed are personal behaviour, social behaviour within the Panth, caste, the sangat, the Gurū Granth Sāhib, rituals, the preparation and consumption of food, women's duties, travel and pilgrimage, false teachers and enemies of the Guru, and attitude towards Muslims. Added to these are sundry prohibitions and miscellaneous injunctions so that hardly anything is left out. The catalogue is very thorough.[14] For a better understanding of the *Rahitnāma*, however, it is necessary to analyse its contents in two parts: (a) the rahit and (b) the two narratives and the tankhā.

An analysis of the two narratives and the rahit would reveal the basic difference between them. Brahmanical myths, beliefs, and attitudes figure prominently in the narratives. They do figure in the other two components, relatively more in the rahit than in the tankhā part, but rather feebly. On the whole, the rahit and tankhā parts conform to the Sikh tradition which gets equated with the Khalsa or Singh tradition. The narrative parts of the *Rahitnāma* are out of tune with the other known *Rahitnāmas*, especially the *Nasīhatnāma*, the *Sākhī Rāhit*, and the *Prem Sumārag*. Basically, the rahit appears to reflect a situation much earlier than that of the narratives which peculiarly reflect the Chhibber concerns. The attribution of an earlier document to Chaupa Singh and the addition of narratives go together. Possibly, Chaupa Singh never composed any *Rahitnāma* on his own, and all by himself. Paradoxically, this leads to the probability of a *huzūrī* Rahitnāma having been compiled after the institution of the Khalsa and before the death of Guru Gobind Singh. The year 1700 as the year of composition in the prologue acquires great importance in this context.[15]

There are several notable features of the first narrative. Importance of the rahit is underscored. The armed Keshdhari Singhs among the Khalsa are presented as the main component. Guruship is given to the Khalsa in the lifetime of Guru Gobind Singh. The purpose of instituting the Khalsa is to establish sovereign rule. This objective, however, is subordinate to the preservation and propagation of the Sikh faith. Unwittingly, the Goddess is made to appear after the institution of the Khalsa. Guru Gobind Singh is presented as performing the *hom*. The position of the Brahmans is sought to be exalted, particularly that of the Chhibber Brahmans who are shown as closely associated with the Gurus. Quietly, Chaupa Singh is introduced not only as the most important Sikh of the Guru but also as the narrator. Consequently, the central position sought to be given to the Goddess in the institution of the Khalsa and the role assigned to the Brahmans become more important than the items of rahit, with the exception of the vesting of Guruship in the Khalsa in the lifetime of Guru Gobind Singh.[16]

The second narrative emphasizes importance of the rahit but adds little to the rahit itself. The political aspect of Guru Gobind Singh's mission is strongly reinforced raising the issue of sin within the Panth and its accommodation through the *mayikī* Sikhs. Chaupa Singh remains the narrator in this as in the first narrative. However, Dharam Chand figures more prominently than Sahib Chand. A written assurance about the future of the Chhibber family is given by the Guru to Dharam Chand.[17] The concern of Gurbakhsh Singh Chhibber with his own family becomes more pronounced in the second narrative.[18] He was not a descendant of Chaupa Singh.

Rahit for the Singhs

The rahit component forms a complete unit by itself. Therefore, we may concentrate on this component for our present purpose. There is no personal Guru now;[19] none should be accepted as Guru;[20] none should set himself up as a Guru.[21] Now there are Sikhs of the Guru, there is rahit of the Guru, there are places associated with the Guru and, above all, there is the shabad-bāṇī of the Guru to be venerated.[22] There are certain categories of descendants of the Gurus, however, who are to be shunned. There should be no association with the Mīṇās, the Dhir Mallias, and the Ram Raiyas. They were kith and kin of the Guru but also his slanderers and enemies. The same tree has leaves, flowers, and thorns. They are the thorns.[23] It is significant to note that the term used for all the Gurus here, as elsewhere, is 'the Guru' in the singular. They are all one, a symbol, an institution. One should pay respect and give consideration to the 'servants' of the Guru whom he called his own. Even the dogs of the Guru deserve consideration.[24] However, there was one category of people closely associated with the Guru at one time who were to be shunned: the Masands, together with their followers.[25] In the absence of the personal Guru, the Guru's *hukam*, his *bhāṇā*, and his *pūjā* acquire a new meaning.[26]

The most important belief shared by all the Sikhs is belief in the shabad of the Guru, his bāṇī. Since a Sikh of the Guru is not to believe in any Guru (other than Guru Nanak and his successors), he should read the bāṇī of the Guru and reflect on it.[27] A Sikh of the Guru should not read or hear any bāṇī, shabad, or sākhī other than that of the Guru.[28] He should talk about the Guru and his bāṇī, commit the bāṇī to memory, and disseminate shabad-bāṇī.[29] He who regards himself as a Sikh of the Guru should regard the shabad of the Granth Sāhib as the Guru[30] and respect the shabad of the Granth Sāhib as he respects the Guru.[31]

A little more than seventy verses are quoted from the Granth Sāhib in support of the rahit prescribed. Among the authors of these verses are Kabir, Farid, Namdev, and Bhikha. However, the bulk of the verses come from Guru Nanak, Guru Angad, Guru Amar Das, Guru Ram Das, and Guru Arjan. There is hardly any doubt that the Granth Sāhib is the *Ādi Srī Gurū Granth Sāhib*. Four other verses are referred to as Gurū ke bachan, sākh Granth Sāhib jī 10', sākh Pātshāhī 10, and sākh.[32]

The Granth Sāhib occupies a central place in Sikh religious life. A Sikh of the Guru should teach *Pothī Granth Sāhib Jī* and kīrtan of shabad-bāṇī not as a pīr or masand but as a fellow Sikh.[33] Since God resides in the Pothī, a Sikh of the Guru should keep himself clean while performing its reading (pāṭh); he should wash his hands if he has touched his nose or any other part of his body.[34] After complete reading of the Granth Sāhib, including the '*siāhī dī bidh*', he should read *Japjī* and end the reading (*bhog*) with *ketī chhuttī nāl*'.[35] This leaves no doubt that the reference is to the Ādi Granth. A Sikh scribe should prepare copies of the Granth Sāhib and give them to other Sikhs as an offering of love.[36] A Sikh of the Guru should write and read the Pothī but should not sell it. He should offer it to others and receive in return whatever is voluntarily given. The sacred word is not to be sold.[37] A Sikh of the Guru should respect the Gurmukhi script. The paper on which Gurmukhi script is written should not come under the feet and should not be used for making a packet.[38] The Granth Sāhib is installed in the dhararmsāls.[39] It serves as the Guru for initiating a Sahajdhari Sikh through *charan-pahul*: the lectern of the Granth Sāhib is washed for the water for initiation.[40] Some parts of the Granth Sāhib are of special importance: the *Japjī*, the *Rahras*, and the *So-Dar*.[41] Faced with a crisis, a Sikh of the Guru should read the entire *Japjī* five times early in the morning, should concentrate on God, and request the Sikhs to pray for him and render service to them according to his means. God may bring relief.[42] A Sikh of the Guru should live strictly in accordance with the teachings of the Granth Sāhib.[43]

The most important institution of the Sikhs is the dharamsāl. Daily visits to the dharamsāl are prescribed in the *Rahitnāma*. After his morning prayers at home, a Sikh should go to the dharamsāl and join the sādh-sangat. He should take some offering with him according to his means: flowers, fruit, grain, or cash.[44] Similarly in the afternoon, if possible, and in the evening without fail, he should go to the dharamsāl to sit in the congregation of Sikhs. He should perform kathā-kīrtan or listen to it.[45] Going to the sādh-sangat is as important as the faith in Gurbāṇī and the external symbols of kesh, kirpān and kachh.[46] When a Sikh of the Guru returns after business in the country or abroad, he should first go to the dharamsāl and then go home. Not necessarily but preferably, he should offer prayer (ardās) in the dharamsāl before setting out on such a business.[47] Sitting among the Sikhs in the presence of the Granth Sāhib in the dharamsāl, a Sikh of the Guru should not feel proud of his merit, wealth, or youth.[48] There is no greater source of merit than joining the sādh-sangat.[49]

To build a dharamsāl was the foremost duty of the Sikhs. 'Wherever there are five, seven, ten or a hundred Sikh homes in a habitation, the Sikhs must build a place for the Guru, a *dharamsāl*'.[50] A suitable person was needed to look after the dharamsāl and manage its affairs for the local community. A Sikh of the Guru in charge of 'the Guru's place' should be kind in disposition and not irritable or greedy.[51] He is called *dharamsāliā*. He should remain celibate so that he has no greed and no pride. He should be a person of moral integrity (*jatī, satī*) and look to the welfare of others (*pasuārthī*); he should have the qualities of patience, detachment, kindness, and restraint. He should observe the rahit. He should overlook the faults of others. He should remain mentally alert and physically clean. He should serve others and share food with them. He should ensure that anything belonging to a visitor from outside is not stolen or misplaced. He should have genuine sympathy for others. The local Sikhs should be considerate and attentive to such a dharamsāliā. On all occasions of some importance an *ardās* should be performed. There should be no women's quarters in the dharamsāl. The Guru's house is meant for the poor Sikhs of the Guru who are in need of help, and who are devout and observe the rahit.[52] At another place, the term *pujārī* is used in the context of the dharamsāl. He should not misappropriate or misuse any part of the offerings that come in the name of the Guru. Such an act results in destruction of intelligence and wisdom (*buddh*). A pujārī should not be proud, ignorant, or dishonest. He should not be lustful or prone to anger, a slanderer or a haughty person.[53] A Sikh of the Guru should not allow himself to be called 'Bhāī' or 'Mahant'. Haughtiness and dishonesty became the cause of the ruin of the masands.[54]

Just as dharamsāl was the place for daily worship and congregation, so the places associated with the Gurus were places of pilgrimage for the Sikhs. If there is a needy Sikh among those who depart from the village for visit to Gurdwaras, the others should take care of his needs. Those who are not accompanying them should contribute according to their means. A village that does not do this is like a *simmal* tree which has no fruit.[55] A Sikh of the Guru should visit the places of his Gurus.[56] The term used most frequently for the individual Sikh is 'a Sikh of the Guru'. It is quite clear, however, that the reference is to the 'Khalsa'.[57] Another term used is 'Gurmukh' with a certain degree of appreciation.[58]

The Sikhs of the Guru are both Keshdharis and Sahajdharis.[59] With the exclusion of the five categories of the excommunicated Sikhs, the only category left there is that of the Khalsa. In other words, the Keshdharis and the Sahajdharis are two components of the community regarded as one.[60] The Sikh women, called Sikhnīs, are a part of this religious community. There is hardly any doubt that the Khalsa came from different castes and pursued diverse occupations.[61]

Whether a Keshdhari or a Sahajdhari, a Sikh of the Guru must bathe early in the morning and recite the *Japjī* five times, and any other bāṇī that he knows by heart. Before going to the dharamsāl he should offer prayer (ardās). In the evening he should recite the *Rahrās* and the *So-Dar* at his place, or join the sādh-sangat.[62] Whether a Keshdhari or a Sahajdhari, a Sikh of the Guru should never smoke tobacco, nor sniff *nasvār*.[63] Whether a Keshdhari or a Sahajdhari, a Sikh of the Guru should follow no other Guru than his own. He should not be misled by the talk of others on this point.[64] The essential difference between the Keshdhari and the Sahajdhari is that the former is initiated through baptism of the double-edged sword (khande dī pahul) and the latter through charan pahul.[65] The former was to keep unshorn hair and a comb (kanghā) to keep them clean. He should regard his kesh as the sacred symbol of his faith (sikhkhī). His proclamation is 'Vāhegurūjī kā Khālsā, Vāhegurūjī ki fateh'.[66] Equally important for him was to bear kirpān and to wear kachh.[67] He should discard the sacred thread. The Sahajdhari had the option to wear or not to wear the sacred thread.[68] A Sahajdhari could use scissors to cut the hair of his body but not his beard. He should not resort to *bhaddan*, and should observe no conventional mourning. He should perform kīrtan and distribute prasād. He should hold bhog-pāth of the Granth Sāhib. He should feed the Khalsa who may offer ardās for the deceased, praying for his abode in the sat-sangat.[69]

A good deal of emphasis in the rahit is on ethical conduct of the individual and his concern for others. A Sikh of the Guru should pursue an honest occupation or trade.[70] He should feed the hungry, and share food with others.[71] He should cultivate humility and shun slander.[72] He should shun thieving, illicit sexual relations, and gambling.[73] He should remain detached in active life.[74] He should work for the welfare of others.[75]

The Guru is pleased with the Sikh who feeds a Sikh.[76] A Sikh of the Guru should give no trouble to another Sikh.[77] A Sikh of the Guru should use a tenth of his savings (dasvandh) for the Sikhs.[78] A Sikh of the Guru should never feel envious or jealous of the Sikhs who are more affluent.[79] On the occasions like betrothal and death, a Sikh of the Guru should offer *tambol* and turban to the concerned Sikh as a Sikh in the name of the Guru.[80] A Sikh of the Guru should serve other Sikhs with a feeling of dedication.[81] A Sikh of the Guru should never turn away from the Sikhs.[82] A Sikh should associate with others Sikhs and treat them with respect.[83] A Sikh of the Guru should prefer his good relations with other Sikhs over wealth.[84] The Sikhs of a habitation should serve a Sikh who has come from outside and meet all his needs. To serve the Sikhs is to serve the Guru.[85] There is no relationship more important than that that of the faith (sikhkhī). A Sikh of the Guru should give his daughter in marriage to a Sikh and not to a *monā*.[86] A Sikh in the service of the 'Turks' should help the Sikhs in whatever way he can. A Sikh sardār, a rājā, or a sāhu should employ only Sikhs in his kitchen (*langar*).[87] A Sikh who wishes to become a sardār should serve the Sikhs.[88]

Baptism of the double-edged sword was not meant for women. The daughter of a mona to be married to a Sikh should be baptized through charan pahul, washing the lectern (*manjī*) of the Granth Sāhib for the water for initiation.[89] A Sikh of the Guru should not kill a girl child and he should have no association with the killer of a girl child. He should never take money for the marriage of his daughter.[90] A Sikh of the Guru should not trust a woman, whether his own or another; he should not share any secret with her, treating her as a source of risk.[91] In other words, a woman could divulge the secret imparted to her. One should be afraid of the woman other than one's own. The ideal household is the one in which the wife is good and comes from a good family.[92]

Whereas the Sikh woman is less privileged than the Sikh male, the Brahman Sikh was to be more privileged than the others in terms of service and honour.[93] A Sikh of the Guru should conduct his affairs in accordance with his varna (*barn-āsram)*. This is supported by the savvayyā in which Guru Gobind Singh says that he is the son of a Chhatri and not of a Brahman and therefore, it is his wish to die fighting in the field of battle.[94] The norms of varna, āshrama, and family are recommended in connection with marriage.[95] At another place, it is stated that a Sikh of the Guru should not become polluted: anger is compared to the chandāl whose sangat is not allowed.[96]

There are some other features which may seem to be Brahmanical. The ashes after cremation are to be taken to the Ganges, though the ceremony after death even for a Sahajdhari is non-Brahmanical. Similarly, the *shradh* on the occasion of the persons to be fed on the occasion are not Brahmans but Sikhs.[97] A Brahman is recommended for performing the marriage ceremony of a Sikh but it is not clear whether or not this Brahman is a Sikh and, therefore, whether or not the ceremony is Brahmanical.[98] For the ceremony of birth and death, there is no role for the Brahman.[99] After *namskār* to the rising sun, a Sikh of the Guru should salute the Sikhs with Vāhegurūjī kī fateh, and similarly after namskār to the new moon.[100] All these features do not amount to much in comparison with the Sikh norms of belief and practice, which remain close to the teachings of the Gurus.

The *Rahitnāma*, sees the Turks as *mlechh* and as the enemies of the Sikhs. A Sikh of the Guru, says *Rahitnāma*, should never regard a Turk as a friend; should never trust him. The text forbids the Sikh to drink water from the hands of a Turk; he should never sleep in a Turk's presence. The oath of a Turk is not be trusted. A Sikh of the Guru should not be taken in by the sweet tongue of a Turk. He is not even allowed to sit with a Turk to eat. He should regard the Turks the Turks as enemies of his faith as they were cow slaughterers. The order of the Guru is to kill them in the field of battle. A Sikh of the Guru should have no association with a Turk woman.[101]

Much of the rahit relates to the religious life of the Khalsa. Belief in the ten Gurus from Guru Nanak to Guru Gobind Singh, the end of personal Guruship after the tenth Guru, and the shabad-bāṇī as the Guru are interrelated and underscore the doctrine of Guru Granth. The Granth of the Tenth Master and some works attributed to Guru Gobind Singh are referred to but the Ādi Granth alone is the Guru Granth. The centrality of the Granth Sāhib in the religious life of the Khalsa gets highlighted in several ways. Interlinked with the Guru Granth is the dharamsāl, the place of congregational worship, kīrtan, kathā, and ardās and the distribution of sacred food. It is also the place where the Sikhs from other places find shelter and sustenance. It is a well-established institution in the life of the local Sikh communities in towns and villages, whether Keshdhari or Sahajdhari.

The basic difference between the Keshdhari and Sahajdhari is the mode of initiation, with the implication of a difference in their external appearance. Though the performance of marriage ceremony by a Brahman is cryptically mentioned, even the Sahajdharis were expected to perform a Sikh ceremony after death, with a central role for the Granth Sāhib and the Sikhs. The importance of personal ethics for the Sikhs in underlined. Even greater importance is given to their mutual regard, respect, and consideration. A few features of varnashrama and popular religion are present but are rather inconspicuous and un-emphatic. Positive hostility is expressed towards the Turks who undoubtedly are Muslim. This social situation is obviously the result of a political confrontation. The rahit, on the whole, presents a predominantly Singh way of life.

Much of the rahit is reinforced in the tankhā part, with some additional obligations. Some of the additional statements are not without significance. A Keshdhari Singh should never wear a *topī* (cap) or a *langot*.[102] A Sikh should never refuse to accept a decision of the sarbat (sangat). He should not touch the feet of a cap-wearer.[103] A Sikh should not watch the dance of a professional prostitute. A Sikh should not call another Sikh by half his name.[104] A Sikh should not leave behind another Sikh who has been wounded in a battle. He should cremate, if possible, a Sikh who has died fighting in the field of battle.[105] A Sikh should never distribute (*kaṛhā*) prasād without reciting the *Ānand*. A Sikh should not mention the name of Sucha of Sirhind or the Sahi Khatri (of Lahore) without cursing him seven times.[106] A Sikh who serves the Turk should seek forgiveness.[107] The tankhā makes explicit statement on Guru-Panth and Guru Granth, underscores the importance of the Granth Sāhib, the sangat in the dharamsāl and the pahul stresses respect for the kesh and arms, especially the sword. The bulk of the tankhā relates to mutual relations of the Sikhs. Carrying the clear implication of dissociation from others, especially in the areas of religion and politics. There is no reference to varnashrama. There are some specific injunctions for women, who are quite visible as a part of the Panth.

On the whole, the early Rahitnāmas present a consensus on the religious, social, and political concerns of the Khalsa who are equated with the Sikh and the Singh as the single category of Sikhs.[108] The Rahitnāma associated with Chaupa Singh makes a distinction between the Keshdhari and Sahajdhari components of the Khalsa and between Sikh men and Sikh women. However, the bulk of the rahit injunctions applies to them all. The Khalsa are different from the contemporaries in terms of their religious beliefs and practices, including some rites and ceremonies. They all have the same ethical concerns and their attitudes are the same in relation to one another, and in relation to others. The identity of the Keshdhari Singhs, who bear and wield arms, is more pronounced; it is spontaneously recognized due to their external appearance.

Notes

1. Karamjit K. Malhotra has collated the text of the *Nasīhatnāma* with MS 29 in the same Library, dated 1831, to prepare a sounder text, consciously following a set of well-formulated criteria. However, she has published only its English translation, with an introduction on the study of Rahitnāmas. See 'The Earliest Manual of the Sikh way of Life', Reeta Grewal and Sheena Pall, eds, *Five Centuries of Sikh Tradition: Ideology, Society, Politics and Culture* (Essays for Indu Banga), New Delhi: Manohar, 2005, pp. 55–81.
2. Ibid., pp. 75–6.
3. Jeevan Deol has missed this point in his article, 'Eighteenth Century Khalsa Identity: Discourse, Praxis and Narrative', in eds, Christopher Shackle, Gurharpal Singh, and Arvind Pal Singh Mandair, *Sikh Religion, Culture and Ethnicity*, Richmond: Curzon, 2001.
4. *The Chaupa Singh Rahit-Nama*, tr. and ed., W.H. McLeod, Dunedin: University of Otago Press, 1987 pp. 29–30. McLeod places the *Sākhī Rahit* in the early 1730s without reference to its actual contents.
5. Ibid., pp. 133–8, 251–2.
6. Gurinder Singh Mann, 'Sources for the Study of Guru Gobind Singh's Life and Times', *Journal of Punjab Studies*, vol. 15, nos 1 and 2 (Spring–Fall 2008), pp. 250–1.
7. J.S. Grewal, 'The *Prem Sumārag*: A Sant Khalsa Vision of the Sikh Panth', *The Sikhs: Ideology, Institutions and Identity*, New Delhi: Oxford University Press, 2009, pp. 158–82.
8. McLeod, *The Chaupa Singh Rahit-Nama*, pp. 25–8.
9. For *Nasīhatnāma*, note 1 above. Guru Gobind Singh is referred to as *tankhā-dhār* in the *Shrī Gurū Sobhā*, ed., Shamsher Singh Ashok, Amritsar: SGPC, 1965, p. 41.
10. McLeod, *The Chaupa Singh Rahit-Nama*, pp. 130–1.
11. Ibid., pp. 251–2.
12. Ibid., p. 31.

13. MS 228, Balbir Singh Sahitya Kendra, Dehra Dun (compiled by Bhagwan Singh as *Bibek Bardhi Granth*).

14. McLeod, *The Chaupa Singh Rahit-Nama*, pp. 32–44.

15. According to Gurinder Singh Mann, the opening two segments of the *Rahitnāma* are claimed by the compilers, including Chaupa Singh who prepared the collaborative statement, to have been completed in 1700. These two segments manifest literary integrity, 'standing as independent units of the text' and having distinctive characteristics of their own. 'Sources for the Study of Guru Gobind Singh's Life and Times', p. 249.

16. McLeod, *The Chaupa Singh Rahit-Nama*, pp. 79–97.

17. Ibid., pp. 116–30.

18. The significance of the categorization of the Sikhs is enhanced by its implication. The *dīdārī* Sikhs remained present with the Guru. The *murid* Sikhs preserved their faith (sikhkhī) in contrast with the *mayikī* Sikhs who become engrossed in māyā.

19. McLeod, *The Chaupa Singh Rahit-Nama*, p. 72.

20. Ibid., p. 62.

21. Ibid., p. 68.

22. Ibid., p. 70.

23. Ibid., p. 58.

24. Ibid., p. 70.

25. Ibid., p. 58.

26. Ibid., p. 77.

27. Ibid., pp. 72, 74.

28. Ibid., pp. 63, 73, 78.

29. Ibid., p. 74.

30. Ibid., p. 76.

31. Ibid., pp. 59, 72–3, 77.

32. Ibid., p. 66.

33. Ibid., p. 76.

34. Ibid., p. 76.

35. Ibid., p. 65.

36. Ibid., p. 65.

37. Ibid., p. 78.

38. Ibid., p. 75.

39. Ibid., p. 60.

40. Ibid., p. 57.

41. Ibid., p. 60.

42. Ibid., p. 78.

43. Ibid., p. 57.

44. Ibid., pp. 57–8.

45. Ibid., p. 58.

46. Ibid., p. 70.

47. Ibid., p. 75.

48. Ibid., p. 77.

49. Ibid., pp. 76–7.
50. Ibid., pp. 62–3.
51. Ibid., pp. 65–6.
52. Ibid., p. 61.
53. Ibid., p. 62.
54. Ibid., p. 70.
55. Ibid., p. 72.
56. Ibid., p. 78.
57. Ibid., p. 57.
58. Ibid., pp. 57, 59–60, 62–4.
59. The evidence of the hukamnāmas of Guru Gobind Singh, Mata Sundari, and Mata Sahib Devi makes it absolutely clear that all the Khalsa were not Singh. The baptism of the double-edged sword was commendable but not compulsory. There were many Sikhs linked directly to the Guru but not yet baptized. The use of the words keshdhārī and sahajdhārī reflects the situation in which the Khalsa consisted of these two components.
60. McLeod, *The Chaupa Singh Rahit-Nama*, pp. 58–9, 61–2, 65, 67, 69, 75.
61. Ibid., pp. 57–8.
62. Ibid., p. 59.
63. Ibid., p. 62.
64. Ibid., p. 65.
65. Ibid., p. 68.
66. Ibid., p. 58.
67. Ibid., p. 60.
68. Ibid., p. 64.
69. Ibid., p. 57.
70. Ibid., pp. 63–4.
71. Ibid., pp. 60, 65.
72. Ibid., p. 69.
73. Ibid., p. 73.
74. Ibid., p. 65.
75. Ibid., p. 61.
76. Ibid., p. 62.
77. Ibid., p. 63.
78. Ibid., p. 64.
79. Ibid., p. 65.
80. Ibid., p. 66.
81. Ibid., p. 67.
82. Ibid., pp. 68–9.
83. Ibid., p. 69.
84. Ibid., p. 75.
85. Ibid., pp. 59–60, 75.
86. Ibid., pp. 59–60.
87. Ibid., p. 75.
88. Ibid., p. 60.

89. Ibid., p. 59.
90. Ibid., p. 69.
91. Ibid., p. 77.
92. Ibid., p. 60.
93. Ibid., p. 72.
94. Ibid., p. 59.
95. Ibid., p. 73.
96. Ibid., p. 63.
97. Ibid., p. 72.
98. Ibid., pp. 63, 65.
99. Ibid., p. 78.
100. Ibid., p. 69.
101. Ibid., p. 59.
102. Ibid., p. 100.
103. Ibid., p. 104.
104. Ibid., p. 105.
105. Ibid., p. 106.
106. Ibid., p. 107.
107. Ibid., p. 108.
108. For the most comprehensive use of the evidence of the *Rahitnāmas*, see Karamjit Kaur Malhotra, 'Social and Cultural Life of the Sikhs in the Punjab During the Eighteenth Century', PhD Thesis, Panjab University, Chandigarh, 2009.

PART FOUR

In the Context of Sikh Rule (1765–1849)

12

The Sikh Faith and the Khalsa Panth

Chhibber's *Bansāvalīnāma*

Rattan Singh Jaggi refers to two opposing evaluations of Kesar Singh Chhibber's *Bansāvalīnāma Dasān Pātshāhīan Kā*: one based on extreme scepticism and the other bordering on credulity. None of these could be regarded as a balanced view. In fact, no serious study of the work could be made in the absence of a printed edition. The primary purpose of its publication, therefore, was to make the text easily available to scholars.[1]

Expressing his own view of the character of this work, Jaggi refers first of all to its title, and the alternate title *Kursīnāma*. Both these are appropriate for a work dealing primarily with genealogies. The author refers to himself as a Brahman Sikh of Jammu and claims that his ancestors were closely connected with the Sikh Gurus. His grandfather, Dharam Chand, was the treasurer (*toshakhāniā*) of Guru Gobind Singh, and his father, Gurbakhsh Singh, had served Mata Sundari and Mata Sahib Devi before he went to Ramdaspur with Guru Gobind Singh's maternal uncle, Kirpal Singh, and served as a *dāroghā*. Furthermore, Dharam Chand's brother, Sahib Chand, had served Guru Gobind Singh as a dīwān. Their father, Durga Mal was the dīwān successively of Guru Har Rai, Guru Har Krishan, and Guru Tegh Bahadur. Sati Das and Mati Das, who were executed in Delhi as the companions of Guru Tegh Bahadur, were Durga Mal's nephews.

Kesar Singh Chhibber completed his work in 1769 at the age of about seventy. Jaggi naturally infers that Kesar Singh was born around 1700. But Kesar Singh does not claim to have seen Guru Gobind Singh. He was in Delhi with his father before they both went to Ramdaspur in the late 1720s. Talking of the events of the 1730s he refers to himself as a youngster. It is not clear when Kesar Singh left Ramdaspur for Jammu.

There is no indication that he participated in any armed conflict against the Mughal administrators. By the time he completed his work, Sikh rule had been established over a large part of the Punjab.

Jaggi regards a few features of Chhibber's *Bansāvalīnāma* as significant. His interest in dates appears to be remarkable but the accuracy of his dates is open to question. They have to be critically examined. The majority of the dates relate to the lives of individuals mentioned in the work rather than to important events. Chhibber's interest is primarily in 'the lives', which would explain his interest in the chains of kinship as well. It is in connection with dates that he refers to the use of a *vahī* in the possession of his family at Jammu, which was destroyed in a fire. Jaggi drives home the point that Chhibber heavily depended on what he had heard from others. Jaggi points out that Chhibber's work does not possess any poetic merit; it consists of mere versification rather than poetry. At places, it acquires the tone of a Rahitnāma.

The contents of the *Bansāvalīnāma* reveal that Kesar Singh Chhibber was possibly a religious man but not a man of letters. He was familiar with the Ādi Granth, the Gītā, the *Bhogal Purāṇa*, the Ramāyaṇa of Tulsi Das, the *Bālā Janamsākhī*, and some of the compositions attributed to Guru Gobind Singh. The form of the *Bansāvalīnāma* is neither that of a *Janamsākhī* nor that of a *Gurbilās* or a Rahitnāma.

Chhibber states that he was asked to provide an exposition of a verse in the compositions of Guru Nanak. This has actually little to do with the work as a whole. His assumption that he understood Gurbāṇī better than others around him is nevertheless important. It gets linked up with the claim that his ancestors were closely connected with the Gurus. His understanding of the bāṇī and his links with the Gurus were a proof of his status as a good Sikh. His work was meant to demonstrate that he understood the Sikh faith and the Sikh tradition better than many others. He is emphatic that he was not seeking patronage from any Sikh ruler. But he seems to protest too much and the purpose cannot be ruled out.

Chhibber wanted to reveal his knowledge of the Sikh Gurus and the Sikh tradition through his work. To make his work inclusive rather than selective, he tended to relate everything that he knew from hearsay or from texts. The heterogeneity of his work appears to spring from his desire to reveal his knowledge as a mark of his nearness to the Gurus and his understanding of the Sikh tradition.

The *Bansāvalīnāma* is divided into fourteen chapters (*chārans*). The last chapter, spread over sixty-one printed pages, discusses the state of the Sikhs in the author's own time. The eleventh, twelfth, and thirteenth chapters deal respectively with Banda Bahadur, Jit Singh, and Mata Sahib Devi, but cover only seventeen pages in print. The first ten chapters, devoted to the ten Gurus, cover 168 pages in print. Out of these, seventy-one are devoted to Guru Gobind Singh alone. The account of Guru Nanak covers virtually five pages.

Guru Nanak

Chhibber provides a clue to his short treatment of Guru Nanak. Any one interested could turn to the *Janamsākhīs* of Guru Nanak for detail. However, no such information was available for Guru Angad, Guru Amar Das, Guru Ram Das, Guru Arjan, Guru Hargobind, Guru Har Rai, Guru Har Krishan, and Guru Tegh Bahadur. Chhibber admits that some of the chapters are long while others are short, and this is primarily due to his tendency to relate all that he knew. He was certainly interested in the lives of all the ten Gurus, but his interest was not confined to them. Indeed, one-third of his work deals with the eighteenth century after the death of Guru Gobind Singh.

That Chhibber's interest was not confined to *bansāvalīs* of the Gurus may be illustrated with reference to what he has to say about Guru Nanak.[2] Giving an exposition of the origin and extent of the universe in terms of the Purāṇic tradition, Chhibber comes to a point that can be regarded as the beginning of the Surajvanshi Raghuvanshis, the family to which belonged Raja Dashrath and his sons Ram, Lachhman, Bharat, and Shatrughan. The descendants of the latter four were the Bedis, the Trehans, the Bhallas, and the Sodhis, that is, the Khatri gotras to which belonged Guru Nanak, Guru Angad, Guru Amar Das, and Guru Ram Das (and his successors up to Guru Gobind Singh). Taking his cue from the *Bachittar Nātak*, Chhibber elaborates the legend according to which the Bedis had promised in an earlier yuga to return the gift of kingship they had received from the Sodhis. That was why guruship (the equivalent of kingship) passed from Guru Nanak to Guru Ram Das through Guru Angad and Guru Amar Das, and stayed in the Sodhi family of Guru Ram Das.

Chhibber's work traces the immediate ancestry of Guru Nanak up to his grandfather. He mentions half-a-dozen dates before the date of Guru Nanak's birth in 1469 in Talvandi, the village of a Bhatti Rajput, Bhoa. The ancestral occupation of Guru Nanak's father, Kalyan Das, was shopkeeping. He was the first in the family to become a patwārī. He had left his father's village for Talvandi. At this point, Chhibber refers to a janampatrī which contained all the facts. A variant reading refers to Miharban, but Jaggi, thinks that the source of Chhibber's work was a *Bālā Janamsākhī*. Conforming to the Bālā tradition, Chhibber mentions the night of the full moon of Kattak (Kartik) as the time of Guru Nanak's birth.

In 1483, Guru Nanak was married to the daughter of Mula, a Choṇā Khatri of Pakhkhoke Randhawe. He went to Sultanpur with Jai Ram, his sister's husband. His elder son, Sri Chand, was born in 1494 as the incarnation (*avtār*) of Gorakh Nath. No date is given for the birth of the younger son, Lakhmi Das. The mother is referred to as 'Mata Sulakhani'. Both the sons were born after Guru Nanak gave her two *laungs* (and not due to any physical union with her). Guru Nanak remained immersed in the stream called Vaein for three days and emerged with a message (received from God). He soon set out with Bala and Mardana to see 'other countries'. Sri Chand practised celibacy. Lakhmi Das was married at the age of eight in 1503 to the daughter of a Sial Khatri. Guru Nanak returned from his first *udāsī*, and lived at home for four months. During his second udāsī, Mardana died in the city known as Khurme and in accordance with his wishes, he was cremated. In 1525, Guru Nanak took up residence in Kartarpur on the bank of the river Ravi. In 1537, he revealed to Angad, who was on a pilgrimage to the goddess, a vision of the goddess, whereupon he returned home. He served Guru Nanak for two years with great devotion and received the robe of Guruship from him in 1539.

Lakhmi Das and Sri Chand remonstrated with their father for bestowing upon a contemptible shopkeeper the important office of Guruship which rightfully belonged to them. Guru Nanak told them that Guruship was a burden placed on Angad's head, while his own descendants were given the boon of 'horses, hawks, and power'; even their dogs would be worshipped. However, this did not placate them and Guru Angad assured them that he was their servant. Guru Nanak's cremation and other rituals were performed by Brahmans, including the recitation of the *Garuṛa Purāṇa*. When all the traditional rites had been performed, the sons of Guru Nanak decided to retrieve the robe of Guruship from Guru Angad. On Sri Chand's demand, Guru Angad gave up the robe but neither Lakhmi Das nor his son Dharam Chand could lift it. Guru Angad lifted it easily. The Bedis were reconciled to his succession, and the mark of Guruship (*tikkā*) was applied on his forehead. Nevertheless, he stayed at Kartarpur for only four months and then moved to Khadur.

Lakhmi Das died at Kartarpur in 1555, and he was succeeded by his son Dharam Chand (born in 1515) who was married in a family of Passi Khatris in 1527. He performed his father's *kiryā karam* as prescribed in the *Shāstras*.

On the whole, though much of the information provided by Chhibber relates to the family of Guru Nanak, his ancestors and his sons and grandsons, there is enough information that is not genealogical.

Guru Hargobind

In Chhibber's treatment of Guru Hargobind, the information on genealogies is overshadowed by other kinds of information. Born to Mata Ganga, the wife of Guru Arjan, in 1590, Hargobind was married at a young age (the printed Sammat 1607 is obviously incorrect) before his father died as a martyr in 1606, having remained on the *gaddī* for twenty-three-and-a-half years. Guru Hargobind's first wife, Mata Madodari, belonged to a Suri Khatri family. At this point Chhibber disgresses from the main theme and discusses incidents related to the enmity of Mughal administrators and their Khatri collaborators with Guru Arjan, Guru Ram Das, and Guru Amar Das. He refers to them as *tatte-khatte* (Muslims and Khatris) at several places in his work.

There was an enemy within the family too: Guru Arjan's elder brother Prithi Chand, referred to as Pirthia by Chhibber. After the death of Guru Arjan, in which Pirthia was implicated, he refused to recognize Hargobind as the Guru. He began to woo the Sikhs so as to get recognition of his claim to Guruship. After performing all the customary rites, Guru Hargobind settled in village Rahela in 1607 and renamed it Sri Hargobindpur. He considered the idea of meeting the Mughal emperor in Delhi to seek justice, but Bhai Gurdas and other prominent Sikhs advised against it. Nevertheless, after contracting a second marriage in a family of Lamma Khatris in 1610, Guru Hargobind proceeded to Delhi. Pirthia came to know of this and he contacted the Sahi Khatris of Lahore, the old enemies of Guru Arjan. Presumably on their behalf, some Puri Khatris of Delhi worked against Guru Hargobind and he was imprisoned in the fort of Gwalior.

Nur Jahan cautioned Jahangir against imprisoning a *faqīr*, but to no immediate effect. A few weeks later, the emperor fell ill and was unable to pass water. He was treated by a Sikh hakīm who was not able to cure him and pleaded helplessness against the spiritual powers of faqīrs. This was a pointer to the cause of the emperor's illness. He ordered the release of all the persons imprisoned in Gwalior. Guru Hargobind refused to leave the fort as he felt that he had not received justice from the court. He was summoned by the emperor. When he appeared before the emperor, he found the Sikh *hakīm* there. Guru Hargobind instructed him to give something to the emperor for his ailment. With the Guru's blessings, the emperor was completely cured. After hearing Guru Hargobind, he issued an order to the governor of Lahore that Guru Hargobind's demands be met. The governor of Lahore handed over the Sahis to Guru Hargobind. The head of the family, Chandu, confessed that he had been misled by Pirthia to work against Guru Arjan. With the sole exception of a daughter-in-law, the entire Sahi family was put to death. Pirthia's son Miharban went to meet the Guru but he refused to see him. Guru Hargobind moved to Ramdaspur in 1611.

The Puris of Delhi, however, continued to be hostile to Guru Hargobind. They reminded Jahangir of the Guru's promise to send gifts of pearls on regaining his property. The emperor sent his soldiers to the Guru, but he dodged them and went to Kashmir. The Puri Mutasaddis remained active in Delhi and the emperor ordered his *ahadīs* to bring the Guru to his court. The Sikhs paid some money to the ahadīs who returned to Delhi. On Nur Jahan's advice, the emperor decided not to pay heed to the enemies of Guru Hargobind. On his return from Kashmir, the Guru contracted his third marriage with a girl of a Marwaha Khatri family of Goindval. Her parents had brought her to Guru Hargobind in the hope that he would accept her.

Guru Hargobind's eldest son, Gurditta, was born to Mata Madodari in 1606. Gurditta's real brother, Ani Rai, was born in 1615. Mata Mahadevi Marwahi gave birth to Surat Singh and Atal Rai (the date given as Sammat 1663 is obviously incorrect). Before he accepted Mata Kaulan as his fourth wife, Guru Hargobind evinced interest in martial activity.

He told the Sikhs not to bring any more offers of marriage. His only daughter Bibi Viro was born to Mata Nanaki Lamma in 1617 and her real brother, Tegh Bahadur, was born in 1621. This was the time when Guru Hargobind began to enlist paid soldiers, and took to hunting. He authorized any five Sikhs of a local congregation (*sangat*) to initiate a willing person into the Sikh faith through the ceremony of *charnamrit*. Many persons adopted Sikhism. They were instructed to associate themselves only with the Sikhs of the Guru. Atal Rai revived a dead child and Guru Hargobind rebuked him; he gave up his life. In 1625, Guru Hargobind decided to get Bibi Viro married into a Bhalla family. Due to the animosity of the close relations of the Sahis of Lahore he went to Kartarpur where Viro's marriage was solemnized. The marriages of Gurditta and Surat Singh were also solemnized at Kartarpur. Around this time, Guru Hargobind prepared to defend himself against any aggressor, which explains why he refused to accept yet another offer of a bride in 1626. However, she was accepted by Gurditta without the knowledge of his father. Guru Hargobind was enraged but he blessed the bride that her progeny would receive great gifts. Ani Rai was married in 1627.

The battle of Kartarpur was fought in 1630 against Painde Khan, the erstwhile commandant in the employment of Guru Hargobind. He had fallen out with the Guru over the issue of a rare white hawk which belonged to the Guru but which was appropriated by Painde Khan's son-in-law, Chiman Khan. Painde Khan decided to support Chiman Khan in the hope of securing a *jāgīr* by gifting the rare bird to the emperor. With the support of the Mughal governor of Lahore, Painde Khan launched an attack on Kartarpur, but was killed in the battle. Chiman Khan took over command of the force, but he too was killed. Guru Hargobind was decisively victorious. He dismissed all his Muslim employees; he decided to leave the plains for the hills and went to Kiratpur.

In 1631, Gurditta's wife gave birth to a son who was named Dhir Mal. Another son, Har Rai was born to Gurditta's second wife. Surat Singh's son, Deep Chand, was born in 1633. Guru Hargobind decided to pass on the mantle of Guruship to Gurditta, also known as Baba Gurditta because of his physical and moral strength. He revived a dead cow and was rebuked by Guru Hargobind, whereupon he decided to end his own life. In 1635, Guru Hargobind bestowed Guruship on his grandson Har Rai instead of a son, or his elder grandson Dhir Mal, because

Guru Hargobind had blessed Har Rai's mother before she married Gurditta. Guru Hargobind himself lived for three years after Har Rai was installed as the Guru. According to Chhibber, Guru Hargobind died in 1638 at the age of forty-eight.[3]

The foregoing paragraphs clearly show that Kesar Singh Chhibber's interest in Guru Hargobind's family is overshadowed by his interest in his activities, including political activity. This interest becomes more prominent in his treatment of Guru Gobind Singh. His interest in genealogies is virtually replaced by his interest in the chronology of the events in Guru Gobind Singh's life.

Guru Gobind Singh and the Khalsa

Guru Gobind Singh was born at Patna on the Triveni in 1661. The Brahmans named him Gobind Rai.[4] Two years later he was taken to the River Beas (Bakala) where he lived for three years. He then went to Makhowal and learnt Gurmukhi and Persian from Munshi Harjas Rai. In 1669, he began his training in the use of arms. In 1673, at the age of 12, he married Sundari. Two years later, Aurangzeb summoned Guru Tegh Bahadur. He preferred to give up his head rather than renounce his *dharam*. When his head was brought to Makhowal, Guru Gobind Singh performed the last rites in accordance with the *Shāstras*. Then he began to practise austerities in seclusion to destroy the Turks. He heard the heavenly voice that he should grasp the double-edged sword.[5]

Guru Gobind Singh came out of his seclusion and asked Pandit Devi Ditta about the auspicious time for ascending the throne of Guruship. The sacred mark (*tilak*) was applied to his forehead at the time of accession. He called for the Chhibber Sikhs. Sahib Chand and Dharam Chand presented themselves. Guru Gobind Singh instructed Chaupa Singh (his old *khidāvā*) to bring *saropās* for the two Chhibbers. Sahib Chand was appointed as *dīwān*, and Dharam Chand as toshakhāniā. Saropas were then given to the Masands who were present on the occasion, and sent to those Masands and Bhāīs who were absent. They were all told to visit Makhowal at the time of Baisakhi. A large number of Sikhs attended the Baisakhi *melā* in 1676.[6]

Pandit Devi Ditta used to perform kathā of the Mahābhārata every day. When he reached the point where Bhim hurled elephants at the enemy, Guru Gobind Singh wanted to know how he had acquired such exceptional strength. Devi Ditta said that all the Vedas, Purāṇas, and Shāstras were unanimous that the source of strength and power was *jagg-hom* (for the Goddess). Guru Gobind Singh wanted to know whether Devi Ditta could make Bhavani appear in person. Expressing his helplessness, he suggested that the Brahmans of Kashi and Kashmir could perform such a feat. Guru Gobind Singh decided to test the Brahmans and invited them to eat food. He offered a sum of money to those who would eat meat, and increased the amount on subsequent occasions. Eventually, only three Brahmans refused to eat meat: Hari Das, Har Bhagwan, and Lachhi Ram. Guru Gobind Singh ordered them to be hanged if they remained adamant. Secretly, however, he instructed the executioners to bring them back if they were willing to die. They were brought back and Guru Gobind Singh washed their feet and drank the charnamrit. They were told that they had passed the test of being true Brahmans.[7]

In 1677, Guru Gobind Singh collected all the material needed for the hom, instructing Dharam Chand to spend Rs 10,000 and send all the material to the temple of Mata Naina Devi. Prominent Brahmans were contacted. Bishanpal came from Kashi with a hundred of his students. Shivbakar came from Kashmir. Many others, including the three who had refused to eat meat, were invited. Gurbakhsh Singh (the son of Dharam Chand and the father of Kesar Singh Chhibber) brought materials worth Rs 10,000 from Delhi. Sahib Chand sent his son Charan Das to Bajwara to procure 10,000 white robes. The Brahmans were told that they had to make 'the Mother' appear. When they informed the Guru that they would try but they could give no guarantee, they were told to go back. However, they observed fast for three days and informed Guru Gobind Singh that Kalakdas, a Brahman in a temple (*thākurdwāra*) of Gujarat, could make 'the Mother' appear.[8]

Kalakdas came, because he looked upon Guru Gobind Singh as an avtār, and not for any material reward. He said that the hom called for a continuous posture (*āsan*) of forty days. Guru Gobind Singh expressed his willingness to do so. Kalakdas asked him why he wanted to see the Goddess. 'To destroy the wicked,' the Guru replied. Kalakdas remarked that the Goddess would destroy the wicked but the Guru would be accountable to Akal Purkh. Guru Gobind Singh told Kalakdas that Akal Purkh had sent him to destroy the wicked. Kalakdas suggested that, being *nirlep* and *nirvair*, Guru Gobind Singh should raise a panth so that he would not be accountable to Dharam Rai for destroying the wicked.

They too were created by Akal Purkh. Guru Gobind Singh approved of the idea.[9]

The new panth was to be established to secure political power. It was necessary to arm this panth. The Goddess would remit the obligation of wearing the sacred thread (*janjū*) and the sacred mark (tilak), and a special symbol could be given to the panth by Guru Gobind Singh. Kalakdas told the Guru that when his panth would come into power, sin (pap) would also raise its head. When sin makes its appearance, the panth would be held accountable by Dharam Rai. Pondering over this, Guru Gobind Singh asked Kalakdas to solve the problem. The Guru was committed to destroy the wicked but not to abandon the panth to Dharam Rai. Kalakdas told him that since sin was inseparable from *rāj*, the only solution was to make some room for sin in the panth. Guru Gobind Singh conceived of the panth as consisting of four categories to confine sin to only one of these. The three constituents which were placed under the protection of Akal Purkh were the *dīdārī*, the *mukte*, and the *murīd* Sikhs. The dīdārīs were those who lived in the Guru's presence and worshipped with him. The mukte Sikhs were those who adhered to their faith in spite of persecution by the Turks. These two categories would establish political power. The rulers who remained detached in the midst of *māyā* and viewed all their possessions as the gift of the Guru, belonged to the category of murīds. Sin was confined to the fourth category, the mayiki Sikhs who, as rulers, would be engrossed in māyā.[10]

According to Chhibber, Guru Gobind Singh believed that he had three fathers and two mothers. Guru Tegh Bahadur was his natural father, Guru Nanak was his father as the Guru, and Akal Purkh was the father of his light (*jot*). Similarly, Mata Gujari was his natural mother and Mata Mansa was his mother as the bestower of intelligence and wisdom.

The wicked people were to be destroyed because of Guru Tegh Bahadur's martyrdom. The Sikhs of the Guru were to be differentiated from the rest of the world and only those who followed the Guru's rahit would be his true Sikhs. On Kalakdas' advice, Guru Gobind Singh wore a new sacred thread (janjū) and prepared himself for the hom.[11]

Guru Gobind Singh sat inside a tent with Kalakdas, Shivbakar, and Bishanpal. Outside the tent 10,000 Brahmans chanted praises of the goddess and behind them sat Sikhs reciting *shabad-kīrtan*. Behind them both were servants and soldiers to prevent anyone from entering the enclosure for forty days. Only Guru Gobind Singh and Kalakdas observed the fast till the end. On the fortieth day, Kalakdas announced that the Goddess would appear and whatever the wish of the Guru, would be fulfilled. Guru Gobind Singh wished that his panth should prevail in the world. Suddenly, there was a great illumination and the Goddess appeared, holding weapons in all her eight hands. Because of the blinding light Guru Gobind Singh could get only a glimpse of the Goddess. Kalakdas, however, stretched out his hands and she placed a double-edged sword in his hands. Had Guru Gobind Singh offered his head to the Goddess, Kalakdas would have brought him back to life and he would have lived for a hundred years.[12]

Guru Gobind Singh instructed Sahib Chand and Dharam Chand to distribute white robes among the Brahmans and to give them charity (*dān*). Pandit Devi Ditta, however, refused to accept the robe and *dakhṇā* on the plea that he had not been invited along with the other Brahmans despite being the pandit of the sacred place (*dhām*). Guru Gobind Singh realized his mistake and composed the savvayyā, '*jo kichhu lekh likhio*', ending with the statement that all Chhatris were created by Brahmans. A new robe was sent to Devi Ditta and he was invited to sit with Kalakdas, Bishanpal, Shivbakar, Lachhi Ram, Har Bhagwan, and Harjas on a high platform. In their praise, Guru Gobind Singh composed the savvayyās starting with '*sev karī inhī kī bhāvat*' and '*judd jitai inhī ke prasād*'. These savvayyas are actually in praise of the Sikhs. Anyway, Devi Ditta apologized for his show of pride and sought forgiveness, saying that Guru Gobind Singh was the perfect avtār of Vishnu. Guru Gobind Singh talked highly of the power of tap and added that he could neither perform it as a Chhatri nor could he renounce his domestic responsibilities. His wish was to die fighting on the battlefield. All the Brahmans acknowledged that Guru Gobind Singh was pre-eminent among the Chhatris. Only he could protect the sacred thread (janjū) and the sacred mark (tikkā).[13]

Chhibber states that there were four *varnas*, four dharmas, and four *āshramas*. The observance of varna-dharma was the test of social responsibility. The Khatri who wielded the double-edged sword, the Brahman who acquired knowledge, the Sikh who conducted himself in accordance with the wishes of the Guru, and the woman who thought of none other than her husband were all praiseworthy. The bards (*chārans*), too, praised Guru Gobind Singh for his magnanimity. He had decided to establish the panth for righteousness (dharam) and whoever joined the panth would be saved from Dharam Rai. His panth would be the true association (sangat) in which Vishnu would dwell all the time. On hearing this, Guru Gobind Singh proclaimed that whoever equated him with God would fall into the pit of hell as there was no doubt that he was God's servant (*dās*). He added that the Brahmans were the masters (*thākur*) and the Khatris were their servants (*chakar*). A true Khatri acknowledged the Brahman as his superior; his duty was to fight and to give alms (dān) to Brahmans. Present on the occasion were all the ten great branches (jāts) of Brahmans, five of the north and five of the south. They praised Guru Gobind Singh before they left Naina Devi.[14]

Kalakdas asked Guru Gobind Singh what he proposed to do about Guruship. The Guru replied that Guruship would come to an end. Guru Nanak had thought of ten bodies (*jāmās*). Since Guru Gobind Singh had decided to destroy the wicked, he would institute a panth. The implication is that the panth would replace the Guru. Kalakdas remarked that the panth would not unite against the enemy. He went on to mention that one of the seven *charanjīts* was in the south. Guru Gobind Singh was aware of him and said that the person referred to would obey his orders and fight against the wicked enemy. The reference is to Banda Bahadur. Shortly thereafter, Kalakdas left and Guru Gobind Singh returned to Makhowal.[15]

Accompanied by Sahib Chand, Dharam Chand and a number of Sikhs, Kirpal Singh, the maternal uncle of Guru Gobind Singh asked Guru Gobind Singh to explain the meaning of his statement that he was not God but only God's dās. The Guru explained that his physical frame was subject to annihilation and all that was destructible was māyā. God alone is not subject to destruction. Thus, he cleared all the doubts of the Sikhs.[16]

Guru Gobind Singh moved to Paonta with his army. Raja Fateh Shah felt offended and decided to fight a battle. There were numerous casualties on both sides. In 1689, Guru Gobind Singh left Poanta and founded Anandpur. In the following year, he married Mata Jito. Fighting broke out between the Jaswals and Katoches and Guru Gobind Singh supported one side. However, when the Rajas made peace with the Turks, Guru Gobind Singh withdrew his support and returned to Anandpur.[17]

In 1693, Guru Gobind Singh resolved to institute a separate panth. He decided that the Sikhs should not observe *bhaddan*. This was a concession from the Goddess because it was difficult to observe the rahit of janjū, tikkā, bhaddan, and kiryā in times of war. As a distinguishing symbol, the Sikhs would not cut their hair (*kesh*); it would be obligatory to carry arms and to bear the name Singh. Also, they would wear the blue dress of Mata Kali and fight to the finish against the Turks.[18]

Hukamnāmas on the new rahit were dispatched to the Masands. Dhir Mal was asked to send the Granth but he refused, saying that if Gobind Singh had become the Guru, he should get a new Granth prepared. Guru Gobind Singh had a copy of the Granth prepared and he also produced a Granth of his own. There were several categories of Sikhs: the followers of Dhir Mal, Ram Rai, and the Mīṇās. Then there were the Masands who did not spare even the daughters and sisters of the Sikhs. Guru Gobind Singh asked them to mend their ways but they did not heed his advice.[19]

In 1697, Guru Gobind Singh decided to give a distinct symbol to the panth to differentiate it from all others, just as Prophet Muhammad had done. The new panth was created to avenge the execution of Guru Tegh Bahadur and to spread the true faith (dharam) by wiping out sin. Distinct from both Hindus and Musalmans, the third panth was created to wage war for the cause of righteousness. Guru Gobind Singh ordered Chaupa Singh to bring water in a clean bowl and stirred it with a dagger (*kard*) while the *Japjī* and the *Ānand* were recited. Sahib Chand suggested that sugar be added to it for taste. Dharam Chand was asked to bring some *patāshā*s which were added to the water. This water was called *pahul*. Chaupa Singh was told to sit down and to place his right hand over the left. Pahul was poured into his palm thrice and he was asked to drink it and to recite Vāhegurūjī kā Khālsā, Vāhegurūjī kī fateh. Five or seven other Sikhs were similarly given pahul at that time. This rite of initiation was prescribed for others as well.[20]

A code of conduct (rahit) was promulgated for the Keshdhari Panth. The Sikh of the Guru was enjoined to do no evil, to have no connection with Musalmans, to fight in the cause of righteousness, to love his own wife, abstain from alcohol and tobacco, not to visit prostitutes, and not to indulge in gambling or stealing. He should be a part of the true congregation (sat-sang) and cultivate love for the sacred word (shabad-bāṇī). He should earn an honest living and appropriate nām, dān, and *isnān*. He should love other Sikhs but none of the enemy. He should share his food with others. He should never discard his faith (dharam), nor should he follow the path of renunciation (*bairāg*). He should have faith only in his Guru and serve no *sādh* or *sant*. Such a Sikh could attain liberation. Indeed, he who joins the Guru's panth attains liberation, and becomes the means of liberation for his family.[21]

The issue of the Masands arose again. A Masand named Chaito did not deliver to the Guru what a rich widow had sent with him, and gave her forged receipts. This came to light when she came personally to see the Guru. Chaito was ordered to hand over the things but the other Masands made a common cause with him out of self-interest. They were confident of the support of their followers. They refused to appear before the Guru, and he ordered them to be brought by force. Some of them were beaten; others were thrown into boiling cauldrons. Only those who ran away or went into hiding escaped death. Guru Gobind Singh sent hukamnāmas to Sikh sangats that they should not associate with the Masands and their followers. At the same time, the Sikhs were ordered not to associate with the Mīṇās, the Dhir Mallias, and the Ram Raiyas. The entire Sikh sangat was the Guru's Khalsa. They were asked to bring *golak* and *dasvandh* personally. The Khalsa of Akal Purkh became purified, cleansed of all sin or blemish. Such hukamnāmas were sent far and wide through special messengers.[22]

Two categories of Sikhs were to be treated somewhat differently. First, a Brahman Sikh was to be accorded special respect and consideration. He could oblige other Brahmans not to oppose the Sikhs, and thereby ensure an increase in their numbers. Second, the entire code was not obligatory for a Sikh in the service of the government; he should help other Sikhs in all matters connected with his office. But even in his case, several obligations were not abrogated: he could not use tobacco, observe bhaddan, kill a female child, cut his hair, or associate with the five excommunicated groups.[23]

On the death of Mata Jito in 1700, all the last rites, including kiryā, were performed in accordance with the Shāstras, but none of the sons of Guru Gobind Singh, who were all Keshdhari, performed bhaddan. Guru Gobind Singh began to observe continence. Some Sikhs offered him a new bride but he did not accept her. On their insistence, she was allowed to serve the Guru. She remained unmarried. In 1701, Guru Gobind Singh's *Samundar Sāgar Granth* was consigned to the river. Only a few leaves were retrieved by some Sikhs. Another Granth, the *Avtār Līlā*, was composed; it was not bound and its leaves got dispersed in a battle. In 1698, the Sikhs had asked Guru Gobind Singh if the two Granths could be bound together. The Guru told them that the Ādi Granth was the

Guru and the other Granth was his 'sport'; it should remain separate from the Ādi Granth.[24]

A large number of Sikhs attended the Baisakhi gathering (melā) at Anandpur in 1702. They carried with them many gifts and offerings. Raja Hari Chand took fancy to a beautiful bird and he wanted to have it. But it was taken by Sahibzada Fateh Singh. Raja Hari Chand approached the chief of Kahlur and they consulted the Katoches and the Hindurias. They decided to approach Aurangzeb to oust Guru Gobind Singh from the hills.[25]

Guru Gobind Singh resolved to hand over rulership to the Panth in 1703. All the four varnas (Khatri, Brahman, Sud, Vais) were represented in the Panth. Rulership could be passed on to the ones chosen by the Goddess. Guru Gobind Singh ordered the Sikhs to offer their heads to the Goddess. Five Sikhs volunteered: two zamīndārs, one Arora, one Khatri, and one tarkhān. This was how rulership was passed on to the Shudras. What was done by the Goddess could not be undone.[26]

Thousands of Sikhs joined the Baisakhi gathering at Anandpur in 1704. They were instructed in the rahit. Among other things, they were told to discard janjū, tikkā, *dhotī*, and *chaukā*, and not to consider varna and jātī while entering into matrimonial alliances. Since the Sikhs did not disregard varna and jati, and a Brahman contracted a relationship with a Brahman and a Khatri with a Khatri, they raised this issue with Guru Gobind Singh. He clarified that all the four varnas belonged to the Panth, and their dharam was not abolished. Guru Tegh Bahadur had sacrificed his life to protect the janjū. Otherwise Aurangzeb would have converted all Hindus to Islam. A Sikh of the Guru was enjoined to carry arms and to live in accordance with the Granth; it was not obligatory for him either to wear or to discard the sacred thread. It was left to the individual's discretion.[27] As for matrimony, a Sikh should contract relationship with a Sikh, keeping in mind the position of the other party. A Brahman Sikh should contract relationship with a Brahman Sikh, and a Khatri Sikh with a Khatri Sikh. The relationship of *sikhkhī* was common to all Sikhs, but matrimonial ties were peculiar to each varna. Chaupa Singh was asked to reduce all the injunctions of the rahit into writing. He compiled a *Rahitnāma* with 1,800 entries. Copies of it were signed by Guru Gobind Singh.[28]

In 1705, the Rajas arrived with the army of the Turks sent by Aurangzeb under the command of Rustam Khan and Dilawar Khan. Guru Gobind

Singh knew that they had an eye on his wealth. Therefore, he consigned all the gold and goods worth Rs 17,32,735 to the river. Cloth worth Rs 4,35,250 was set on fire. Battles were fought every day. Pamma, the vazīr of Raja Hari Chand, offered safe evacuation. Guru Gobind Singh was aware of his evil intentions but the Sikhs were not. The Guru decided to send women with boxes full of shoes and stones to expose Pamma. They were attacked. When accused of the attack, the Rajas attributed it to outsiders. They gave an oath in writing, and so did Rustam Khan and Dilawar Khan. Against Guru Gobind Singh's better judgement, the Sikhs insisted on evacuation. In the darkness of the night, Mata Gujri's carriage lost its way. Accompanied by the two younger Sahibzadas, she was taken to Nawab Wazir Khan at Sirhind by the Ranghars of village Saheṛī. Guru Gobind Singh went towards Ropar, pursued by the army of the Rajas.[29]

In the battle of Chamkaur, Jit Singh and Jhujar Singh fought courageously. On the third day of the battle, Jhujar Singh died fighting. Jit Singh slew Raja Gaj Singh. Sangat Rai, a Khatri Sikh, put up a brave fight. Here, Chhibber refers to the heroes of the battle of Bhangani fought in 1688 and refers to the *Bachittar Nātak* which had been composed before 1700. Jit Singh too, died fighting. Guru Gobind Singh now decided to leave Chamkaur. Accompanied by four Sikhs, two of them Keshdhari and two Sahajdhari, he entered the camp of the Turks amidst cries of '*Hindū bhāgā, Hindū bhāgā*'. While the Sikhs fought his pursuers, Guru Gobind Singh reached Mācchīwāṛā. From there he went to Dīnpur where he was joined by four or five Sikhs who had survived the attack on Chamkaur. They recounted the deeds of others. Guru Gobind Singh praised the Sikhs who had died fighting at Chamkaur and told the survivors to ask for a boon. They requested that the paper on which the Sikhs had put their signatures to disown the Guru at Anandpur before its evacuation be torn. Their wish was granted.[30]

Meanwhile, Suchcha Puri persuaded Nawab Wazir Khan not to spare the two younger Sahibzadas and they were executed at Sirhind. Zorawar Singh was nine years old and Fateh Singh was seven-and-a-half. Suchcha Puri was related to the Sahis, the old enemies of the Gurus. Mata Gujri consumed poison and died. From Dīnpur, Guru Gobind Singh went to Muktsar, but the Turks pursued him. He moved to Kangar where he composed 1,400 couplets. Daya Singh Sobti agreed to carry this compilation to Aurangzeb. He dressed himself as a Muslim pilgrim (*hājī*) and placed the book over his head as if it were the *Qur'ān*. He was able to meet Aurangzeb at Aurangabad. The emperor accepted the book with great veneration, but when he began to read it, he died of shock.[31]

Guru Gobind Singh sent a hukamnāma to the Khalsa in the army of Bahadur Shah at Kabul. They informed the prince that the throne had been given to him by Guru Gobind Singh. He expressed his gratitude and left Kabul to fight against his brother, the rival contender for the throne. He emerged victorious.[32]

Guru Gobind Singh went to the country where the charanjīt Lachhman Das lived in the guise of a bairāgī in a thākurdwāra with a disciple. The Guru held consultation with Sahib Chand, Dharam Chand, Darbari and Gharbari, Kripal Singh, and Nand Chand. The question he put before them was: 'Who should be asked to bear the burden of Guruship?' They submitted that he knew better. Guru Gobind Singh proposed the name of the bairāgī who was a detached charanjīt. They approved of his choice. Guru Gobind Singh then went to the garden surrounding the thākurdwāra, and placed a cot on the seat (*āsan*) of the bairāgī. When the bairāgī entered the garden, he was asked to sit on the cot but he sat on the floor. Guru Gobind Singh told the four Sikhs who had accompanied him to leave them alone. They had a private discussion. Following this, the bairāgī bowed to him, took pahul and became a staunch Sikh. Entrusting 'the burden' to him, Guru Gobind Singh moved on.[33]

At Burhanpur, the Sikhs were instructed to go to Delhi. Mata Sundari did not wish to go because she was missing her son Jit Singh. A Sikh named Jit Singh was standing there. Guru Gobind Singh told Mata Sundari that she could take Jit Singh to Delhi. She accepted him as a son and left for Delhi with the other Sikhs. From Burhanpur, Guru Gobind Singh travelled to Nander. There he encamped in a graveyard to the chagrin of the Turks. Guru Gobind Singh told them that this place had belonged to him. To substantiate his claim, he dug out a *gangā-sāgar* and a chaukī from under the grave, and pointed out that this sacred place had been misappropriated by the Turks. A township was founded there.[34]

Guru Gobind Singh resolved to give up his physical body. He began to incite the sons and grandsons of Painde Khan, who were in his service, that the murder of one's ancestors should be avenged. The Guru appointed them as his personal bodyguards so that they could attack him. One of them attacked Guru Gobind Singh with his dagger. But he was slain by the Guru with his sword. Guru Gobind Singh had his wounds dressed. When Bahadur Shah learnt of the incident, he sent his personal physicians (hakīms). They dressed his wounds and were handsomely rewarded before they left.[35]

Guru Gobind Singh asked the Sikhs to arrange five maunds of sandal wood (*chandan*) as if he wanted to perform a hom. He also instructed them to bring some bows. Despite their protests, he tested the bows and the wounds opended up. Guru Gobind Singh bled profusely. In their anxiety, the Sikhs asked him who would look after the sangat. Guru Gobind Singh told them: 'The Granth is the Guru, and take refuge in Akal. The Guru is the Khalsa and the Khalsa is the Guru.' They were told to follow the rahit of the Guru and to believe in none other than Vaheguru. They talked for several hours before his light mingled with the light of Akal Purakh. His body was cremated before daybreak.[36]

After Guru Gobind Singh

Chhibber's work reveals his respect for Banda Bahadur who is referred to as Guru Banda Sahib or Guru Sahib Banda. He invoked the idea of revenge to secure the support of those who professed to be Sikhs. When Sirhind was captured, even the daughters and daughters-in-law of Suchcha Puri were humiliated and ill-treated. Chhibber justifies this by explaining that the deeds of one generation affect the fate of another. Banda Bahadur avenged the atrocities perpetrated by the Turks on the Sikhs though he lost his own life. He represented the sword of Guru Gobind Singh. Chhibber adds that he did not hesitate to punish those Sikhs who had become unjust after the acquisition of power. The Guru's injunction for the ruler was to be just. Banda Bahadur was besieged in Gurdaspur in 1718 (actually 1715). Many Sikhs were put to death because of their sins. Banda Bahadur was captured and taken to Delhi along with hundreds of other Sikhs. They were executed in batches of five every day but no one betrayed his faith. Banda Bahadur, too, courted martyrdom. All these martyrs were reborn and became rulers in Chhibber's time. Banda's rāj lasted for nine-and-a-half years. Many Sikhs referred to him as the eleventh Pātshāhī.[37]

Chhibber devotes a separate chapter to Jit Singh, the adopted son of Mata Sundari. Sikhs used to attend his court (*darbār*) in Delhi. Jit Singh once ordered a Muslim faqīr to be thrown into a well and all the Muslim faqīrs of Delhi made a representation to the emperor against Jit Singh.

His *derā* (camp) was plundered. Jit Singh went into hiding in the house of a *kalāl* (vintener) who betrayed him. When he was being taken for trial, he died of fright. His son, Haṭhī Singh, fled from Delhi to Mathura. According to Chhibber, Jit Singh exercised Guruship in Delhi for sixteen years, with a large number of followers known as Jit Mallias.[38]

When Mata Sundari died, the Sikhs began to attend the darbār of Mata Sahib Devi who advised them not to organize Diwali and Baisakhi gatherings in Delhi. The underlying reason was to forestall a situation similar to the one that had led to Jit Singh's death. A decision was taken to hold these gatherings at Amritsar. In 1727, Kirpal Singh arrived in Amritsar and made new arrangements with the assistance of the panchas of the town. Gurbakhsh Singh Chhibber (Kesar Singh's father) was appointed as dāroghā of the *go-khāna*, *kārkhāna*, and the *khazāna*. Arrangements for regular *ardās* and *sadā-barat* were made with the new sources of income.[39]

After finalizing all the arrangements, Kirpal Singh returned to Delhi, and Chaubanda arrived in Amritsar with his followers. There were three categories of Sikhs in the town: the Jit Mallias, the Bandais (in the Jhanda Bunga), and the Akal Purkhias (in the Akal Bunga). All were keen to acquire control of the sacred space. The watchword of the Akal Purkhias was Vāhegurūjī kī fateh, and that of the Bandais was fateh darshan. Bhai Kahn Singh (Trehan) tried unsuccessfully to resolve their differences. The number of Akal Purkhias began to increase. In 1731, Mata Sahib Devi died. By that time, Kirpal Singh had also passed away. In Amritsar, the Akal Purkhias triumphed over all others. As all Sikh individuals of any consequence had died, the Panth now held the field.[40]

Talking of contemporary Sikhs, Chhibber relates an incident involving a Mazhabi Sikh who posed as a Sandhu Jatt and dined with Sikh Jatts. However, he was discovered, humiliated, and hanged by Bhai Kahn Singh much to the satisfaction of all the Sikhs in Amritsar. They were asked to keep the incident a secret lest the Turks should interfere.[41] In another incident, however, the Turks became involved. Some Sikhs took mulberry fruit forcibly from Chuhar Mal Ohri's orchard. His son lodged a complaint in Lahore. The Chaudhari of Patti accompanied by Diwan Har Sahai and Aslam Khan, the *sūbedār* of Lahore, arrived in Amritsar. The Sikh gathering was attacked and the town was besieged. The Sikhs assaulted the Turks after Har Sahai was struck by lightening. Aslam

Khan was forced to retreat. Chhibber comments that Vaheguru protects his Sikhs. Therefore, the Sikhs of the Guru should practise dān, *pun*, and dharam. They should not associate with a Musalman, whether a man or a woman.[42]

The Turks returned to set up a *thāṇā* at Amritsar, and began to persecute the Sikhs. Majha was scoured for Sikhs, and they were killed. In 1736, the Turks marched from Lahore to Amritsar, killed many Sikhs, and laid siege to the town. Chhibber, 'a small boy', was with his father in Amritsar at that time.[43] He praises the Sikhs for going without food for days rather than eating impure food. It was due to their merit (*tap*, *bhajan*, and martyrdom) that the Turks were eventually destroyed. Bhai Taru Singh was eminent among the martyrs.[44]

Any Sikh who associated with Musalmans was considered an enemy of the Guru because the Turks had killed thousands of Sikhs and had not even spared the young sons of Guru Gobind Singh. The injunction of the Guru was to kill all the mlechh. Chhibber rues that sikhkhī ended with the death of Nawab Kapur Singh in 1746, having remained an integral part of *singhī* for forty-eight years. Chhibber recounts the atrocities committed by the Turks, including the desecration of *amritsar* in 1736, and the execution of Bhai Mani Singh and Bhai Tara Singh. There was no compatibility between the Turks and the Sikhs: 'We read Pothī-Granth, Shāstras, Vedas and Purāṇas; they observe circumcision and fasting, and read the Qur'ān and other books.' The Sikhs should follow the Gurū Granth Sāhib. The Sikh of the Guru should avenge himself on the enemies of the Guru. If he is not in a position to do so, he should at least have no association with them.[45]

Chhibber's explanation of Bhai Mani Singh's martyrdom is interesting. The Bhai gave no cause of offence to the Turks and yet he was hacked to pieces. He had arrived in Amritsar in 1725 and collected the scattered leaves of Guru Gobind Singh's *Avtār Līlā Granth* including some pages carrying the Guru's signature. He had them transcribed. However, he made the mistake of excluding the bhagat bāṇī from the Ādi Granth and bound the rest of the Ādi Granth and the *Dasvīn Pātshāhī dā Granth* together. When a humble Sikh saw this bound volume he inquired why the Bhagats had been excluded. Offering an explanation, Bhai Mani Singh said that the Bhagats were servants of the Gurus and, therefore, they could not sit with him. Hearing this, the Sikh said that if the master adopted the servant as a child and nurtured him as his own, would

Bhai Mani Singh ask the servant to go away? Bhai Mani Singh was silenced. Since the Sikh had uttered words to the effect that Bhai Mani Singh deserved to be hacked to death for infringing a tradition sanctified by the Guru, Bhai Mani Singh prayed that he may preserve his faith when his body was cut into pieces. The Sikh reassured him that his sikhkhī would remain firm. Many years later, Bhai Mani Singh was taken to Lahore and his body was cut into pieces limb by limb. He remained firm in his faith.[46]

At several places in his work, Chhibber underlines the unity of Guruship from Guru Nanak to Guru Gobind Singh, treating them as the embodiment of one single spirit and light. Nevertheless, he talks of the tenure of Guruship of Banda Sahib for nine years, of Jit Singh for sixteen years, and of '*Guru ke ghar*' for twenty-five years.[47] That explains why he has devoted separate chapters to Banda Bahadur, Jit Singh, and Mata Sahib Devi.

Of the four categories of Sikhs, two are easy to define: those who remained present with the Guru (dīdārī) and those who were willing to die for the cause of righteousness (mukte). Contemporary Sikhs fell into two categories. The murīd Sikhs recognized the Granth (as their Guru), served the sikhs, the sants, and the sādhs, and looked upon their wealth and power as a gift from Vaheguru. The mere possession of wealth and power, thus, did not make them māyikī, that is, they who forgot the Guru on acquiring rulership, did not serve the sādhs, the sants, and the sikhs, and had no love for the Granth. They attributed their success to themselves and forgot the bestower of rulership. Chhibber underlines the inexorability of the law of karma to induce the rulers to do good deeds.[48]

Chhibber was not optimistic about the future. He invokes the authority of the Ādi Granth to forecast the increasing influence of the Kaliyuga. All distinctions of varna would be demolished as described in the *Bhogal Purāṇa* too. There would be no sat, tap, or dharam. The Shastras and the Vedas would speak the language of the mlechh. There were already signs of the Kaliyuga. Just as Hindus had gone over to the Musalmans earlier to safeguard their mundane interests, so also the Musalmans were coming over to the Hindus. Both sides had adopted evil conduct. When the *Qur'ān* was current, there could be no sikhkhī. The Sikh of the Guru should not discard his dharam; he should flee from sin and *adharm*. Each *yuga* had its own peculiar dharam. For the Kaliyuga it was the dharma of the *Atharva Veda*.[49]

Towards the end of his work, Chhibber accords great importance to the Guru and, therefore, to *Guru Granth*. The Guru is God; in fact, higher than God. The Tenth Master handed over the gaddī of Guruship to the Granth Sāhib. Therefore, the Granth is manifestly the Guru and one who turns away from the Granth is lost for ever. One should follow the teachings of the Granth to the best of one's capacities. The Sikhs should not recognize any other authority. The younger Granth was compiled in 1698. Despite a request from the Sikhs, it was kept separate from the Ādi Granth. No one knows the reason for this. But Guru Gobind Singh did regard his Granth as very dear to him. Therefore, Chhibber suggests that both the Granths could be regarded as the Guru.[50]

The Faith and the Panth

It is clear from the foregoing pages that Chhibber's detailed account of Guru Gobind Singh provides many dates, and it dwells on kinship.[51] But the authenticity of this information cannot be accepted as established. To give only a few glaring examples, he places the death of Guru Gobind Singh in 1709. Banda Bahadur for him was still alive in 1718. Sango Shah, the son of Guru Gobind Singh's sister, who had died fighting at Bhangāṇī, is associated with the battle of Chamkaur. Chhibber's detail is impressive merely because of its plausibility. More often than not, its authenticity is dubious.

The episode of the Goddess is the most detailed in Chhibber's account of Guru Gobind Singh and yet there is no proof of its authenticity. The Goddess granted a boon to enable Guru Gobind Singh to create the Khalsa and yet there is no single event in Chhibber's account that can be viewed as marking the institution of the Khalsa. The Goddess was invoked in 1678. Guru Gobind Singh decided to establish a separate Panth in 1693. Hukamnāmas on the new rahit were sent to the Masands in 1696. The rite of pahul was introduced in 1697 when the new rahit was promulgated for Keshdharis. The Masands were punished and removed in 1698. The five volunteers offered their life to the Goddess on the Guru's call in 1703.

Chhibber tries to establish an essential link between the Khalsa and the Goddess. Apart from the boon that the Panth of Guru Gobind Singh would destroy the wicked Musalmans, the blue dress of the Khalsa also comes from the Goddess. She relaxed some obligations of kiryā-karam to accommodate the Khalsa. Virtually, she chose the five potential martyrs whose martyrdom and piety were instrumental in bringing about political change. It is she who bestows rāj on the Shudars.

The Goddess episode underscores the importance of the Brahmans. Only they can perform hom, and they are given preference over Sikhs. They create Chhatris and they are acknowledged as superior to Chhatris. Only a Brahman can make the Goddess appear; without her aid Guru Gobind Singh, or his Sikhs, cannot overpower their enemies. Kalakdas shows Guru Gobind Singh the way to avoid accountability to God and how to accommodate sin in his panth. Wealth and riches can be sanctified by the Guru, but not power. Kalakdas throws hints about the institution of Guruship in the future. He points to the role that Banda Bahadur could play after Guru Gobind Singh.

Chhibber looks upon Guru Nanak as the fountainhead of Sikhism and does not find any difference between him and his nine successors. They all represent one and the same light. No rival claimant to Guruship is acknowledged. The followers of Prithi Chand, Dhir Mal, and Ram Rai are excommunicated by Guru Gobind Singh. Nevertheless, Chhibber refers to the duration of Guruship of Banda Bahadur, Jit Singh, and Mata Sahib Devi. Chhibber does refer to the Khalsa as the Guru but makes no reference whatever to their authority in any situation. He is emphatic about the Ādi Granth as the Guru but he also brackets with it the 'Book of the Tenth Master'.

Chhibber's attitude towards the 'Book of the Tenth Master' is very significant. As we noticed earlier, he refers to two Granths composed by Guru Gobind Singh: the *Samundar Sāgar* which was consigned to the river, and the *Avtār Līlā* which was lost in a battle presumably after the evacuation of Anandpur. At the time of Guru Gobind Singh's death there was only one Granth, that is, the Ādi Granth. Much later, Bhai Mani Singh collected the scattered leaves of the Granth or Granths of Guru Gobind Singh, had them transcribed, and bound them with the Ādi Granth. Where was the Granth of the Tenth Master? Chhibber takes its existence for granted though his own account does not support its existence. Besides the *Bachittar Nātak* and the Savvayyās of Guru Gobind Singh, Chhibber was familiar with the literature on Chandi. This could serve as the basis for introducing the entire range of Brahmanical literature as authoritative. In any case, Chhibber brackets with the Granth Sāhib not only the works attributed to Guru Gobind Singh but also the Vedas, the Purāṇas, and the Shāstras.

Chhibber's presentation of the Khalsa tends to Brahmanize the Sikh tradition. He does talk of the kesh, the pahul, the epithet Singh, the injunction to carry arms, and several other items of the Khalsa rahit, the five volunteers, the boon of rulership, the end of personal Guruship, and the vesting of Guruship in the Khalsa and the Ādi Granth. But he presents them in a manner that robs them of all significance. The kesh are an alternative to janjū and tikkā. But his attitude towards janjū and tikkā is ambivalent. The pahul remains unconnected with the five volunteers (and, therefore, with the idea of *āpe gur-chelā*). Instead of looking at singhī as subsuming sikhkhī, Chhibber views singhī as an adjunct of sikhkhī.

Further, Chhibber draws a clear distinction between sikhkhī as a religious faith and the practice of varna-dharma in the social sphere. Consequently, the ideal of equality gets shorn of all its social meaning. The varna norms of commensality and connubium reintroduce the principle of inequality. It is not surprising that Chhibber pleads for special privileges of the Brahman Sikhs. The Sikh tradition of one single ethical principle for all members of the Sikh social order is negated by Chhibber. Portraying the Khalsa as a political spearhead of the Goddess, he appears to present an antithesis of the Khalsa as an egalitarian socio-political and moral order based on the monotheistic conception of the Deity. Whether consciously or unconsciously, Kesar Singh Chhibber makes a consistent attempt at Brahmanizing the Khalsa tradition.

Significantly, however, Chhibber looked upon the Khalsa Panth as distinct from both Hindus and Muslims as the Third Panth. For him, the inegalitarian Khalsa order he himself advocated did not have any bearing on its distinct character. He has a soft corner only for Brahman Sikhs and not for all Brahmans. He remains torn between his Brahmanical heritage and his affiliation to the Khalsa Panth. The faith is common but not the social norms. This basic contradiction is the source of many other contradictions in the *Bansāvalīnāma*.

Notes

1. Kesar Singh Chhibber, *Bansāvalīnāma Dasān Pātshāhīan Kā*, ed., Ratan Singh Jaggi (published in ed., S.S. Kohli, *Parkh*, bol II), Chandigarh: Panjab University, 1972, Preface by Jaggi.

2. Ibid., pp. 1–15.
3. Ibid., p. 125.
4. In the hukamnāmas of Guru Tegh Bahadur, the name given is Gobind Das and not Gobind Rai.
5. *Bansāvalīnāma*, pp. 99–101.
6. Ibid., pp. 101–2.
7. Ibid., pp. 102–4.
8. Ibid., pp. 104–5.
9. Ibid., pp. 107–10.
10. Ibid., pp. 110–12.
11. Ibid., pp. 112–13.
12. Ibid., pp. 113–16.
13. Ibid., pp. 116–19.
14. Ibid., pp. 119–22.
15. Ibid., pp. 122–3.
16. Ibid., pp. 123–4.
17. Ibid., pp. 124–5.
18. Ibid., pp. 125–6.
19. Ibid., pp. 126–7.
20. Ibid., pp. 128–9.
21. Ibid., pp. 129–30.
22. Ibid., pp. 130–2.
23. Ibid., pp. 132–3.
24. Ibid., pp. 134–6.
25. Ibid., pp. 136–7.
26. Ibid., pp. 137–8.
27. Ibid., pp. 142–3.
28. Ibid., pp. 146–7.
29. Ibid., pp. 148–50.
30. Ibid., pp. 151–2.
31. Ibid., pp. 153–4.
32. Ibid., pp. 155–6.
33. Ibid., pp. 156–7.
34. Ibid., pp. 157–8.
35. Ibid., pp. 162–3.
36. Ibid., pp. 163–4.
37. Ibid., pp. 170–8.
38. Ibid., pp. 178–81.
39. Ibid., pp. 182–4.
40. Ibid., pp. 184–6.
41. Ibid., pp. 187–8.
42. Ibid., pp. 189–90.
43. If Kesar Singh was a young boy in 1736 he could not have been born around 1700. Or, he was confused about the time of the event.
44. Ibid., pp. 190–3.

45. Ibid., pp. 193–7.
46. Ibid., pp. 135–6.
47. Ibid., pp. 197–8.
48. Ibid., pp. 199–201.
49. Ibid., pp. 202–6.
50. Ibid., pp. 115, 177.
51. Chhibber refers to the marriage of Guru Gobind Singh to Jito at 'Lahore', a township raised for this specific purpose near Anandpur, in 1685. The birth of Jit Singh to Mata Sundari is placed in 1688; the birth of Zorawar Singh to Mata Jito, in 1696; the birth of Fateh Singh to Mata Jito, in 1698; and the death of Mata Jito, in 1700.

13

Sovereignty of the Third Panth

Bhangu's *Gurū-Panth Prakāsh*

Ratan Singh Bhangu finalized his *Gurū Panth Prakāsh* in the Bunga of Sardar Shiam Singh at Amritsar in 1841. Bhai Vir Singh chanced upon a copy of 1858 that appeared to have been prepared in haste. He corrected what he regarded as the mistakes of the copyist and published it in 1914. He came upon another manuscript of 1866 and used it to make improvements in the second edition in 1939. He chose to give the title *Prachīn Panth Prakāsh* to this work, presumably because the *Panth Prakāsh* of Giani Gian Singh, already known to the readers of Punjabi, was composed later.[1]

A new text of Bhangu's work has been published recently, edited by Balwant Singh Dhillon. He points out that the doctoral work of Harinder Singh Chopra on the editing of the *Panth Prakāsh* by Bhai Vir Singh casts doubt on the authenticity of the text. Therefore, an authentic edition was called for. The new edition is based on two manuscript copies of the *Panth Prakāsh*, one at the Panjab University, Chandigarh, and the other at Guru Nanak Dev University, Amritsar, collated with the text of Bhai Vir Singh. He also takes into account the quotations given by Harinder Singh Chopra from yet another manuscript used by him. On the whole, the new text published as *Srī Gurū Panth Prakāsh* is more useful for analysis.[2]

Bhangu expected his work to be read and recited. The faith of the reader and the listener was expected to become firm. The listener would fight valiantly in battle and join the company of martyrs.[3] This function of the work was not unrelated to the purpose for which it was composed. Colonel David Ochterlony and Captain Murray were keen to obtain accurate information on the Sikhs. Bhangu was particularly keen about one specific issue: the true source of Sikh sovereignty. Possibly, he perceived a threat to Sikh sovereignty in his own time, particularly after the death of Ranjit Singh in 1839.

Creation of the Khalsa

At the very outset, Bhangu invokes the aid of Guru Nanak and the other Gurus to enable him to write on 'the creation' (*utpatī*) of the Khalsa.[4] Evidently, the creation of the Khalsa and the issue of sovereignty were inseparable for Ratan Singh Bhangu. This linkage carried the implication that the Khalsa never submitted to the Mughals.

The perfect and the true Guru created the Panth forwar (*juddh*) because sovereignty (pātshāhī) cannot be attained without armed struggle.[5] The Mughal rule had lost its legitimacy. Bhangu believed that sovereignty had been conferred on Babur by Guru Nanak, the lord of both temporal and spiritual power (mīrī and pīrī), because of his disapproval of Afghan rule. Babur and his descendants were to rule beyond seven generations only if they did not oppress the followers of Guru Nanak.[6] This condition was infringed first by Jahangir who came under the influence of *mullās* and *qāzīs*. He played false with Guru Arjan but used the agency of a Khatri *(dīwān)* to assign the blame to him. Shah Jahan converted many Hindus to Islam. Aurangzeb persisted in his hostility towards the Gurus. He called Guru Har Krishan to Delhi where the latter ended his life.[7] Because of Aurangzeb's persecution of Hindus, Guru Tegh Bahadur willingly sacrificed his head for the sake of *dharam*.[8] There was no longer any moral justification for Mughal rule.

The roots of Mughal rule dried up when Aurangzeb executed Guru Tegh Bahadur. Guru Gobind Singh decided to take up the sword to cut down the tree of the sovereignty of the 'Turks'. He did not need rulership for himself because, as a successor of Guru Nanak, he was far superior to any earthly ruler. In fact, like Guru Nanak, he could bestow Pātshāhī on others. He initially considered the Rajput Rajas but they would not be willing to become Sikhs. Therefore, he turned his attention to the poor Sikhs who belonged to the lower castes or even to people outside the four *varnas*. When they were told to take up arms against the 'Turks', they were struck with fear. 'We are sparrows and they are hawks', they said. 'Can the deer ever kill the lion?' The Jatts, Nāis, and Tarkhāns, who were not used to arms, were no match for the Mughal and Pathan soldiers.

Guru Gobind Singh was aware that this attitude was due to *charan-pahul* which encouraged them to be peaceful (*shānt*) and induced kindness (dayā) in them. This had to be changed.[9]

To make the Sikhs an awe-inspiring entity, it was necessary to introduce a new form of initiation, the baptism of the double-edged sword (*khande pahul*); to make their appearance warlike, it was necessary to wear kesh and turban and to adopt the name 'Singh' which was used by Chhatris. Every Khalsa horseman would then become a sovereign ruler. Steeled through the baptism of the double-edged sword, they would be always to use the *khandā*. They would bow to none except the True Sovereign. They would not believe in evil spirits, or in Gugga, sacred thread, and the sacred mark; they would all dine together. With this idea, Guru Gobind Singh chose an auspicious moment to select at Kesgarh five *bhujangīs* belonging to five different *jātīs*: a Khatri, a Jatt, a Chhīmbā, a Nāī, and a Jhīwar.[10] The Guru himself prepared pahul by adding sugar to water and stirring it with a double-edged sword, while reciting the '*pritham bhagautī*' *pauṛī* to invoke the help of his nine predecessors, the *32-Savvayyās*, and the most forceful stanzas of the *Chandī-bāṇī*. The pahul was sprinkled over the eyes of the five and over their heads five times before they were asked to taste it. At the same time, they were told to shout '*Akāl, Akāl*' and 'Vahegurūjī kī fateh'. They were instructed to discard the notion of the four varnas and the four āshramas, together with the sacred thread and the sacred mark.[11]

Guru Gobind Singh instructed them not to have any connection with the Mīṇās and the Masands.[12] To associate with the Ram Raiyas, the killers of female infants, and the smokers of *hukkā*, was degrading for the Khalsa. They should contribute to the Guru's golak according to their capacity, and serve *kaṛhā* to the Khalsa. They should wear *kachhherā* and turban, and remain devoted to the Guru Granth. They were enjoined to recite the *Japjī*, the *Jāp*, the *Ānand*, the *Rahrās*, and the *Chandī-bāṇī* in the morning and evening; to tie the turban twice every day, to take care of their weapons all the twenty-four hours of the day; to drink *sudhā* and to go ahunting; to eat *jhatkā* mutton and not to touch *kuththā* meat; to take care of the kesh and never cut it; to discard traditional rites and to concentrate their thoughts on the feet of the Guru; and to prescribe penance (*tankhā*) for those who deviate from the true path. Just as he had administered pahul to the five bhujangīs, so he received pahul from them in the same manner. That was why he was known as '*āpe gur-chelā*' (he himself was the Guru and the disciple at the same time). Just as Guru Nanak had become the disciple of Guru Angad, Guru Gobind Singh became the disciple of the Khalsa.[13]

Bhangu says that the Khalsa began to increase from the very day of its creation. The Sikhs were administered pahul and became Singhs in groups of five to raise the daily number to fifty or even a hundred. They were sent in all directions and appointed mukhtiārs everywhere, particularly at places associated with the Gurus, like Amritsar and Patna. Written instructions were sent to all Sikh sangats to be baptized by the double-edged sword. As representatives of the Guru, the five bhujangīs were entitled to administer pahul to others. The offerings received by the Gurdwaras were placed at the disposal of the Khalsa: they sent to the Guru whatever they could save. The sangats were also asked to go to the Guru to become *tejdhārī* through the new baptism and to subdue the 'Turks'. Satisfied with the creation of the Khalsa, the Guru asked them which territory they would like to rule. They asked for the Punjab. The Guru advised them to increase their numbers first and then to rise in arms against the rulers.[14]

Political Activities

The Singhs began to plunder the villages around Anandpur. The hill chiefs, who were defeated in an open battle, approached the Mughal emperor to represent that the Guru was increasing his resources to put an end to Mughal rule. He styled himself as 'the true king' to imply that Aurangzeb was a mere pretender. Aurangzeb was alarmed. Eventually, Anandpur was besieged by the combined Mughal and hill forces. Guru Gobind Singh was keen to stay on but the people wanted him to evacuate the town. He failed to convince even his mother that the enemy was only deceiving them by promises of safety. He asked the Sikhs to sign a written statement that they were not his Sikhs. The Singhs resolved to remain with the Guru and to go with him. Most of them died fighting. The Sahibzadas Jhujar Singh and Zorawar Singh also attained martyrdom (*shahīdī*).[15]

Guru Gobind Singh left Chamkaur with the help of Ghani Khan and reached Dīnā in the Tappā of Kāngaṛ where he was joined by Singhs. The younger Sāhibzādas had been betrayed by a Brahman cook of the Guru to Jani Khan and Mani Khan, the Rangharṣ of Morinda, who took them to Sirhind. Suchcha Nand, the Dīwān, prevailed upon Wajida

(Wazir Khan) to slay them. The Malerkotla Afghans, however, refused to perform such a heinous act. The Sāhibzādas were told to embrace Islam. When they refused, they were slaughtered in the open court. Their grandmother died of shock on hearing the news. The murder of the Sāhibzādas led to the ruin of the 'Turks'. The Malerkotla Pathans became firmly rooted because of their refusal to be a party to Wazir Khan's crime. At Dīnā, Guru Gobind Singh wrote a letter to Aurangzeb and sent it through Dayā Singh. The emperor died on reading this letter containing admonition and advice in addition to an account of the battles.[16]

An increasing number of Singhs had joined Guru Gobind Singh before the batlle of Muktsar. Forty of them resolved to fight unto death. They were lying wounded when Guru Gobind arrived. Their only request to the Guru was to tear the paper disowning the Guru which they had signed at Anandpur. After granting their wish, Guru Gobind Singh moved to Talvandī Sābo. Many Sikhs received pahul from him, including a few Sodhis, and Tilok Singh and Ram Singh, the ancestors of the Phulkian

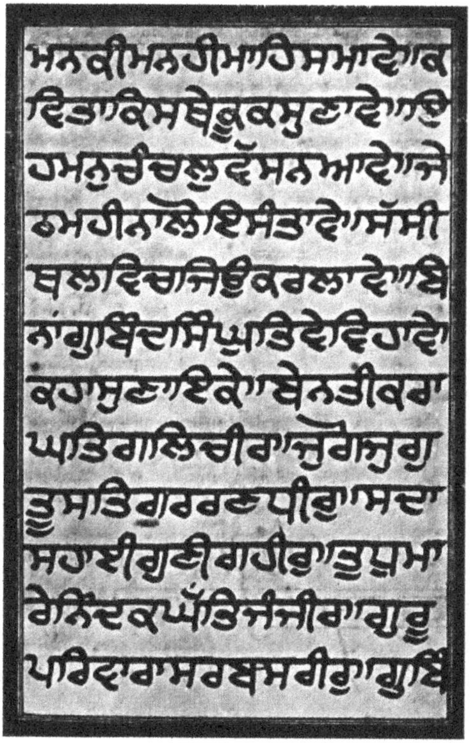

Fig. 13.1 The Gurmukhi script evolved at Damdama Sahib in the late eighteenth century

chiefs. The place came to be known as Damdama and the Guru's Kanshi because the Guru had lived there and had continued his literary activity. Having stayed there for nine months and nine days, Guru Gobind Singh moved towards the south.[17]

Banda Bahadur

Ratan Singh Bhangu gives much importance to the time of Banda Bahadur. We may note only the most significant aspects of his Sākhīs related to Banda. Guru Gobind Singh was warned by Mahant Jet Ram at Dādū Duār against Narain Das Bairagi of Nander who enjoyed tormenting holy men. The warning, however, had the opposite effect. Guru Gobind Singh was determined to meet Narain Das and to guide him to the right path. All the supranatural powers of Narain Das failed to work against the Guru and he submitted in all humility: 'I am your *bandā*; I am your Singh and you are my Guru.' He was informed that the Sikh faith was sharper than the double-edged sword. Banda made repeated requests for the Guru's order. He was assigned the service of subduing Sirhind and the surrounding hills with the support of Singhs. Banda is told that 'there is no difference between them and me; I am with them and they are with me.' Baba Binod Singh, Baba Kahn Singh, Daya Singh, and Baj Singh, among others, were sent with Banda. He was told that he would be happy as long as he made the Singhs happy. He was one of them, and not superior to them. All the prayers of the five Singhs would be answered.[18]

Banda reached the Punjab accompanied by the Singhs. There was an enthusiastic response to his call. The first to join him were the Banjārā Singhs, followed by the Malwa Singhs who were closer, and then the Majhail Singhs who were opposed by the 'Turks' on their way. Samana was the first place to be sacked, followed by Sadhaurā and Banūṛ. The Singhs then defeated the Malerkotla Pathans in a battle near Ropar. Chhatt was plundered before Wazir Khan was defeated in the battle of Chappar Chiri and put to death. Baj Singh was appointed Diwan of the Sarkar of Sirhind and two of his brothers were made *thāṇadārs*. The Singh thāṇadār of Pail punished a Ram Raiya Masand who was hostile to the Singhs. Malerkotla was not plundered but its inhabitants had to hand over their wealth. Fateh Singh was made head of the Malwa Singhs and appointed to Hisar, with the title of Nawab. Many of the parganas of the Sarkar of Hisar were occupied. Banda conquered the Doaba and the upper Bari Doab with the support of the Singhs. Serveral thāṇas were established in the fortresses. The call to prayer could not be heard from Panipat to Patti and Pathankot. Banda subdued Kahlur and remained active in the hills for three years.[19]

In relation to Banda's early activity, Bhangu emphasized the motive of revenge, the strong support received by him from the Khalsa and the establishment of sovereign rule. In his account of Banda's activity in the hills, his supranatural powers are emphasized. Bahadur Shah was reluctant to act against Banda, but he was pressed to do so by the mullās and qāzīs. He looked upon Banda as the slave of that Guru who had bestowed Pātshāhī on the emperor. He wrote to Banda that they were both Sikhs of the Guru. Banda agreed to leave the Punjab and retain only the hills. Bahadur Shah reached Lahore but only to die there. His grandson, Farrukh Siyar who ascended the throne, was initially inclined to follow the mild policy of his grandfather. But when Banda was temporarily imprisoned in Kullu, Farrukh Siyar was persuaded to recover the Mughal territory from the Singhs. Banda retaliated and killed the three Afghan *faujdārs* who were active on behalf of the Mughal emperor. The 'Turks' approached Mātā Jī in Delhi and she agreed to send a hukamnāma to Banda under the Guru's seal. But he refused to submit. He declared that he was not a Sikh but a Bairāgī, and that he was capable of establishing his own rule.[20]

This alienated the Khalsa from Banda. Mātā Jī wrote to them that the Guru had given 'service' to Banda and not Pātshāhī. Indeed, the true king had bequeathed Pātshāhī to the Panth. Banda, on the other hand, thought that he would treat the Singhs as his servants. He wanted to replace the Khalsa by his own panth. He replaced the blue dress with a red one, coined the slogan 'fateh darshan' to replace 'Vāhegurūjī kī fateh', introduced vegetarian diet in place of meat, and the Vaishnava way of *chaukā* instead of the *sarbangī* tradition of the Khalsa in which all the four varnas intermingled and ate together. Banda proclaimed himself to be the Guru. Consequently, many Singhs left him and decided never to trust him. Banda thought of eliminating the Singhs before seizing Lahore, but he was defeated. The Singhs remained in Amritsar, and vowed never to compromise their objective of sovereignty.[21]

The 'Turks' made an all-out effort against Banda, appealing to the religious sentiments of Muslims through their religious leaders. A message was sent to Banda that all Muslim *pīrs* and *faqīrs* wanted to pay homage to him. Banda was deceived and allowed the enemy to come closer to him. The Turks lulled him further by informing him that the Mughal emperor had decided to issue a farmān, conferring all the hill areas on him. Meanwhile the Mughal forces surrounded him. His followers urged him to fight an open battle but he preferred the safety of the fortress. His followers repulsed an attack. However, 4,000 of them could not withstand the might of 4,00,000 'Turks'. They were prepared to die fighting. The 'Turks' suffered immense losses and decided to starve Banda to submission. Eventually, he was captured, locked up in a cage and taken to Delhi along with his followers. He was blinded, tied with a rope to a horse, and dragged till he died. This was the mode of death that Banda had used for Wazir Khan and this was the way in which Farrukh Siyar met his end later.[22]

Bhangu lists ten reasons for Banda's downfall: first, he annoyed Mātā Jī; second, he lost the status of a celibate; third, he lost the power to fly; fourth, he was deprived of the advantage of the *pothī* which gave him occult knowledge and power; fifth, he spoke ill of the Guru; sixth, he displeased the Khalsa Panth; seventh, he established his own panth; eight, he killed a female infant; ninth, he had received *siddhī* without earning it; and the last, he stopped earning merit. Bhangu makes a clear distinction between magical power exercised temporarily for a particular purpose and spiritual power attained through intense devotion to be exercised throughout one's life. In short, Banda fell because he deviated from the path set for him by Guru Gobind Singh. Banda's political failure was the outcome of his moral failure. Bhangu extols the bravery of the followers of Banda, but he leaves no doubt that the ultimate victory had been prophesied for the Khalsa.[23]

The Tat Khalsa

The followers of Banda were bound to go down before the Tat Khalsa who were deceived neither by Banda nor by the 'Turks' in their single-minded dedication to the Guru's cause. After Banda's downfall, his followers wanted to remain separate and to increase the strength of their panth. Their conflict with the Tat Khalsa was inevitable. Baba Kahn Singh, who had separated himself from Banda, invited the Khalsa to Amritsar. During a festival, the Banda-panthīs asked for a share of the offerings.

They were told that they had no valid claim as they did not belong to the Khalsa Panth. At another gathering, they came in greater numbers and encamped near the Jhanda Bunga. The 'Turks' were interested in creating a rift between the Sikhs. They incited the followers of Banda against the Tat Khalsa. The Bandaīs asked for half the share of the offerings. Both sides were willing to fight over the issue. On advice from seniors, they agreed to leave the decision to God. Papers of both sides, with 'fateh Gurū' written on one and '*fateh darshan*' on the other, were thrown into the pool. The piece with 'fateh Gurū' surfaced to the top and the other sank to the bottom of the pool. Some of the Singhs who had remained with Banda deserted the Bandaīs and joined the Tat Khalsa. But the verdict of the 'papers' was not accepted by the Bandaīs. A wrestling match at the Akal Bunga, between Sangat Singh of the Bandaīs and Mīrī Singh, son of Baba Kahn Singh, of the Tat Khalsa, also went in favour of the latter. The Bandaīs were told to leave but they refused. In the fight that followed, all the armed Bandaīs were killed. The others either fled or joined the Khalsa. Bhai Mani Singh occupied the place where the Bandaīs had installed their gaddī. Amrtisar came under the undisputed control of the Tat Khalsa.[24]

Ratan Singh Bhangu draws clear boundaries not only between the Tat Khalsa and the Banda-panthīs, but also between the Tat Khalsa and the followers of Gulab Rai, the grandson of Guru Hargobind. He claimed to be the Guru, and purchased 60 *ghumāons* of land in Anandpur to occupy the gaddī of Guru Gobind Singh; he administered *charan-pahul* instead of baptism of the double-edged sword, and was generally hostile to the Khalsa. He met a miserable end.[25]

Similarly, Gangūshāhī Kharak Singh believed that the Sikh sangat had become a 'widow' because no Sodhi Guru was on the gaddī. Claiming to be the Guru, he tried to lure even the Singhs. While he offered blessings and boons, the Khalsa offered constant struggle (*dangā*). Whereas the Khalsa claimed victory, Kharak Singh asserted that they had been defeated. He also contested the claim of the Khalsa that the prayers offered by five Singhs were efficacious. Once when he tried to convert a Singh through charan-pahul, a Kumhar Singh of Delhi, named Mihar Singh, appeared on the scene with about ten armed Singhs. Mihar Singh, a bhujangī, was opposed to the Ram Raiyas and the Gangūshāhīs. He would sing the Guru's shabads and play on the rabāb. He would offer ardās and proclaim 'Guru fateh'. Carrying a staff in his hand, he wore a sword, and blue dress, including a *kachhehrā* of a yard and a quarter of cloth. He was afraid of none. He associated with the Sangat of the Tenth Guru and shunned the Mīṇās and the Masands as well as the killers of infant daughters. He demonstrated to the people that the prayers of the five Singhs were efficacious, not the boons of Kharak Singh.[26]

Gangu had been blessed by Guru Amar Das but his successors became hostile to the Khalsa of Guru Gobind Singh. Similarly Hindal of Jandiala had been blessed by Guru Amar Das but his descendants were hostile to the Khalsa. In fact, Hindal produced a Janamsākhī in which Guru Nanak was portrayed as a servant of Raja Janak in a previous life and Hindal himself as his son-in-law, like Sri Rama. In other ways too he tried to demonstrate that he was superior to Guru Nanak. Hindal's followers were known as Niranjanias and not Sikhs. His grandsons substituted Kartār for Vāhegurū. They associated with Musalmans and ate with the Sultānīs, that is, the devotees of Sākhī Sarvar. Harbhagat Niranjania was instrumental in the killing of many Singhs by the Mughal administrators. Kirpal and Dayal assisted Ahmad Shah against the Khalsa. Dayal Das, son of Sharan Das, was a reprobate drunkard who had no regard for the sangat.[27] In Bhangu's account of the opponents of the Khalsa, the differences are not merely political. Matters related to belief and practice sharply differentiate the Khalsa from all others.

The Tat Khalsa or the bhujangī represents Bhangu's ideal Singh. He strictly observes the rahit. He wears the blue dress and carries arms. He is devoted to both the Guru and Gurbāṇī. He is true to his word. He fights in the front. He is not afraid of death and never submits to the 'Turks'. He upholds the claim of sovereignty. He helps the oppressed. He venerates the Sangat like the Guru and is always keen to serve the Khalsa. He cannot hear denigration of the Singhs. He holds his kesh dearer than his life. He is intent upon *dharam-juddh*. He bathes in the pool of his Guru instead of the Ganga or the Jamuna. He hears only the Guru's shabad and does not meditate upon Rama or Krishna. Above all, he remains a celibate and devotes his entire life to the service of the Panth. He is the stuff of which martyrs are made.[28]

The Singh Martyrs

Martyrdom was in a sense the most important aspect of the Sikh tradition for Ratan Singh Bhangu. Guru Tegh Bahadur sacrificed his life for the good of others (*parsuārth*): he saved the *dharm-karam* of Hindus. The story of the Brahmans approaching Guru Tegh Bahadur for protection in the face of persecution by the Mughals and the resolve of the Guru to sacrifice his life, his refusal to embrace Islam, and his strategy to have his head cut off, saved not only the dharm-karam of the Hindus but also his own. Tara Singh became a martyr, upholding the ideal of sovereignty in opposition to the supporters of the Mughal administration and Mughal rule. Against overwhelming odds, not once did he think of escaping. In fact, he inspired twenty-two other Singhs to join him. He followed the example of Guru Tegh Bahadur: he sacrificed his life but did not give up his resolve. Bhai Mani Singh tampered with the body of the Granth and the sangat declared that his own limbs would be separated in the same way. He requested the sangat to pray that his faith may remain perfect (*sikhkhī sābat rahe*). When he was finally arrested, not only did he decline to pay any money but also refused to accept Islam. He offered his limbs to be chopped into pieces till his head was severed as one piece. Reciting the *Sukhmanī* all the time, he felt no pain. He was hailed as the *sardār* of *shahīd*s or the prince of martyrs.[29]

There are numerous examples of martyrs in the *Gurū Panth Prakāsh*. Bota Singh was enraged when he heard someone saying that no true Singh was to be seen around. He announced his presence by collecting duty on the highway to Lahore and died fighting, along with a Ranghreta Singh, against a large Mughal contingent. His martyrdom upheld the ideal of sovereignty. Sukha Singh, a Tarkhān, joined hands with Mahtab Singh to slay Massā Ranghaṛ in the Harmandar (later the Golden Temple) which he was desecrating, he took a dip in the holy tank at Amritsar as a challenge to the Mughals, killed an Afghan in a duel, and died fighting in search of Ahmad Shah Abdali on the battlefield. Bhai Taru Singh, who was dedicated to his faith and the Khalsa Panth, did not fear death and he died with his kesh.

Ratan Singh Bhangu reveals his philosophy or metaphysics of martyrdom through his asides and reflections. When Guru Tegh Bahadur gave his head for the sake of dharam, cries of the people reached the true court and God shifted the pīrs and prophets of the Turks from the Sachch Khand to the rear of the court. From that moment, the Pātshāhī of Delhi began to decline and the power of the 'Turks' began to diminish. It is in this context that Tara Singh said that his deliberate sacrifice would be held against the Turks. Bhai Mani Singh became the *deoṛhīdār* of the

Sāhibzādas after his martyrdom. Similarly, Bota Singh reached the derā of the shahids who held the pīrs and *paighambars* in siege.

The Singhs of Padhana suggested to Bhai Taru Singh, who was being taken to Lahore, that they would kill the *ahadīs* to secure his release. He told them that the Gurus had sacrificed their lives for the Sikhs and, since he belonged to their panth, he would prefer death over escape. The Gurus had made great sacrifices to save the panth in order to destroy the 'Turks'. After his martyrdom Bhai Taru Singh went to the Divine Court to seek redress against the 'Turks'. Bhai Mahtab Singh also sought martyrdom along with Bhai Taru Singh. The wise began to say that the rule of the Mughals would not survive. Even the Prophet would be consigned to hell if he attempted to intercede on behalf of the Nawab (Zakariya Khan). When he was ailing and he invoked the aid of pīrs and paighambars, the Singh shahīds inflicted greater pain on him. Only a Khalsa could relieve his pain. The honour of the Khalsa Panth was saved, and the 'Turks' were disgraced. Bhai Taru Singh was taken to Sachch Khand in a procession of shahīds. Like Bhai Mani Singh on the right, Bhai Taru Singh became a deoṛhīdār of the Sāhibzādas on the left. The *pīrī* of the *pīrs* was destroyed. All one's wishes were granted through vows of offering to Bhai Taru Singh Shahid. Indeed, all one's wishes were fulfilled through offerings at a *shahīdganj*.[31] Anthropology had its counterpart in cosmology.

In this connection, it is significant to note that the Khalsa Panth raised *dehurās* on the various sites of martyrdom. Bhangu refers to a *gurmatā* by which a darbār was constructed on the site where the younger Sāhibzādas were slain in Sirhind. After holding a dīwān, a *takht* was raised and five weapons were placed on it to be worshipped like the Guru. A Singh was deputed to look after the place. The Panth made generous offerings and all their wishes were fulfilled. *Rabābīs* were appointed for regular recitation of shabads. In this way, the dehurā was rejuvenated. Revenues were assigned for the maintenance of the Gurdwara.[32] A shahīdganj was constructed by the Singhs on the spot where Nihang Gurbakhsh Singh and his martyr companions were cremated in Amrtisar after their defence of the Harmandar against the Afghans. Nihang Gurbakhsh Singh was taken to Sachch Khand by Bhai Mani Singh and Bhai Taru Singh, and was persuaded by the True Guru to be born again as the king of kings, to exercise supreme authority over the Khalsa. He was born as Ranjit Singh.[33]

According to Ratan Singh Bhangu, the fact and the concept of martyrdom were central to the Khalsa tradition. A martyr (shahīd) by definition was a Khalsa who was always ready to lay down his life not for any personal gain but for the sake of the oppressed, the Sikh faith, and the Sikh Panth. Though closely associated with martyrdom, the idea of sovereignty had originated with Guru Nanak and had been passed from one successor to another. Guru Arjan, Guru Har Krishan, Guru Teg Bahadur, and Guru Gobind Singh, whose four sons attained martyrdom, put this idea into practice.[34] The moral triumph of the martyr strengthened the position of the Khalsa in relation to God and weakened the position of their adversaries. Consequently, martyrdom enhanced the power of the Khalsa on the earth to ensure their sovereignty. The martyrs being close to the Guru and God could fulfil the wishes of those who made earnest supplication to them. This provided the basis for prayers offered at a shahīdganj.

Sovereignty of the Guru-Panth

With or without martyrdom, the idea of sovereignty is underlined by Bhangu throughout his work. The idea that Guru Gobind Singh had prophesied mīrī or Pātshāhī for every Khalsa horseman is reiterated elsewhere. Sovereignty could not be attained without armed struggle; therefore, the Khalsa were prepared to fight and to die fighting. Indeed, dangā was their *jāt* and *got*; they could not survive without dangā. Dangā leads to martyrdom which is the means to sovereignty. The Khalsa could not be defeated because they were destined to rule. The Khalsa were not prepared to accept *nawābī*; the Guru had made them sovereign.

The claim of sovereignty was sustained by the trust of the Khalsa in the prophecy of Guru Gobind Singh; they could be indifferent to suffering in the hope of Pātshāhī. Bhangu had no appreciation for the Sikh rulers who like Ala Singh of Patiala, submitted to any earthly ruler.[35] The belief of the Khalsa in the prophecy about sovereignty was a part of their general faith in the words of the Guru. The Guru had prophesied that a dog from Kabul would be instrumental in destroying the Mughals. The invasion of Nadir Shah appeared to be a fulfilment of that prophecy. The time had come, they thought, for the triumph of the Khalsa. The prophecy that 'ploughs drawn by donkeys shall be witnessed at Sirhind before long' encouraged the Khalsa to attack the city despite their small

Fig. 13.2 Raja Ala Singh, the founder of the Patiala State (d. 1765)

Fig. 13.3 Sardar Jassa Singh Ahluwalia, the most eminent Sikh leader of the eighteenth century, who founded the Kapurthala State

numbers and they emerged victorious. In a critical situation, the only support of the Khalsa was gurbachan, the words of the Guru. The Guru had said that the brave who fight dauntlessly in battle attain sovereignty; and every Singh was ready to fight against 1,25,000 men. The Guru had also said that the Panth would increase despite all odds. The words of the Guru never remained unfulfilled. It was on the basis of this faith that the Khalsa approached the Guru Granth for guidance and blessing (*vāk*).[36]

Bhangu takes it for granted that Guruship was vested in the Granth at the end of the line of the ten Gurus. The Khalsa read and recite the bāṇī of the Guru Granth, and worship it as others worship Lord Ganesh. They do not consult anyone for an auspicious time (*mahūrat*): they listen to the vāk of the Guru Granth. The Granth for them is the true body of the Guru. Therefore, the Sikh sangat asks for the true *vāk*. They are gratified when 'the Guru' assures them of triumph in their campaign against the Afghans of Kasur. The Guru Granth was their ultimate refuge in all situations. Bhangu nowhere talks of the *Dasam Granth* or the Granth of the Tenth King. He makes it clear that the recension known as the Ādi Granth is the Guru. He refers to the presence of Amritsari and

Fig. 13.4 The Gurmukhi script used by Kashmiri scribes in the early nineteenth century

Damdami recensions during the *ghallūghāra*, or the great carnage, of 1762. Both these were recensions of the Ādi Granth.[37]

The importance accorded by Ratan Singh Bhangu to 'the five' may be reiterated. When Subeg Singh approached the Khalsa on behalf of the Mughal governor of Lahore, the Khalsa asked the five bhujangīs to impose tankhā on him. When Kapur Singh accepted the *khil'at* brought by Subeg Singh with the title of Nawab, Kapur Singh got it sanctified by placing it at the feet of five bhujangīs before donning it. Before Sukha Singh engaged a Durrani in a duel, Charhat Singh requested five Singhs to offer ardās. The Guru had told the Khalsa that he would reach wherever five Sikhs joined hands in prayer. The five Sikhs have the same power as Gurbāṇī. The prayer of five Sikhs is heard in the true court.[38]

The concept of *gurmatā* is linked to the belief in the doctrines of Guru-Granth and Guru-Panth. Ratan Singh Bhangu uses the word matā for the decisions of Sikhs and non-Sikhs alike. The word gurmatā is reserved for the resolutions of the largest possible number of the Khalsa, generally at the Akal Takht. There is a general statement that the Khalsa used to visit Amritsar on Diwali and Baisakhi after their campaigns in the country, to listen to the Guru's words in the Harmandar, to hold dīwāns at the Akal Bunga, to adopt gurmatās and to administer justice. On the Baisakhi day in 1760 (actually, 1763), a Brahman of Kasur approached the dīwān of the Khalsa at the Akal Bunga to seek redress against the Afghans of Kasur who had forcibly taken away his wife. The Khalsa took vak and decided to sack Kasur and to give justice to the Brahman. For the sack of Sirhind, the gurmatā was adopted in the field. The gurmatā to oppose Ahmad Shah Abdali on his return from Sirhind in 1766 was also adopted presumably outside Amritsar. Significantly, the occupation of territories by the Khalsa was based on a gurmatā at the Akal Bunga. The first Singh occupant of any territory was not to be dislodged. Consequently, the smaller sardārs occupied small territories in villages and the bigger sardārs occupied large territories, including cities and towns. Those who reconciled the subject people struck firm roots but those who alienated them were soon dislodged. In the case of an unfair ejection, the *misl* to which a sardār belonged could intervene in favour of the first occupant.[39]

The Gurmatā is morally binding on all because the Guru is present in the sangat. There is no difference between the Guru and the sangat: the

Guru is the sangat, and the sangat is the Guru. What is true of the Panth is true of the sangat. The power of the Guru is in the Panth. The sants who change the age (*jugg*) are the Khalsa. The Guru is the Khalsa and the Khalsa is the Guru; there is no difference between the Guru and the Khalsa.[40] The Guru-Panth can be nothing but sovereign.

Identity of the Khalsa

Ratan Singh Bhangu was familiar with the Gurū Granth Sāhib and some of the compositions attributed to Guru Gobind Singh. There are quotations from the *Bachittar Nātak*, the *Zafarnāma,* and a work entitled *Chandī-Astotar*. Bhangu refers the reader to the *Gurbilās* of Sukha Singh for further information. Most of the time, however, he eagerly provides additional information. This information came from his father and mother, his ancestors, the venerable old Sikhs, and others.[41] In other words, the main source of Bhangu's work was oral information and tradition. Therein lies the significance of his work, with all its strengths and limitations. There is some hearsay, which the author points out, and there is much graphic detail which could come ultimately from first-hand observation. Not only action but also sentiments, beliefs, ideas, and emotions come into play to make the *Srī Gurū Panth Prakāsh* a rare kind of document. It embodies an understanding of the Khalsa tradition by a respectable member of the Khalsa who was deeply religious in his feelings and acutely political in his outlook on the world.

Ratan Singh Bhangu subscribes to the idea that Guru Gobind Singh invoked the aid of Chandī for making the Khalsa strong. The term used is awakened (*jagāī*). All the four sons of the Guru were given in bhet to Chandī. There was no difference between the Singhs and the sons of Guru Gobind Singh. Therefore, he committed 1,25,000 Singhs too for *bhet*. He who 'awakens' Chandī is committed to slake her thirst for blood. It is dangerous but necessary, because he who slakes her thirst becomes a supreme sovereign. Her thirst could be slaked in two ways: martyrdom, and slaugher of the enemy. That is why the term *'Chandī-bhet'* is used for the slaughter of both the 'Turks' and Bandaīs at one place.[42] Chandī or Kali has no other role to play in the narrative of Bhangu. It is relevant to add that several Sikh writers had referred to the invocation of Chandī by Guru Gobind Singh, like Koer Singh, Kesar Singh Chhibber, Sarup

Das Bhalla, and Sukha Singh. In fact, Bhangu refers to Sukha Singh as his source of information. Chandī's limited role is subsumed by the basic purpose of Guru Gobind Singh's mission.

Bhangu refers to God's incarnations. Just as Narsingh was the incarnation of God in the Satyuga, Ram in the Treta, and Krishan in the Duapar, so Nanak was his incarnation in the Kaliyuga. The supreme deity for Bhangu is Akal Purkh. The *Srī Gurū Panth Prakāsh* opens with invocation to Guru Nanak and the other Gurus. Guru Nanak was the true Guru who made a large number of people his Sikhs who became devoted to shabad, Sākhī, and saçhch. For him, Hindus and Musalmans were alike. He taught them *bhagtī* and *bandagī*. The service of *pīrs* and *paighambars* and of devīs and devs came to an end, along with the worship of Bīrs, Siddhs, Gugga, and evil spirits. He was followed by nine true Gurus as his successors. The Tenth Guru vested Guruship in the Khalsa and the Granth. With sovereign rule as their objective and their willingness to die for it, the Khalsa constituted a political community rooted in religious faith. A new baptism, a new appearance, and a new way of life distinguished them from others, even those who claimed to be Sikhs but believed in the Guruship of an individual.

Bhagu explicitly refers to the Khalsa as the third panth (*tisara panth*), the other two being Muslims and Hindus. He also brackets skills with Hindus. It seems, therefore, that the Khalsa were Hindu in relation to Musalmans as the non-Muslim inhabitants of Hind or Hindustan. In relation to Hindus, the Khalsa had a distinct identity of their own.[43]

Notes

1. *Prachīn Panth Prakāsh*, ed., Bhai Vir Singh, New Delhi: Bhai Vir Singh Sahit Sadan, 1993 (called 'new edition' but actually a reprint), Preface, pp. 471–2.
2. Balwant Singh Dhillon, *Srī Gurū Panth Prakāsh*, Amritsar: Singh Brothers, 2004, Preface, pp. *cha-chha* (in Gurmukhi).
3. Ibid., p. 436.
4. Ibid., pp. 1–6.
5. The need of physical force for attaining sovereignty is a recurring theme in Bhangu's work.
6. Ibid., pp. 259–70.
7. Ibid., pp. 271–2.
8. Ibid., pp. 24–9.
9. Ibid., pp. 29–32.

10. Ibid., pp. 33–4. Bhangu does not mention how the five were chosen. At another place, however, he refers to the call for heads, and the five Sikhs who offered themselves were given the status of shahīds, ibid., pp. 171–3.

11. Ibid., p. 35.

12. Bhangu places the removal of the Masands after the creation of the Khalsa. Ibid., pp. 41–3.

13. Ibid., pp. 35–6. The event is placed by Ratan Singh Bhangu on the Baisakhi day but in Sammat 1752 (AD 1695).

14. Ibid., pp. 36–8.

15. Ibid., pp. 43–6.

16. Ibid., pp. 47–59.

17. Ibid., pp. 60–7.

18. Ibid., pp. 68–79.

19. Ibid., pp. 80–115.

20. Ibid., pp. 116–27.

21. Ibid., pp. 128–34.

22. Ibid., pp. 134–56.

23. Ibid., pp. 138–9.

24. Ibid., pp. 157–65.

25. Ibid., pp. 166–70. Gulab Rai was encouraged by Bahadur Shah to assume guruship. Ibid., pp. 167–8.

26. Ibid., pp. 173–8.

27. Ibid., pp. 178–83.

28. These traits are praised by Ratan Singh Bhangu in the individual Singhs who dedicated their lives to the cause of the Khalsa Panth.

29. Ibid., pp. 26–9, 183–93, 215–20.

30. Ibid., pp. 234–59, 272–85.

31. The shahīdganj of Sikh martyrs presents an alternative to worship at the places of Muslim shahīds like Sakhi Sarvar.

32. Ibid., pp. 380–2.

33. Ibid., pp. 386–94.

34. Ibid., p. 258. Guru Gobind Singh held a unique position insofar as he 'saved the panth at the cost of his family' (ansh). Ibid., pp. 29–30.

35. Ibid., pp. 31, 33, 78, 128–9, 132, 134, 157, 160, 184, 190, 193, 197, 207, 224, 228–9, 235, 238, 248, 250–1, 273, 388, 390. For *hanne hanne mīrī*, ibid., pp. 129, 194, 196, 394.

36. Ibid., pp. 53, 60, 68, 146, 178, 214, 218, 222, 279, 303, 354, 360–1, 379, 382.

37. Ibid., pp. 279, 281, 362, 384, 388.

Bhangu does not refer to any compilation at Talvandi Sabo. He refers to the Damdama at Anandpur also. Indeed, several recensions of the Granth from the pre-Khalsa years are known. It is not necessary, therefore, to maintain that Guru Gobind Singh prepared the first recension of the Granth at Talvandi Sabo. Bhangu does not refer to the Granth of the Tenth Master but he does refer to several of the works now included in the *Dasam Granth*.

38. Ibid., pp. 34, 36–7, 79, 108, 175–6, 207, 216, 243, 279, 282.
39. Ibid., pp. 214, 311, 372, 377, 379–80, 399, 414.
40. Ibid., pp. 77, 133, 216, 280–1.
41. Ibid., pp. 1, 220, 302, 385, for example.
42. Ibid., pp. 3, 29, 38, 147, 160, 253, 258.
43. Ibid., pp. 1, 4–6, 14–15, 17, 19, 29, 31, 195.

PART FIVE

In the Context of Colonial Rule (1849–1947)

14

An Argument for Sikh Nationality

Nabha's *Ham Hindū Nahīn*

Bhai Kahn Singh Nabha is known by his magnum opus, *Gurshabad Ratanākar Mahān Kosh* (*The Encyclopaedia of Sikh Literature*), published in 1930. However, his literary career had started four decades earlier, and before the end of the nineteenth century he had published two seminal works. The *Gurmat Prabhakār* (1898) was a collection of verses from the Gurū Granth Sāhib given under nearly a thousand themes arranged in alphabetical order. The *Gurmat Sudhākar* (1899) covered a larger

Fig. 14.1 Bhai Kahn Singh of Nabha, the most eminent scholar of the Singh Sabha Movement, who published the *Gurshabad Ratanākar Mahān Kosh* or *The Encyclopaedia of Sikh Literature*

number of themes on the basis of Sikh literature produced during the precolonial period, starting with the works of Bhai Gurdas in the early seventeenth century and ending with the works of Bhai Santokh Singh in the early nineteenth century. Thus, before 1900, Bhai Kahn Singh Nabha was thoroughly familiar with the bulk of literature analysed in the present study.

Born in 1861 in a village of the Patiala state, Kahn Singh shifted to Nabha where his father was the Granthi of an important Gurdwara. Within five years, by the age of ten, he had studied both the *Gurū* Granth Sāhib and the *Dasam Granth* line by line. He learnt Sanskrit, and took interest in Vedantic philosophy, besides learning grammar and poetics. At the age of twenty, he went to Delhi and Lucknow to learn Persian. In 1883, he went to Lahore, and came into contact with Professor Gurmukh Singh, the leading light of the Lahore Singh Sabha. The inspiration he derived from the constructive work of the Singh Sabha remained with him for the rest of his life. He was closely associated with Max Arthur Macauliffe who published his magnum opus, *The Sikh Religion*, in 1909 as the most influential work on the Sikh tradition. Bhai Kahn Singh was also closely associated with the Khalsa College at Amritsar.

Fig. 14.2 Max Arthur Macauliffe, the author of *The Sikh Religion* (1909), who devoted his life to the study of the Sikh tradition

Fig. 14.3 Khalsa College, Amritsar, the premier Sikh educational institution of the colonial period

The Issue of Hindu-Sikh Identity

Bhai Kahn Singh's *Ham Hindū Nahīn*, published in Devanagri in 1897 and in Gurmukhi in 1898, was written to promote one of the basic concerns of the Singh Sabha reformers, that is, the issue of Sikh identity.[1] The title serves as a reminder that the book was first written in Hindi, addressed more to Hindus than to Sikhs. It was published in Punjabi in 1898 but the title was retained. In a later edition, Bhai Kahn Singh used its Punjabi form (*asīn hindū nahīn*), but not in the title. The Punjabi work was addressed not to the Hindus so much as to the Sikhs. This was because Bhai Kahn Singh knew that the Sikhs were being told that they were 'Hindu'. Being ignorant of Sikh scriptures and Sikh history, many Sikhs accepted the interpretation of Sikh tradition put forward by parties who were actually inimical towards Sikhism. These parties were anxious to see the Sikhs merged with the Hindu 'nation' (*qaum*). Evidently, Bhai Kahn Singh Nabha was responding to the claim being made that the Sikhs were 'Hindu'.

Presumably on a complaint from Bhai Kahn Singh's opponents, his book was officially examined from the viewpoint of his intention and its effect. The official who read it in English translation expressed the view that it was not intended to hurt the feelings of others and it contained nothing derogatory to the faith of the Hindus. Some 'Hindus' tried to refute Bhai Kahn Singh's arguments in the press. His opponents also contrived that the Maharaja of Nabha may take action against him. The Maharaja asked the Sikhs of Amritsar for their views about the book. They were unanimous in support of Bhai Kahn Singh's exposition and submitted their own evidence to support the view that the Khalsa Panth was distinct from both Hindus and Muslims: it was the 'Third Panth'. Bhai Kahn Singh sent a copy of his book to the Khalsa Diwan of Lahore. Its Joint Chief Secretary expressed the view that the distinct identity of the Khalsa Panth was well established in this publication with appropriate evidence from Sikh sacred literature. The Sarbat Khalsa of Gurdwara Tambu Sahib at Muktsar praised Bhai Kahn Singh for demonstrating that the Khalsa Panth was distinct and separate from Hindus and Muslims as the 'Third Panth'. This was the view of the Sarbat Khalsa at Damdama Sahib, Keshgarh Sahib, and Huzur Sahib (Abchalnagar). A large number of individuals wrote letters to Bhai Kahn Singh to support his view.

The fifth edition of *Ham Hindū Nahīn* was out in 1920. Easily among the most influential Sikh publications of the early decades of the twentieth century, it has been reprinted several times afterwards for wide dissemination. Referred to as 'Panth Ratan, Bhai Sahib, Bhai Kahn Singh Ji, Nabha', the author is looked upon as a venerable scholar and his *Ham Hindū Nahīn* as a classic statement of Sikh identity. To look upon it as a polemical vernacular tract is to miss its real significance.

Bhai Kahn Singh presents his thesis in the form of a dialogue between a Hindu and a Sikh. This enabled him to give a comprehensive treatment to the subject. All possible arguments in support of the proposition that Sikhs were Hindu come from the Hindu speaker and all possible arguments in support of the proposition that Sikhs have a distinct identity come from the Sikh. The book appears to reflect the whole range of arguments used on both sides in the debate during the late nineteenth and the early twentieth century. That may partly be the reason why *Ham Hindū Nahīn* became the most comprehensive statement on the subject of Sikh identity.[2] Our purpose is to analyse his exposition of Sikh identity and to assess its significance.

Debate in General Terms

Nabha's *Ham Hindū Nahīn* may informally be divided into two parts. The first part of about twenty pages relates to Sikh identity in rather general terms. According to the Hindu participant in the debate the Sikhs are Hindu because they have emerged from the Hindus, they eat food with Hindus, they enter into matrimony with Hindus, and they live in 'Hindustan'. Only recently have some Sikhs begun to talk of their separate identity. He goes on to add that the word 'Hindu' was derived from Sindhu, a Sanskrit word which means 'the conquerer of the wicked' and 'brave warrior'. The Sikh participant in the debate gives a longish reply. Talk of distinct identity was not an innovation of the contemporary Sikhs; they were simply following the injunctions of their Gurus. He quotes the Ādi Granth to the effect that 'we are neither Hindu nor Musalman'. He quotes Bhai Gurdas to the effect that Sikhs are distinct from both Hindus and Muslims. In further support of his argument he quotes from a *Janamsākhī*, the *Thirty-Three Savvayyey* of Guru Gobind Singh, the *Rahitnāmas* of Bhai Chaupa Singh and Bhai Dayā Singh, the *Bhagat Ratnāvalī*, the *Panth Prakāsh*, and the *Gurpratāp Suriyā*.[3]

On the point that the Sikhs had emerged from the Hindus, the Sikh participant refers to the semitic religions in which Christianity emerged from Judaism, and Islam arose out of both. In other words, just as Christianity and Islam were distinct religions so was the Sikh *dharam*. Furthermore, when a Hindu became a Christian or a Muslim he was not regarded as Hindu. Therefore, a Hindu who becomes a Sikh cannot be regarded as Hindu. On commensality, the Sikh participant refers to the *Rahitnāmas* which instruct the Khalsa not to observe distinctions of caste and not to eat with those who cut their hair. Similarly, on the question of matrimony the instruction is to have connections only with the Sikhs and not with those who cut their hair. If Sikhs are Hindu because they live in 'Hindustan', why the Christians and the Muslims who live in this country are not Hindu? The name 'Hindu' was given to the people of this country by outsiders. It does not occur in the ancient Indian scriptures and the epics. That was why the Arya Samajists insisted that they should not be called 'Hindu' and their country should not be called 'Hindustan'. However, the Sikhs had no objection to the use of the word 'Hindustan' for the country and, they had no objection to the term Hindu being used for them if 'Hindu' is equated with 'Indian'.[4]

Another line of argument which Bhai Kahn Singh puts into the mouth of his Hindu participant brings in the evidence of Sikh scriptures. '*Hindū sālāhī sālāhan*' in the Granth Sāhib is taken to mean that Hindu beliefs and practices are approved. The Sikh participant quotes the whole passage to show that far from being a praise of Hindu *mat* the passage in question underlines the importance of praising God and appropriating the True Name. The Hindu participant then quotes from the *Chhakke Chhand*, attributed by him to Guru Gobind Singh, to the effect that the Khalsa Panth was meant to spread Hindu dharma. Therefore, Sikh mat was a Hindu panth, like the Bairāgī and Sanyāsī panths. The Sikhs, who equated panth with qaum, did not realize that it was necessary to have larger numbers to be a qaum. The Sikhs counted merely in lakhs. The Sikh participant points out that the *Chhand* in question was not an authentic composition of Guru Gobind Singh. Even if taken to be authentic for the sake of argument, this composition refers to the triumph of the Khalsa as '*the third panth*'. The other two panths being Hindu and Muslim, it was clear that the Sikh Panth was to be treated as a qaum. According to the Hindu participant, innumerable *sākhīs* proved that Sikhs were Hindu. The Sikh participant responds to this general observation by saying that the Sikhs regarded as authentic only those parsangs which did not contradict the Gurbāṇī. According to the Hindu participant Guru Tegh Bahadur sacrificed his life for the sake of Hindus precisely because he was a Hindu. The Sikh participant replies that it was a cardinal principle of Sikh dharam to protect the oppressed. Guru Tegh Bahadur sacrificed his life for a principle and not for the sake of Hindus. This was the principle for which the Sikhs made sacrifices for the country and in the cause of justice. They looked upon Hindus as their 'brothers', but they were not Hindu in terms of religion (mazhab). They look upon Christians and Muslims also as their 'brothers'.[5]

Argument in Detail

About a score of points are discussed in the second part of over a hundred pages. It may clarify the two opposing viewpoints better if we take up each set of arguments together. Understandably, the arguments in support of the proposition that the Sikhs are Hindu are less elaborate. Nevertheless, a number of issues are raised by the Hindu participant in the dialogue. It is important to note that the Hindu participant is not an Arya Samajist but a Sanatanist.[6]

The first issue relates to scriptures by Bhai Kahn Singh. The references to the Vedas in the Ādi Granth, it is contended by the Hindu participant, are only to those hymns which talk of *giān*. But the scope of the Vedas is not confined to giān for they deal with karma and *upāsanā* as well. The implication is that the Vedas are not criticized in their entirety. Alternatively, the authors of the Ādi Granth did not have a thorough knowledge of the Vedas. In any case there are several statements in the Ādi Granth which recognize the sanctity and authority traditionally associated with the Vedas. As many as eight quotations are given from the Ādi Granth which do give the impression as if the authority and sanctity of the Vedas is acknowledged. The Shāstras, Smritīs, and Purāṇas are included in a few of these quotations. There is a reference also to the six schools of philosophy. Another line of argument is that Guru Nanak was a Bedi. Obviously, his ancestors at one time were known for their knowledge of the Vedas and their adherence to the Vedic Dharma. The *Bachittar Nātak* is quoted on this point: 'They who mastered the Vedas came to be known as Bedi; they propagated actions based on *dharma*'.[7]

The second issue relates to the system of caste (*jātī-varahn*) among the Sikhs. The Hindu participant argues that the claim that the Sikhs did not subscribe to the varnashrama ideal stands refuted by Guru Nanak's regret about the obliteration of varna-*maryādā* in his days. He castigates the Khatri for discarding his dharma and adopting the language of the mlechh: 'the whole world has become one caste and there is no *dharma* left'. In the *Janamsakhi* of Bhai Bala, Lalo the carpenter presumes, as a Shudra, that Guru Nanak would not eat food cooked by him and suggests that Guru Nanak himself may prepare his food. He had seen the sacred thread (janjū) worn by Guru Nanak. The point at issue therefore is whether or not high caste Sikhs wore the sacred thread, a practice which had a bearing on the question of varna-maryādā. A quotation allegedly from Guru Nanak's compositions is cited to confirm that he used to wear the sacred thread. In the *Bachittar Nātak* it is stated that Guru Tegh Bahadur sacrificed his life to save the *tilak* and *janjū* of the Hindus. Guru Gobind Singh wrote savvayyās in praise of Brahmans and instructed his followers to give *dān* to them. In the *Sukhmanī* the Sikhs are instructed to revere the *pandit* who understands the Vedas, Smritīs, and the Purāṇas.[8]

The third point as given by Bhai Kahn Singh relates to the idea of incarnation. Several parsangs in the *Dasam Granth* prove, it is contended, that Guru Gobind Singh believed in *avtārs*. A quotation carries the import that one could attain liberation from transmigration by worshipping Krishna. Even in the Ādi Granth there is a passage in which various avtārs are mentioned with the idea that they were to be worshipped. The fourth point was that of the worship of the Goddess among the Sikhs. There is a statement in the *Bachittar Nātak* that Guru Gobind Singh invoked the Goddess (*Kālikā*). The whole of his *Chandī Charitra* is written in praise of the Goddess (Chandi): the merit of reciting her praise is underlined. Above all, in the Sikh prayer (*ardās*) the Goddess (Bhagvatī) is invoked first of all. Since the term used in Gurmukhi is *bhagautī*, the Hindu participant suggests that Guru Gobind Singh originally wrote it in the Persian script in which it was hard to make a distinction between bhagvatī and bhagautī, and the Gurmukhi scribe accepted the latter reading out of ignorance.[9]

The fifth point relates to idol-worship. It is stated in the Granth Sāhib that Namdev realized God through the worship of an idol and that Dhanna found God in a piece of stone. The references in the *Vārs* of Bhai Gurdas to Dhanna and Namdev prove further that the Sikhs had no objection to idol-worship. Furthermore, the Sikhs regard the Granth Sāhib as the physical form (*sarūp*) of the Guru and offer *kaṛhā* in a dish by way of bhog to the Granth Sāhib. This is similar to idol-worship.[10] According to a Hindu participant, Guru Nanak observed his father's *shradh* only two days before his own death. The Sikh Gurus used to go to sacred places for pilgrimage. In a composition of Guru Amar Das there are clear instructions regarding what was to be done after his death, including the *kathā* of the Purāṇa by Keso Gopal. The verse also refers to pind, pattal, *kiryā*, *dīvā*, and *phull*.[11] This shows that these practices were observed commonly by Hindus and Sikhs. Indeed, the Hindu participant asserts that no injunction of the Gurus forbids Sikhs to perform their rites in accordance with the Hindu Shāstras, and there was no injunction to have separate Sikh rites (Gur-maryādā). The *chhants*, *ghoṛiān*, and *lāvān* composed by the Gurus and recited by the Sikhs at the time of marriage, were not meant to be taken literally for the actual conduct of rites (*vivhār*); they were meant to be taken as metaphors. Even if it is conceded that Sikhs have their own *sanskārs*, the symbols like the kesh and the kachh were adopted as temporary measures in a situation of armed conflict. They were no longer necessary. Similarly it was not necessary to keep uncut hair; the first nine Gurus had no kesh.[12]

The Hindu participant raises three more points according to Bhai Kahn Singh. The first relates to the basic principles of Hindu Dharma which, he maintains, are shared by the Sikhs with the Hindus. The first principle was to regard the Vedas, which formed the basis of Hindu Dharma, as true and the second was to subscribe to belief in God, good and evil, heaven and hell. The five other basic principles were: to seek *muktī* from transmigration, to regard *varnashrama* as the ideal social order, to cremate the dead, to protect the cow, and to uphold the idea of purity and pollution. The second point made by the Hindu participant is that even if the Sikh dharam, Sikh principles, and Sikh rites and ceremonies were different from those of the Hindus, the Sikhs were governed by the Hindu Law. The third point was that it was not really politic on the part of the Sikhs to separate themselves from the Hindus. All such attempts increased mutual hostility. The Sikhs were small in numbers and they were bound to suffer great loss through separation from the Hindus. By aligning themselves with the Hindus, who had now become important, the Sikhs could increase their own importance.[13]

Beliefs and Practices in Early Sikh Literature

According to the Sikh participant, who is Bhai Kahn Singh himself, the Sikhs have their own scripture, the Gurū Granth Sāhib. Other religious books among the Sikhs are judged as authentic to the extent to which they accord with the Granth. Justification for this exclusive status of the Granth Sāhib is found in the compositions of the Gurus and in other Sikh literature. Guru Amar Das emphasized the superiority of the bāṇī of the Guru over other bāṇīs which are looked upon as 'unripe' (*kachchī*). Gurbāṇī is the light of the world; it leads to the Divine Name. According to Guru Ram Das, Gur-shabad is above everything else. The Sikhs of the Guru regard it as true: the Creator himself made the Guru to utter it. What the Gurus say about other scriptures should be seen in conjunction with the indispensability of the true bāṇī underlined by the Gurus. About a score of quotations from the Ādi Granth, the works of Bhai Gurdas, the *Bachittar Nātak*, the *Rām Avtār*, and the *Thirty-Three Savvayyey* underline the inefficacy of the Vedas, Smritīs, and Shāstras for attaining liberation. The semitic books are often bracketed with Hindu religious scriptures. Bhai Gurdas includes the Purāṇas, the Epics, and the Gītā in the list of religious books which stood rejected in comparison with Gurbāṇī. The Sikh participant goes on to explain that the entire message of Gurbāṇī is meant for all human beings. Furthermore, the Sikh conception of *karma*, *upāsanā*, and giān is totally different from what they mean among the Hindus. The lines and phrases quoted by the Hindu participant are refuted by the Sikh participant either by providing the full text to explain the correct meaning or by quoting other passages for clarifying the meaning, or by doing both. The final conclusion drawn on the point of scriptures is that the only valid religious book for the Sikhs is Gurū Granth Sāhib, and no other scripture.[14]

On the issue of the varna system, the Sikh participant quotes passages from Manu and other authorities which exalt the position of the Brahman and his rights and privileges, and which underline the disabilities of the Shudra and his over-all depression and deprivation. The message of Guru Nanak is meant for all the four varnas and even for the chandāls. The path is open to all because the whole of mankind is believed to have been created from the same light. Guru Nanak castigated the Khatris for abandoning their faith. Had he believed that Persian language was *mlechh-bhāshā* he would not have composed in Persian, and Guru Gobind Singh would not have written his *Zafarnāma* in Persian. The idea of equality in the Sikh Panth is underlined at many places in the Ādi Granth and in the Vārs of Bhai Gurdas. More than a score of quotations on this point are given from these and other sources like the *Akāl Ustat*, the *Gurpratāp Suriyā*, and the *Rahitnāmas* of Bhai Chaupa Singh and Bhai Daya Singh. The Sākhī of Lalo the carpenter demonstrates that Guru Nanak ate food cooked by a Shudra. For that reason alone the point about the sacred thread loses its significance. The line quoted from the Ādi Granth by the Hindu participant, placed in its proper context, also shows that Guru Nanak discarded the distinctions of caste. In the *Bachittar Nātak*, quoted by the Hindu participant, *tilak* and *janjū* were clearly the sacred mark and the sacred thread of the Brahmans who had approached Guru Tegh Bahadur for help. An incident narrated in the *Dabistān-i Mazāhib* indicates that Sikhs attached no sanctity to the sacred thread even before the Khalsa was instituted. Furthermore, the Gurus wanted their Sikhs to give dān not to Brahmans but to Sikhs. The savvayyās of Guru Gobind Singh were not in praise of Brahmans but in favour of the Khalsa who were to receive all kinds of gifts. In the *Sukhmanī* too Guru Arjan emphasizes the qualities which make any person a true brahman (and not the Brahman of varna order). The pandit of the Hindu social order is denounced by Guru Nanak and his successors. Appropriate quotations are given from the compositions of Guru Nanak, Guru Amar Das, and Guru Arjan on the point.[15]

The idea of incarnation stands discarded in Sikh dharam. God is never born; he never dies; he does not take any form. The so-called avtārs are God's creatures, and they too are in search of emancipation. In support of this view, quotations are given from the Ādi Granth, the *Shabad Hazāre*, the *Thirty-Three Savvayyey* and the works of Bhai Gurdas and Bhai Nand Lal. If Krishna is mentioned in the *Krishan Avtār*, it must be remembered that this work was meant to be a free version of a received account, and the ideas it contained could not be taken as the views of Guru Gobind Singh. In the *Mārū Sohle*, Guru Arjan refers to beliefs prevalent among others; his own view is expressed in the last line, indicating his preference for the True Name. The use of epithets for God derived from the names of avtārs did not mean that God of the Sikh dharam becomes equated with them. Rather, a new meaning is given to those epithets. The transformation in the meaning is comparable to the transformation of allah as the divinity of pre-Islamic Arabs into Allah of the Prophet Muhammad, or the transformation of the Teuton 'god' into the Christian God in English.[16]

As God's creatures, gods and goddesses stand bracketed with avtārs. They were all a part of māyā. Like the other creatures of God, they seek emancipation. Neither Brahma nor Bishan nor Mahesh can be equated with God. They all serve God who alone is to be worshipped. These ideas find support in the Ādi Granth, the *Akāl Ustat*, the *Thirty-Three Savvayyey*, the *Jāp Sāhib*, the *Shabad Hazāre*, the *Rahitnāma* of Bhai Dayā Singh, and the works of Bhai Gurdas and Bhai Nand Lal.[17] The term Kālikā in the *Chandī dī Vār* is used for Akāl Purkh and not for the Goddess. Durga in the same composition is mentioned as created by God. Since the *Chandī dī Vār* was a popular version of the *Durga Saptshatī*, every idea mentioned in the composition could not be ascribed to Guru Gobind Singh.[18] In the *Bachittar Nātak*, Guru Gobind Singh is explicit on the point that none other than God is to be worshipped.[19] To argue that ritualistic purification was hygienic was a futile rationalization because the ritual itself was based on superstition.[20] Similarly, the practice of plastering the ground with cow dung and drawing a circle around (*chaunkā-kār*) which, among other things, was insisted upon by Manu was denounced by the Gurus. Bhai Chaupa Singh in his *Rahitnāma* forbids the use of cow-dung in the langar. The author of the *Gurpratāp Suriyā* states that the Sikh sacred food (deg) was meant for all the four varnas. The author of the *Dabistān-i Mazāhib* also conveys the impression that there was no restriction on food among the Sikhs. The only criterion was that it should not be harmful for the body.[21] Quotations from the Ādi Granth, the Vārs of Bhai Gurdas, the *Rahitnāma* of Bhai Dayā Singh, and the *Gurpratāp Sūriyā* support the view that fasting on days like the Janamashtmi, Ram Naomi, and Ekadasi was rejected by the Gurus and their followers. Observing fast was a sign of ignorance (agiān)[22] as also the notion of auspicious and inauspicious days and times. Quotations from the Ādi Granth, the works of Bhai Gurdas and Bhai Nand Lal, and the *Gurbilās Pātshāhī Chhe* show that the notions of muhūrat, *tith*, *vār*, and sagan were discarded by the Gurus and their followers.[23] The idea of the efficacy of *mantras*, *tantras*, and *jantras* in enhancing the spiritual and physical prowess of individuals, giving them supranatural powers or longevity or sexual virility, stood discarded in *Gurmat*.[24] The performance of *hom* or *yagg* was also discarded. These views are supported with quotations from the Ādi Granth, the works of Bhai Gurdas and Bhai Nand Lal, and the *Dabistān-i Mazāhib*.[25] In response to Swami Dayā Nand's insistence on *hom* as the key ritual of the Aryas, it is argued that the supposed purification of the atmosphere involved a great loss of materials which could be more useful to human beings if put to their ordinary use.[26]

The rites of kiryā, shrādh, and *tīrath* are taken up together as related to death by Bhai Kahn Singh. The *Janamsākhī* statement that Guru Nanak observed shrādh for his father only two days before his own death is not based on authentic information. The correct position is depicted in the *Gurū Nānak Prakāsh* in which Guru Nanak rejects the practice of shrādh. The *Sadd* of Guru Amar Das in *Rāg Rāmkalī*, which is supposed to prescribe kiryā after his death, is not properly understood. It was written with reference to a hymn of Guru Nanak in which 'Keso' refers to God. Therefore the 'Keso Gopal' of the *Sadd* is no other than God. Furthermore at several places in his compositions, Guru Amar Das himself denounces the pandit and what he does.[27] Mourning with loud lamentations was denounced by Guru Nanak. He prepared kaṛhā parshād after Mardana's death, according to a *Janamsākhī*. According to the *Giān Ratnāvalī*, *kiryā* was replaced by ardās, kīrtan, and kaṛhā parshād. The ceremony of bhaddan was not to be observed, according to the *Srī Gur Sobhā* and Bhai Chaupa Singh. The Gurus went to the places of Hindu pilgrimage not as pilgrims but to preach their own message to the people assembled there.[28]

The Gur-maryādā regarding birth, initiation, and marriage had nothing to do with Hindu mat. Guru Amar Das uttered the *Ānand* at the birth of his grandson and instructed the Sikhs to recite this composition at the birth of a child. Guru Arjan did this, as referred to in one of his hymns, at the birth of his son Hargobind. Guru Ram Das composed chhants, ghoṛiān, and lāvān for the occasion of marriage. A close attention to these compositions makes one realize that they were meant to be used on the occasion of marriage. They refer to the bridegroom and the marriage party, the young married couple, and the custom of displaying dowry (*dāj*). Guru Gobind Singh performed the marriage of a Sikh girl in accordance with this rite. Bhai Daya Singh in his *Rahitnāma* insists that Sikhs should not adopt any ceremony of marriage other than '*ānand*'. For initiation Guru Nanak introduced the practice of charan pahul, which was followed by all his successors before Guru Gobind Singh introduced *khande ka amrit*. He also instructed the Sikhs to observe rahit and adopt certain symbols like *kachh* and *kaṛā*. There is no evidence to suggest that Khalsa symbols were meant to be a temporary measure for the times of war. There was no certainty that wars had ended for all times to come. The Sikh Gurus used to keep uncut hair (kesh). There are several references in the Ādi Granth to the long hair serving metaphorically as a fan or a chaur.[29]

Responding to the seven 'universal' principles mentioned by his Hindu counterpart, the Sikh participant denies that the Vedas are the basis of Sikh dharam. Belief in God, *pun* and *pāp*, or reward and punishment, is not confined to Hindus or Sikhs. Similarly, belief in transmigration was not confined to Hindus and Sikhs in the history of mankind. The Sikhs did not subscribe to the ideal of varnashrama. Cremation was not the only practice among either Hindus or Sikhs. While *jal-parwāh* was known to both Hindus and Sikhs there were Hindus who practised burial rather than cremation. Cow protection was rationally desirable, but the Sikhs did not have the same kind of attitude towards the cow as the Hindus. The dung and urine of the cow were not used by the Sikhs in any way similar to their use among the Hindus. In the Vedas, there are references to *gomedha* and *goghaṇā*, the former in the context of ritual sacrifice and the latter involving the slaughter of a cow for entertaining a special guest. Finally, the Sikhs did not subscribe to the idea of pollution. Thus, the basic principles mentioned by the Hindu participant as common to both Hindus and Sikhs were not upheld in Sikhism and were not prevalent among the Sikhs. The Sikh participant goes on to add that the principles to be found among the Hindus were innumerable like the Hindu gods. Consequently, even the census reports failed to clarify one's ideas about who was a Hindu. That there was no acceptable definition was not surprising, because the word 'Hindu' did not occur in the sacred books of the Hindus. They were the only people in the world to have accepted a name given to them by outsiders.[30]

On the question of Hindu Law being applicable to the Sikhs, the Sikh participant points out that the law operative in the country was no longer the Hindu Law. It was mostly customary law that was operative among the Sikhs. There were no legal codes based entirely on religious books. Laws based on religious books did not come into operation immediately on the appearance of a new religious system. This did not happen in Islam or Christianity. So far as the Sikhs were concerned, the basic principles had been enunciated in Gurbāṇī and the *Rahitnāmas*. The Anand Marriage Act had also been passed. Thus, the possibility of preparing a Sikh code of laws had been created. Lepel Griffin had observed that the Sikhs had abandoned the Hindu faith, and the system of laws based on that faith; for fifty years the Sikh chiefs had followed laws of succession which were altogether different. A Hindu could not invoke the authority of Manu and the Shāstras after becoming a Sikh just as a Muslim could not invoke the sharī'at after accepting the Sikh faith.[31]

Was it politic on the part of the Sikhs to insist that they must be treated as a separate people? The answer is quite unambiguous. No progress (uṇtī) is possible without becoming independent (*sautantar*). To be a branch (*shākh*) of another qaum is to remain in slavery (*ghulāmī*), and such subordination involved all kinds of depression. The Sikhs loved their neighbours and looked upon their tribulations as their own, but they could not be treated as a part of another people in terms of religious and social principles. They had already suffered for becoming one (*ikk-mikk*) with the Hindus. The Sikhs lost in numbers, and their wealth went into the hands of Brahmans through dān and *dakshiṇā*. The vested interests among the Hindus made every possible effort to dissuade Sikhs from retaining their religious symbols. Many Sikh families reverted to the Hindu fold and many others entered into matrimony with Hindus. While the Sikhs were told that Sikhism did not lie in the kesh or the kachh, no one told the Hindus that their dharma did not lie in the sacred thread (janjū) or the tuft (*bodī*). If mutual hostility was increasing it was due to the hostile attitude of some Hindus towards the Sikh faith. Aggression came precisely from those Hindus whose interests were bound to be hit if Sikhs were treated as a separate qaum. They were keen to own the Sikhs in self-interest. They were joined by the self-styled gurūs among the Sikhs in self-interest. They published books and articles to show that the Sikhs were Hindu.[32]

Not to create hostility among various religious communities was in the interest of the country as a whole. Differences of religion should not be allowed to become a cause of conflict. Everyone should have the freedom to pursue and propagate one's religion. However, everyone should do this in such a manner that does not create resentment among others. The Sikhs should know that they are not Hindu, but they should also know that it is their duty to love their countrymen as brothers and to look upon all the peoples of Bharat as inseperable organs of the same body.[33] These obviously are the views of Bhai Kahn Singh himself, expressed directly in his 'appeal' to the reader in 1920. Sikh dharam is different from others and Sikhs are a separate qaum. But they should not criticize other faiths or oppose other people. We have one father, and we are all his children. All are our friends and we are friendly towards everyone. Not to regard the *desh-bhāī*s as a part (*ang*) of the same body is to invite curse from the land of one's birth (*janam-bhūmī*). They who create animosity and division by mixing up matters of religion (dharam), politics (*nītī*), and society (*samāj*) are bound to suffer here (*lok*) and in the hereafter (parlok). They do not deserve the title of 'human beings', much less the title of 'God's progeny'. They who belong to different faiths and yet regard themselves as a part of one 'Nation' receive respect and honour from civilized nations.[34]

The Basic Thesis

We have closely followed the text of *Ham Hindū Nahīn* to ensure that no relevant point in Bhai Kahn Singh's exposition of Sikh identity is missed. If we set aside the sequence of his arguments and omit minor detail, we can present his basic thesis in clear terms. Bhai Kahn Singh wrote his book at a time when communitarian consciousness was gaining ground among an increasing number of people in the Punjab, as in the rest of the country. In other words, the emergence of communitarian consciousness was not confined to the Sikhs.

Bhai Kahn Singh argues that distinctive Sikh identity was not a new thing. The authorities which he invokes in support of this argument were nearly all pre-colonial: the Ādi Granth, the works of Bhai Gurdas, the compositions of Guru Gobind Singh and others in the *Dasam Granth*, the works of Bhai Nand Lal, the *Srī Gur Sobhā*, the *Rahitnāmas*, the *Gurbilās Pātshāhī Das*, the *Gurbilās Pātshāhī Chhe* and the works of Bhai Santokh Singh. At a few places the evidence of Janamsākhīs is also invoked. This literature was not only precolonial but also voluminous, and it covered a wide range.

Sikh literature according to Bhai Kahn Singh underlines belief in one God, rejects the existence of gods and goddesses as independent entities, discards the idea of incarnation, and rejects idol-worship. Pilgrimage to places traditionally regarded as sacred has no merit and is, therefore, denounced and discarded. The only authoritative scripture for the Sikhs, the Ādi Granth, came to be regarded as the Guru. The Sikh mode of worship consisted of the recitation of Gurbāṇī after a bath early in the morning, participation in kīrtan and recitation of Gurbāṇī in the evening. The Sikh mode of initiation consisted of baptism (amrit), as *charan-pahul* first and then as khande kī pahul. The Sikh code of conduct related to the personal and social life of the Sikhs. In the religious symbols of the Sikhs, three items are specifically mentioned as important: kesh, kachh, and kaṛā. With the kesh was associated the turban, and *kanghā*. The identity indicated by these items is the Khalsa identity. However, Bhai Kahn Singh is quite categorical on the point that the pre-Khalsa Sikhs also possessed a distinctive identity.[35]

For the rites of passage, Bhai Kahn Singh refers to Guru Nanak's denunciation of mourning as the basis for the rites after death. For birth, his earliest reference is to Guru Amar Das; for the rites of marriage he refers to Guru Ram Das. By the eighteenth century there was a good deal of insistence on all the Sikh rites of passage. For commensality, the principle was to make no distinction of caste. The Sikhs used to eat together in the langar. For matrimony, Sikhs were to confine their relations to Sikhs. All human beings were God's children and the path of liberation was open to them all. The caste system was discarded by the Gurus and their followers. Thus, the distinct identity of the Sikhs was based on their religious beliefs and practices, their exclusive scripture which guided them like the Guru, their distinctive rites of passage, and their social usages. This distinctive identity was deliberately created by the Gurus.

Recent Historiographical Perspectives

The question of Sikh identity has been discussed by a few scholars in recent decades. We can turn to them first. Daljeet Singh has discussed Sikh identity with reference to the spiritual experience of the Gurus and their concept of God, their ideology, the character of the Sikh religious system, scripture, and the Sikh Panth and its institutions. His discussion ends with the time of Guru Gobind Singh, carrying the implication that Sikh identity was clearly established during the sixteenth and seventeenth centuries. In his view, the principal attributes of God and the spiritual experience of the Gurus gave an identity to Sikhism that was new in Indian history. The repeated stress of the Gurus on 'the reality of the world' was an important departure from the Indian religions of their times. The goal of Sikhism was to work in accordance with God's 'altruistic will'. This too was an important departure from the goal generally prescribed in Indian religions, that is, merger in Brahman or extinction in Nirvāṇa. Ethics were placed at the centre of Sikhism: 'Everything is lower than truth; higher still is truthful living or conduct'. The ideal man of Sikhism, the Gurmukh, carried out the 'altruistic will' of God. Like Judaism and Islam, Sikhism was a whole-life system. Unlike them, it was free from exclusiveness and monasticism. Indian systems were dichotomous, making a sharp distinction between the spiritual and the empirical life. But Guru Nanak organized a system of householders who participated in all walks of life and remained socially responsible. The Sikh scripture, *Gurū* Granth Sāhib, is the most emphatic pronouncement about 'the distinct and independent identity of Sikhism'. The foundations of a new social order were laid by Guru Nanak himself with the institutions of sangat, *langar*, Guruship, and the ideal of social commitment. From this foundation, the Sikh Panth logically developed into the order of the Khalsa by the end of the seventeenth century. Sikh identity, thus was not something created by external circumstances: it was consciously created by the Gurus themselves on the basis of their thought and vision.[36]

According to W.H. McLeod, the permanence of the Nanak Panth was ensured by ritual and administrative measures introduced by the early Gurus. The twin concepts of sangat and kīrtan are emphasized in the Janamsākhīs as a regular feature of the corporate life of the Nanak Panth. The Sikhs had their distinctive mode of salutation and places of worship called dharamsāls: they cherished the characrteristically Sikh ideal of nām-dān-isnān. By the end of the sixteenth century, the leaders of the Nanak Panth had developed a strong sense of Panthic identity. In general terms this identity was defined by a common loyalty, common association, and common practice. The path enunciated by the Gurus was open to men and women of all castes. In other words, caste had nothing to do with access to liberation. However, it did not mean a total obliteration of caste identity. Also, the general body of the believers was not so clearly conscious of distinct identity as the elite of the Panth. The institution of the Khalsa by Guru Gobind Singh sharpened the distinctive identity of his followers. They also remained visible throughout the eighteenth century. By the end of the century the Khalsa ideal was clearly dominant and to some foreign observers it seemed that all Sikhs were in fact Sikhs of the Khalsa. Actually, however, the non-Khalsa Sikhs too were there as members of the Sikh Panth. But the dominant Sikh identity was the Khalsa identity. This was the position in the early nineteenth century when the British annexed the Punjab.[37]

In Harjot Oberoi's view 'the Khalsa was instituted to finally end the ambiguities of Sikh religiosity'. The Khalsa was a new person with a concrete identity. His 'personhood' came to be confirmed through an unusual initiation ceremony, called khande ki pahul, 'the like of which had never existed before in South Asia'. The Khalsa was to maintain unshorn hair and to carry arms on his person. The Khalsa brought forth its own dharam, giving it the distinctive name of rahit. The manuals called *Rahitnāmas* cover all domains of human life, ranging from how the Khalsa shall eat to laying down the nature of piety. The Khalsa introduced new rites, particularly to mark birth, initiation, and death. These rites gradually turned 'a fluid identity into a distilled, enduring form, supplemented by a long inventory of tabooed behaviour. The Khalsa established their own control over Sikh sacred space and laid down norms for its management. Contemporary records point towards Khalsa identity gradually 'becoming hegemonic within Sikh tradition'. The ideas of the Guru Granth and the belief in the Guru-Panth provided links with the early Sikh tradition.

Unlike McLeod, Oberoi thinks that the Khalsa tradition gave place to what he calls the Sanatan Sikh tradition. The Sahajdhari Sikhs came to occupy a more important position in the Santan tradition in the late eighteenth and the early nineteenth century. Ideological differences and 'deviant' practices were tolerated much more in this tradition than among the Khalsa of the earlier eighteenth century. The Sanatan Sikh tradition was more tolerant of caste distinctions too. There were several identities among the Sikhs during the early nineteenth century, all more or less equally important.[38] Oberoi's treatment of Sikh identity ignores the fact that the majority of the members of the Sikh Panth were Singhs and not Sahajdharis even during the early nineteenth century.

Despite the differences of detail, emphasis, and perception among the three scholars in their treatment of Sikh identity, it is clear that the issue of Sikh identity did not emerge for the first time in the colonial period. Our own analysis of Sikh literature in the earlier chapters of this book shows that consciousness of a distinct identity began to emerge in the sixteenth century; it was emphatically articulated by Bhai Gurdas in the early seventeenth century; it was asserted in literature related to Guru Gobind Singh and the Khalsa. The term tīsar panth (the third Panth) makes its appearance around 1700 to remain in use in the literary works of the late eighteenth and the early nineteenth centuries. The colonial context did not throw up the issue of Sikh identity; it provided a new perspective for looking at religious identities.

The Political Perspective

The term 'Hindu' does not occur in the ancient Indian scriptures. It was used by outsiders for 'Indians'. Its use was quite common in Persian and Arabic literature by the tenth century. The term used for the country was either 'Hind' as in al-Beruni's *Kitāb al-Hind* or 'Hindustan' as in the *Tuzuk-i Bāburī*. With the coming of the Turks, Persians, Arabs, and others into India and the conversion of a considerable number of Indians to Islam, 'Hindu' came to be distinguished from 'Muslim'. The term 'Hindu' is used in this sense by all the Persian writers of the period.

Amir Khusrau refers to himself as an 'Indian Turk'. Babur refers to an Indian Muslim as 'Hindustani'. The label 'Indian' came to be shared by Muslims, and the term 'Hindu' began to acquire other connotations when this identity was accepted by some of the people who were called 'Hindu'. One connotation of 'Hindu' was a person who followed Brahmanical beliefs and practices, whether a Vaishnava, a Shaiva, or a Shakta. 'Hindu', thus, began to acquire a religious connotation.

During the nineteenth century, the term 'Hinduism' came into currency. It was meant to refer to the 'religion of the Hindus'. But there was no single religious system that could be called 'Hinduism'. The process of exclusion and inclusion began almost simultaneously. Affinities were perceived between Vaishnavism, Shaivism, and Shaktism, and differences were noticed between all these on the one hand and Buddhism, Jainism, and Sikhism on the other. The equation of Brahmanical traditions with 'Hinduism' was reinforced. The major Sanskrit texts 'rediscovered' by the Europeans appeared to support this construct.

Furthermore, the western writers who took interest in 'Hinduism' were often Christian missionaries, full of evangelical fervour and optimistic about a dramatic success in their missionary enterprise. For various reasons, they generally attacked 'Hinduism' in strong terms, trying to demonstrate that it was spiritually bankrupt and morally corrupt. Before long, educated Indians rose in defence of 'Hinduism', unconsciously accepting the monolithic construct in the process. The beginning of this development can be seen in the career of Raja Ram Mohan Rai from a cosmopolitan humanist to the founder of the Brahmo Samaj. In spite of all their catholicity and appreciation for Christianity, the Brahmos worked for 'reformed Hinduism'.

Many people in the Punjab felt attracted to Brahmo 'reform'. The most notable Sikh who dedicated his life to the Brahmo Samaj was Dyal Singh Majithia. He is remembered every year by the trustees of *The Tribune* which was his creation, besides the Dyal Singh College and the Dyal Singh Library. On his death in 1898, his widow went to the court to contest his will for creating these institutions with his property. She lost. It was popularly believed that she lost because Dyal Singh was regarded as a Hindu. This, *inter multa alia*, became a cause for the passage of the Anand Marriage Act in 1909. It is relevant for our purpose to note that, 'reformed' Hinduism as a monolithic construct was seen by many Sikhs as a threat to their own separate identity.

Threat to the separate existence of Sikhism was reinforced by Swami Dayanand. He had no appreciation for any of the existing religious traditions. Though his criticism of the Sikh faith was milder than his condemnation of Christianity, Islam, and the Purāṇic Hindu tradition, it was enough to indicate that the Sikh tradition had no place in his 'reformation'. It is true that Swami Dayanand never talked of Hinduism, and he did not like even the use of the term Hindu. But this literal accuracy can lead us astray from his essential position. He stood for one religion for all the people of the country. His trinity of Arya Dharma,

Arya Bhasha (that is, Hindi), and Aryavarta was meant to revive the glories of India in all spheres of life. The more militant among the Punjabi Aryas had no hesitation in criticizing the Sikh Gurus and the Sikh scriptures in rather strident terms. Sikhism in their view had outlived its purpose. The Arya programme of shuddhī, a purificatory rite meant to bring into the Arya fold all converts to Christianity and Islam, was logically extended to Sikhs in due course.[39] Whereas the Brahmans used to ask the Sikhs to remove their kachh and kaṛā temporarily for ritual purposes, the Aryas were prepared to remove their *kesh* permanently and deliberately in public. The symbolic significance of '*shuddhī*' was not lost on the Sikhs.

Two years after the foundation of the Arya Samaj in Lahore, a Singh Sabha was founded at Lahore in 1879. The Lahore Singh Sabha leaders were rather militant, like the Aryas, and they contested every inch of the ground with them. The last two decades of the nineteenth century were marked, among several other controversies, by the Hindu-Sikh controversy over matters religious and social. The Sanatan Dharmi Hindus asserted that Sikhs were Hindu.[40] Bhai Kahn Singh wrote his *Ham Hindū Nahīn*, responding to what he perceived as a threat to a tradition that he cherished. He was not alone. He represented the views and feelings of an increasing number of Sikhs who prized the Sikh tradition. They gave great importance to the Ādi Granth as the exclusive scripture of the Sikhs, and to the Khalsa identity as the preferred Sikh identity. Neither the doctrine of Guru Granth nor the Singh identity was new. What was new was the emphasis laid on both.

A far more serious concern of Bhai Kahn Singh was the recognition of the Sikh Panth as a political community. To be recognized as a qaum on the basis of their identity was in the best interests of the Sikhs. The Sikh Panth of the sixteenth and seventeenth centuries was a distinct entity. The Khalsa of the eighteenth century was a political community. Therefore, the word panth was synonymous with qaum, that is, a socio-religious community which was also a political entity. The Indian Nation consisted of three 'nationalities' (qaums): Hindu, Muslim, and Sikh. Indian Nationalism as a common enterprise of all these nationalities should empower all of them alike. What was new in Bhai Kahn Singh's book was his view that Sikh identity made the Sikhs a political community. His *Ham Hindū Nahīn* can be appreciated as a conscious argument for Sikh nationality based on a distinct Sikh identity.

Notes

1. Shamsher Singh Ashok, 'A Life Sketch of Bhai Kahn Singh' (Punjabi), in *Gurshabd Ratnākar Mahān Kosh*, Patiala: Punjab Languages Department, 1999 (6th impression). Pritam Singh, *Bhai Kahn Singh Nabha: Pichhokaṛ, Rachnā te Mulankaṇ* (Punjabi), Amritsar: Guru Nanak Dev University, 1989. It may be added that the *Gurmat Prabhākar* and the *Gurmat Sudhākar* have been reprinted by Bhai Chatar Singh-Jīvan Singh of Amritsar in 2005.
2. Kahn Singh, Bhai, *Ham Hindū Nahīn* (Pbi), Amritsar: Dharam Parchar Committee (SGPC), 1981 (rpt of the 5th edn). Prefaces to the 1st and the 5th edition, and pp. 34n1, 39n1, 77n1, and 160n1.
3. Ibid., pp. 34–7.
4. Ibid., pp. 47–51.
5. Ibid., pp. 51–5.
6. There is a general but wrong impression that the Arya Samajists alone were contesting the issue of Sikh identity.
7. Ibid., pp. 58–64.
8. Ibid., pp. 69, 77–9, 81–2.
9. Ibid., pp. 86–7, 97, 100.
10. Ibid., pp. 108–9.
11. Ibid., p. 132.
12. Ibid., pp. 146, 151.
13. Ibid., pp. 152–3, 158.
14. Ibid., pp. 55–65.
15. Ibid., pp. 65–84.
16. Ibid., pp. 85–9.
17. Ibid., pp. 89–105.
18. Ibid., pp. 105–10.
19. Ibid., pp. 110–11.
20. Ibid., pp. 111–13.
21. Ibid., pp. 114–17.
22. Ibid., pp. 118–23.
23. Ibid., pp. 123–6.
24. Ibid., pp. 138–42.
25. Ibid., pp. 142–5.
26. Ibid., pp. 143–4n2.
27. Ibid., pp. 127–8.
28. Ibid., pp. 149–51.
29. Ibid., pp. 146–9.
30. Ibid., pp. 153–6.
31. Ibid., pp. 156–8.
32. Ibid., pp. 158–63.
33. Ibid., p. 163.
34. Ibid., p. 13.
35. Ibid., pp. 43n1, 74n2.

36. Daljeet Singh, *Essentials of Sikhism*, Amritsar: Singh Brothers, 1994, pp. 255–65.

37. W.H. McLeod, *Who is a Sikh? The Problem of Sikh Identity*, Oxford: The Clarendon Press, 1989, pp. 7–68.

38. Harjot Oberoi, *The Construction of Religious Boundaries: Culture, Identity and Diversity in the Sikh Tradition*, New Delhi: Oxford University Press, 1994, pp. 47–71, 137–8.

39. Kenneth W. Jones, *Arya Dharm: Hindu Consciousness in 19th Century Punjab*, New Delhi: Manohar, 1976. Bhagat Lakshman Singh, *Autobiography*, ed., Ganda Singh, Calcutta: The Sikh Cultural Centre, 1965.

40. Sheena Pall, 'The Sanatan Dharm Movement in the Colonial Punjab: Religious, Social and Political Dimensions', PhD Thesis, Panjab University, Chandigarh, 2008, pp. 260–86, for the concern of the leaders of the movement for Hindu identity, and their conscious concern on treating Sikhs as 'Hindus'.

Epilogue

Recapitulation

We may recapitulate the gist of the foregoing chapters to make a few observations on the links between Sikh history, literature, and identity. In the compositions of Guru Nanak we find a comprehensive critique of contemporary religion, social order, and polity. The two things which he categorically denounced were inequality and discrimination in the socio-religious and political order. This critique was only the reverse of his ideology which is strictly monotheistic and projects a new conception of liberation, underscoring the importance of altruistic action after the experience of liberation-in-life. He introduced a form of worship in which his own compositions (*bāṇī*) were recited individually and sung in congregation (*sangat*). Based on the idea of equality his path was open to all human beings irrespective of their caste, creed, or gender. In the community kitchen (*langar*) too anyone could eat irrespective of his or her social background or position. Guru Nanak emphatically rejected the ideal of renunciation. His ideal was to cultivate detachment amidst social commitment and activity. He claimed to be the herald and minstrel of God and adopted the position of a formal guide. He looked upon his path as different and distinct from what the others were following and called it the Gurmukh Panth or the path of those who have turned to God through the Guru. There is no doubt that a new socio-religious fraternity came into existence during the lifetime of Guru Nanak. Before his death he installed one of his disciples, Lehna, in his place as Guru Angad.

Guru Angad composed verses as 'Nanak', making it clear that he was not different from Guru Nanak, holding the same office, the same authority, and the same status. His *shaloks* indicate that he had internalized the ideology of Guru Nanak. Guru Angad's theology and his conception of liberation are the same. He strengthened the institution of congregational worship and community meal. He projected the path of Guru Nanak as the most efficacious for liberation and his bāṇī as the revelation of Truth. Before his death, Guru Angad installed his disciple Amar Das as the Guru in his place. Guru Angad's interpretation and representation of Guru Nanak was crucial in strengthening the foundations laid by him.

Writing as 'Nānak', Guru Amar Das elaborated the conception of God and the concept of liberation. He treated the compositions of the Guru as the only true bāṇī. The sangat and the Sikh or Gurmukh figure very prominently in the bāṇī of Guru Amar Das and he invites the *pandit*, the shaikh, and the *jogī* to follow the path of Guru Nanak. The *Ānand* of Guru Amar Das is important for its liturgical status as well as for Sikh theology. The line drawn between the Sikhs and the others is of their faith. He is emphatic that the path shown by Guru Nanak and advocated by his successors is the only efficacious path for the Kaliyuga.

As the fourth 'Nānak', Guru Ram Das carries forward the scriptural and institutional heritage of his predecessors, giving explicit expression to the Sikh way of life and Sikh rites and rituals, and paying studied attention to the Sikhs and the sangat. He equates bāṇī with the Guru and he equates the Sikh also with the Guru; emphasizes that God is present in the sangat. In his theology, grace appears to become a little more important than *hukam*. The dispensation of the 'House of Nanak' tends to become an expression of divine grace for the redemption of the world. With these concerns and assumptions, the Sikhs of the Guru could not be bracketed with any other category of people in the world. They stand apart as instruments of God's will.

Guru Arjan elaborates the ideology of his predecessors in terms of the conception of God with equal emphasis on his power and grace. He makes a clear statement on the essential conception of Nām and its multilayered signification: its equation with shabad, and of both these with the 'revealed' bāṇī of Guru Nanak. The bāṇī of the Guru as the source and instrument of redemption, is compiled in a Granth which is seen as the abode of God. Guru Arjan lays great stress on the institutions of sangat and *ardās*. He identifies himself with Guru Nanak and his successors, and with their followers. His pronouncement, 'we are neither Hindu nor Musalman' is declaration of a distinct identity. The scripture, the institutions, the wide network of Sikh sangats, their resources and their organization, represent the entire dispensation. Guru Arjan refers to it as *Halemī Rāj*, a dispensation that was not only different and distinct from other religious dispensations but also parallel to the state. The martyrdom of Guru Arjan was symbolic of his commitment to uphold and propagate this dispensation.

In the phase of confrontation with the state during the early seventeenth century, the Vārs of Bhai Gurdas, who was a contemporary of Guru Arjan and his son and successor, Guru Hargobind, show his deep veneration for Guru Nanak and his successors. Bhai Gurdas emphasizes that they are one. He notices the split in the Panth of Guru Nanak, denounces the 'rebels' most vehemently and justifies the measures of Guru Hargobind. The spiritual and temporal concerns of the Gurus represent two sides of the same ideological coin. The faith of Guru Nanak and his successors transcends all earlier dispensations of the world and the Sikhs of the Guru constitute a distinct Panth. Their guiding principle is par-upkār which makes them unique in the world. Dissent within the Sikh Panth makes Bhai Gurdas all the more emphatic about the distinct identity of the 'Sikhs of the true Gurus'.

Guru Tegh Bahadur composed bāṇī in a critical and grave situation. He succeeded to the position of Guru Har Krishan who had been called to Delhi by Aurangzeb. Before long, Aurangzeb started his measures of coercion againt non-Muslims and non-Sunnis. Guru Tegh Bahadur stood for toleration and freedom of conscience. In this tense situation, he dwells on detachment and fearlessness. Both of these are old Sikh ideals but they become more important in a situation of confrontation. The trenchant statement of Guru Tegh Bahadur, 'frighten no one and be afraid of none', sums up his response to the situation. He reassures the people, the Sikhs in particular, that what matters in the end is their commitment to the values of life cherished by them as devotees of God. His martyrdom was a deliberate and, in a sense, a political act. He was opposed in principle to the policy of coercion followed by Aurangzeb.

The *Bachittar Nātak* was composed at the court of Guru Gobind Singh in 1696 as a part of the larger interest in the Purāṇic lore that was popular among the Vaishnavas, the Shaivas, and the Shaktas. Much of this literature related to divine intervention in human affairs. The instruments chosen for divine intervention were authorized to make use of physical force in support of the good against their enemies. They were also endowed with great martial prowess, like Rama, Krishna, and the Goddess (Kalka or Chandī). However, the *Bachittar Nātak* underlines that these instruments of divine intervention had themselves become the objects of worship. There were many others in the world who had deviated from the worship of God to the worship of beings created by him. Guru Nanak had shown the right path to redeem humankind through divine will, and his dispensation was to be preserved and propagated. The enemies of this dispensation were to be destroyed. This was the mission of Guru Gobind Singh. He was a human being, a servant of God, commissioned by him to empower his followers and others to fight against the forces of evil. His battles were a part of this *dharam-yudh*; he was under divine protection; and his success was inevitable. This is what the *Bachittar Nātak* essentially proclaims.

The *Vār Bhagautī*, generally regarded as a late eighteenth century work, appears to have been composed originally in the time of Guru Gobind Singh. In any case, it depicts the triumph of the Khalsa created by him to destroy the wicked enemies of the true faith of Guru Nanak and his successors. The author, who calls himself 'Gurdas', is concerned with liberation and sovereign power. For him, the Khalsa embody both. Their faith leads to liberation and their action leads to sovereign rule. The Sikh faith is the 'third religion' (tīsar mazhab) and the Khalsa Panth is the 'third community' (tīsar panth) as different and distinct from Hindus and Muslims.

The author of the *Srī Gur Sobhā*, Sainapat, who wrote during the first decade of the eighteenth century, is concerned primarily with the wondrous deeds of Guru Gobind Singh who is seen as closely allied with God. The institution of the Khalsa is his most wondrous achievement. It is through the Khalsa that the purpose of destroying the enemies of the Sikh faith can be fulfilled; they are prepared to fight and to die for the cause. They inherit the position of the Guru and, thereby, attain a sovereign status. Though Sainapat underlines that the primary connotation of the Khalsa is direct affiliation with the Guru, he equates the Khalsa with the Singh. He brings the political character of the Khalsa to the fore and cherishes the ideal of their sovereign rule.

The *Rahitnāma* literature was a part of the literary upsurge of the time of Guru Gobind Singh. No *Rahitnāma* appears to have been dictated by Guru Gobind Singh but the composers tried to remain close to his ideas and injunctions. There is a vast difference of detail in the short and long

Rahitnāmas but the scope of the short Rahitnāmas too is wide enough to cover the religious life, social attitudes, and political aspirations of the Khalsa. On the whole, the Rahitnāmas lay stress on the belief in Akal Purkh and his worship to the exclusion of all other deities and objects of popular worship. The most important institution of the Khalsa is the dharamsāl. The importance of the shabad and the sangat is underscored even if the Granth or the Khalsa is not always equated with the Guru. The authority of the Granth is invoked for the authenticity of beliefs and practices. Certain rites and rituals are recommended in which the Brahman has no role and Gurbāṇī occupies the central position. The political character of the Khalsa, who are generally equated with the Singhs, is clearly projected. Their objective is to acquire political power sooner or later. Their identity is distinct from the rest of the people.

The *Bansāvalīnāma Dasān Pātshāhīan Kā* appears to have been written by Kesar Singh, a Chhibber Brahman, in the hope of patronage from the newly established Sikh rulers. The author tries to impress upon the reader that he is thoroughly familiar with the Sikh scripture and other religious works. He speaks authoritatively as a Sikh and advises the Sikh rulers to rule with justice and in Sikh interests, especially in the interest of Brahman Sikhs. He recognizes the presence of both the Sahajdhari Sikhs and the Keshdhari Singhs among the Khalsa, but talks almost entirely about the Keshdhari Singhs. When he makes a difference between *sikhkhī* and *singhī*, he seems to be making a distinction between faith and political conduct. This explains his preference for the faith but he looks upon the Keshdhari Singhs as a distinct entity (tīsar panth). He does not see any contradiction between the faith and ethics of the Khalsa and his advocacy of conformity to the Brahmanical norms of commensality and connubium. Even as a Brahman Sikh, however, he recommends uniform faith and ethics for all the Sikhs, including the untouchables of the traditional order.

Writing in the early 1840s, Ratan Singh Bhangu in his *Gurū Panth Prakāsh* hammers the basic point that the Khalsa, who stood equated with the Keshdhari Singhs, were meant to be sovereign. Incessant fighting and sacrifices were the means through which sovereignty was attained. The unity among the Khalsa was made possible by their common belief in the doctrine of Guru-Panth, and the ever present source of inspiration for them was the Guru Granth. The Gurmatās of the Khalsa possessed such a moral authority that no member could disobey them. Martyrdom was built into the institution of the Khalsa and it was the highest form of *par-suārath*. This selfless sacrifice could be made for the Sikh faith, the Sikh Panth, the Sikh sacred space, Sikh sovereignty, and for the injustice done to any individual or group of individuals, whether Sikh or non-Sikh. The Guru-Panth was a distinct entity (tīsar-panth) and it was meant to be an egalitarian social order in every sphere of life. Ratan Singh Bhangu's emphatic assertion of the sovereignty of the Khalsa may be partly due to the threat to the sovereignty of the Sikh state in the Punjab from the British.

The issue of Hindu-Sikh identity cropped up under colonial rule when all the religious communities of the Punjab were redefining identity because of its practical implications for entry into educational institutions, offices of the colonial government and later on, into municipal and legislative bodies. A new dimension to this concern was added by a religious resurgence in which theologies, beliefs, and practices were sought to be reinterpreted in the light of scriptures. The Sikhs were never confused with Muslims but the lines of demarcation from Hindus were not always clearly perceived. That was why the issue of 'Hindu-Sikh' identity cropped up, though 'Sikh-Muslim' identity never became an issue. The Aryas as reformists made little difference between outcaste Hindus, Sikhs, and Muslims for the purposes of reconversion (*shuddhī*) which was meant to bring them back to the Arya fold. The orthdox (Sanatanist) Hindus, on the other hand, argued that the Sikhs were Hindu. Therefore, claims and counter-claims were put forward largely by Sanatanist Hindus and the reformers associated with the Singh Sabha movement.

Bhai Kahn Singh Nabha took up the issue on behalf of the Singh reformers. He tried to establish that in terms of scriptures and doctrines, beliefs and practices, rites and rituals, social order and consciousness of distinction the Sikhs had never bracketed themselves with the Hindus. But they belonged to the same country, like Muslims and Christians. The common bond between all the religious communities of India could be provided by patriotism, that is, concern for the welfare of the country as a whole. In religious terms, however, the Sikhs had been different from Hindus, like Muslims and Christians. In his view, the distinctive identity of the Sikhs was not a new thing. But the new situation demanded that the Sikhs should be regarded as a separate community for political purposes. In other words, what was new in Bhai Kahn Singh Nabha's exposition was his rational argument that distinct identity entitled the

Sikhs to be recognized as a political community or a nationality within the Indian Nation.

The historians and scholars who have taken serious interest in the identity of the Sikhs in the pre-colonial period do not agree entirely with Nabha, but they do not support the popular view that the Singh reformers were the first to claim that Sikh identity was different from that of the Hindus. Even in the earliest phase of Sikh history, Guru Arjan had declared, 'we are neither Hindu nor Musalman'. This appears to be a very moderate statement. The conception of *Halemī Rāj* as a dispensation parallel to all other religious systems and the state leaves no room for identification of the Sikhs with any other set of people in the world. Yet, the use of the phrase 'tīsar panth', the Third Community, makes its appearance in Sikh literature for the first time in connection with the Khalsa. But the Khalsa are seen as a continuation of the earlier sangat with the difference that the former were consciously political and politically far more active. They shared their religious faith with the earlier Sikhs of the Gurus from Guru Nanak to Guru Gobind Singh, but a new dimension to their way of life was added by the political role associated with them. The identity of the tīsar panth, the Khalsa identity, was conceived in religious, social, and political terms. At the same time, it needs to be emphasized that there was no argument for any demands on the basis of that identity. The acquisition of political power required no rational argument or justification in the pre-colonial period.

In the twentieth century, however, an increasing number of Sikhs began to demand participation in the power game on the rational argument of a distinct Sikh identity. What was new in the situation was not 'Sikh identity' but the political argument on its basis. This was precisely the position of Bhai Kahn Singh Nabha.

In Retrospect

We can see that the earliest phase of the Sikh movement synchronized largely with the expansion of the Mughal empire. The relative peace in a large part of the Indian subcontinent provided a context in which the movement could spread wide across the Mughal empire resulting in the proliferation of local congregations and *dharamsāls*. The Gurus appointed their representatives to look after the local congregations and bring their offerings to the Guru. The growing human and material resources of the Gurus enabled them to undertake large projects and to develop institutions. Emergence of autonomons towns and the institutions of Guruship, Gurdwara, and the Granth made the Sikhs visible as a social entity. The compositions of Guru Nanak's successors reflect and promote these developments. Seen from inside, the dispensation of Guru Nanak or *Halemī Rāj* was the instrument of universal redemption; seen from outside, the Sikh Panth appeared to be 'a state within the state'. Being a parallel entity to the Mughal state, this dispensation enabled the Gurus to react to state interference in a manner that politicized the Sikh movement. The self-image of the Sikhs and their objective differences made them increasingly aware of their identity and their role in history.

Jahangir talks of the popularity and influence of Guru Arjan; Bhai Gurdas underscores the poise with which he suffered torture and death. Writing after the martyrdom of Guru Arjan, Bhai Gurdas applauds Guru Hargobind's policy of confrontation with the state. In his eyes, there is no difference between Guru Nanak and Guru Hargobind, and the Sikhs who do not follow him are base 'rebels'. Bhai Gurdas, thus, gives eloquent expression and support to martial activity in defence of the dispensation of Guru Nanak and his successors. Guru Tegh Bahadur is acutely aware of the situation of growing tension with the state. He is emphatic about liberation as 'the state of fearlessness'. Political power, like all worldly things, is the shadow of a cloud. It is of little consequence in comparison with the fundamental purposes and concerns of human life. The bāṇī of Guru Tegh Bahadur comes as a message of reassurance in a situation of confrontation between the Sikh Panth and the Mughal state.

The martyrdom of Guru Tegh Bahadur added a new dimension to the situation. Aurangzeb's professed motive for Guru Tegh Bahadur's execution was religious; Guru Tegh Bahadur's deliberate decision to court martyrdom underscored his concern for freedom of conscience. Guru Gobind Singh's response to external threat is not simply martial but also constructive. The literature produced at his court embodies a declaration of dharam-yuddh, the goal of sovereign rule, a celebration of political and religious freedom, the ideal of martyrdom, and a well-defined way of religious, social, and political life for the Khalsa, with a pronounced consciousness of distinct identity. The spirit of triumph (*chaṛhdī-kalā*) is the hall-mark of this literature.

The writers of the period of Sikh rule, Chhibber and Bhangu, feel concerned with the past, present, and future of the Sikh Panth. Writing at the beginning of the period, Chhibber advises the Sikh rulers to remain steadfast in their faith and to promote Sikh interests through their policies. He does not favour the idea of employing Muslims and Hindu Khatris in the administration of Sikh territories; he is opposed even to the use of Persian for administrative purposes. He advocates a conservative social policy, insisting on the observance of caste norms and patterns for commensality and matrimony. Writing in the 1840s, Bhangu perceives a serious threat to Sikh sovereignty and emphasizes thesis that the Khalsa Panth was created to be sovereign. The incessant struggle of the Khalsa and their sacrifices were meant to realize this essential purpose. By implication, Sikh sovereignty was to be defended now at all costs. Bhangu dwells on the egalitarian principle and practices of the Khalsa. Though silent about matrimony, he underlines that commensality was extended to all the Khalsa irrespective of their caste background. Both Chhibber and Bhangu subscribe to the doctrines of Guru Granth and Guru-Panth. Whereas Chhibber talks more of Guru-Granth, Bhangu lays equal emphasis on both. Chhibber notices the presence of Sahajdhārīs among the Khalsa but Bhangu talks only of the Singhs. Both Chhibber and Bhangu look upon the Khalsa as the Third Community (tīsar panth).

The historians who have concentrated on the colonial period to the exclusion of this background tend to see the issue of Sikh identity as something new. They look upon Bhai Kahn Singh Nabha's *Ham Hindū Nahīn* as a polemical pamphlet to claim distinct identity for the Sikhs. Our study of Sikh literature clearly shows that his argument was based largely on this literature. Furthermore, what was new in his argument was not distinct identity but his insistence that this identity made the Sikhs a political community, a qaum or nationality, which entitled them to a share in political power as an integral part of the Indian Nation.

This study indicates that the consciousness of identity among the Sikhs was a product of their religious beliefs and institutions, their social order, and their political role. Present even in the literature of the earlier period, this consciousness crystallized in the eighteenth century as the tīsar panth. It may only be added that the author of the seventeenth century *Dabistān-i Mazāhib*, who was a Parsi, the author of the eighteenth century *Jangnāma*, who was a Muslim, and the author of the nineteenth century *Chār Bagh*, who was a Punjabi Hindu, looked upon the Sikhs in the pre-colonial period as distinct from both Hindus and Muslims.

Glossary

abchal	stable, everlasting
abchal nagarī	eternal city (the everlasting dispensation of Guru Nanak)
abhai dān	fearlessness as the result of liberation through God's grace
achal amar nirbhai pad	the state of fearlessness that is ever stable and everlasting
ād purkh	the primal being, an epithet for God
Ādi Granth	the Sikh scripture, compiled by Guru Arjan in 1604 (containing the compositions of the first five Gurus and a number of *bhaktas*, *sants*, and *sūfīs*) and authenticated by Guru Gobind Singh with the compositions of Guru Tegh Bahadur. It is now known as Gurū Granth Sāhib
ahankār	pride of possessions or power
ajūnī	one who never takes birth, who does not incarnate; an attribute of God
akāl	not subject to death or destruction, everlasting, eternal, God
Akāl Takht	the platform constructed by Guru Hargobind to preside over the temporal affairs of his followers. The practice was revived by the Khalsa in the early eighteenth century. A structure raised on the spot came to be known as Akāl Bungā where all important meetings of the Khalsa were held. It served as the headquarters of the Akālīs till the early nineteenth century
Akālī	a staunch follower of Guru Gobind Singh; equated with the Nihang in the early nineteenth century; in the twentieth century, initially a volunteer to take over Sikh Gurdwaras and afterwards a member of the Shiromani Akali Dal

alakh	unseeable, God
alipt	unattached, detached from creation, God
amr	immortal; order, generally a royal order; a metaphor for divine ordinance
amrāpad	the state of immortality, an everlasting state; used for the state of liberation in Sikh thought
amrit	the drink that imparts immortality or everlasting life, nectar; used as a metaphor
amritsar	literally the pool of the water of immortality; the term originally used for the tank constructed by Guru Ram Das; the usage was extended to the town of Ramdaspur (Amritsar) by the early nineteenth century
amrit-bachan	the nectar-like utterance (of the Guru), the Guru's shabad, the Guru's order
amrit-bāṇī	the nectar-like utterance (of the Guru), the Guru's shabad, divine utterance (for God's creation)
amrit-nām	the nectar-like name (of God), the Name that imparts immorality
anahad shabad	the unspoken word that is heard in the state of liberation, the state of being one with God
ānand	happiness, bliss, experienced in the state of liberation
anbhai	without fear, fearless in the state of liberation
anbhau nagar	the city in which there is no fear; the state of liberation; a metaphor for Guru Nanak's dispensation
anahad-bāṇī	divine self-revelation, the utterance of the Guru, the Guru's shabad that leads to liberation
anbhau pad	the state without fear, the state of liberation
ang	a part, a limb; an inseparable part
anjaṇ māhi niranjaṇ	pure amidst impurities, detached
antarjāmī	one who knows the innermost thoughts, an epithet for God
āp chhoṛ jīvat marae	discarding the self and thereby dying while alive, alive to the divine presence and divine will
āpe gur-chelā	he who is both the Guru and the disciple; used generally for Guru Gobind Singh but applicable also to Guru Nanak and his successors
āratī	the rite of offering food, fruit, flowers, and fragrance to a deity while singing its praises, generally an idol; a hymn of praise

ardās	supplication, prayer; generally made by a Sikh sangat, standing with hands joined in the presence of the formless God; an essential part of worship in the Sikh tradition
ardāsiā	literally one who offers ardās; a person employed for this purpose
āsā māhi nirās (*āsā vich nirās*)	without hope amidst hope, detached from personal interests but attached to God; the state in which one performs all social acts in a detached manner
ashtpadī	a composition of eight padas or verses
atal	immoveable, stable, an epithet for God
aukhad	medicine; metaphorically, the Guru's shabad and the divine name
auliyā	plural of walī, a friend of God; eminent Sūfīs and even a single Sūfī great importance
avadhūt	an ascetic who has attained a high spiritual status
avtār	birth, incarnation; the ten incarnations of Vishnu, especially his human incarnation Rama and Krishna
ayāṇā	a child or a young person, one who has no knowledge
Bābar-bāṇī	four compositions of Guru Nanak, assumed to have been composed in connection with the sack of Saidpur (later Eminabad) by Babur, but actually expressing Guru Nanak's response to several events; the phrase comes from one of the compositions in the sense of 'Babur's order'
bādshāh	king, emperor, used generally for a Mughal ruler
bairāg	the feeling of separation from God seen as a mark of spiritual awakening
bairāgī	a person who practises bairāg, a renunciate; generally, a Vaishnava; used also for the Sikh and even God as a metaphor (as in *rassik bairāgī*)
Bais	the Punjabi form of Vaishya, the third caste in the hierarchical fourfold vārna order
bājīgar	from the Persian bāzīgar, a juggler; used as a metaphor for God
bakhshī or *mīr-bakhshī*	the officer in charge of the army affairs in the Mughal times; he was directly responsible to the emperor
bandā	a slave; a devotee of God

bandagī	the state of slavery, acting as a slave; total submission to God as the only Master, devotion, worship
bāṇī	utterance; divine self-revelation through creation the utterance or the word of the Guru; generally equated with Gurbāṇī
bāṇīa	one who conducts trade, generally a shopkeeper or a merchant
bāṇī-shabad	utterance and the word; generally used for Gurbāṇī.
bāolī	a well with steps for easy accessibility to water simultaneously for several persons; the well constructed by Guru Amar Das at Goindval, which came to be regarded as sacred
barat	vow; fasting, in various ways on different occasions, regarded as meritorious in the Brahmanical systems, like *rozah* in the Islamic tradition
beohār	convention, conventional social behaviour in specific situations, sanctified by long usage
bhaddar (*bhaddan*)	shaving the head, tonsure; especially as a ritual after the death of one's father
bhagat	one who is devoted to God; used generally for Vaishnava *bhaktas*, but the term is used for the Sikh, too, in Gurbāṇī
bhagat-jan	the devoted ones; used for the Sikhs too in Gurbāṇī
bhagtī	also *bhaktī*, loving devotion and dedication to God
bhagtī-jog	the path of bhagtī that leads to union with God
bhai-bhanjaṇ	the breaker of fear; God
bhajan	a song in praise of God, singing of God's praises; uttering God's name
bhandār	store; a storehouse; a place for the preparation and distribution of food in religious institutions
bhāo (*bhāv*)	love, loving devotion directed towards God
bharam (*bhram*)	illusion, belief in a thing that does not exist
bhau (*bhai*)	fear; fear of God, awe
bhekh	garb, a particular kind of outward appearance as a mark of identity, generally of a religious person
bhet-kār	offering made out of one's earnings
bhog	conclusion of the reading of Ādi Granth, followed generally by singing of hymns, an *ardās*, and distribution of Kaṛhā Prashād
bhog-pāṭh	the reading of the Granth Sāhib as a part of mortuary rites

bhogī	one who indulges in the pleasures of life, a married person
bhujangī	a young man who has taken pahul or amrit, that is, baptism of the double-edged sword; a reckless warrior too
bibhūt	the ash used by ascetics to smear their bodies, a practice common among the Gorakhnāthī Jogīs
chakras	the cycles believed to be functioning in the human body, and used in ascetical practices for concentration
chalīhā	a rite performed on the fortieth day after death; offerings on that account, kept for the Guru
Chandī-Bāṇī	three compositions in the *Dasam Granth* related to the Goddess Chandī
Chandī-bhet	the offering of blood to the Goddess Chandī to appease her
Charanamrit	nectar of the foot; also called charan pahul
Charanjīt	a person believed to possess powers of the supranatural order, including the power to incarnate in different forms
charan pahul	the practice of drinking the water in which the toe of the gurū has been dipped, symbolizing humility and dedication on the part of the initiate. Also called charanamrit
chaudharī	the hereditary headman of a group of villages for collecting revenues on behalf of the government
chaukā	a square drawn on the ground and plastered with cow-dung generally by a Brahman for eating food with the idea that all impurities would be kept out
chaukā-kār	a line drawn on all the four sides for protection
chaupaī	a unit of four lines, with the rhyme scheme of a a, b b, in a poetical composition called chaupai
chaur	a fly-whisk used as a symbol of royalty or great position.
cherī	a female sevak or disciple
chhatar	an umbrella used as a symbol of royalty
Chhatri (Kshatriya)	the warrior or ruling caste of traditional Hindu society; the Khatris in medieval Punjab derived their origins from the Kshatriyas but followed trade, shopkeeping, and other professions, including administration
dakhna	from *dakshina*, reward given to a Brahman for performing a ritual service
dargāh	the place of a pīr who is no longer alive; a holy place, court

dārоghā	a superintendent or head of an organization
darvesh	a pious Muslim, generally a Sūfi; a pious person
Dasam Granth	the term used for the compilation earlier called the Book of the Tenth King (dasven pātshāh kā granth); its compilation is attributed to Bhai Mani Singh; the authorship of its contents (a number of independent compositions) and the date of its compilation have been the subject of debate
dāsī	a female slave or servant
dasvandh	one-tenth, offering of a tenth of one's income to the Guru, or for purposes commended by the Guru
dātā	the giver, the giver of all gifts, God
deg-tegh	cauldron-and-sword as symbols of charity and power
dehura	a structure raised on a spot of cremation
deoṛhīdār	the keeper of the gate; a person in charge of a palace or the house of an important personage
derā	a camp; a religious establishment
des	country, the real country, God's country (in contrast with the earth as a place of sojourn)
dhādhī	a singer who generally used a miniature drum (*dhadh*) while singing of love or war for the entertainment of his patrons; used as a metaphor for the Guru as the singer of God's praises, and also for his Sikh
dharam	a whole complex of religious and social ideas and practices, used for the dispensation of Guru Nanak and his successors
dharam juddh	war for the sake of faith, struggle in a righteous cause
dharma	duty, moral obligation; a set of religious beliefs, and social practices prescribed for each vārna of the Brahmanical fourfold social order
dharamsāl	the place for earning merit; Sikh sacred space or the Sikh place of worship in early Sikh history; synonymous with Gurdwara
dharmyudh	war in a righteous cause
dhotī	the spotless sheet worn by the Brahman round the lower body to conduct religious worship
dīdārī, māyikī, mukte, and *murīd*	categories of Sikhs in the *Rahitnāma* associated with Chaupa Singh and also in Chhibber's *Bansāvalīnāma*; the first and the third category belonged to the past as having lived in the presence of the Guru or having died for his cause; the second category consisted of those

	Sikh rulers who were engrossed in māyā to the exclusion of dharam, and the fourth category consisted of those Sikhs who preserved their dharam in the time of Sikh rule
dīwān	an office, a court, a royal court; the person holding the position next to that of the king in his realm; the keeper of a treasury; the head of the finance department; an honorific given to Hindu nobles by Mahāraja Ranjit Singh and his successors
dohrā	a rhyming couplet of a certain measure, popular in Punjabi poetry
dubidhā	duality, dual affiliation, the tension between affiliation to māyā and devotion to God
duhāgan	a woman who is unhappy because she is not loved by her spouse; a metaphor for the person who has not turned to God through the Guru
dūja bhāo	affiliation with māyā and not with God; an object of worship other than God
faqīr	one who practises *faqr* or renunciation and austerities; a darvesh; a pious person; a devotee of God; used generally for a Muslim mendicant
fātihā	the opening sūrah of the Qur'ān used at the beginning of an undertaking, and in prayer for the dead
faujdār	one who keeps troops; a military officer under the Mughals whose duty was to maintain law and order and to assist civil authorities; the office survived into the early nineteenth century Punjab
gaddī	a cushioned seat; a throne; the seat of the head of a religious fraternity
gat (gatī)	a state or condition; the state of liberation
ghallughara	a stream of blood, carnage, a great massacre; used for two such events in Sikh history, in 1746 and in 1762.
gharī	one sixtieth of a day, equal to 24 minutes
ghoṛiān	songs sung when the bridegroom mounts the horse to lead the marriage party to the bride's place or home
ghumāon	a unit of land, somewhat smaller than an acre but much larger than a *bigha* which was double the area of a *kanal* of 500 sq. yards
giān	knowledge, knowledge of God; enlightenment
giānī	one who possesses knowledge (giān); a liberated person; a person well versed in the Sikh scripture

go-khana	the place where milch cows are kept
golak	cash offerings deposited in a box from time to time to be carried to the Guru; a receptacle for offerings generally placed in Gurdwaras
gopī	the wife or daughter of a cowherd; a milkmaid; any girl of Braj in love with Krishna
gotrā	subdivision of a caste; subcaste; an endogamous group
granthī	a professional reader of the Granth; the functionary in charge of a Gurdwara
Gurbāṇī	an utterance of the Guru
Gur-bachan	the Guru's speech; the Guru's word equated with shabad; the Guru's command equated with hukam
Gur-bhagtī	loving devotion to the Guru; the path of loving devotion shown by the Guru
Gur-bhāī	a fellow disciple of the Guru, given great importance in the Sikh tradition
Gurbilās	a poetical work written in praise of a Guru or the Gurus
gur-chelā, chelā-guru	the syndrome peculiar to the Sikh tradition in which the Guru becomes a disciple and a disciple becomes the Guru
Gurduārā	through the Guru, his grace
Gurdwara	'the door of the Guru'; the Sikh sacred space where kīrtan, kathā, and ardās are performed, and community meal is cooked and eaten by all; generally the centre of social activity too
gurmatā	decision of a general body of Sikhs, generally taken in the presence of the Gurū Granth Sāhib
Gurmat	the Guru's instruction, the Guru's wisdom; Sikh thought as a whole
Gur-maryādā	the norms of Sikh beliefs and practices, based on the Gurū Granth Sāhib and the Sikh tradition
Gurmukh mārag (Gurmukh-panth)	the path shown by Guru Nanak and followed by those who have turned to the Guru
Gursikhkhī	the faith of the Sikh of the Guru; his beliefs and practices.
Guru	preceptor; religious teacher; an epithet used for the founder of Sikhism and each of his nine successors, and also for the Granth Sāhib and the Panth
Gurupdes	the Guru's instruction, generally in the form of his shabad
gurz-bardār	a mace-bearer, generally used as a special messenger by the emperor

halāl	the traditional Muslim mode of slaughtering animals for meat; anything lawful, as opposed to *harām* (prohibited)
Har-jan	God's devotee; used for both the Guru and the Sikh
Har kā nām	the name of God; the Name
Harmandar	'the temple of God'; the central Sikh shrine in Amritsar popularly known as the Golden Temple
haumai	a kind of self-centredness in which everything is attributed to oneself to the exclusion of God's will
hom	a sacrificial act; the ceremony of chanting Vedic hymns around a fire kept burning with oblations of wood, ghee, incense and other such materials, regarded as a way of pleasing gods or God through the god of fire
hukam	order, divine order; the principle that the power of God remains operative all the time in the physical and the moral world
hukamnāma	a written order; generally used for a letter of the person exercising moral and spiritual authority, like the Guru.
in'ām	literally, a reward; an assignment of revenue distinct from jāgīr and dharmarth
jagg (yagya or *yajna)*	the ceremony of sacrifice to the fire amidst chanting of Vedic hymns to please gods or God through the god of fire (Agni)
jāgīr	an assignment of land revenue in lieu of salary for performing service for the state
jāgīrdār	the holder of a jāgīr, with the right to collect revenues from a given piece of land in lieu of salary for service to the state
jajmān	the patron in a client-patron relationship; the person who makes payment for services rendered manually or by performing a ritual, like the marriage ceremony performed by a Brahman
jajmānī	also called *sepī*, the system in which customary payment was made for services rendered by Brahmans and others over the year; the patron is referred to as jajmān
jal-parwah	consigning to water, the practice of consigning a corpse to a running stream or river as a mode of disposal of the dead, as distinct from cremation, burial or exposure
janaeu (janjū)	the sacred thread worn by higher caste men after the formal ritual performed by a Brahman
Janamsākhī	a collection of episodes associated with the life of Guru Nanak, meant primarily to depict his doctrines, ethics,

	and his spiritual status; several traditions of this genre developed in the seventeenth and eighteenth centuries
jangam	a category of the ascetical followers of Shiva and Gauri, conspicuous for their peculiar garb
janjū	the thread worn by the upper caste Hindus as a sacred symbol
jantar	instrument, device
jap	recitation, used in connection with nām
jas	praise; praises of God; kīrtan
jāt (jātī)	an endogamous group, constituted by a number of septs, following generally the same occupation and placed in one of the four Vārnas as a mark of its social position in relation to others, popularly called caste in English
jāt-baran	an endogamous group placed in the fourfold hierarchical order in relation to other such groups
jhatkā	the mode of slaughtering an animal for meat with one stroke of the sword or some other weapon; the traditional non-Muslim mode of slaughtering animals in India. Unlike *halāl*, it did not carry any religious significance
jīvan-muktī	liberation-in-life
jog	union; the practices of ascetics known as Jogīs with the objective of union with God
jogī	from yogī, or one who practises yoga; a person belonging to any of the twelve orders of the followers of Gorakh Nath
jugg	from yuga, one of the four cosmic ages; a very long span of time
kabitt	a poetical form of four lines with a set rhyme scheme
kādar	from qādir, all-powerful, God
kalal	the distiller or the seller of alcohol; a person belonging to that occupational group as a *jati*
Kaliyuga	the fourth and the last cosmic age, traditionally regarded as the age of degeneracy in religion, ethics, and social norms
Kalma (kalima)	a word, saying, discourse; the confession of faith in Islam 'there is no god but Allah and Muhammad is Allah's messenger' (*lā-ilāh illilah Muhammad ar-rasūlillah*)
kanghā	the comb kept by a baptized Sikh as one of the five Ks

kautak	an extraordinary deed, a wondrous demonstration
kāparī	robed renunciates, as opposed to the naked
kār (kār-bār)	work, occupation; an offering made out of one's earnings
kaṛā	the iron bracelet worn by a baptized Singh as one of the five Ks
Karam-dharam	action and faith; coming to the stage of adulthood in life when certain prescribed practices are observed
kaṛhā parshād	sacramental food distributed in Gurdwaras to all persons present, generally prepared with equal quantities of wheat flour, sugar, and ghee
karīm	one who shows mercy (karm), an attribute of God
karkhana	a place of work, workshop
karma	an act, a deed; the law of karma, according to which living beings take birth in different forms, with human birth as the best; that is why it is regarded as a rare opportunity for emancipation or release from the chain of transmigration
kartā	the doer, the only doer, God
kathā	an exposition of the Guru's verses, generally in connection with the life of the Guru; a religious discourse
kathā-kīrtan	a performance in which narration and singing are combined; generally using episodes from the life of the Guru and his shabads
khān	a title given to a member of the ruling class in medieval India
Keshdhārī (*keshdhārī*)	a baptized Singh who keeps long unshorn hair
Khalsa	a Sikh directly affiliated to the Guru and not through the mediacy of a Masand; the Sikh brotherhood instituted by Guru Gobind Singh; used for an individual as well as the collective body
khande ki pahul (khandedhār-pahul)	baptism of the double-edged sword, introduced by Guru Gobind Singh for initiating Sikhs and others into the Order of the Khalsa
khazāna	a treasure, used also as a metaphor for something precious
khidāwā	a person employed to look after a child and to keep him busy in one or another kind of activity
khel	a play, a sport; used for the universe and whatever goes on within it as the sport of God

khil'at	a dress of honour, containing articles of costume generally numbering three to twenty-one, including even arms or horses, and bestowed by a superior on an inferior as a mark of distinction; a robe of honour
Khulāsā	a term used for Sikhs not initiated through baptism of the double-edged sword and, consequently, not keeping unshorn hair, and not bearing arms or the epithet 'Singh'
kīrat	praise; to sing God's praises; singing God's praises through the shabads of the Guru, generally called kīrtan
kirpā	kindness, grace
kīrtan	the singing of hymns from the sacred scripture of the Sikhs; hence kīrtan darbār for an elaborate performance
kiryā	performance of Brahmanical rites prescribed for a particular occasion
kos (*kroh*)	a measure of distance equal to 2¼ miles or about 3½ kilometres
kuththa	meat of an animal slaughtered with one stroke of the sword or some other such weapon; also called *jhatka*, and distinguished from the Islamic practice popularly known as *halāl*
langar	community kitchen; the open kitchen in a Sikh dharamsāl
laung	clove; believed to have been made instrumental by Guru Nanak for pregnancy without physical intercourse
lāvān	a composition of Guru Ram Das which uses the metaphor of marriage for conveying a spiritual message, and which is now used for the Sikh marriage ceremony in which each of the four stanzas are recited for each circumambulation of the Granth Sāhib by the bridegroom and the bride
madad-i ma'āsh	literally aid for subsistence; most commonly used in the Mughal times for land-revenue alienated in favour of a religious personage or institution
malik	a title of honour given to a member of the aristocracy
mamtā	the feeling of a mother for the child; affection for kith and kin
manmukh	one who goes by his own inclinations as opposed to the Gurmukh who follows the Guru's instruction and cares for others as well

maṛhī	the spot where a corpse has been cremated; sometimes a small structure was raised over it for lighting a lamp
maryādā	limit, boundary; bounds (of law, usage); custom; convention; traditionally correct behaviour; the Sikh code of belief and conduct
masāṇ	a corpse; the place where corpses are cremated; a sepulture raised over a spot of cremation
Masand *(masand)*	a representative appointed by the Guru to look after the affairs of a local congregation of Sikhs, or a number of such congregations
Maulā (*maulā*)	master, God
mauṇ-dhārī	one who observes silence as a part of austerities
māyā	all creation, all earthly things; seen as the source of entanglement in the cycle of death and rebirth; treated in the Sikh tradition as 'false' in contrast with the eternal truth of God
mehtā (*muqaddam*)	the headman of a village or a part thereof
Miṇā (*mīṇā*)	a derogatory epithet used for Prithi Chand, the elder brother of Guru Arjan who refused to acknowledge Guru Hargobind; used also for his successors and their followers
mīrī-pīrī	leadership in both the spiritual and temporal realms, generally associated with Guru Hargobind and his successors
misl	a unit of fighting men; used generally for the unit of government of the Sikhs in the late eighteenth century; the system is called *misldārī*, but the concept is not clear
mlechh	impure; a derogatory term used for an outcaste or a foreigner, both were regarded as outside the four-tier varna order
moh	affection, love, attachment to kith and kin
monā	one who cuts off his hair
muktā	a liberated person; in Sikh history, anyone of the martyrs of Muktsar
muktī	release, emancipation, liberation
mullā (*mullā*)	a Muslim priest and teacher; generally in charge of a mosque
mūlmantar	the basic statement; the invocatory statement at the opening of the Granth Sāhib, generally regarded as the essence of Sikh theology as it refers to the most

	important attributes of God, the one eternal and true doer who is devoid of fear and enmity, the immortal who does not take birth, who exists by himself and is known through the Guru's grace
mundrā	a large earring, generally worn by a Gorakhnāthī jogī, a mark of his status as an adept
muqaddam (mehtā)	the headman of a village or a part thereof
mutasaddī	an official; an accountant
nād	a horn, a musical instrument; music
nadar	from *nazr* in Persian, sight, a kind glance, grace
nāīb	a deputy, the provincial governor as a deputy of the ruler
nām, dān, isnān	these three terms embody the essential ideas of Guru Nanak for the Sikh way of life: worship through the Name, contribution from rightful earning towards the welfare of others, physical and moral purity
namāz	one of the five daily prayers in Islam
nīch jāt	a person who belongs to the lowest caste in the varna order, generally used for an outcaste
nihang	a militant follower of Guru Gobind Singh who was regarded as a reckless warrior; nihangs were employed in the army of Ranjit Singh and received jāgīrs from the state
nindak	a back-biter, a slanderer; one who talks ill of the Guru
nirbāṇ (nirbāṇ pad, pad nirbāṇ)	detached, unattached; liberation, the state of liberation
nirmal	absolutely pure, with no trace of impurity
Nirmala *sādhs*	the ascetics and renunciates belonging to the Nirmala order among the Sikhs
nirol	distinct; unlike anything else
nirvāṇa	the state of liberation in Buddhism; liberation from the cycle of transmigration
pādhā	a Brahman teacher
pahar	one-eighth of a day; a duration of three hours
pahul	water used for initiating a person as a Sikh (charan pahul) or a Singh (khande kī pahul)
paighambar	one who carries a message, a messenger; used for the prophet of Islam as the messenger of Allah; extended to other prophets of the semitic tradition
palīt	from *palīd,* impure; a person who commits a sin and thereby becomes impure

pancha	one of five; member of a *panchāyat*; the headman of a village or one of its subdivisions
pandit	a learned Brahman
Panth	a path, the people following a particular path; collectively the followers of the Gurus; the Sikh community
parsād	sacred food; food of the langar
pāṭh	reading, reading of the Granth Sāhib; reading of the Granth Sāhib on a particular occasion
Pātshāhī	(from *badshahi*) rulership; a metaphor for the tenure of the Guru in the Sikh tradition; anyone of the ten Gurus
pattal	a tree leaf used as a plate
pauṛī	a stanza
pind	a ball of rice for feeding Brahmans as a part of mortuary rites
pīr	*shaikh* or guide among the Muslim mystics who leads on the path to union with God; a shaikh who is no longer alive but his tomb has become a place of pilgrimage for the people who believe in his power to confer blessings
pūjā	worship, adoration of a deity, an idol; homage
pun	a virtuous act believed to be rewarded in life hereafter
Pūrab dī sangat	the sangat of the east, used for the Sikhs of the Gangetic plain (and Assam)
Purāṇs	the *Purāṇas* in general, whether Shaiva, Shakta, or Vaishnava
purohit	the Brahman who performs the customary duties for a family, or a number of households
qaum	a social group; a nationality; a nation
qāzī	the judicial officer who pronounced judgement on the basis of the provisions of the sharī'at as expounded by a muftī; an important official in the administration of justice under Turko-Afghan and Mughal rule
qila'dār	the holder of a fort; generally used for an officer in charge of a fort
qudrat	God's power manifested in the creation; his omnipotence
Rabābī	one who plays on the stringed instrument called *rabāb*; Mardana was the first Rabābī in the Sikh tradition; a person employed for this service in a Gurdwara was called Rabābī, while the singer of *shabads* was called Rāgī

rāgī	a singer, particularly of the hymns of the Sikh scripture
rahit	way of life, used especially for the Sikh way of life in accordance with the philosophic and ethical principles advanced by the Gurus
Rahitnāma	a written code of norms for the Sikh way of life based on the principles of Sikhism
rai'yat	the subject people in a monarchical rule; the common people
rākhī	literally 'protection'; believed to be a transitional arrangement in the 1750s, signifying essentially the Sikh leader's claim to a part of the produce from land in return for protection against all other claimants
razā	wish, God's will
sādh	a mendicant; a recluse; a pious person; a devotee of God; the Guru; the Sikh of the Guru
sādh-sangat	an association of the pious; used generally for the Sikh congregation for worship through kīrtan and kathā
sādiq	one who is absolutely sincere and steadfast in his faith
sahaj	a state in which there is no tension; the state of liberation as a state of bliss; the state of union with God
Sahajdhārī	the term used in the early eighteenth century for a Sikh directly affiliated to the Guru but not yet baptized through the rite of the double-edged sword and therefore, not a 'Singh' with the obligation to bear arms; used later for a Sikh who was not a Singh
sahlang	an associate; a person admitted to the Sikh faith by a representative of the Guru on his behalf
samyā	the arm-rest used the ascetics, especially the Jogīs
sāng (*suāng*)	impersonation; a character in a theatrical performance, a role
sangat	an assembly, a religious congregation; a congregation of Sikhs; the collective body of Sikhs at one place
sanjam	restraint, moderation
sanyāsī	a Shaiva renunciate who practises austerities
sant	a pious person; the figures like Namdev, Kabir, Ravidas, and Dadu; equated with Sikh in the Gurū Granth Sāhib, and now with an eminent Sikh known to be pious
sarbangi	a gathering in which all are treated as equals, whether for worship or for eating food, in opposition to the

	Brahmanical practice of *chaukā* (eating square) symbolic of isolation from others
sardār	a leader; a Sikh ruler; any Khalsa Sikh
Sarkār-i ā'lā or *sarkār-i wālā*	literally His Exalted Majesty; a term used for Mahāraja Ranjit Singh by officials who drafted his orders
sarrāf	a money-changer; a jeweller; a metaphor for God
Satgurū (*satgurū*)	the true Guru, used for God, and for Guru Nanak and his successors
satnām-mantar	the mantra of the true name; the Sikh faith, the Sikh scripture
sat-sangat (*sādh*-sangat)	the true association, generally used for the Sikh congregation for worship
sat-shabad	the true word, used for the bāṇī of the Guru
Satyuga	the first of the four cosmic ages, regarded as the age of truth or virtue, the golden age
sevak	one who serves; a devotee of God; a follower of the Guru.
shabad	the word; divine self-revelation through creation; a composition of the Guru
shabad-kīrtan	the praises of God sung through the shabad of the Guru in a Sikh congregation
shabad marae	one who dies in the shabad (to live for ever)
shahīd	a martyr in the Muslim tradition as an object of veneration, with his tomb as a place of pilgrimage
shahīdganj	a structure, generally a Gurdwara, built in commemoration of a martyr
shahīdī	martyrdom in the Sikh tradition
Shaikh (*shaikh*)	the guide on the Sūfī path, also called pīr, and generally having a *khānqah* where his disciples pursued the path as a regular discipline
shalok	generally a couplet, but can be a composition of several couplets
Shāstar	(shāstra) a Brahmanical work in general
Shiqdār	a person appointed by the king under Afghan rule to look after the civil and military administration of a territory called *shiqq*
shrāddh	the rite in which the dead ancestors are fed through the mediacy of Brahmans
shuddhī	purification, especially in the context of reconversion
siddh	a person who has attained high spiritual state so as to command supranatural powers

siddhī	the status of a *siddh* or a Shaiva renunciate who has attained liberation; possession of supranatural powers
sikdār	from *shiqdār*, the holder of a shiqq; the person in charge of a particular area for government and administration during the period of Afghan rule
sikh	a disciple; used generally for a follower of Guru Nanak; also for the instruction of the Guru
sikhkhī	the faith of the Sikh
singī	a horn; the horn blown by the Jogīs
singhī	the faith of the baptized Singh
simarnā	to recite, to recite the name of God
Smritīs	used generally for the Brahmanical works supposed to be based on the Shāstras
suchajjī	a woman who has good manners and skill and, therefore, knows how to please her spouse
Sūfī	a mystic of Islam
sultān	the ruler, the king in the pre-Mughal times
sunnat	true to the tradition of the prophet Muhammad; popularly restricted to the practice of circumcision
sūtardhār	a person with the sacred thread; the person who introduced the play in the traditional Sanskrit Drama
takht	a throne; used metaphorically for the seat of the Guru; one of the five important religious centres of Sikhism
taksāl	a mint; used metaphorically for the dispensation in which human beings are turned into Sikhs as true coins
tankhāh	literally payment for service or salary; among the Khalsa, it was used for the penance prescribed for a defaulter for his spiritual benefit
tankhāhia	a person who becomes liable for *tankhāh*
tantar (*tantra*)	the diagrams used generally by the *vām-maragī*s or the left-handers, particularly among the Shaktas
tap	practice of austerities
Tat Khalsa (*tat khālsā*)	the staunch Khalsa; used for the Khalsa of Guru Gobind Singh who opposed Banda Bahadur and his followers in the early eighteenth century, and also for the Singh reformers of the early twentieth century
tej	fire, passion; used in connection with the temper of the Khalsa instituted by Guru Gobind Singh
tejdhārī	a person who appropriates *tej*

tilak	the sacred mark on the forehead of a Brahman, an upper caste Hindu, or the member of any religious sect
tilak-janjū	the sacred mark and the sacred thread which mark the superiority of the twice born or the upper castes; symbols of the Brahmanical faiths
tikkā	mark on the forehead, regarded auspicious; a prerogative of the upper castes, and a distinguishing mark of the sectarians
tith	an auspicious day in a phase of the moon
tīsar panth	the third path or the third collective entity; used for the Khalsa as a community representing the third dispensation as distinct from the Islamic and the Hindu
toshakhana	a store-house, a treasure-house
toshakhānia	the person in charge of a *toshakhāna*, a treasurer
Tretayuga	the second of the four cosmic ages in which virtue began to decline
Turk	used for Muslim rulers in general
Turk-Pathanī'aml	the phrase used by Guru Nanak for the rule of the Afghans who were Muslim by faith (not to be taken literally as Turko-Afghan rule)
Udāsī	a renunciate belonging to an order tracing its origin to Guru Nanak through his son Sri Chand and not through Guru Angad and his successors
'ulamā	plural of *'ālim*, a learned person; a person adept in Islamic learning
upāsana	worship of a deity through praise; ritual worship in Vaishnava bhaktī
uttam jāt	the highest caste in the varna order
Vāhegurū mantar	the mantra of 'Vāhegurū'; the Sikh faith
Vahis	account books, books; records kept by Brahmans or Bhatts of the families of their clients from generation to generation
Vanjara	also *banjārā*, a trader; a trader who moved from place to place with a caravan, or an army camp, to sell goods of various kinds, especially grain
Vār	a literary genre, generally used for heroic poetry; Guru Nanak used it for his religious compositions; the most famous Vārs in Sikh literature were composed by Bhai Gurdas in the early seventeenth century for celebrating Sikh Gurus and the Sikh Panth; also used for a day of the week

varna	literally, colour; one of the four tiers of the ideal Brahmanical social order
varnashrama	the fourfold division of society into varnas and of human life into āshramas, with duties associated with each
Vedas	used generally for the Brahmanical scriptures regarded as revealed
wājā	a musical instrument
zamīndār	literally the holder of land; applied alike to the intermediary who collected revenue on behalf of the state, a vassal chief, and a peasant proprietor
zikr	remembrance; reciting of God's names, the practice of Muslim mystics to remember God

Bibliography

Ādi Srī Gurū Granth Sāhib, Amritsar: Shiromani Gurdwara Prabandhak Committee (standard pagination).

Ashok, Shamsher Singh, *Shrī Gurū Sobhā*, Amritsar: Shiromani Gurudwara Prabandhak Committee, 1967.

Attar Singh, Sir, 'The Travels of Guru Tegh Bahadur and Guru Gobind Singh', *The Panjab Past and Present*, vol. IX, pt 1 (April 1975).

Bhangu, Ratan Singh, *Prachīn Panth Prakāsh*, ed., Bhai Vir Singh, New Delhi: Bhai Vir Singh Sahit Sadan, 1993 (rpt).

_________, *Srī Gurū Panth Prakāsh*, ed., Balwant Singh Dhillon, Amritsar: Singh Brothers, 2004.

Bhuyan, Surya Kumar, 'Guru Tegh Bahadur in Assam', *The Panjab Past and Present*, vol. IX, pt 1 (April 1975).

Chhibber, Kesar Singh, *Bansāvalīnāma Dasān Pātshāhīan Kā*, ed., Rattan Singh Jaggi (*Parkh*, ed., S.S. Kohli, vol II), Chandigarh: Panjab University, 1972.

Dabistān-i-Mazāhib in *Sikh History from Persian Sources*, trans. Irfan Habib and eds, J.S. Grewal and Irfan Habib, New Delhi: Tulika/Indian History Congress, 2001.

Deol, Jeevan, 'Eighteenth Century Khalsa Identity: Discourse, Praxis and Narrative', *Sikh Religion, Culture and Ethnicity*, Christopher Shackle, Gurharpal Singh, and Arvind Pal Singh Mandair, eds, Richmond: Curzon, 2001.

Dil, Balbir Singh, *Bāṇī Gurū Amar Das Jī dā Teeka*, Patiala: Punjab Languages Department, 2004.

Fauja Singh, 'The Martyrdom of Guru Tegh Bahadur', *The Panjab Past and Present*, vol. IX, pt 1 (April 1975).

Ganda Singh, 'Guru Tegh Bahadur', *The Panjab Past and Present*, vol. IX, pt 1 (April 1975).

_________, 'The Martyrdom of Guru Tegh Bahadur', *The Panjab Past and Present*, vol. X, pt 1 (April 1976).

_________, ed., *Srī Gur Sobhā*, Patiala: Punjabi University, 1967.

Grewal, J.S., *Sikh Ideology, Polity and Social Order*, New Delhi: Manohar, 2007.

Grewal, J.S., 'Guru Gobind Singh: Life and Mission', *Journal of Punjab Studies*, vol. 15, nos 1 and 2 (Spring–Fall 2008).

_________, *The Sikhs: Ideology, Institutions, and Identity*, New Delhi: Oxford University Press, 2009.

_________, ed., *The Khalsa: Sikh and Non-Sikh Perspectives*, New Delhi: Manohar, 2004.

Harbans Singh, *Guru Tegh Bahadur*, New Delhi: Sterling Publishers, 1982.

Jaggi, Rattan Singh, *Guru Granth Vishvkosh*, Patiala: Punjabi University, 2002.

Jodh Singh, *Vārān Bhai Gurdas: Text, Transliteration and Translation*, 2 Vols, Patiala: Vision and Venture, 1998.

Malhotra, Karamjit K., 'The Earliest Manual of the Sikh Way of Life', Reeta Grewal and Sheena Pall, eds, *Five Centuries of Sikh Tradition: Ideology, Society, Politics and Culture* (Essays for Indu Banga), New Delhi: Manohar, 2005.

Mann, Gurinder Singh, 'Sources for the Study of Guru Gobind Singh's Life and Times', *Journal of Punjab Studies*, vol. 15, nos 1 and 2 (Spring–Fall 2008).

McLeod, W.H., *Textual Sources for the Study of Sikhism*, Manchester: Manchester Universtiy Press, 1984.

_________, *The Sikhs: History, Religion and Society*, New York: Columbia University Press, 1989.

MS 228, Dr Balbir Singh Sahitya Kendra, Dehra Dun (compiled by Bhagwan Singh as *Bibek Bardhi Granth*.

MS 1192, Panjab University, Chandigarh.

Murphy, Anne, 'History in the Sikh Past', *History and Theory*, vol. 40 (October 2007).

Narotam, Tara Singh, 'Gurdwāre Nauvīn Pātshāhī De', *The Panjab Past and Present*, vol. IX, pt 1 (April 1975).

Oberoi, Harjot, *The Construction of Religious Boundaries: Culture, Identity and Diversity in the Sikh Tradition*, New Delhi: Oxford University Press, 1994.

Puran Singh, 'The Life and Teachings of Sri Guru Tegh Bahadur, the Ninth King Spiritual', *The Panjab Past and Present*, vol. IX, pt 1 (April 1975).

Sabinderjit Singh Sagar, *Hukamnamas of Guru Tegh Bahadur: A Historical Study*, Amritsar: Guru Nanak Dev University, 2002.

Shabdarth Srī Gurū Granth Sāhib Jī, 4 Vols, Amritsar: Shiromani Gurdwara Prabandhak Committee (standard pagination of *Ādi Srī Gurū Granth Sāhib*).

Singh, G.B., 'Sikh Relics in Eastern Bengal', *The Panjab Past and Present*, vol. IX, pt 1 (April 1975).

Sohan Singh, *Āsā di Vār*, Amritsar: Guru Nanak Dev University, 1982.

Srī Dasam Granth Sāhib, eds, Rattan Singh Jaggi and Gursharan Kaur Jaggi, New Delhi: Gobind Sadan, 1999.

The Chaupa Singh Rahit-Nama, W.H. McLeod, ed., and tr., Dunedin: University of Otago Press, 1987.

Vārān Bhai Gurdas., ed., Giānī Hazara Singh, Amritsar: Khalsa Samachar, 1962.

Index

1 *Chelas* of Bal Nath come to meet Guru Nanak, Acc. No. 4072 (1).
Courtesy: Government Museum and Art Gallery, Chandigarh

2 Guru Nanak with Sufis at Uchch, Acc. No. 4072 (6).
Courtesy: Government Museum and Art Gallery, Chandigarh

3 A king pays homage to Guru Nanak, Acc. No. 4072 (3).
Courtesy: Government Museum and Art Gallery, Chandigarh

4 Golden token with the image of Guru Nanak, Acc. No. 85.26.
Courtesy: National Museum, New Delhi

5 **Guru Gobind Singh on horseback, Acc. No. F-48.**
Courtesy: Government Museum and Art Gallery, Chandigarh

6 **Guru Gobind Singh in court.**
Courtesy: Gurinder Singh Mann

7 Guru Nanak and his successors, Acc. No. 3787.
Courtesy: Government Museum and Art Gallery, Chandigarh

8 **An illuminated folio of Guru Granth.**
Courtesy: Gurinder Singh Mann

9 **Jassa Singh Ramgarhia, Acc. No. 60.543.**
Courtesy: National Museum, New Delhi

10 **Jai Singh Kanhiya, Acc. No. 250.**
Courtesy: Government Museum and Art Gallery, Chandigarh

11 **Mahan Singh Sukarchakia, Acc. No. 364.**
Courtesy: Government Museum and Art Gallery, Chandigarh

12 **Maharaja Ranjit Singh's court, Acc. No. 3772.**
Courtesy: Government Museum and Art Gallery, Chandigarh

14 **A fresco from Atal Sahib.**
Courtesy: Malkiat Singh